The Reconstruction of the New York Democracy, *1861-1874*

Jerome Mushkat

Rutherford • Madison • Teaneck
Fairleigh Dickinson University Press
London and Toronto
Associated University Presses

Associated University Presses, Inc.
4 Cornwall Drive
East Brunswick, New Jersey 08816

Associated University Presses Ltd.
69 Fleet Street
London EC4Y 1EU, England

Associated University Presses
Toronto M5E 1A7, Canada

Library of Congress Cataloging in Publication Data

Mushkat, Jerome.
The reconstruction of the New York democracy, 1861-1874.

Bibliography: p.
Includes index.
1. Democratic Party. New York (State)—History. 2. New York (State)—Politics and government—Civil War, 1861-1865. 3. New York (State)—Politics and government—1865-1950. 4. New York (City)—Politics and government—To 1898. 5. Tammany Hall—History. I. Title.
JK2318.N7 1861 329′.3′009747 79-16826
ISBN 0-8386-3002-2

Printed in the United States of America

To Linda, Steven, and Ivan

Contents

Preface

Despite the many able political histories written concerning the North during the Civil War and Reconstruction years, few have concentrated upon Democratic party politics and even fewer on the state and local levels. Where Democrats do appear, most historians portray them as obstructionists and racists, who reacted to Republican-inspired policies on the basis of expediency and ultra-conservatism. From these works, a picture emerges of a Democratic party in shambles during the war, one that failed to help the Union and often flirted with treason, a party that afterwards united in defense of the white South through President Andrew Johnson and followed the politics of blind reaction. Such a picture fails to reflect the historical record. This book examines the New York Democracy from 1861, when the crisis of disunion threatened to destroy the party, through 1874, when it fully reconstructed itself and set a political pattern that lasted in most instances well into the next century. Although the work is limited to that state, I trust my findings apply beyond its borders.

This study begins with the premise that New Yorkers were a contentious people. Many of their quarrels stemmed from hostility between New York City and upstate, loosely defined as the area beyond city limits. Regional differences had abounded since the colonial period because of the state's diversity in religion, ethnicity, cultural beliefs, demographic migrations, economic systems, stages of urbanization, and geographic interests. By the 1860s, such conflicts were unabated and produced issues that divided New Yorkers to near the century's end. Among these were disagreements over home rule for New York City, allocation of state funds, regulation of liquor, supervision of education, machine politics, the role of state government as an instrument of reform, economic policies including taxation, and legislative apportionment. As a result, much of this study deals with the nature of downstate-upstate political rivalries, particularly the feuds between Tammany Hall and its opponents. One cannot deal with New York politics during this period, or any other period, without concentrating upon the city because Tammany was the heart of the state Democratic party, and its operations, for better or worse, directly shaped the entire course of state politics.

Additionally, political developments in New York, important in themselves, become even more significant when considered within the context of national events. Although the local Democracy was but a part of the larger story of countrywide developments, it typified many party characteristics: interest group composition, organizational network and structure, partisan maneuverings, orientation on issues, ideology, and leadership. Moreoever, New York affected politics throughout the United States because of its large bloc of electoral votes, its wealth, and the ability and ambition of its leaders, many of whom automatically became presidential contenders or candidates on their ability to carry the Empire State. In many ways, then, the history of the New York Democratic party presents a microcosm of the problems that perplexed Americans during the years of Civil War and Reconstruction.

In dealing with the New York Democracy's structural dynamics concerning local and national issues, and by putting its successes and failures, its strengths and weaknesses, into perspective, several themes run through this study.

First, the Civil War and Reconstruction experiences did not mark a dividing point in the party's history. After initially succumbing to confusion in early 1861 because of the national party's fragmentation, Abraham Lincoln's victory, secession, war, and Republican-induced pressure to forgo normal partisanship for the nation's sake, Democrats rallied behind the standards of traditional party beliefs and used them to preserve the organization. The upshot was that the Democracy's programs and values followed well-delineated lines of consistency and continuity between where the party had been in the 1830s and what it became in the 1870s and beyond. In the process, the Democracy's political philosophy remained the central core of party loyalty and the most powerful determinant of organizational cohesion. For Democrats, their ideology performed several vital functions. It laid down fundamental moral precepts for designing governmental policies; determined positions on issues; defined individual and constitutional rights; and legitimatized partisan behavior. Above all, it strengthened the idea that the party was a vehicle for implementing a belief system in which the government derived its will from the people, and the people designated governmental options. Thus Democratic ideology, articulated by leaders and broadly shared by members, gave the organization its sense of purpose and convinced Democrats that their party was an organic entity that must be preserved. Seen in that light, the Democracy was not merely a political party, but a way of life.

Second, although the Democracy remained true to its traditional principles, it could not escape the problem of party fragmentation that resulted from the sectional conflict over the extension of slavery and its consequences. Here, Democrats had to counter the voters' loss of faith in the party's operations, its principles, and its leaders. During the Civil War, the questions that divided Democrats and Republicans, and Democrats among themselves, did not simply revolve around support for the Union. Rather, the political struggles involved a complex interplay of forces concerning how the two-party system should function; the roles that Democrats would play as the legitimate opposition; the changes that Democrats were willing or unwilling to accept as the fruits of war; and the place of traditional Democratic ideology in setting the bounds for partisan behavior.

In the various stages of Reconstruction, the New York Democracy was not a monolith geared to white Southern wishes nor did it have a program with predictable answers. Democrats sought to revitalize the organization by reestablishing the active competition implicit in a two-party system; validating the relevance of party principles; attracting former members now Republicans; and readmitting ex-Confederate states without undue erosions of conservative constitutional guarantees. Democratic efforts became more complex because of their ambiguous relationship with President Johnson and their uncertainty about handling state-instituted reforms which had widespread appeal among certain groups the party courted. Compounding these knotty problems, a leadership struggle erupted that distracted Democratic hopes to form a coherent policy reflecting the electorate's concerns. Under those conditions, Democrats searched for issues with broad support while avoiding those which proved divisive.

These attempts remained incomplete until 1874. By then, Democrats finally proved that they had kept faith with long-time ideological commitments and had detailed programs for social justice. Furthermore, able men now led the party, whose organizational skills and devotion to principles achieved unity and brought to an end the difficulties that had plagued the organization for nearly two decades.

Third, Democrats throughout much of the Civil War and Reconstruction did not apply principles such as freedom and equality toward blacks until necessity forced the party to reassess its views. Consequently, this issue, among others, indicated the reciprocal nature of local and national issues. Like most Democrats, New Yorkers were motivated by a mixture of virulent racism, pseudoscientific rationalizations, conservative state sovereignty theories, and the belief that the continual uproar for black citizenship detracted attention from pressing white needs. Only when the federal government guaranteed black civil and political rights did New York Democrats adopt new attitudes and end the party's overt racism. Taken as a whole, the manner in which local Democrats grappled with race relations, one of the critical problems in this period of American history, trace how New Yorkers — as well as many other white Northerners — dealt with racial attitudes and policies.

Fourth, as Democrats contended with such issues, they developed two major models of political behavior that guided the post-Reconstruction party: machine politics epitomized by Tammany Hall, and the Bourbon Democracy symbolized by Samuel J. Tilden and, later, Grover Cleveland. In that sense, New Yorkers supplied the national Democracy with models of political behavior for practical politicking, buttressed by traditional principles, that enabled the organization to operate in the chaotic, industrialized, urbanized, and technological world of late nineteenth-century America.

Fifth, despite a shared moral code and a tight-knit organizational structure which left little to chance, Democratic politics suffered from endemic political factionalism and interest group conflict. Many things divided Democrats: the scramble for spoils, personality clashes, different interpretations of principles, the rival claims of antagonistic groups, the rift between rural and urban factions, soaring ambition, and battles between Tammany and intraparty reformers. Often, these internecine struggles weakened party loyalties and confused rather than clarified many issues. As a result, Democrats frequently could not overcome personal hatreds and the scars of previous fraternal combat. At times, these men risked defeat in order to beat party rivals, real or imagined. Even so, because the stakes of victory were so high, New York Democrats generally managed to find common ground by fabricating an acceptable internal program based on collective beliefs and, above all, collective principles. What appeared to an outsider as political anarchy, to New Yorkers seemed a normal reflection of a heterogeneous society.

Since each author approaches a subject with certain key questions and interests, these frequently shape the sources used and the conceptions emphasized. Methodologically, I have relied heavily upon primary manuscripts and the contemporary press, plus key secondary literature, for this book's analytical framework. Furthermore, I assume that one cannot separate political history from human behavior. In the largest sense, I believe that the politicians described in this study were men who hoped their efforts would accomplish specific goals because of specific beliefs and specific interests. Nevertheless, as in any human effort, what they wanted and what they achieved often came about through unanticipated factors including irrationality, compromise, delusion, ambition, revenge, and, above all, paradox. I also believe that interest group conflict best characterized New York's pluralistic society, although I recognize that not all interest groups had equal access to decision-making. Finally, I have chosen a descriptive, narrative approach to describe New York's structural politics for three reasons: it allows me to blend nation, state, and local developments; it suggests the complexity Democrats faced as they dealt with problems with no easy or sure solutions; and their endeavors become clear through the words and feelings of the people involved. In organizing these materials and ideas, I used chapter one to set the stage for the Democracy's entire range of political problems and operations from 1861 to 1874. Chapters two through eight concentrate upon the task of party reconstruction.

During the course of my research, I received cordial assistance from a number of librarians and libraries. I am particularly grateful to the following for permission to quote material from their manuscript holdings: the Henry E. Huntington Library; the Manuscript Division, Library of Congress; Special Collections, Columbia University Library; the New-York Historical Society; Manuscripts and Archives Division, The New York Public Library, Astor, Lenox, and Tilden Foundations; the New York State Library, Albany; Department of Manuscripts and University Archives, Cornell University; the Cincinnati Historical Society; and the Rush Rhees Library of the University of Rochester. I owe special gratitude for the generous help afforded me by the University of Akron for interlibrary loan assistance, faculty research grants, and a research leave. Without compromising them, I am indebted to Dr. Robert H. Jones and Dr. James F. Richardson for their thoughtful criticism and help. Indispensable typing and clerical assistance was provided by Mrs. Garnette Dorsey. Above all, I thank my wife Barbara, my children Linda and Steven, and my friend Ivan, for their understanding and patience.

1
Parties in Transition

THE secession winter of 1860 culminated a decade of escalating crises for the New York Democratic party. While thoughtful citizens were horrified by the prospect of a national breakup, many Democrats thought their party had the political tools to save the Union. Democrats were proud of their oganization. At rallies throughout the state, party orators emphasized the Democracy's illustrious past and invoked the names of leaders such as Thomas Jefferson, Martin Van Buren, Andrew Jackson, and Silas Wright as touchstones to rally support for a sectional compromise. But now, in November 1860, everything had turned sour. Sitting in his study in Binghamton, former United States Senator Daniel S. Dickinson shrewedly pinpointed the Democracy's weakness. To Albany banker Thomas Olcott he wrote: "*political parties,* in the old sense of the term, are to exist *no more in this country.* The trouble is first now, that we are in transit from where old organizations left off to where the popular sense should begin."[1]

The sources of the political malaise that prompted Dickinson's observation lay in a series of factors that had grown progressively worse during the 1850s. During that decade, a series of partisan disruptions ushered in an era of voter realignments which momentarily flared into multiparty organizations. New issues, centered around ethnocultural, regional, and economic differences, symbolized by nativism, prohibitionism, and most particularly the extension of slavery, challenged traditional values and forced many Americans to reassess their deepest beliefs.

Few New York Democrats doubted their party's ability to solve these problems. Looking backward to the early 1820s when Van Buren had organized the Democracy, Democrats recalled their assets. The state party, as well as the national organization, was a diffused collection of persons consisting of multiple, overlapping interest groups, that cut across lines of class, religion, ethnicity, and section. Even more, the party acted as the agent of a coherent political philosophy that defined its legitimacy. As in any national institution that drew its members from such a diverse constituency, factionalism was a recurring theme in party history. Yet Democrats prided themselves on the fact that no matter how often they had bickered among themselves, they had always managed to reconcile their differences. It was for these reasons that Democrats assumed their party would become the vehicle for some sort of sectional accommodation. Swift-breaking events, however, proved that such hopes were illusionary.

Democratic problems began with a national organization in shambles. Ideally, the Democracy was a united party formed by various state parties, led by professional politicians, which agreed on certain underlying principles. Practically, such was not the case. Even with its superstructure of a national committee, a national chairman, and centralized methods of fund raising, the national party was a diffuse collection of state associations that temporarily cooperated every four years. Then, too, the national party, because of the heterogenous nature of state constituencies, found it difficult to deal with key issues, much less those of a controversial character. These weaknesses became accentuated when the Democracy grappled with the issue of extensionism. Unable to resolve Southern Democratic demands for a federal slave code in the territories, the party split between the followers of Stephen A. Douglas and John C. Breckinridge.

The disruption of the national Democracy was ominous for New Yorkers. By the sheer arithmetic of the Electoral College, New York plus the normally Democratic South, along with swing votes in a few critical states such as Pennsylvania, Ohio, Indiana, and Illinois, had supplied enough votes since the time of Andrew Jackson to elect presidents. Thus, any danger to the alliance between New York and the South threatened the entire party. By these standards, New York Democrats continually defended Southern institutions, notably slavery. By 1860, however, many New York Democrats recognized that their long-time reliance on the South needed modification. In practical terms, the local Democracy acknowledged that sectional differences over extensionism had contributed significantly to intraparty cleavages and hence to the spectre of national suicide.

Since the national party could not advance initiatives to prevent secession, New York Democrats tried to rely on local leaders to effect a compromise. Despite such optimism, state Democrats had many reasons for apprehension. The most striking aspect of the 1850s was the local Democratic party's accelerating disintegration. After the Kansas-Nebraska bill's passage in 1854, the party split into three factions: the Hards, led by Dickinson, who felt that Congress lacked any jurisdiction over the South's right to expand; the Softs under Secretary of State William Marcy, Governor Horatio Seymour, and John Van Buren, the former president's son, in favor of Congress setting a formula for expansion based on popular sovereignty; and many Barnburners turned Free Soilers, dedicated to the containment of slavery and its ultimate extinction. When the Democracy proved unresponsive to their ideas, most Barnburner-Free Soilers led an exodus of the party's left wing and fused with the fledgling Republicans.

The Democracy's embarrassments were not over. By 1860, bitter factionalism flared. The Hard-Soft controversy grew in bitterness, and the emergence of three other groups complicated the already chaotic situation: pro-James Buchanan Half Shells, under city Congressman Daniel Sickles; Mozart Hall, under New York City Mayor Fernando Wood, out to supplant Tammany Hall as the heart of the state party; and the conservative Stuyvesant Institute, a mixture of Hards and Softs, encouraged by state chairman Dean Richmond of Buffalo, which under city merchant Augustus Schell opposed both Tammany Hall and Mozart Hall. Making the situation more explosive, the New Albany Regency, the Democracy's upstate executive arm, under Richmond and Erastus Corning, and bankrolled by the New York Central Railroad, locked in a bitter battle against western Erie Canal groups, centered in Buffalo and Rochester, for control of the rural organization. As a final blow to Democratic harmony, both the canal and railroad groups resented New York City's influence in party affairs, and both sought to undermine the city Democracy's importance.

The Republican party was the chief beneficiary of Democratic fragmentation. Since its formation in 1854, the party elected two governors, including incumbent Edwin D. Morgan, a city merchant; carried the state in the 1856 presidential election for John C. Frémont; demolished the Know-Nothing party which consisted of many conservative Whigs; controlled the majority of upstate counties; and dominated the legislature. Only Democratic linkages to federal patronage through President James Buchanan prevented a complete rout.

Ordinarily, Tammany Hall's control of New York City, where the Democracy's heavy concentration of votes usually offset losses upstate, should have stemmed Republican gains and supplied the glue to hold the Democracy together. But while Tammany Hall had fabricated a powerful urban machine whose pluralities provided the nucleus around which the party built its state organization, the Hall was actually too weak and divided in 1860 to help at the moment of the Democracy's greatest need.

Tammany's problems partially flowed from state interference in home rule because of the Republican-dominated legislature's imposition of the Charter of 1857 on the city. Under the charter's terms, administrative chaos reigned. The charter diffused executive authority by dividing the municipal government, which included the mayor, department heads, and the Board of Aldermen, from the county, by creating a bipartisan, twelve-man Board of Supervisors that by fiat always consisted of six Democrats and six Republicans. The mayor lacked control over key municipal functions: the board of education, the corporation council, the almshouse, and the departments of fire, welfare, and police. Even taxation schedules were independent of the mayor and rested with the Board of Supervisors. On the positive side, Tammany gained strength by cutting through this clutter, and, by working outside the system, developed an alternative approach to the confusion and decentralization implicit in the municipal government. On the other hand, since authority rested in so many agencies, the Hall could not ease the cultural and ethnic antagonisms inherent in the chaos of rapid urbanization, ameliorate the growing pains of a metropolis in which vital city services failed to keep pace with demands, or create reform programs to solve ever-increasing problems. Then, too, the endemic corruption that flourished at every level of municipal rule due to the lack of accountability led to continual political instability and disillusioned the public.

As a result, Tammany's mastery of the city rested on an infirm foundation. To exploit the situation, anti-Tammany Democrats, such as Wood, Republicans, and reformers of various hues, sought power by taking advantage of the Hall's inability to govern the city and county. Under those conditions, Tammany could neither fully dominate the city nor give the state party dependable pluralities until the legislature provided the city with a fresh charter geared to competent government through increased local autonomy, executive authority, and consolidated power. As the *New York Herald* noted in 1874, New York City was "the main pivot of the politics of this State. The Democrats cannot carry the State until they give a reasonable guarantee of good government in this city."[2]

Tammany's second structural fault rested in the peculiar political composition of the city and state party. Because of the city's heterogeneous population, no single local politician ever fully represented its varied interest groups, nor could any escape the internecine nature of ward politics. From Aaron Burr and DeWitt Clinton to Fernando Wood and William Tweed, New York City devoured its best talent and prevented any local politician from establishing a state or national reputation as a party leader. Since upstaters avoided the city's bitter intraparty battles, however, they staked claims to predominance and customarily became candidates for choice offices as senators and governors, while city Democrats took secondary slots. The upshot was massive regional jealously between the city and state that often sapped the entire party's vitality.

With their organization at every level in confusion, Democrats looked inward toward their political philosophy for sources of strength and guidance. Starting in the 1790s under Thomas Jefferson's tutelage and reinforced in the 1830s with Andrew Jackson, Democrats had evolved their ideas into a shared political philosophy, with deep ideological roots, that not only established the role and function of their party, but hardened the brittle nature of factional ties. The key element in Democratic ideas began with the premises that all men deserved equal rights, and that a just society was one where the government preserved individual freedoms. In specific terms,

Democrats believed in local autonomy, state sovereignty, limited executive power, negative government, a weak judiciary, and frequent elections to prevent abuses by officials. The same approach applied to people. Human beings were good; hence, the Democracy stressed the collective wisdom of the populace through majority rule, unlimited white manhood suffrage, and reliance on popular opinion as the sole guide for political behavior.

These ideas formed the basis for Democratic policy-making. The party demanded frugality on all levels of government spending, public expenditures based on the ability to pay without incurring long-term debts, a small standing army, a revenue tariff system that bordered on free trade, decentralized, laissez-faire government that did not interfere with matters of private religious or moral beliefs, complete separation of state and federal banking, rotation in office, and state-sponsored internal improvements. The Democracy stressed that these ideas identified majority rule with individual freedom, total self-government, and state sovereignty, all of which they considered embodied in the Constitution. For those reasons, the Democracy guarded the Constitution against all changes and fought any effort to diminish the rights it guaranteed.

Democratic ideology and policy, party members assumed, would create a good society, one in which people lived together in a series of primary relationships that they understood and accepted. In such a system, citizens through a process of accommodation and compromise generated values which in turn forged fair economic, social, and political institutions. It was, furthermore, a decentralized, pluralistic system that welcomed careful innovations as a means of reform, and rewarded talent while at the same time cherishing human rights.

Taken as a whole, Democratic principles formulated the organization's concept of a biparty nation. Democrats felt that a political party's chief function was to serve as an instrument of popular will regulated throughout by values that could be either explicitly expressed or taken for granted by its members. The chief role of party leaders was to negotiate with various internal groups and work out compromises that bridged multiple demands. An opposition party also had its place; it checked the party in power, presented alternative policies, and prevented the rise of entrenched power.

Two major inconsistencies plagued Democratic principles. As they pictured politics, Democrats considered power a dangerous commodity, they denied government any discretionary behavior, and they felt that liberty consisted of free individuals who guarded their autonomy against the intrusions of organized institutions. But power and the right to rule were there the objects of any political party, and once in office few men were willing to relinquish their positions. To cut through this thicket, Democrats maintained that the major test of political behavior rested on three interrelated variables: the pursuit of power was legitimate insofar as it did not infringe on people's rights; the use of power hinged on moral behavior; and the contest for power demanded the formation of mechanisms that allowed peaceful rivalries to exist which destroyed neither the social fabric nor the parties involved.

The ferment of antiextensionism revealed the second inconsistency in Democratic principles — the extent to which equal rights applied to blacks. Democrats did believe that social justice was synonymous with equality for all, but they excluded blacks whom most white Americans considered biological inferiors and outside the social order. Whether or not Democrats were active or passive racists, they followed three ideas regarding blacks: the nation had more pressing problems than slavery extensionism to consider; any political rupture over the status of slaves would harm the New York-Southern alliance; and abolitionism was an invidious distraction from pressing white needs.[3]

As Democrats, then, faced the crises of the 1850s, they sought to use their principles as a means of solving political issues. Among these values were state autonomy, which Stephen A. Douglas's followers reinterpreted as popular sovereignty; governmental noninterference with private morality, to counter prohibitionism and nativism; opposition to federal centralism as a means of protecting property rights, including slavery, and capable of blunting the creation of a congressional paternalistic economic system hostile to laissez-faire; and the doctrine of equal rights to ensure equality of opportunity. If Democrats were morally myopic about slavery, they nonetheless shared the Republican faith, which in many ways derived from Jacksonianism, in the superiority of Northern free institutions. But unlike the Republicans, the Democrats were limited by their links to Southern whites and their common ideology. Where factional Republicans found common agreement over the containment of slavery, factional Democrats could not find a unified formula based on party principles to satisfy its varied constituency.

In this fevered atmosphere, the New York Democracy crumbled in the fall campaigns of 1860. Tammany, the Regency, the state's Democratic business community, led by banker and national chairman August Belmont, and most Softs supported Douglas for president. The Hards, including Tammanyites James Brady and former Barnburner John A. Dix, soon to become Buchanan's secretary of the treasury, and most Half Shells supported pro-Southern John C. Breckinridge. A third group of conservative Democrats and old-line Whigs backed the Constitutional Union party. Blurring party lines even more, Daniel S. Dickinson, who normally should have supported Breckinridge because of past ties to the Southern Democracy backed Douglas. Even more confusing, Mayor Wood, firmly pro-Southern, sulked after the Democratic convention at Charleston barred his insurgent delegation and refused to commit his organization to any candidate.

During August and September, Democrats made one final, convulsive effort to save the state from the Republicans. Each group knifed through a web of mutual suspicions and agonizingly formed a fusion electoral ticket. However, while common concerns created fictional harmony in the presidential race, the Democrats did not erase their disunity. They managed to find a proportional formula to share electoral votes, but they split over financing the campaign, what issues to stress, or which local candidates to support. Their failure proved expediency was not the answer to disorganization. Although the party carried the city easily, it lost the state to Abraham Lincoln, Morgan won reelection, and Republicans retained the legislature.

The election confirmed New York's voting realignments. Setting a pattern for the future, a general mosaic of partisan behavior emerged. The southeastern part of the state, including New York City, Brooklyn, and the Delaware River valley region, along with Troy, Albany, and Utica, plus several counties in southern and western New York, were Democratic. Republican strength rested in northeastern and central counties, a few medium-sized cities such as Rochester, Syracuse, Auburn, Poughkeepsie, and Binghamton, and parts of the Hudson Valley and Long Island. The area including Buffalo was a section that swung between the two parties.[4]

The Democracy's inability to counter the secessionist movement bore mute testimony to its disarray. Unity was impossible because each party faction advanced different and often contradictory solutions. New York City corporation lawyer Samuel L. M. Barlow, an influential member of the party's establishment with many Southern connections, attempted unsuccessfully to prevent disunion by stressing common business needs among Northerners and Southerners. Mayor Wood worked counter to Barlow and helped the emerging Confederacy when he made a startling proposal to have the metropolis withdraw from the Union and make the city free since secession was unavoidable. Tammany downplayed the national crisis and used the mayor's suggestion to destroy Mozart Hall. Conservative businessmen support John A. Dix's futile efforts to forge some accommodation with the Confederates through the constitutional guarantees that John C. Crittenden of Kentucky advocated. Moderate centrists fearful of war called for a "re-construction" of the Union based on the Confederate constitution. White supremacists and dogmatic states' righters huddled around Ben Wood, the mayor's brother, who used his editorship of the *New York Daily News* to demand total acquiescence in all Southern demands.[5]

All these conflicting positions came to a head in Albany during a special state convention held in January 1861. The delegates did agree that a sectional compromise was necessary, but bogged down on any workable details beyond a pious wish to maintain national integrity. Through all these confusing sounds, three notes were clear: Democrats were generally anticoercionists who felt that war was avoidable; they blamed Republicans for fomenting secession; and they placed their faith for a solution in the give-and-take within the political system.[6]

The traditional party system, however, was dead, as Dickinson had noted, and so were the relatively clean-cut issues that had formed it during the 1830s. Instead, confusion held sway, bitter personal recriminations were the norm, and uncertainty ruled. Whatever illusions Democrats had about using their party to save the nation now turned to ashes. The Democracy not only had failed the Union; it had failed itself.

In the emotional surge of patriotism that followed the outbreak of war, New York Democrats abandoned partisanship and pledged defense of the Union. Yet Democrats were politicians who dealt in power, and as emotionalism cooled they reassessed the situation. They faced awesome tasks. As their first priority, Democrats had to somehow unify their shattered organization by absorbing logical allies, such as the conservative Constitutional Unionists and Breckinridgeites, regain former Democrats, particularly the Barnburner and Free Soil Republicans, and mediate the split between Tammany Hall and Mozart Hall. In terms of local issues, the Democracy needed to come to terms with nativism and prohibitionism, neutralize the corruption, within the municipal government, and forge a new charter for New York City based on home rule.[7]

The war presented Democrats with crisscrossing difficulties. First, Democrats had to emphasize their commitment to the Union, yet carry on traditional partisanship in a manner that separated legitimate dissent from disloyalty. Second, Democrats sought a policy to parry Administration efforts to create wartime coalition politics through the formation of one national Union party. Next, Democrats had to determine what changes they were willing to accept as the consequences of war, notably in their attitudes toward slavery, decentralized federal power, and constitutional rights. Finally, the Democracy searched for a formula to regain its customary national role as the majority party. In that regard, Democrats needed a means to fight the Confederates in a way which would not alienate their prewar allies.

Long-range problems had equally sharp edges. Democrats were convinced that the party's disruption was a temporary aberration and did not automatically mean its obliteration. But the sweep of events preceding the war tended toward that end. In general terms, Democrats intended to revive their party, embarrass the Republicans wherever possible, and use old partisan traditions to return to power. The specific means to accomplish this goal lay in Democratic attempts to reconstruct the party based on the continuity in traditional principles and issues.[8]

Facing such enormous difficulties, party leaders recognized that they needed a clear, well thought out, all-inclusive program, rather than a random throw of the dice every time one of these questions clamored for attention. Yet beyond such a realization lay five profound questions linked inexorably to the Democracy's eventual reconstruction: for what ends did the party exist; what visions of the future did it hold; how could old partisan traditions operate in wartime; what principles could Democrats plausibly emphasize in an era of instability; what changes could Democrats accept as the results of war?

These questions had no predictable answers or timetables. Even worse for Democrats, as political issues shifted from the question of slavery extension to the question of preserving the Union, party leaders encountered unprecedented problems that distracted them from their first priority, rebuilding the organization. As a result, the story of the New York Democracy's role during the Civil War was a story of conflicting views, deep stresses and abrupt transitions in factional alignments, erosions of traditional principles, deep-seated racial prejudices, and uncertain leadership. Under those conditions, Democrats could not reconstruct and revitalize their party until they came to terms with the war's political dimensions and then settled its consequences. Although Democrats lacked the ability to read the future, that task remained incomplete until 1874.

In the meantime, Democrats had to start somewhere. They began within their own organization. The Civil War and its aftermath, as far as most New York Democrats were concerned, was not only a battle to save the Union, but also a battle to save the Democratic party. Yet as events quickly indicated, the war had disasterous consequences for the Democracy and fundamentally reordered its priorities. As a result, the party could not rebuild itself in any permanent fashion until the war ended.

State chairman Dean Richmond, the party's titular head, took the Democracy's first tentative step in policy-making. Through his organ, the *Albany Argus* and its editor William Cassidy, Richmond strongly endorsed the war and supported Lincoln's preliminary efforts to save the Union. At the same time, Richmond wanted to draw a distinction between Republicans and Democrats. Initially, he failed. Yet the *Argus* did touch two issues, antiemancipation and defense of civil liberties, with enormous possibilities. For the moment, the paper argued that the war's only legitimate end was restoration of the Union, not "the preaching of a negro crusade," nor did Lincoln have the right to suppress civil rights.[9]

Richmond's efforts, however, made little impact in New York City. Despite their show of nonpartisanship in the war's early months, local Democrats could not erase either past problems or ingrained habits. Still bound by disorganization, the party floundered over finding a suitable war policy. The situation was particularly intense because city Democrats and the Albany Regency had different perceptions. In the city, politics revolved around the power struggle between Mozart and Tammany. Upstate, Richmond sought to mute that conflict while finding a way to coalesce with the Breckenridge Democrats and the Constitutional Unionists.

Ironically, Republicans gave Democrats a reprieve. Before the war, factionalism hounded the New York Republican party. One wing, generally former Whigs, led by upstaters Thurlow Weed, the editor of the *Albany Evening Journal,* and Senator William H. Seward, now secretary of state, along with moderates Governor Morgan and Henry J. Raymond, editor of the *New York Times*, sought to dominate the party. Opposing them was a second wing concentrating around former Democrats such as Preston King and William Cullen Bryant of the New York *Evening Post,* along with social reformers including the *New York Tribune's* powerful but erratic Horace Greeley. Between the wings, a shifting group of prohibitionists and nativists existed who usually, but not always, supported Greeley. In the period between Lincoln's election and the firing on Fort Sumter, Republicans quarreled bitterly over divisions of spoils and control of the legislature. Weed was notably angry. To Governor Morgan he complained: "There is less disposition to harmonize among our friends than with Southern Union men."[10]

Lincoln's call for troops temporarily cooled the feud. But as passion waned, Republican woes increased. It quickly became apparent that they had factional differences over the war's purposes, the manner in which the Administration should fight it, and their vision of postwar America. The major bone of contention rested on war policies, notably emancipation. The Weedites, generally drawing conservative and moderate support, favored a military victory that would not disrupt Southern institutions and might revive the old Whig party coalition. On the other hand, the more radical Republicans, around Greeley and Bryant, favored a strong war effort aimed at fundamental changes in the Confederate states, including slavery's elimination.[11]

Despite such disagreements, patriotism and nationalism usually held Republican internal divisions at a safe political level. With that in mind, Republicans sponsored the formation of a nonpartisan "Union party" with the Democrats. On August 6, 1861, the Republican state committee issued a formal invitation to the Democracy to attend a joint convention and form a single ticket dedicated to saving the Union. "What are all our past party differences," Bryant asked, "compared with this momentous subject of national existence?"[12]

Democrats had no intention of abandoning their party. By July, they began to flesh out their role as the legitimate opposition. The *Argus* and the *New York Leader,* Tammany's mouthpiece edited by William Clancy, seized upon four issues — the Administration's growing centralism, arbitrary arrests, suppression of civil liberties, and the threat of emancipation — to define themselves politically. As for the proposed Union party, Richmond's official reply to Republicans reeked with partisanship. While accepting the premise that the North fought to preserve the Union and the Constitution, he charged that the Republicans had fomented the war because of their "fanatical sectional policy." Seen in that light, he concluded, a viable two-party system was an indispenable function of a free society.[13]

Although Democrats had passed one crisis, another quickly developed that further shattered party unity. While Tammany and the Regency supported the war, significant groups in the state felt that coercion was not the answer. Before the war, many of these people had supported slavery either out of business needs, political associations, or racism. Ben Wood was their spokesman. The issue before the public, he wrote, was "between a useless and destructive war and a prosperous and enduring peace." Emancipation was a curse "to northern industrious white inhabitants." Lincoln's arbitrary arrests were totally unjustified. The only way, Wood concluded, to restore the Union was through the election of "conservative men" who would seek common ground with the Confederates through an armistice followed by a new sectional compromise.[14]

Although a federal grand jury through Postmaster General Montgomery Blair denied the *Daily News* mailing privileges, which forced the paper to suspend operations for over a year, neither prowar Republicans nor Democrats could silence the questions Ben Wood raised. In one sense he was a dissenter, a threat to national unity, but he nevertheless reflected a growing disillusionment among many Democrats against unthinking patriotism, Republican conduct of the war, and other Democrats who accepted the Administration's views. Then, too, Wood believed in party integrity and distrusted any attempts to disrupt normal politics or to use the war as a pretext to create social upheavals. Along with him were party ideologues who refused to compromise their Jacksonian principles, or their view of a static society guided by an unchanging Constitution. Soon called Peace Democrats, these men felt the North should fight the war on a conservative basis defined as the defense of state sovereignty, protection of constitutional liberties, reunion through an armistice and compromise, and antiemancipation. In so doing, they evoked two questions based on traditional party principles: What were the limits of federal authority? What were the consequences of unchecked power?

The Peace Democratic emergence had many long-range effects on the Democracy. Upstate, their strictures, which many prowar voters felt synonymous with treason, forced Richmond to redouble his efforts to find new allies. In the city, Tammany used its loyalty to the Union to undermine Mozart Hall, which it claimed covertly back Ben Wood. On an overall basis, the questions Peace Democrats suggested indicated the Democracy's difficulty in convincing the public that any censure of the Administration was legitimate dissent, not treason. In that sense, Peace Democrats trod a delicate path. For despite their legitimate reservations about war policies, many Peace Democrats failed to understand that the sacrifices both sides made outmoded their program. Moreover, some of them ultimately sought to fulfill their prophecies of doom by weakening the Union's war efforts in ways that went beyond questioning the justice and expediency of the war. When that happened, Peace Democrats not only engaged in obstructionism, but tarnished the entire party with treason.[15]

Meanwhile, the Republicans steadily sought to create the semblance of a bipartisan war effort. At their state convention, they endorsed a platform — with the aid of some Constitutional Unionists and prowar Democrats such as Dickinson, now called Union Democrats, who placed nation above party — whose planks endorsed Administration policies and carefully avoided emancipation. In that spirit, the party then nominated a nonpartisan ticket. Immediately, five prominent prewar Democrats switched to the new Union party: Congressmen Daniel Sickles and John Cochrane from the city, former Jacksonian George Bancroft, John A. Dix, a long-time Van Burenite, and James T. Brady, an influential Tammanyite. The Republican's major coup came from a totally unexpected source, Fernando Wood. Worried about reelection, Wood decided to cast his lot with Unionism. He confided to Isaac Sherman, Weed's confidant, that Mozart was determined to destroy Tammany "by advocating the most vigorous prosecution of the war." In return, Wood exacted no terms beyond an unstated understanding that in the December municipal election "he may want on our part [Republicans] some alliance with his organization."[16]

In contrast, the fall campaign began badly for Democrats despite a promising start. Before the convention, Richmond managed to ease some disunity when the Breckenridge state committee, plus the Hards and Softs, agreed to back the ticket without reservations. Trouble erupted, however, from the city. Despite Fernando Wood's seeming conversion to Unionism, he sent a Mozart delegation to challenge Tammany's status as the regular organization. In the end, the delegates accepted prowar Tammany because they feared Ben Wood's activities might alienate voters. Yet while Tammanyites basked in party approval, the fact remained that the city organization was still in shambles.

Harmony within the ranks was not to be for other reasons. In response to the Peace Democrats, a counter group, the Tammany-led War Democrats emerged, committed to preserving the Union while opposing the Administration. Yet the War Democrats were far from united. Tammanyites were generally firm patriots, while upstaters, taking their cues from former governor Seymour and party strategists such as Samuel J. Tilden and state assemblyman Francis Kernan of Utica, backed the war provided Lincoln did not tamper with constitutional liberties. In many ways, most War Democratic ideas overlapped Peace Democratic values except for three major differences: War Democrats were avowed nationalists who could not accept the Confederacy's permanence; they did not confuse criticism of war policies with support for disunion; and they felt their principles were flexible enough to withstand the shock of war. In policy terms, they felt the Democracy could defend the Union and constitutional liberties, maintain traditional principles, seek conservative allies, and wherever possible carry out legitimate opposition against clearly Republican partisan ends. Even so, the line between Peace and War men was not hard and fast. As a minority party, the Democracy could not afford factionalism, and its two wings often coalesced by sacrificing key beliefs. Among the issues that brought them together were racism and conservative constitutionalism.[17]

In retrospect, the convention underscored the party's disorganization. Although Richmond had ended the old Hard-Soft split and won Breckenridgeite support, the struggle between Tammany and Mozart remained. In dealing with war-related issues, the Democracy was split over tactics; it had divided leadership; it lacked a united program to criticize the Administration; and it proved unable to lure conservative Republicans and Constitutional Unionists. Even more significant for the party's future was the surge for Unionism. Although the Democracy did its best to convey the idea that a two-party system was a vital check on the excesses of one-party government, many voters felt the Democracy's only concern was self-preservation. The *Argus* might claim, then, that "the Democracy is the only party that can carry on a successful war, or secure an honorable peace," but most loyal New Yorkers agreed with Weed that voters backed "uncompromising friends of the Union, irrespective of party."[18]

Democrats absorbed stunning losses throughout the state in the November elections. To soften the blow, however, the Democracy drew some encouragement from another development, a growing rupture over emancipation between conservative and moderate Republicans, who opposed it under all circumstances, and radicals, who favored it as a war measure. Just as promising, one Breckenridge Democrat, now a

Unionist, warned Dix, the issue could alter "the alliance of men behind Lincoln who believe in the Constitution, and the Union, but abhor Emancipation."[19]

The political focus now shifted toward the city's municipal election where unlike the state canvass, localism and personality took precedence over war-related issues. Trouble abounded for War Democrats because Tammany faced conflicting leadership claims. Elijah Purdy, a long-time party strongman, and editor Clancy favored the nomination of a forthright war supporter but lacked a popular candidate. Opposing them was Supervisor William M. Tweed, Purdy's one-time protégé, just nearing political maturity, who wanted to fuse with Weedites. Yet Tweed, too, ran into trouble when Dix, the only suitable candidate for such a fusion, declined. In the end, the Hall compromised on C. Godfrey Gunther a German Democrat, who satisfied neither Purdy nor Tweed. As for Republicans, they settled grudgingly on George Opdyke, a former Democrat and anti-Weedite, who had strong backing from the city Custom House, headed by Collector Hiram Barney. Only Mozart remained firm and renominated Fernando Wood.

When the smoke cleared, Tammanyites were clearly routed. Opdyke won the mayoralty, a Mozarter beat Tweed for sheriff, and Abraham Oakey Hall, a Weedite running with Mozart's aid, became district attorney. At the end of 1861, then, the New York Democracy found itself facing a new dilemma: without control of New York City, the party's citadel, the Democracy faced the bleak prospect of political impotence.[20]

In short, the Democratic party faced the problem of sheer survival as a credible party because it had failed the key test of any viable political organization — the ability to shape unified policies that created interfactional harmony. This failure amounted to an internal party ambivalence that bordered on suicide. Yet in another sense, the conflicting, but often overlapping, Democratic alignments indicated that such instability might end under strong leadership and the right set of issues based on the party's traditional principles. For the moment, these factors were not apparent.

It was not surprising that the Republicans were the chief beneficiaries of Democratic fumbling. Yet internal party variable prevented Republicans from capitalizing on the situation. Unionism had proven a remarkable achievement, but few politicians knew whether it would become a permanent fact or prove to be a temporary ploy. Moreover, the quarrel between radicals and conservatives was too personal and deep-seated for an easy cure. Just as dampening, the emancipation question threatened to further split the party.

As a temporary device, both War and Peace Democrats, no matter their differences, experimented with antiemancipation in early 1862 in order to revive their party. They did so for three reasons. Antiemancipation, they reasoned, could lure back Union Democrats. Furthermore, white supremacy might form the glue to reunite party factions. Finally, Republican inability to agree on the status of blacks could bring their internal discords to a painful head. Yet emancipation was a theoretical question so far, and would not become tangible until either Congress or the President acted.

The upshot of this development was continued Democratic drift. In the spring, War Democrat Samuel Barlow sent Sam Ward, an influential lobbyist and a close friend of General George B. McClellan, to assess the mood in Washington. Events were not encouraging for War Democrats, Ward reported. Admitting that he wished the general had "more dash," Ward nonetheless felt "Radical Republicans" conspired against his success because of his Democratic connections. Prospects for peace were even more clouded because the radicals lusted for emancipation as the first step in the destruction of traditional Southern institutions and wanted to prolong the struggle for that end. On the basis of what he saw in the Confederacy on a recent business trip, Ward glumly concluded both sides could only fight a long war to a bloody finish.[21]

National chairman August Belmont confirmed Ward's gloom. Prodded by Barlow, Belmont approached President Lincoln through Seward and Weed, with two alternatives for peace: negotiations, which Belmont favored, to restore the "Federal Union," and, failing that, total war "to crush the rebellion." Showing a slow drift to Peace Democratic ideas because of a string of recent Northern defeats, Belmont emphasized the need for an armistice, followed by a national convention, where the delegates would make changes "as our late sad experience had demonstrated to have become necessary." Lincoln was unsympathetic. The Confederates, he countered, showed no inclination for compromise; the Union's only recourse lay in a war of conquest. Frustrated, the War Democrats now awaited some new shift in the political spectrum to influence the Administration.[22]

Peace Democrats were equally disarmed. Unable to convince the President that their ideas were valid, many lapsed into sullen, nonconstructive criticism or frank racists attacks on the government. More trouble loomed for Fernando Wood. Bereft of patronage to discipline his factious followers, Wood watched as Mozart shattered into four splinter groups: armistice-at-any-price Peace Democrats led by his brother; expedient ward plug-uglies out for themselves; quasi-War Democrats seeking a deal with Tammany; and white supremacists preaching hate against all Republicans. With disaster facing him, Wood straddled the fence. He pledged his support to Lincoln, assailed the "ultra radical abolitionists" for disrupting the war effort, and secretly reassured Peace Democrats by bankrolling their activities.[23]

While Democrats floundered, Republican problems gave them some leaway. In the legislature, a rift developed between old-line Whigs and former Democrats over funding the state's war debt. Misunderstandings existed on the meaning of Unionism. Some Union Democrats balked at clearly partisan Republican bills, while regular Republicans, assuming that the Unionists lacked options, tried to convert fusion into a permanent force, dedicated to traditional Republican ends. At the conclusion of the session, however, Union Democrats issued a manifesto that reaffirmed their allegiance. Henry J. Raymond was elated. To Lincoln he gushed: "Political affairs in this state were never more promising. A thorough union on principle has been affected between Republicans & the Union men."[24]

Suddenly, the situation changed. Forces outside the state restored Republican factionalism and gave the Democracy an opportunity to revive party unity. Trouble began for Republicans in April and May 1862 when General David Hunter issued two separate but related orders that freed slaves in his military district. Local Republican reaction fell along predictable lines; radicals attacked Lincoln for rescinding the order, conservatives and moderates applauded. Democrats also reacted predictably and formed a solid front against emancipation. Yet as Democratic anger mounted, one paradoxical fact emerged. Despite all the vociferousness, both Peace and War Democrats were actually pleased with Hunter because he unwittingly supplied the party with its long-sought catalyst to create factional unity.[25]

The entire Democracy quickly exploited the situation by calling protest meetings throughout the state culminating in a massive unity rally in New York City under Tammany's nominal leadership. Avoiding Peace Democratic extremism, the steering committee, through Barlow's direction, adopted resolutions that pledged the Union's preservation but rejected emancipation in any form. Tammany's Independence Day celebration continued the work. With prominent Peace Democrats in attendance, the Hall promised that all Democrats regardless of "past divisions" intended to fight "for the suppression of the rebellion and the supremacy of the law." Of more importance, Tammany muted its strong War Democratic stance, with Richmond's approval, and invited Peace Democrats to join them through "honorable means."[26]

Without losing momentum, the united Democracy increased its aggressive tactics. In truth, the Administration supplied two ready targets when it proposed a draft to shore up the flagging volunteer system and with Lincoln's preliminary Emancipation Proclamation on September 22, 1862. Even better by Democratic standards, the President split his party. Although most Weedites swallowed their chagrin and accepted the Proclamation "as an extreme act of war," they clearly disagreed with Greeley and Bryant, who considered it "a sublime act." These wrangles, a former Breckenridgeite told Barlow, signalled the death "knell of the Republican party" and heralded the Union party's demise.[27]

In the midst of the Democratic revival, a new factor emerged within leadership ranks. For several years, upperclass Democrats, called the "swallow-tails," including Tilden, Richmond, Belmont, and Barlow, had grown progressively disillusioned with the rampant corruption within both Tammany and Mozart. Moreover, these men were irked by the willingness of city Democrats to accept their money, but surrender little influence in return. To remedy this situation, the swallow-tails craved an independent newspaper, representing the "better element," that could rise above petty ward squabbles, one that could simultaneously counter corruption and direct public opinion toward issues of party regeneration. They found their man in Manton Marble, a young intellectual with a sure grasp of traditional principles, bankrolled by Barlow, who became the editor of the struggling *New York World*. Along with the *Argus* and the *Buffalo Daily Courier*, the Regency now had three powerful newspapers to express its point of view and check the city Democracy's influence.[28]

For the moment, such intraparty rivalry was a luxury Democrats could scarcely afford. All factionalism became secondary to fusion based on antiemancipation, and Democratic editors played the issue with reckless abandon. The *Argus* and *World* wrote that Lincoln had illegally tampered with the Constitution because of the repulsive influence of "insane radicals," who had reneged on their containment principle. Then, too, the Proclamation destroyed property rights, thus proving, Marble charged, that the President was "fully adrift on the current of radical fantacism." The influential and politically independent *New York Herald* concurred. Calling the Proclamation "a sop to the abolitionists," the paper suggested that Republicans had altered the war's entire nature and advised Democrats to seek common ground with the Weedites.[29]

The Democracy gained one final advantage from the Proclamation. From the standpoint of timing, it coincided with the Republican state convention and created the impression that the Administration supported radicals. Greeley and Bryant made the most of it. Along with upstate radicals, they secured the gubernatorial nomination of former Barnburner James S. Wadsworth, an outspoken emancipationist. The choice strained Unionism, but not to the breaking point. Dickinson disliked both Wadsworth and emancipation, but urged voters to back each in order to accomplish the "great work before us." In contrast, Democrats rejoiced. By nominating Wadsworth, the Republicans guaranteed emancipation as the key issue in the fall campaign and alienated Weed. With proper "management," Belmont urged, conservative and moderate Republicans might coalesce with the Democracy.[30]

Intense harmony gripped the Democratic convention where the delegates nominated the chronically reluctant Horatio Seymour for governor on a platform stressing home rule, state sovereignty, antiemancipation, and support for the war on a conditional conservative basis. Equally vital, the party fulfilled Richmond's search for allies by fusing with many former Constitutional Unionists including such important one-time Whigs as former governor Washington Hunt, ex-President Millard Fillmore, and William Prime, editor of the conservative *New York Journal of Commerce*. Robert Stevens, the man most responsible for wooing his fellow Constitutional Unionists into Democratic ranks, felt one factor might mar the alliance. Many of these former Whigs theatened a walkout unless the Democracy committed the organization to drop those "intensely corrupt men" who dominated Tammany and Mozart. Yet Stevens admitted that was unlikely. "Our most reliable men," he concluded, were so fearful of being "swamped in the quicksands of abolitionism" that they would join the devil to defeat Wadsworth.[31]

The gubernatorial campaign degenerated into a bitter contest. Republicans, thoroughly frightened by the prospect of losing the state, coalesced and made Seymour's patriotism the campaign's chief issue. Setting the party line, Greeley pictured him as an ultra-Peace Democrat whose victory "would be hailed beyond the lines of the Union armies." Conservative Republicans, plus many prohibitionists who despised Seymour's veto of a temperance bill when governor in 1854, echoed Greeley. As Raymond put it, Seymour devoted "ten times as much space and labor to the condemnation of our Government as he does to that of the Rebellion."[32]

Democrats answered back on two levels. As constitutionalists, they defended property rights, civil rights, decentralized government, and state autonomy. As antiemancipationists, they raised racist fears and portrayed Seymour as the white laboring man's savior. The Democracy added a further wrinkle in the city. Using emancipation as an excuse, Tammany and Mozart ignored past positions on the war and shared the congressional and municipal tickets.[33]

While the Democrats held all the advantages, some party leaders such as Belmont feared that Republican attacks on Seymour might sway impressionable voters. Other Democrats were alarmed over Unionism. Such forebodings were real. The Union State Committee asked Lincoln to dispatch General Franz Sigel of Missouri to sway German Democrats, while Bryant pleaded for some military victories to stiffen Republican resolve. Greeley had a firmer grip on the situation. The Democrats would win, he complained to abolitionist upstater Gerrit Smith, because "the Rum-sellers, the Irish and the Slavery idolators make a big crowd and they are fiendish in their vote against the president's proclamation of freedom."[34]

Greeley was correct. Democrats rebounded throughout the state, Seymour won easily, and in the city both Woods gained congressional seats. In legislative races, Democrats made startling gains, but not enough to offset Republican control on a forthcoming joint ballot to elect a new senator. As a result of Administration policies, then, Democrats had reversed the entire thrust of state politics in the period between April and November 1862. Nonetheless, party unity was cosmetic; shrewd political observers believed that the simple desire to win was the prime factor holding the Democracy together. The real eruption, sure to come, lay in how Democrats interpreted their triumphs.[35]

The fall election of 1862 proved the last major Democratic triumph during the Civil War years. Despite the surface appearance of a revitalized party, the Democracy was more on the defensive than it realized. As a protest vehicle, the party had reaped success by combining racial fears and public disillusionment over a stalemated war into a telling indictment against all Republicans and Union Democrats. Yet as the war dragged on into 1863, the necessities of war transformed the struggle into a truly total effort that invalidated Democratic philosophy. Now forced to mobilize the Union for a centralized war effort, Lincoln and Congress passed a series of laws — the draft, a high protective tariff, a national banking system, an unprecedented internal revenue act, and a legal tender act unsecured by specie — that fundamentally eroded Democratic values such as state sovereignty, decentralism, free trade, limited government, property rights, individual liberty, and the divorce of state and federal banking. Just as damaging to Democratic beliefs in laissez-faire, the Republicans allied themselves to the Northern business community by accepting the old Whig idea of an activist government that stimulated the economy.

The Democracy was appalled but disarmed. In Congress, most Democrats acted as the loyal opposition, sustained laws they thought necessary to prosecute the war, and tried to prevent Republican abuse of one-party rule. But because Congress operated under Republican majorities, Democrats, bereft of their Southern wing and split over Unionism, lacked enough votes to sustain the traditional functions of a two-party political system. As a result, congressional actions had grave partisan overtones for all Democrats because these laws involved the allocation of power that undercut the party's principles and its traditional localism.

As Democratic principles and programs crumbled under the impact of war, then, the party faced three major imponderables that symbolized its plight. Democrats were forced to ask themselves if their philosophy of decentralism, forged in peacetime, was a working alternative to centralism as a means to win the war? Or did centralism and the growth of federal authority, as Republicans contended, provide the only approach to victory? Equally complex was the problem that, if Republican values worked, the people might become so conditioned that a return to Democratic principles once the war ended might be impossible.

In New York, the situation was particularly grave. Since the War Democrats dominated the Democracy because of Seymour's victory, they could not shirk the responsibility for beginning the process of intraparty regeneration. It was precisely at this point that party leaders had to again ponder the key questions they faced: for what ends did the party now exist; what visions of the future did it hold; what principles could it plausibly emphasize; how could traditional politics bridge the gap separating War and Peace Democrats while regaining the Unionists? How well the Democracy met those challenges would not only determine Seymour's success as governor, but lay the groundwork to unseat Lincoln.[36]

Seymour's term began under almost impossible conditions. Both Democratic factions demanded exclusive patronage, and the party's regional jealousies made his appointive policies a nightmare. Even Republicans were involved in Seymour's woes. Lincoln dispatched Weed to sound the governor out about his forthcoming program and hoped to influence him with the need to sustain the war. The meeting proved disappointing. Weed reported that the governor was "morbid" over the suppression of civil rights; he felt the radicals who had

"Nigger on the Brain" dominated the Republicans and were "laboring to destroy the Government and the Union." Seymour's legislative address indicated how little impact Lincoln's messenger exerted. The governor chided the President for misusing executive powers, condemned arbitrary arrests, argued that generals abused martial law, defended the spirit of decentralism in the volunteer system for troop recruitment, and concluded that "fanaticism at the North" prolonged the war.[37]

Seymour's address was less a statement of goals than a manifesto of Democratic grievances. As such, it projected him as a key leader of the national War Democrats and possibly the Peace Democrats. Locally, however, the message served an unanticipated end; the opposition used it in the legislature to form a solid front against Democrats. Their unity increased with Weed's resignation from active editorial control of the *Evening Journal.* Although he remained politically involved and continued to blast radicals, his retirement gave most Republicans and Democratic Unionists a reason to table their policy quarrels in order to preserve the Union "on a solid and permanent foundation."[38]

Democratic troubles escalated during Seymour's first months in office. War and Peace Democrats were unsatisfied with his evenhanded patronage and distracted his attention from policy-making. In the city, Tammany, Mozart, and the swallow-tails fell into a bitter disagreement over local leadership. Worse, upstaters and city Democrats became more estranged over dividing the spoils. The party's inability to govern, coupled with Seymour's criticism of the Administration, disillusioned many Democrats. Led by John Van Buren, they siphoned off a large number of War Democrats who joined Republicans and Union Democrats to form a branch of the Loyal Union League, which pledged nonpartisan support for the war.[39]

Democrats tried to end this erosion by their own form of propaganda. Some conservatives organized a new pressure group, the Society for the Diffusion of Political Knowledge. Intended to "promote sound political education" about the dangers of "arbitrary and unconstitutional measures," the Society issued over one hundred pamphlets in English and German, written by a variety of men including Tilden, Seymour, and Washington Hunt. Another group surfaced among ultra Peace

Democrats, led by Gideon Tucker, Ben Wood's crony and a former *Daily News* editor. These men formed the Anti-Abolitionist State Rights' Association, issued racist pamphlets, and labored for a negotiated peace. The formation of these two groups, so close in time that they overlapped, confused the public which considered them synonymous. Tilden might argue, then, that the "calamity of our times is that the people have outgrown their knowledge of their own civil institutions." But the *Herald* lumped both groups together and asked "how do they propose to save the Union? Why, by a revolution against the government." In short, the Democracy had failed to establish a unified system of legitimate dissent.[40]

At the same time, the Union's inability to score a decisive victory increased Northern defeatism. The Peace Democrats made the most of the opportunity and tried to mold the party in their image. Fernando Wood set the pace. In Congress and at a series of public meetings that reached a peak at a mass state convention in July 1863 dedicated to "Peace and Reunion," Wood ticked off a litany of Peace Democratic attacks against the Administration and the War Democrats. Left unsaid but clearly implied was Wood's drift to extremism, peace without reunion. That is, if negotiations failed, renewal of the war was fruitless; the Union's only recourse was Confederate independence.[41]

Wood's prestige increased when General Ambrose Burnside arrested Ohioan Clement Vallandingham, a leading national Peace Democrat, for disloyal statements. Immediately, New York Democrats of all factional labels erupted in angry protest meetings. Despite that, the basic differences within the party remained. While War Democrats bitterly assailed the Administration for abusing constitutional guarantees of free speech, they had no intention of falling under Peace Democratic sway. For their part, Peace Democrats used Vallandingham as a martyr to increase their stature as party leaders and defied War Democrats to stop them.[42]

The War Democrats met the challenge. They lashed back by calling a special meeting of the state committee which they controlled. In particular, the committee passed two resolutions that reemphasized the need to restore the Union on a constitutional basis, consistent with party principles. Moreover, the committee pinpointed the Peace Democrats' weakness by pointing out that their program rested on Confederate willingness to compromise, a willingness not apparent. In citing the Vallandingham case, the committee concluded that Wood's fervent efforts hid a sinister desire for "dishonorable peace." Tammany Hall followed the same course. For the past several months, William M. Tweed had attempted to form a working agreement with the Woods. These efforts angered men such as Purdy and Clancy, who forced Tweed to join them in denouncing both Woods. Simultaneously, Clancy indicted Fernando Wood as a "Rebel sympathiser" and cautioned Democrats to avoid him.[43]

Yet one issue, opposition to the draft, tended to draw the two factions together. War Democrats condemned conscription as an invasion of state autonomy, while Seymour termed it another example of unwarranted centralism. Peace Democrats lost restraint. In particular, they blasted the section that exempted a draftee if he bought a substitute or paid a $300 commutation fee. Almost daily, their newspapers, notably Ben Wood's, damned the war as a poor man's fight, aimed at freeing blacks, who would then move to New York to replace white laborers. Against this backdrop, the governor ignored Mayor Opdyke's warning of a possible riot when the draft began. Instead, Seymour heaped fuel on a combustible situation by making a speech at the New York Academy of Music destined to haunt him for the remainder of his career. "Remember this," he said, "that the bloody and treasonable doctrine of public necessity can be proclaimed by a mob as well as government." Few people were prepared for what happened next. In a city long conditioned to riots, with a police force wise in the ways of mass frenzy, New Yorkers watched in agony as a three day explosion of hate created an orgy of looting and murder that scandalized the entire Union.[44]

The Republicans pounced on the riot with the same fervor Democrats used against emancipation. All sections of the party charged Seymour with complicity, argued that he "disgraced his high office," and exulted that he had "killed himself and his party." Furthermore, they maintained the Peace Democrats had provoked lawlessness to endanger the war effort. Greeley was even bitterer and singled out the Irish as the main culprits. Reeling under these attacks, Democrats lamely defended themselves. War Democrats blamed the Administration for "arbitrary" centralism which transformed "law-abiding people into a mob." Peace Democrats nodded in agreement and suggested the riot indicated New York's growing antiwar spirit. Seymour defended his "honor" and upheld his right to denounce unfair laws, but promised to abide by the draft's provisions when it resumed. As for the Irish, they argued that nativism, not patriotism, prompted Republican attacks.[45]

Things got worse rather than better for Democrats. Republican strategists, aware that the riot had ignited full-scale public indignation, especially after the recent Union victory at Gettysburg, quickly adapted to the new swing in public opinion. To symbolize their cause, the Republicans formally adopted the label of the Union party at their state convention. If anything, however, Weed dominated. Following his advice to broaden appeal, the delegates downplayed all controversial issues including emancipation and nominated a ticket that excluded radicals. Greeley was so upset, a Weedite reported, that he "declared it to be the last State Convention that he should attend." Despite this, one paramount fact emerged — Republicans intended to win; all other questions were secondary.[46]

By contrast, Democrats labored under several debilitating miscalculations. Despite the seeming popularity of Peace Democratic ideas earlier in the year, the draft riot marked their apex and became the turning point in Wood's struggle with Tammany. For his part, Fernando Wood, not Seymour, became the riot's chief victim within the party because his main power base, the Irish, could no longer back him without appearing unpatriotic. With that in mind, the Irish formed a new faction under John McKeon, an influential lawyer, opposed to both halls.

Neither the Regency nor Tammany realized Wood's decline and both proceeded to compound Democratic mistakes. Tweed reneged on the War Democrats by making a deal with Mozart to freeze the McKeonites out by forming a joint convention delegation without reference to national issues. Equally damaging, Tweed forged an agreement on the local ticket with Mozart that gave Wood the bulk of municipal offices in return for his support of Tweed's mayoral candidate. The Regency was just as inept. It placated Peace Democrats by passing a resolution that favored a compromise, but later reversed positions by adopting a plank that supported the war along conservative lines. Then Richmond, working with Wood, Tilden, and Tweed, formed a state ticket that included a Constitutional Unionist, a War and Peace Democrat, and a Union Democrat. Seymour was elated. "Everything looks well in the State," he told a supporter. "Our friends are confident and united."[47]

Seymour fooled himself. The convention revealed the Democracy's lack of consistency, the Regency's equivocation angered both War and Peace men, and Tammany's deal with Mozart solved nothing beyond local divisions of spoils. James Gordon Bennett, the shrewd owner and editor of the *Herald,* understood public opinion far better than any Democratic politician. "Many thousands of the loyal Democracy, national in their views and independent in their judgment," the paper intoned, were "dissatisfied" with the party's blatant expediency made at the expense "of the only great issue now great enough and grand enough to absorb popular attention — the issue of war for the Union or peace at the price of dissolution."[48]

Both parties locked into a desperate struggle, each realizing the effect a resounding victory might have on national politics. The Democrats, however, went down to painful defeats. In November, the Union party swept to victory, although the joint Tammany-Mozart slate managed to salvage some local contests. But in the December mayoralty election, the voters rebuffed Tweed's expediency and elected McKeonite C. Godfrey Gunther by a split vote in a three-man race. As a consequence, many War Democrats stirred with anger and several ward committees sought Tweed's ouster from the Hall's leadership circle. Assessing these developments, the *Herald* concluded: "The old Democratic party is dead as the old Whig party, and thus Tammany, Mozart and the Albany Regency amount to nothing."[49]

Democratic leaders immediately understood the threat to their political futures. Manton Marble symbolized that awareness. He theorized that the Democracy could never revive unless it unequivocally rejected the Peace Democrats. To that end, he launched a boom, with the aid of Barlow and Belmont, for the presidential nomination of their friend General

McClellan. Although the general proved coy, he left no doubt he welcomed the chance to oppose Lincoln. Nevertheless, Marble labored against two difficulties; the Peace Democrats and Democratic Unionists considered McClellan unsuitable, and some War Democrats, who agreed with Marble that the party must end its ambiquities, failed to see how they could support the war without also endorsing emancipation. Marble did not back down. He felt the general was the only person the Democracy could back, and "any man who runs for the Presidency on an open Peace Platform . . . is doomed to an utter rout at the polls."[50]

Tweed agreed. Although he was a key figure in Tammany because of his chairmanship of the Hall's General Committee, the city Democracy's ruling body, and controlled many patronage slots due to multiple office holding, Tweed did not dominate the total organization. Moreover, his destructive flirtation with Mozart had lowered his prestige. It was time for action.

Along with his close associate, Peter B. Sweeny, a man the public considered the brains behind him, Tweed laid out fresh tactics. He now wanted close cooperation with War Democrats and meant to defeat both Woods as men and as symbols when they ran for congressional reelection. Tweed began by using his chairmanship to decentralize the General Committee by increasing its membership, which added many War Democrats, and he allowed ward committees more authority. His purpose was not as egalitarian as the *Leader* claimed. By enlarging the General Committee, he made it too unwieldy for decision-making, hence minimizing the chances for rivals to oust him. Moreover, he regained the gratitude of War Democrats, and he removed old committeemen who challenged him. Finally, Tweed reserved two vital functions to Tammany's three-man Committee on Organization, which he and Sweeny controlled: it had the right to discipline rebellious ward representatives and it selected delegates in contested elections. In short, Tweed had created the possibility of bossism; he could discipline Tammany, but Tammany could not discipline him.[51]

At this critical juncture in February 1864, the Democracy held its state convention to name national convention delegates. If the party was ready to take a firm stand, it could find no better time. Instead of making an effort to regenerate the party around prowar issues, however, the Regency revealed a weakness that bordered on political bankruptcy. The first sign of Richmond's irresolution occurred when the credentials committee considered which competing New York City delegates to admit: prowar Tammany, Peace Democratic Mozart, or the McKeonites, a mixture of both positions. The committee took the easy way and evasively split the delegates among the three. The McKeonites and Mozart accepted; Tammany balked. When the question reached the floor and the convention refused an override, Tammany withdrew. Purdy, the Hall's "Old Warhorse," stalked from the meeting and muttered to reporters that Tammany could not accept a compromise full of "dishonor and disgrace," one tantamount to a surrender of "the cause of the Union." With that settled, the Regency formed an uncommitted delegation, minus Tammanyites, bound by the unit rule under Richmond's control, and the convention adjourned without any statement of principles.[52]

In a way, Richmond's strategy made sense. With the party so fragmented, he bought time to see how events developed. Then, too, the lack of any endorsement gave him the flexibility to prevent a stop-McClellan movement. On the other hand, the Regency did not grapple with vital war-related issues, which diminished the party's standing as an effective political organism. What the delegates failed to grasp was that the Democracy could not revive old partisan traditions, nor deal with wartime changes, until its commitment to saving the Union was clear. Until it did, its opposition to Lincoln smacked of disloyalty, and the entire organization could not plausibly defend its conservative principles nor the normal processes of a two-party system. Only Tammany and Marble emerged with a sense of the future. In stressing their devotion to the Union, they indicated the only means toward party reconstruction.

Republicans were understandably thrilled by Democratic actions, but a variety of internal problems prevented them from exploiting the situation. In New York, the radicals and Democratic Unionists, led by Cochrane, along with the Weedites, opposed Lincoln's renomination for different reasons. The radicals and Democratic Unionists, fearful that Lincoln was ineffective, and angry at his easy Reconstruction plan, supported Salmon P. Chase. When he withdrew, they turned toward John C. Frémont and supported his independent third party ticket. The Weedites, furious that the President's local patronage policy seemed to prefer "his enemies over his friends in this State," also sought to block Lincoln. In the end, however, the conservatives came to his side because they lacked an alternative. Yet Weed was completely disillusioned. "I fear that we have as little to expect," he lamented to Senator Edwin D. Morgan, "from Mr. Lincoln even after a re-nomination."[53]

The Union national convention did not end factionalism. The delegates selected Lincoln, and wrote a broad platform that among its planks branded slavery as the cause of the war and called for its complete eradication through a constitutional amendment. Then, in a move that appeared an insult to New York radicals and Democratic Unionists, the delegates rejected Daniel S. Dickinson, the state's favorite son, for vice president and instead named Andrew Johnson. The radicals and Democratic Unionists were not satisfied; they still backed Frémont. Weed matched them in sowing dissension. He charged the radicals with fomenting secession and then prolonging the war in order to create the bitterness necessary for a harsh peace. He also accused Greeley and Opdyke of war profiteering in "cotton speculations" and sales of inferior goods to the military. At once, an angry war of words erupted that grew so bitter that Henry J. Raymond, chairman of the Union National Committee, despaired of victory and informed Lincoln "the tide is setting strong against us."[54]

With things going so badly, some pro-Lincoln Republicans began an effort to woo War Democrats. To that end, Postmaster General Montgomery Blair, a former Jacksonian and Barnburner, used his long friendship with Samuel Barlow to reach national chairman August Belmont. Lincoln and the Union cause were so identified in the popular mind, Blair wrote, that his defeat would encourage the Confederates. Under those conditions, the patriotic as well as logical choice for War Democrats, one that would remove the taint of disloyalty, lay in "rallying wholeheartedly with the President." By supporting Lincoln, moreover, the War Democracy could prevent "the revolutionary spirit prominent in some portions of the North" from using slavery as a partisan trick to divide parties in the future. That meant War Democrats must acknowledge slavery's demise; thus, by seeking merely to free blacks as a nonpartisan military issue, the War Democrats would "demonstrate the North is not fighting for Negro equality." Settling that question would realign the political system, Blair implied, because Northern public opinion rejected black equal rights. Since the radicals favored it, they would split the Union party and the Democrats could then rebuild a fresh national coalition based on new questions arising from the Confederacy's defeat.[55]

Blair's proposal perplexed Barlow. He did recognize the plan's many advantages, but was more conscious of its disadvantages. Barlow knew his friends were committed to McClellan, and that out of emotional loyalty they could not abandon the Democracy. Above those, they were uncertain what principles might justify fusion, particularly since emancipation seemed the antithesis of party doctrines. All these factors forced Barlow to reject Blair's ideas. Yet in writing to Blair, Barlow unwittingly revealed how deeply racism clouded the Democracy's future. Lincoln's renomination, he explained, was an endorsement of every "fallacy & monstrosity, which the folly of fanaticism of the Radicals may invent, including miscegenation, negro equality, territorial organization and subjugation."[56]

Even if the War Democrats wanted to find common ground with some Unionists, two events precluded such a possibility. The government suspended the *World* for publishing a bogus Presidential proclamation, and the military issued a warrant, which General John A. Dix quashed, for Barlow's arrest for complicity. Even if Barlow wished to follow Blair's advice, he could not without seeming a coward. The Unionists were not, however, dissuaded. Since Democratic leaders were unresponsive, they decided to appeal directly to the rank and file.[57]

Yet on the whole, Unionist prospects grew more bleak. The army's bloodbath in Northern Virginia increased defeatism and strengthened Peace Democrats. In Washington, a group of Republicans gave up on Lincoln and issued the Wade-Davis Manifesto that called on him to withdraw. Weed shared their convictions. In a signed editorial in the *Evening Journal,* he branded the Administration a failure, urged Lincoln to retire out of patriotism, and implied conservatives might back a proper War Democrat. To initiate further action, Weed visited the President and reemphasized that his election was "an impossibility" because the people were "wild for Peace." For once, the radicals accepted Weed's analysis. According to Bryant, the Democrats could win by rallying men "dissatisfied with the present administration of affairs" around a "sound, honest, capable War Democrat" on the simple platform of "unconditional submission to the Constitution and the laws."[58]

War Democrats were elated by Unionist problems, but cautious. "There is quite a difficulty in their ranks that will widen," Richmond observed, "untill [sic] we have a man in the field. When we do they will try to settle." What Richmond feared was the national Peace Democracy's startling surge of popularity caused by massive defeatism. Alexander Long and George H. Pendleton of Ohio, along with the Woods, cleverly manipulated this feeling and put the party on record that they would not tolerate "a war platform upon which to place a military hero." Rather, Long wrote a supporter, Peace Democrats were determined to block McClellan and secure "a peace candidate & a peace platform."[59]

In New York, Peace Democrats deceived themselves. As Bennett cannily noted, no matter how robust the national Peace Democracy appeared, they had lost momentum locally. Tammany agreed. It waged a relentless war against Peace Democrats, using cajolery, force, and naked patronage against their followers. Mozart cracked under the pressure and its fragmentation, which had begun earlier, now became complete. In desperation, Fernando Wood sought Lincoln's help to reestablish his credentials as a party leader. The President was willing to do so, the *Herald* observed, "to break up the Democratic party and secure his re-election." Yet nothing really helped. Many New Yorkers rejected the Peace Democrats because they could not justify their sacrifices if the Confederacy won at the bargaining table. Others assumed that slavery was doomed, and the real question, which only a united Democracy under the general could handle, lay in preventing black equality. Still others, who demanded a "change in rulers," felt the Peace Democrats, while they might grumble, dared not bolt.[60]

Unfortunately, the Regency failed to realize how badly Peace Democratic stock had fallen. Speaking for Richmond, the *Argus* editorialized that peace, "honorable to both belligerents," must come about "through the medium of a National Convention," which would "terminate strife" and restore "fraternal relations on the basis of a continuance of the Federal Union."[61]

To the utmost chagrin of the Regency, however, this statement created a storm of protest. On one side, the Peace Democrats were unappeased. Wood and others warned Richmond they would not tolerate McClellan, nor any "war candidate or platform." While the Regency might have expected such a reply, it was unprepared for War Democratic reactions. In the city, the *Leader* announced that Tammany had "two enemies: the abolitionists . . . and the Regency." Upstate, another War Democratic revolt stirred when Joseph Warren, the editor of the *Buffalo Daily Courier,* chided Richmond for failing to deal with issues other than those the Peace Democrats raised. Shifting the focus, Warren asked the Regency how it proposed to reconstruct the nation once the Confederacy died. Specifically, Warren wanted to know what policies the Regency envisioned on economic matters, and the role of traditional principles in reviving the organization. Only by grappling with such questions, Warren argued, could the Democracy survive. Manton Marble was another Regency critic. Despite his friendship with Richmond, Marble suspected the Regency secretly supported Seymour for president. Fully aroused, Marble also assumed that Richmond and Belmont had delayed holding the national convention until September as a step in that direction. The postponement even angered Barlow. He feared the move gave Peace Democrats time for more mischief, and contributed to a swing against McClellan.[62]

Flushed into the open, the Regency revealed that it had none of these things in mind. The problem was that its circuitous, often convoluted, strategy, confused others. Richmond and Belmont shifted the convention's date, not to mollify Peace Democrats but in hope that added time might turn the public against their strident arguments. Even so, the Regency had no intention of writing them off; it believed that a minority party could not ostracize a sizable faction and still win. With that in mind, Richmond wanted a "composite" ticket headed by the general with some prominent Peace Democrat for vice president. As for new issues, the Regency avoided them because it thought the public would respond to safe questions such as opposition to emancipation and centralism, plus defense of civil liberties and the one-term presidential tradition. Marble was a regrettable problem, but Richmond assured him that Seymour was not a candidate. In regard to Tammany, the Regency let

Purdy know that although the Hall was not represented at the convention, the party intended to seek its advice. Richmond made himself clear on the eve of the Chicago convention when he informed reporters the Regency solidly endorsed McClellan. Making the point firmer, Belmont publicly bet $4,000 that the party would nominate and elect the general. At last, the Regency's critics grew silent.[63]

Few things in politics are certain. Although Belmont remarked that the general's nomination "will not be as easy as we thought," his backers, confident of success, counted on winning over Peace Democrats primarily because he was the only man capable of gaining "any large portion of the army vote in the field." Hoping to avoid any unforseen complications chiefly over the platform, Barlow erred by assuring McClellan he saw "no harm by advocating commission, convention or any other ordinary or extraordinary [measures] looking to peace," provided the delegates kept "the Union in view." On the eve of the convention, a reporter wrote Lincoln, "both war and peace men appear to be agreed upon an armistice as one of the steps to peace, and that will undoubtedly be embodied in their platform."[64]

It quickly became apparent that McClellan's backers paid too stiff a price for such harmony. The delegates did select him and balanced the ticket with Peace Democrat George H. Pendleton. But War Democratic mistakes on the platform proved ominous. Peace Democrats wrote practically the entire document, notably the Second Resolution, which condemned the war as a costly failure and virtually accepted the Confederacy's independence. McClellan was cornered. As he pondered his options, advice poured in. "Throw the Chicago platform overboard," one Tammanyite pleaded. Cassidy denounced the platform as "a horrid piece of patchwork," and admonished McClellan to reject it. Barlow cautioned restraint. In the end, after shifting positions erratically, McClellan let his emotions rule and rejected the Second Resolution.[65]

War Democratic newspapers quickly sprung to the general's defense and laid out the main thrust of the party's campaign. They maintained that the Democracy was intent on preserving the Union and denied Republican charges that McClellan was a Peace Democratic captive. By electing him, Warren added, the new president would strike down the barriers Lincoln erected "between the Southern people and their return to allegiance," eliminate the threat to both "the property and lives of the Southern people," and end the war in the "simplest forms of submission to the Constitution and adhesion to the Union." Republicans, realizing the magnitude of the Democracy's trouble, refused to let McClellan off so easily. Greeley scoffed that Democrats favored unilateral surrender to Confederates at the price of national suicide.[66]

At the same time, New York Peace Democrats were furious but impotent. Not only had the delegates ignored Fernando Wood, but recent Union victories robbed them of their chief issue. At this critical point, they held a strategy meeting in the city. It was a time for decisions, but they found none. Although Ben Wood and the McKeonites denounced McClellan and War Democrats, local problems prevented even partial cooperation. Even worse, Fernando Wood broke with his brother to support the ticket. The War Democrats were elated. The intense rivalry among Peace Democrats removed them as potential rivals; their hostility to McClellan absolved him of disloyalty; and some of them, chiefly Fernando Wood's followers, backed into the War Democracy as supplicants. After reviewing the situation, Barlow gloated that "Ben Wood's opposition here helps rather than hurts us." Warren agreed. He charged Ben Wood with being a party traitor who led "a flank movement for Lincoln." In that sense, loyal Democrats judged the Peace-men as renegades to both nation and party.[67]

In contrast, Tammany Hall regained its position as the center of the local Democracy. The *Herald* commented that the Hall "stands for the Union, for the War and for McClellan, while the speculating, bargaining, copperhead concerns are for dis-union, for peace on the rebels' terms, for whoever will buy them and against McClellan." Tweed capitalized on the situation, and pressed for a permanent party realignment. The means to accomplish that, the *Leader* suggested, lay in "a wise, generous and magnanimous" policy to unite all Democratic factions under Tammany's "umbrella."[68]

In the interim, Republicans, as Richmond surmised, ended their factionalism with the Democratic convention. At their state convention, they accepted rival New York City radical and conservative delegations on equal terms, and easily nominated radical Congressman Reuben E. Fenton of Jamestown, a former Free Soiler, for governor. The platform backed the war, lauded the Administration, endorsed the proposed Thirteenth Amendment, and belittled Seymour's record. Once more, Weed was not satisfied. He favored the unavailable Dix for governor, but accepted Fenton as a lesser evil than other radicals. Through these maneuvers, party unity held. Weed might grouse to Lincoln that the radicals were like "rats" who would "not be with us an hour after they think your success doubtful," but he avoided any conflicts that might compromise the election. The radicals were equally cooperative. At the end of September, they encouraged Frémont's withdrawal. In sum, Republican concord strengthened because each faction scented victory and none wanted responsibility for failure.[69]

The state Democracy's convention met in less harmonious circumstances. As in the past, the first item concerned the seating of New York City delegations, a problem compounded by six groups, each claiming regularity. Barlow recognized the danger. If the delegates split the vote as they usually attempted, Tammany would, he felt, boycott the election. With that, the party would forfeit much of its hard-won prowar credentials, and the resultant proliferation of groups would prevent the Hall from delivering its needed pluralities. Moreover, the five anti-Tammany delegations sprang from the splintered Peace Democrats, who might not support the general even if admitted. Barlow took matters into his own hands. Using his prestige as a key member of the national Central Campaign Committee, which masterminded McClellan's campaign, Barlow forced the reluctant Richmond to accept only Tammany. At once, the others departed. Most delegates were unconcerned; the majority of Peace Democrats, they felt, "are rapidly falling into our ranks." Tweed's triumph became complete when Fernando Wood, shorn of power, slowly walked out of the building accompanied by hisses and groans.[70]

The party's prowar policy, however, was deceptive. After the usual criticism of Lincoln and fulsome praise for Seymour, the platform included one plank stating the Democracy "was unalterably opposed to the rebellion," but shortly reversed itself with another that accepted compromise "as the first step to peace and concord." The delegates then overwhelmingly renominated the reluctant Seymour, and set up a special committee, which Tilden headed, to gain "the critical soldier vote." Barlow was grim. He felt Seymour a liability to the national ticket, and suspected the Regency was more concerned with state victories than electing the general. A Democratic Unionist confirmed Barlow's fears. "I have been in Albany a few days among the [New York] Central Rail Road Democrats," he told Seward, "and I am entirely satisfied that they have no confidence whatever in being able to elect McClellan."[71]

During the relatively short campaign, Democrats dropped misgivings about such matters, followed Marble's admonition "to close up the ranks," and emphasized national issues such as free trade, inflation, centralism, and liberating slaves. Then, too, they charged the Administration used "despotism" to create a "sectional social system on all men," and manipulated the draft to silence war critics. The election's only issue, therefore, was "McClellan, with Peace as soon as it can be obtained on the basis of Union, or Lincoln with war until Slavery is destroyed." To emphasize the importance of the black question, ultra Peace Democrats stirred racist fears when they claimed Lincoln favored miscegenation and planned to make it official Administration policy once reelected. Even the army's recent victories were suspect in Democratic eyes; they were "manufactured to help Lincoln." Tactically, Democrats left no stone unturned. In the city, Tammany increased the tempo of illegal naturalizations, and Marble tried to goad Greeley and Odyke into attacking Weed by repeating his charges about their purported profiteering. Upstate, the Democracy gained the endorsement of the New York State Anti-Prohibitionist Central Committee, and labored for the military vote. The swallowtails were equally energetic. They used contacts to increase the party's coffers and immersed themselves in directing McClellan's national campaign.[72]

Faced by such Democratic efforts, the Union State Committee moved boldly. It sneered that McClellan was incompetent and pointed out that both the national and state platforms committed him to two conflicting policies toward ending the war and preserving the Union. Then, too, Democratic policies left Southern loyalists and black Union troops unprotected if the Confederacy survived. Beyond that, Unionists demanded that the Democrats be specific. Charging that the party was merely obstructionist, Unionists demanded to know what alternatives Democrats proposed as necessary war legislation. Here, the Democrats were cornered; the reality of the Civil War was that their principles were too inflexible, and the party lacked an alternative to centralism.

Democratic Unionists proved to be the major weapon against Democrats. Working through the masses, their message of nonpartisanship, coupled with Union victories, impressed many voters with the need to sustain Lincoln, not so much as a politician but as a symbol of nationalism. The Democratic Unionists culminated their efforts at a gigantic rally in New York City. Speakers including former Democrats such as Dix, Francis Cutting, Daniel Sickles, and Daniel S. Dickinson swore that their activities conformed to traditional principles laid down by Jefferson and Jackson. They had not deserted the party, the party had deserted them. In contrast, the Regency and Tammany, by opposing the Administration, led the Democracy down the same road Federalists trod to the Hartford Convention. Thus, the men who had served the Union in war using time-tested principles earned the right to reconstruct the Democracy in peace.[73]

The election was closer than anyone expected. Tammany elected five out of six congressmen, lost "but one warrior" in the county races, yet failed to offset the Unionists upstate who carried New York for Lincoln and Fenton by less than 10,000 votes. Equally damaging, the Unionists retained control of the legislature and dominated the state's congressional representatives. The Democracy's only solace was that the Peace Democrats were swamped; the Woods and other "irregulars" lost.[74]

The Democrats' first impulse was to blame their defeat on Unionist manipulation of the soldiers' vote, plus the presence of federal troops to "supervise" the election in the city. In a way, the party had a point. As one Unionist boasted to Lincoln, he had voted twice thanks to the military, once "for myself" and again for "an absent soldier." On second impulse, Democrats felt sorry for themselves. The nation, not the party, had lost, Barlow consoled McClellan. Because of Lincoln's reelection, "I see little prospect of anything but fruitless war, disgraceful peace, & ruinous bankruptcy."[75]

Behind these rationalizations lay a more far-reaching crisis. The experience of a nation at war confirmed the fact that the conflict reflected major divisions in a society undergoing rapid economic, social, political, and racial transformations. The situation changed all previous ground rules, and challenged the validity of Democratic principles. Since these principles were the glasses through which Democrats viewed the world, the party either had to accommodate those principles to changing realities and use them to reflect and influence policy, or lapse into sullen reactionism. Despite the closeness of the election, then, the Democracy's identity crisis intensified because it had not answered the four basic questions of 1861: for what ends did the party exist; what visions of the future did it hold; what principles could it emphasize; how did the old partisan traditions operate? To make solutions to those questions more difficult, party leaders faced three additional imponderables: what issues would divide voters once the war ended; had the Democracy gained a reputation for obstructionism because of its inability to clarify its position on the war that threatened its survival in peacetime; and, worst of all, had the entire Democracy outlived its usefulness?[76]

For Democrats, then, the presidential election underscored the point that the party had not recovered from the bitter internal struggles of the 1850s. The party, in November 1864, was still divided over policies, leadership, and direction, problems that became sharper by the taint of Copperheadism and the erosion of principles.

Under those conditions, the Democracy needed a new approach to state and national policies, consistency to reconstruct the party, and continuity in principles to justify its existence. But when party leaders sought help, confusion reigned. Diehard Peace Democrats rebuffed any idea of peace save on their outmoded terms and repeated the same shopworn arguments. As Ben Wood put it, "the practical fact [is] that the Union has become a thing of the past." Tammany Hall felt party regeneration rested on two factors: purging the Peace Democrats and restoring the prewar Democracy by accepting the inevitable — slavery was dead. With that question "as forever out of the way," the party could revive "Democratic principles" which "will rally to the old Democratic party the good and true men of the land . . . not only at the South, but at the North." Horace Greeley, for different motives, brought the black question into deeper focus. Pointing out that Jefferson Davis's request to the Confederate Congress for authorization to "arm and drill" slaves as soldiers meant that slavery was moribund, Greeley suggested that even "the dullest intellect must now comprehend that the restoration of a pro-slavery Union will be an impossibility."[77]

The points Tammany and Greeley raised — the nature of postwar America and the end of slavery — were the cutting edges of future politics. Standing on the threshold of a new political era, however, the Democracy bound itself with ambiguity. Ohio Congressman Samuel S. Cox, soon to move to New York City, articulated that attitude. To Marble, he asked: "Will you take judgment by Default against the States in rebellion by voting the constitutional amendment abolishing slavery: or would you go for party principles now to vote to 'eliminate' the slavery question out of our politics for the purpose of future success?" Momentarily, the Democracy had no answer.[78]

The Republican party had its own crisis. Since its formation, factionalism had wracked the organization. During the war, party unity generally prevailed because Republicans, augmented by Democratic Unionists, accepted the old Jacksonian idea of the majority's right to unlimited rule and coupled it to the Whig belief in an activist legislature to save the Union. But with the war nearly over, factionalism reappeared. Congressional radicals, Blair informed Barlow, wanted vengeance — disfranchisement of whites, territorialization of the former Confederacy, and black equality. Raymond and Weed had other goals. The ideal policy for Republicans and Union Democrats, Weed counseled Seward, lay in conservative programs that rebuffed radicals. Some Union Democrats pursued their own dreams. For one, John A. Dix suggested to Lincoln that the Union party provided a perfect model for postwar politics. The Republican crisis had another dimension. In destroying slavery, Joseph Warren shrewdly noted, the Republicans had severed the one link that held their party together. What then, he asked, would Republicans do when slavery "ceased to be a vital question"? Just like the Democrats, the Republicans lacked answers.[79]

Both parties, then, faced a new political era, with the old issues nearly resolved and new ones just forming. Since the Republicans were in power, they had responsibility for solving two immediate political questions: what policy did the Administration have in mind for national reconciliation, and how did it propose to treat blacks, once slavery died, in white America? On those questions hung the realignment of the two-party system.

2
Political Restoration: *1864–1865*

BEFORE Democrats grappled with the Thirteenth Amendment, several lingering but recurrent problems clamored for attention. Fortunately, the Peace Democrats solved one when they committed political suicide by sticking to their hackneyed arguments. Realizing the impossibility of the situation, ex-Congressman Fernando Wood deserted his brother and left on an extended trip overseas in the hope that with time voters would forgive him.[1]

Democrats could not solve other problems so easily. In the city, Tammany faced a new challenge. The Irish, a key group in party politics, distrusted the Hall, feeling that the organization prized their bloc voting but did not give a fair share of patronage in return. Moreover, they suspected the Hall's Protestant establishment. Fenianism was another source of friction. Many Irish-American zealots were emotionally committed to liberate their home land from British rule by conquering Canada as ransom for freedom. While these men made no overt move in that direction yet, they viewed Tammany's support for an independent Ireland as a political ploy.[2]

The swallow-tails and the Regency had other problems. Both groups resented Tammany Hall. They sought to regenerate politics through honest government by changing the structure and leadership of the municipal party, plus concentrating on economic issues such as free trade, hard money, lowered taxes, and fiscal retrenchment. To their dismay, Tammany blunted this attack when other concerned New Yorkers, led by ironmonger Peter Cooper of the influential Citizens' Association, dedicated to municipal reform, accused the Democratic-controlled Board of Supervisors of graft possibly running as high as $250,000. At once, the Hall claimed that the Association, and by implication all reformers, were Republicans in disguise. By that reasoning, any agitation against local corruption played into the opposition's hands. Forced on the defensive, the swallow-tails and the Regency grudgingly played a waiting game to give Tweed enough time to discredit himself. Yet the swallow-tails were not totally passive. Under Marble's leadership, they organized a new political and social club, the Manhattan, designed for upper-class elites, as a counter to the Tammany Society.[3]

In the interim, the local Democracy turned its attention to congressional debate over the Thirteenth Amendment. This issue gave the nation an index to judge how well the Democracy responded to changing political realities. The manner in which the party reacted would go far in determining its ability to revitalize itself, and perhaps the United States, once the war and war-related questions ended.

Until December 1864, congressional Democrats had managed to table the amendment. But then their delaying tactics failed. In Washington the radicals, working with the President's blessing, pressed acceptance. Secretary of State Seward was just as active and mounted a powerful lobby in New York. To make matters worse for hesitant Democrats, Jefferson Davis's proposal heralded the institution's death no matter what Northern action or inaction. Caught in these crossfires, the Democracy, divided along factional lines, beset by conflicting interest group pressures, and haunted by a leadership vacuum, could not formulate a consistent policy.

Upstate, the party split into two camps. One, clustered around Warren, considered slavery "doomed." Even so, Warren felt the amendment was superfluous owing to Confederate action. The second, headed by Richmond and Seymour, abrogated leadership. Richmond did agree with Warren that slavery was finished, but he also assumed that Democrats, from a constitutional standpoint, could not erase their traditional defense of state sovereignty and property rights. As his way out, Richmond lamely suggested that the party avoid a stand and allow each congressman to decide for himself because "there is so much diversity of opinion among our own party on the subject." Seymour feigned indifference. William Bilbo, Seward's chief lobbyist, informed Lincoln that "if it passes he [Seymour] would have no regrets." Such studied ambiguity carried its own liabilities. "We must have new leaders," a disappointed Warren told Marble, "and a more decided policy."[4]

In the city, the Democracy also split. As expected, Ben Wood never wavered. Slavery was a state institution, he warned. "No Democrat must violate constitutional guarantees," nor tamper with a "higher law" of nature that separated the races. Other Peace-men, just as bigoted and bound by conservative constitutionalism as Wood, were more moderate. Impressed by the arguments of some War Democrats that blanket opposition "will damn the Democratic party," they tended toward removal of slavery as a partisan issue.[5]

Tammany favored the amendment. Intent on reducing dangerous and divisive national problems such as slavery as a prelude to rebuilding the party around long-time localism, the Hall maintained that slavery had sundered the Democracy, cost it two presidential elections, and turned the state into a Republican preserve. As for state sovereignty, the amendment was necessary because slavery, "being a Constitutional right . . . could only be Constitutionally abrogated." Then, too, the Hall warned that Republicans might use Democratic intransigence to impose a harsh peace. Finally, Tammany recognized that the Republican party, built on the slavery issue, might not survive the disappearance of that question.[6]

Former Democrats backed the Hall's brief but for different reasons. Montgomery Blair, speaking for many old Jacksonians and Democratic Unionists, pleaded with Barlow to back the amendment. Blair's aim, however, was the reorganization of parties, not sympathy for blacks. When slavery was gone, he wrote, conservatives could "reconstruct parties" by opposing any black equality, particularly suffrage. Since the President rejected radical moves in that direction, the issue would split the Republicans, and the Democrats could join Lincoln's supporters in a new conservative party. "This would certainly bring about the reconstruction of the Union with the rights of the states unimpaired," Blair concluded. Other former Democrats increased the pressure. George Bancroft implored Cox to work for the amendment as a means to rebuild the old Jacksonian Democracy. William Cullen Bryant culminated the parade. Free Soil Republicans, he commented, had not irrevocably committed themselves to their new organization because old loyalties lingered. Many former Van Buren Democrats still watched the Democracy to judge if its action now merited their support. As one letter to the editor in the *Evening*

Post put it, once slavery ended, "the re-union of all who love Democracy is inevitable. It is sure to carry the country by an immense majority at the next election."[7]

Manton Marble epitomized the cross-currents that washed through the party. Personally opposed to the amendment, he wavered erratically. In December 1864, he termed it unneeded because of Confederate action. If Congress passed the amendment, however, further amendments would be necessary to clarify the status of blacks. The nation's best course, under those circumstances, lay in doing nothing and letting slavery die a natural death.

Such a timid and irresolute reaction only confused the question, and showed that the party was as unprepared for peace as it had been for war. In contrast to Tammany and Samuel S. Cox, who called on Marble to accept the amendment, Barlow rejected Blair's advice and backed the *World.* Yet Seward's operatives put unrelenting pressure on Marble. In mid-January, he made a subtle shift. The paper announced that the Democracy was never "pro-slavery" but upheld the constitutional principle of "non-interference" in state concerns. But Congress had the power to amend that position, and he implied that each congressman was free to follow Cox's lead. Having taken the plunge, Marble stopped short of an outright endorsement. As a result, he as well as the Regency and the Peace Democrats, forfeited a major opportunity to stunt the Hall's drive for party leadership.[8]

In the end, the Democracy was as confused as when debate began. In Congress, the New York delegation hopelessly splintered. Reaction in the state was mixed and again underscored the party's lack of direction. Upstate, the *Daily Courier* and *Argus* accepted the amendment's passage and urged the party to redirect its energies toward conservative economic issues. In the city, Wood flayed the few Democrats who had voted for the amendment as traitors to "the creed of their party." The *World* wasted little time in introspection but pointed out that without a speedy reconstruction of the Southern states, the process of ratification would be prolonged. Tammany was elated. Past issues were dead, the *Leader* wrote, and the Democracy would vault into power by stressing the party's traditional "principles of finance, of economy and accountability, of executive and legislative power, and of personal and political rights." The *Herald* endorsed the Hall's reasoning. With the nation no longer distracted by slavery, Bennett observed, economic issues were the cornerstones of the future. Upon them, the Democracy should rebuild the party as Tammany suggested.[9]

Mixed as these viewpoints were, several points emerged about the state of Democratic politics. With varying degrees, the party accepted the Thirteenth Amendment and anticipated a fresh era unconnected to slavery. Yet the Democracy's continued ambivalence over leadership raised serious questions about its ability to forge factional unity while reorganizing the two-party system. Beyond that, Tammany's surging prestige, marked by a commensurate decline among the Regency and the swallow-tails, accentuated the party's regional and political divisions. To perplex Democrats even more, Secretary of State Seward, working with Weed, plunged ahead in trying to create a new force in the state by constructing an alliance between conservative Republicans, War Democrats, and Unionists, while isolating the radicals, Peace Democrats, and Tammany.[10]

On the surface, Democratic prospects shone brightly. The Republican wing of the Union party shattered over state patronage, and Opdyke widened the rift by suing Weed for libel. Then, when conservatives and radicals began a bitter war of words about what obligations the government owed freed blacks, the Republican party seemed on the verge of its predicted disintegration. These developments appalled Union Democrats. Many of them agreed with Bryant's observation that a majority of ex-Democrats would shortly "betake themselves to other political organizations." Such problems were sweet to Democrats. Positive that the opposition's breakup was just a matter of days, Warren welcomed back all former Democrats with the warm embrace of brotherhood.[11]

In their elation, Democrats neglected sobering signs of a Republican renewal. Many Republicans had accepted slavery's end as a turning point in politics, and sought to rebuild the party on a fresh basis. Under radical auspices and exploiting the same type of centralism that had transformed the nation during the war, the followers of Governor Fenton used the legislature to create institutional reformism — the belief that changes in the institutions of government, directed by central authority, could usher in meaningful social changes — to both retain wartime power and retool the Republican party. Their moves were loaded with partisan dynamite. On one hand, they struck at the Democracy's soft underbelly, Tammany's corruption; and, on the other, at Seward's attempt to rebuild the Republican party into a conservative-moderate organization, directly linked to the presidential Union party of 1864.

The major target of institutional reformers lay in New York City, particularly its inefficient municipal government, the corruption rife in all its departments, the misery of urban life, and Tammany's culpability. As a start, the reformers aimed at changing the city's anachronistic volunteer fire system into a professional force. The reform package, however, had other long-range aims: a municipal health act, a voter registration law to eliminate purported illegal immigrant voting, an excise law to cut Sunday sales, a tenement act to set minimum building codes, and, above all, the implementation of these laws, through state commissions, based on the Republican-drawn Metropolitan Police Act of 1857, which created a supposedly nonpartisan board, under control of the legislature and governor. From the standpoint of urban needs, reformism was an issue whose time had come. As a result, these ingenious steps reaped immediate political capital among many groups that Democrats wooed. Bennett, Bryant, and Raymond endorsed the Fentonian program, fought for it on humanitarian, not partisan grounds, and urged the commission system to rout corruptionist "rascals."[12]

Many anti-Tammany Democrats secretly sympathized with the Fentonians. But they realized the party had to defend the Hall because it was the organization's core. Moreover, they recognized that the commission system was the antithesis of party principles, notably home rule. In particular, they resented the entire philosophy behind the commission system because it gave appointive officials more control over municipal and county expenditures than the elective mayor and aldermen. In that sense, the entire thrust of institutional reformism denied both the validity of party politics and the implications of majority rule. Reluctantly, then, the Regency, Warren, and even the swallow-tails criticized the legislature by defending the right of local self-rule. In that sense, the radicals, who were the main force among institutional reformers, were not interested in good government so much as in reaping partisan gains through unconstitutional centralism and antiurban prejudice. As for Tammany, the *Leader* emphasized its belief in popular responsibility at the grassroots, and stressed that its own brand of social reform, geared to its ability as a power broker, better served human needs than outsiders.[13]

Democratic efforts proved futile and the fire department bill passed. Nonetheless, the Hall felt it could finesse the radicals because it thought the governor, guided by past precedents, would appoint a bipartisan board. The governor, however, had one example to dissuade him; Tweed had bribed Republican supervisors to turn a supposedly nonpartisan board into a Democratic stronghold. It came as a complete shock to Tammany, then, when Fenton used the commission for his own ends and appointed three radicals and one Unionist.[14]

With state politics suddenly so dangerous, Democrats turned to national issues to revitalize the party. All Democratic factions agreed on a peace settlement without vengeance to restore old alliances with their prewar Southern colleagues. As Warren put it, "Reconstruction is synonymous with radicalism, restoration with conservatism." In specific terms, Marble added, the Democracy favored conditional restoration of the former Confederacy based on its acceptance of the Thirteenth Amendment, no black equality in any form, reestablishment of state sovereignty, probation toward rebel leaders until they proved repentant, no military occupation, "amnesty to the Southern people," and invalidation of the Confederate debt. If the United States did those things and rejected the "theoretical schemes of pseudo-philanthropy" rife among the radicals, the *Leader* concluded, all American citizens could "congratulate each other upon a restored Union and a regenerated Democracy."[15]

A large part of Democratic calculations hinged on President Lincoln, who had not yet established a rigid policy toward the defeated Confederates. The Democrats also assumed that he was more conciliatory concerning the rebels than Andrew Johnson, who seemed firmly radical. Then, too, all Democratic factions considered Johnson unfit for high office because of his intoxicated behavior during his vice presidential inauguration.

The *Leader* observed that "prayers" for Lincoln's continued good health "have become very fervent." The reason, Ben Wood explained, was that if by chance the President died, Johnson would shame the Republic "beyond endurance."[16]

Lincoln's death was a national tragedy and a Democratic dilemma. In political terms, "What will Andrew Johnson do?" became the paramount question. The Democracy was uncertain, but agreed it was vital to establish a rapprochement with the new President. Reflecting that idea, Barlow told Blair "our duty is apparent. Can there be any longer any party in opposition to Mr. Johnson?" Other Democrats swallowed the harsh words they had uttered scarcely a month earlier and assured Blair, Johnson's close friend and advisor, that New York Democrats intended to give the President "cordial support." After reading these responses, Blair told Barlow not to despair, no matter how radical the President seemed, because he was still a Democrat at heart. Thus, if the "Democrats are true to their principles, [they] must sustain Andrew Johnson."[17]

Such promises of Democratic aid were inevitable given the circumstances of Johnson's sudden thrust into the presidency. Yet the intensity of their views indicated that many now believed that Johnson was a Unionist in name only and would waste little time in declaring himself a true Democrat. Tammany Hall epitomized the party's changing view of Johnson. The *Leader* pronounced him "a thoroughly ingrained Jacksonian Democrat," who typified wartime Democratic Unionists sure to return to prior "loyalties and antecedents." To reassure the party, the paper noted his record. He was "no negrophile"; he opposed most Republican "economic legislation"; and he was "against wasteful extravagance in internal matters of government." In their haste, Tammanyites made one blunder: Blair cooperated with Barlow, Tilden, and Richmond and considered them the party's natural leaders. As a result, if Johnson proved a Democrat, the swallow-tails and the Regency, not the Hall, would garner credit for reviving the party and with it a lock on critical federal patronage.[18]

There was as much speculation and hope as to what Johnson intended amoung other interest groups. Many Republican Barnburners, Free Soilers, and Democratic Unionists expected Johnson to steer his Administration between both Democrats and Republicans and build Unionism into a third political force unconnected to either party. Conservative Republicans, mainly Seward and Weedites, agreed with that assessment and thought the President backed their efforts to rid the Union party of radicals. Radical Republicans, in contrast, took Johnson's past statements about punishing treason at face value and assumed he favored a harsh peace.

Some Democrats dissented from all these assumptions. Warren, for one, took sharp issue with the party. Although Johnson "still claims to be a Democrat" and "it seems improbable" he "will fall into the hands of the ultraists," Warren cautioned, the Democracy must judge him on acts not expectations. A great deal of how Democrats would respond, the *Argus* and the New York City *Irish-American* concurred, depended on two variable — the President's treatment of radicals and his restoration policy.[19]

As things stood, then, Johnson inherited massive public sympathy following Lincoln's assassination. But each faction in both parties expected contrary things from him. Under these circumstances, the President needed great political skill and firmness, plus the ability to read public opinion correctly, if he was to expect success.

Although New York Democrats decided to give Johnson time and scope to shape restoration, they did not intend to remain passive. Rather, they turned their attention to the problem of party reorganization. Immediately, sparks flew over which faction controlled policy-making. Based on its war record, Tammany staked claim to leadership. The *Leader* maintained that Tammany presented "a nucleus" for party reorganization, while the "temporizing Regency" and the traitorous Peace Democrats had disqualified themselves. A great party could not be constructed "upon shifting sands of expediency," as they sought, the paper announced, "but upon the eternal rocks" of Jacksonianism, sound finance, and generous restoration. As part of that restoration, the Democracy must reach out and find allies among conservative Republicans and regenerate Union Democrats.[20]

The Regency and swallow-tails scorned the Hall's pretensions and sought reorganization through an alliance with President Johnson. Yet they were uncertain of how far to commit themselves, as Warren suggested, without a direct sign of the

President's support. Certain factors chilled their ardor. Johnson continued military courts, he refused to restore the writ of *habeas corpus,* he established a military commission to prosecute Lincoln's assassins, and he countermanded General William Sherman's generous peace terms toward the last Eastern Confederate army command. With that in mind, the Regency and swallow-tails pressed Johnson in a variety of ways, to emphasize that he could not automatically expect Democratic aid. Marble cautioned him that the rebellion was over and the "necessity" for extralegal judicial practices had also ended. It was time for him to "revive the law." The *Argus* chimed in that he must restore constitutional legal forms to "re-inspire" the nation's confidence in its "institutions" and "rulers." Even Barlow was wary. To Blair he wrote that the President must bend because a "huge feeling" existed among Democrats against infractions of civil law. Did not Johnson realize, Barlow asked, that the war was over?[21]

In Washington, Montgomery Blair assessed the New York situation and decided to continue support for the Regency and swallow-tails. That created serious repercussions in the state because he failed to appreciate the dynamics of local politics. Mistakenly informing Johnson that the city Democracy was "demoralized," Blair compounded his blunder by assuring him that the Regency was in the "ascendant." Beyond that, Blair's greated folly lay in thinking that the swallow-tails, chiefly Barlow, wielded real power within the city organization. This was simply not true. Even though Tweed was a controversial figure, he was a professional; Barlow was not. As he admitted to a friend, "I am overwhelmed with [legal] work and have no desire to take part in politics whatever." Thus, while Barlow only dabbled in party reorgaization, and while Marble thought the *World* had effective influence, neither man was a policymaker. Tammany accepted their advice only if it fit the party's needs.[22]

Yet in a larger sense, none of the Democratic factions controlled party regeneration. William Cullen Bryant, who loomed large in their plans of regaining former Democrats, illustrated the party's problems. Bryant initially encouraged the Democracy's expectations. The Republican party, he announced, was dead because it no longer had a "distinctive creed to express, or any peculiar function to fulfill." But he shocked Democrats by saying their party was also finished. Except for its hunger for spoils, the Democracy had "no collective unity or life," it "proclaims no great ends," and must give way "to another, fresher, more pertinent and more earnest organization." In a philosophic sense, Bryant totally demolished Democratic hopes. Expressing the equalitarian spirit of Jacksonianism, he said that party labels were meaningless. Instead, one party would adopt the "true democratic ideas" embodied in "the freedom, the equality and the right of every individual worked out and sustained by equal laws and impartial institutions." A second party would then emerge, one based not on the idea of "equal rights," but "in the dictates of expediency or in an assumed devotion to the general good of society." The "great majority" of the people, he concluded, favored the former.[23]

By shifting the question of party reorganization from factionalism to principle, Bryant pinpointed the Democracy's structural weakness. As Marble noted earlier, ending slavery created a chain of consequences about the status of freedmen that the nation could not ignore. Even so blatant a racist as James Gordon Bennett realized the problem's dimensions. In a breathtaking piece of advice, considering the source, the *Herald* instructed Democrats that their goals hinged on ending the black question by giving freedmen "a share in the political right of the ballot-box." Racial justice played no part in Bennett's reasoning. Restoration could not begin because radicals, he felt, intended to keep ex-rebel states out of the Union under the guise of federal protection for blacks. At the same time, the paper scoffed at white fears that "negro social equality" would follow black suffrage. "Society will take care of itself in this matter," he forecast. Bryant made the message even clearer. If postwar white Americans wanted "peace and prosperity," they must "look to it that all men shall have equal rights" including "universal suffrage."[24]

Democrats turned deaf ears to these arguments, partly because of ingrained racism, partly because of traditional principles. Representing the viewpoint of many Democrats, Samuel S. Cox sympathized that "the blacks are as much misplaced in their freedom as they were in slavery." But he came to the conservative conclusion that the whole question was a state, not federal, matter. Democratic white supremacists found their spokesman in James Brooks's *New York Express*: "The objection to negro suffrage is not ignorance or poverty, but race." Democratic antisuffrageites, however, tended to follow Manton Marble, who based his position on what he inferred lay in Johnson's mind. Speaking as a states' righter, Marble said that suffrage was a local concern. The federal government could not infringe on the "seminal" rights "small communities" exercised in self-determination. Defense of that principle, Marble felt, "is almost as important as the principle itself."[25]

Once again, Democrats floundered over the application of their ideology, chiefly equal rights, to concrete circumstances. Temporarily, it seemed the party would not suffer because the President seemed amenable to Marble's view. In May, when Johnson refused to take position on suffrage in a meeting with visiting blacks, John Dash Van Buren, a distant cousin of John Van Buren, whom people often mistook for his kinsman, gloated to Blair: "The President's speech to the darkies is excellent in what it says & what it omits." For the moment, then, Johnson had cooled both sides of the suffrage question because each did not wish to antagonize him while his position was so imprecise.[26]

Despite the lull, the Democracy's antisuffragism, whether based on principles or racism, loomed as a major political issue with vast potential. Evidence from past state elections when voters turned down amendments easing the state constitution's property qualifications for free blacks, plus the lack of consensus among Republicans concerning suffrage, indicated the question's explosiveness. As a result, New York Democrats were determined to manipulate the issue to split Republicans, while most Republicans, outside of the radicals, were evasive until public opinion hardened. Yet of the two parties, the Democracy was in greater peril over the black question. As the party faced the many problems that ending the war had created, Democrats took it for granted that black welfare was secondary to the welfare of whites. What Democrats failed to realize was the essential fact that the organization could not return to conventional economic and political issues, nor validate traditional principles, until it forged a consistent policy based on settling the full constitutional status of blacks because this problem directly related to the nation's entire postwar tasks. Under those conditions, black suffrage was an inevitable issue that both parties faced, and neither could totally solve other political questions until the nation resolved the matter.[27]

As things stood, Democrats reverted to their prewar attitude of white Southern apologists. Party editors, notably Warren, Cassidy, and Marble, developed various explanations based on principle and racism. They contended that slavery had left blacks unable to cope with freedom; if left to themselves, blacks would face racial extermination. Southern whites, by habit, training, and self-interest, would save then, and, in the process, restore prosperity. As for blacks, the unconstitutional radical agitation for suffrage, land confiscation, and redistribution hindered racial progress and contributed to an increasing death rate. Applying that reasoning to the Freedmen's Bureau, Democrats charged that the agitation undermined local self-government and gave black false notions about rights they must earn, not inherit, since they were not yet citizens. Turning to white Southerners, Democrats suggested they must face reality, beginning with the awareness that the Thirteenth Amendment benefited both races. For whites, it ended the wasteful plantation system; for blacks, Marble wrote in the spirit of emerging social Darwinism, "it opens the door for the full development of the capacity of the negro race; if that race possesses the elements of enduring strength; or for its gradual extinction by the silent operation of natural causes."[28]

On May 29, 1865, President Johnson broke his silence about restoring the Confederate states by issuing two policy guidelines. One defined amnesty as a Presidential prerogative based on excluded groups, not individuals. The second outlined the process of restoration in North Carolina with preconditions that implicitly denied black suffrage. Democrats lauded the President's program, although some expressed dismay over his definition of amnesty. Even so, one visitor to New York was so impressed with Democratic praise that he told Johnson, "all conservative elements of the Country will enter actively upon an open support of the government."[29]

Republican rejoinders followed factional lines. New York conservatives backed the President, while radicals cried that the proclamations were defective because Johnson had not come out for universal suffrage and had thus placed in power many former Confederates. Bryant took a centrist position. The President, he wrote, did have the right to determine readmission policies. Nevertheless, "harmony and tranquil co-operation" in the South hinged upon the doctrine of equal rights. Yet until the President became more specific, Bryant adopted a wait-and-see attitude, and reenforced Democratic beliefs that the Barnburner and Free Soul Republicans would ultimately rejoin the party.[30]

James Gordon Bennett watched these developments with a craftsman's eye. Determined to reflect public opinion at the proper hour to sell newspapers and enhance his personal reputation as a political seer, Bennett felt the time was ripe and converted the *Herald* into Johnson's most vociferous local backer. In one way the paper's endorsement was vital for the President because of its importance as a political independent. But in other ways Bennett did him a disservice. Despite the paper's huge circulation, the largest in the the state, it rarely influenced policy-makers in either party. Above that, Bennett was undependable and often took contradictory positions to promote his paper, not advance the Administration's needs. Where Bennett was irreplaceable, however, lay in his ability to spot a trend, base his editorials on ideas the public was predisposed to accept, and then gain plaudits for influencing developments that actually began without his aid. By June 1865, Bennett declared that Johnson's "sagacious reorganization policy" was producing a national miracle involving sectional reunion. On that basis, the paper performed a gigantic transformation that recast the President's image from an accidental chief executive into the nation's legitimate leader.[31]

Blair was elated. He wrote to Barlow that Bennett fully favored their plan "to restore the old Democracy & lead the reunion." But Barlow was still uneasy about the President's reluctance to commit himself and increased efforts to get a hard policy outline. Blair, aware of his feeling, did his best to reassure the New Yorkers by having prominent Democratic leaders interview Johnson. By the end of July, Barlow seemed satisfied, but only to a point. In a veiled threat to Blair, he said that while Democrats fully intended to "support the Administration," the President "alone will be to blame" if that did not happen. At once, Blair arranged further meetings. By September, Johnson's visitors, including Tilden, agreed that he seemed receptive to such Democratic ideas as immediate seating of Southern congressmen from restored states, ending military tribunals, the restoration of *habeas corpus,* suffrage left to the states, and reorganization of his cabinet with Seward ousted.[32]

On the eve of the Democratic state convention, the swallowtails and the Regency succumbed. They felt any futher clarification would be self-defeating and might antagonize Johnson. Tilden, Barlow, Marble, and Cassidy now put themselves on the line when they drew up a series of pro-Johnson resolution for the delegates to endorse. Their only remaining task lay in convincing Tammanyites.

That proved difficult. Even though the Hall had clambered aboard the Johnson bandwagon at the start, Tammany was furious that its foes had emerged as the party's driving force because of their association with the President. Moreover, they resented Bennett's carping against "spoilsmen and plunderers" who "disgraced the city" in the "management of our municipal government." Tammany's stubbornness appalled Richmond and Barlow, and they held a meeting in New York City to resolve matters. Pragmatically, the Hall backed down. Recognizing the brute fact that most party workers favored the President, the Hall dared not risk disfavor without any more excuse than a squabble over local leadership. Yet in accepting the inevitable, Tammany merely bought time until it could defeat the swallow-tails and the Regency on grounds it chose.[33]

Former Peace Democrats played no part in these calculations. Although other Democrats realized the opposition could win enormous support by associating the entire organization with disloyalty, men such as Ben Wood reasoned that their ideology and static view of society fit into Johnson's restoration formula. Despite that, Tammany, the Regency, and the swallow-tails rejected their aid and called them a "squad of disorganizers" whom all loyal Democrats shunned.[34]

Concurrently, Thurlow Weed matured plans to reorganize the Union party in order to protect Seward, isolate the radicals, and quash the Democracy's absorption of Johnson. In mid-August, Weed gained a vital edge when the President reshuffled the New York Custom House by replacing Collector Simeon Draper, a moderate friendly with radicals, with former

Barnburner Preston King, a firm conservative. With this control of a major source of local patronage, Weed increased his efforts. For several months, Tammany encouraged him and even Bennett assumed fusion was possible based on mutual support for Johnson. Positive that his plans were working, then, Weed told Seward that Richmond and he "do not differ much in our view of the course things will take." Weed wallowed in an illusion; Tammany and the Regency courted him to lure Democratic Unionists, nothing more. Regardless of the advantages involved, however, neither Barlow nor Blair, who opposed Seward and Weed for a variety of political and emotional reasons, favored the ploy. Even so, Weed exuded confidence. To Seward he confided: "We are all right in the State, our only need is to be left alone."[35]

One reason for Weed's ebullience lay in his assumption that Democratic Unionists, who supported Johnson, lacked an alternative to coalescing with conservative Republicans. The reverse was true. Unionists indeed supported the President, but many of them including Sickles, Cochrane, James Brady, and Edwin Croswell, the *Argus*'s former editor, felt the Union party had lost its identity. Dickinson told Johnson the party had died with Lincoln; therefore, former War Democrats and Union Democrats sought "a new hearty organization of democratic tendencies," chiefly with conservative Democrats who would then realign parties by supporting Presidential restoration. Just like Bryant, these Democratic Unionists planned a new party within the old parties, with the child devouring the parents.[36]

The Democratic state convention, held in September, was a strategic victory for the Regency and swallow-tails. The delegates adopted their pro-Johnson resolutions without any changes. Among these planks were praise for the President, the idea that suffrage was a state concern, demands for full and quick repayment of the national debt, charges that Republicans had rigged the state census to deprive New York City of its legitimate legislative representatives, and acceptance of the Thirteenth Amendment as removing the last obstacle to "amicable feelings among the states."[37]

From the standpoint of tactics, the delegates ignored the Peace Democrats and formed a ticket which emulated the 1864 Union party by remaking the Democracy along bipartisan lines. The slate included one conservative Republican, one Loyal League Democrat, one Irish Democrat, and one Union Democrat, plus a sprinkling of War Democrats. Every party newspaper, except the *Daily News,* which eventually came around, outdid each other in lauding the convention's actions. Equally encouraging, most moderate and conservative Republican newspapers congratulated the Democracy for the quality of its candidates. Bennett had the last word. Both Democrats and Republicans wanted to ride the President's "coat tail," he wrote, but by meeting first, the Democrats "have taken a full and strong hold of the tail of President Johnson's coat" and left Republicans "grief-stricken" over their "lost opportunities."[38]

Blair was equally overjoyed. "The resolutions are capital & the whole movement eminently judicious," he told Barlow. Yet the New York Democracy could not relax because "everything depends on your vote this fall." If the party carried the state, Presidential restoration was safe from radical attacks; if not, "we may have a most serious struggle between the Executive and Congress." The Regency was aware of more dangers. Supporters from other states warned them that their dependency on Johnson could be self-defeating because he lacked the will to "hold out" against critics. Barlow shared that concern. At the same time that he reassured friends that the President had promise Tilden "all that we could ask," Barlow was still uncertain whether Johnson's actions matched his words. Somewhat somberly, he cautioned Blair "we shall carry the State unless the President unwisely allows the Custom House here and other Federal patronage to be exerted against us." However, these alarms, serious though they were, did not invalidate the excellent start the swallow-tails and the Regency made toward reorganizing the party. Now, all depended on winning.[39]

Weed controlled the Republican convention and dictated a platform that closely resembled that of the Democracy. With the aid of Senator Morgan and Congressman Henry J. Raymond, Weed then selected the ticket, comprising conservative Republicans and Democratic Unionists headed by a former Democrat, Major General Francis Barlow. Judging by radical reaction, it became clear that they wanted to avoid a confrontation with the conservatives even to the extent of remaining silent about black suffrage. In contrast, Weed felt conservatives did not need radical aid; even if they bolted nothing was lost. On the sidelines, Bryant took an ambiguous stance. He considered the platform overly "prolix in style" but admitted it "excellent in sentiment." In regard to candidates, the *Evening Post* confessed they were of above "average merit" but carefully skirted any endorsements and created the impression it could just as easily back Democrats. Bryant's equivocation ran counter to conservative plans. To prevent any slippage, Raymon clung to the President's coattails, denounced the Democrats for insincerity, and lectured Bryant that Johnson needed his total support for reviving the Union party.[40]

Democratic reaction was predictable. Furious that Weed failed to endorse any of their candidates in the spirit of pro-Johnsonism, Cassidy and Warren suggested that Weed's desire for personal aggrandizement instead of bipartisan fusion hurt the entire nation. Moreover, they argued that Weed insulted Democratic Unionists by ignoring some of their stronger leaders in nominating the clearly lesser Barlow. As a result, the Democratic editors claimed the old Union party was as dead as slavery. Tammany joined the attack after sulking over its minor role at the convention. The *Leader,* hoping to goad radicals into assailing conservatives, insinuated that the mounting Republican reluctance to face suffrage indicated a loss of will identical to a party death wish. To Raymond's claim that conservative Republicans controlled Johnson, Marble retorted: "Blood is thicker than water, and upon the issues of to-day President Johnson and the Democracy are firmly united."[41]

All these claims and counterclaims angered Bennett. Pointing out that each ticket in a practical sense had endorsed the President and rejected radicalism, the *Herald* maintained that political reorganization was complete and New York set a national pattern. Both the old Democratic and Republican parties were dead, never to be resuscitated. Now, the United States entered a period of a one party system, similar to President James Monroe's "Era of Good Feeling" with "President Johnson as its leader and champion." The paper concluded: "Prepare, then, we say to all old politicians, to make way for the new and magnificent party of the future." Only time could tell how well Bennett functioned as a political oracle.[42]

Since both Weedites and Democrats pegged politics on Presidential restoration, the key variable in the state election hinged upon the reaction of Southern whites. By October 1865, the situation came into focus. The ex-rebels interpreted restoration solely on their terms, and, encouraged by Johnson's leniency, made a series of blunders harmful to moderates in both parties. Among them were black codes that blatantly reinstitutionalized racism, truculent defiance of the North as if defeat had no meaning, and the election of many congressmen who had served in the Confederate administration or military.

These actions dismayed New York independents, moderates, and Weedites. Bennett called Southern intransigence "stupid" and warned the Southerners that they had destroyed any chance Congress might adopt Presidential restoration. Bryant was equally infuriated; he called for biracial "equal justice" in the South, and alienated Democrats by endorsing the opposition's ticket. Raymond, in his dual capacity as congressman and editor, spoke for Weed. Although disturbed by Southerners, the *Times* trusted the President and avoided any attempt to inject black issues into the campaign. Concentrating instead on Democrats, Raymond ridiculed them for having demeaned a man they now proposed to support. Only the radicals were happy. Instead of dealing with the local election, their newspapers devoted attention to reports that ex-rebels exulted over their easy return to power and their suppression of blacks. Implicit in such tactics was the radical idea to give Weedites enough room, given Southern blunders, to turn the voters against them.[43]

Most Democrats were equally angry at the white South because it hurt restoration. Nevertheless, the imperatives of party politics forced the Democracy to defend Southerners in terms of state autonomy. Above all, loyalty to Johnson was the Democracy's touchstone. In a key speech that drew applause from such disparate observers as Bennett, Cassidy, and Bryant, John Van Buren claimed that conservatives and moderates supported the President and planned to "nominate him in 1868." For all the party's self-confidence, Johnson's refusal to commit himself as a Democrat made the situation highly fluid. In that regard, the *Evening Post* plausibly refuted Van Buren by claiming the President was a "good old-fashioned democrat who believes in principles rather than parties, and who will stick to his principles until parties come up to them." Again, Barlow was perplexed. After all Johnson's assurances, Barlow felt Johnson meant to back Democrats. But as it became clear that he remained aloof from state politics, even allowing King to use patronage against the Democracy, Barlow's disillusionment grew despite Blair's soothing words. With that in mind, one of Barlow's friends concluded "that the President himself desires, and is laboring for, your defeat."[44]

Other events perplexed Democrats. In the city, an unlikely combination of Irish, radicals, and Bennett bellowed against Tammany's corruption. Moreover, the *Herald* hurt both Weedites and the Hall when it charged they had formed a "new ring," along with the aid of Fernando Wood, who was now back home, to defeat the radicals. The accusation, although false, gained credence when Ben Wood ran for the state senate despite the *Leader's* official statement that Tammany opposed him. Nonetheless, Dean Richmond believed the *Herald* and felt the Hall wanted to embarrass the Regency. In a heated exchange with Tweed, Richmond snapped "He'd be dam'd to hell if they [Tammanyites] should dare nominate any peace man for the Legislature." Again, the Hall denied the charge, but it could not prove its innocence, and the twin taints of corruption and disloyalty tarnished its image.[45]

Governor Fenton's mounting efforts to remove corrupt municipal officials and enforce a new voter registry bill ended Tammany's problems. To combat him, the swallow-tails and the Hall warily joined forces. Both agreed with John T. Hoffman, the popular young recorder, the chief officer of the city's criminal court, who had gained immense prestige as a responsible civil servant after the draft riot by prosecuting offenders, that the governor lacked removal powers. The registry bill also aided the Hall. Despite their unhappiness with Tammany, many Irish recoiled from registry as nativism in disguise. As a result, the Hall defused their rebellion by defending the rights of "adopted citizens." On the other hand, the Republicans, chiefly the Fentonians, committed an egregious blunder. Instead of competing for the immigrant vote, which was up for grabs, they foolishly considered it a Democratic preserve, and gave the Irish no alternative to Tammany other than the Wood brothers.[46]

On election day, Weed scribbled to Seward: "Union majorities in the State probably over twenty thousand." Weed was correct. The Union party did score a decisive victory; it elected the full state ticket by over 27,000 votes, and retained control of the legislature by better than two to one. Only in New York City did Unionism fare badly. Tammany supplied its traditional plurality on the state ticket and won the majority of legislative races. Only Ben Wood's triumph as an independent senate candidate marred its record.[47]

Conservative Republicans congratulated themselves and Weed basked in approval. Even so, he was worried that Collector King, whose patronage gave Unionism the edge, hovered on insanity. One week later, King committed suicide and threw Weedites into confusion over his successor. In a series of editorials that appeared over the next two months, the *Times* tried to repair the damage. Raymond pronounced the Democracy dead, reemphasized the President's dependence upon conservative and moderate Republicans, and lectured Democrats they must prove their principles by aiding Johnson "out of office as well as in."[48]

The radicals drew separate conclusions. Unwilling to give Weed any credit, they groused that conservatives won because the voters feared Democrats. Beyond that, the radicals seethed with fury against restoration. When Congress opened, they were determined to deny admission to ex-Confederates and seek a direct confrontation with Johnson and his allies.

On the Democratic side, Barlow was infuriated at the turn of events. Although professing to take the defeat in stride, he told Blair the President was wrong to accept Seward's attempt to "build up a Johnson party in the North without us." Then, too, Barlow issued a subtle warning to Blair, which he knew the President would hear, that Democrats might support his "wise and just" policies but reject him personally if he did not replace King with a Democrat. Once more, Blair calmed his friend. Democrats lost because of residual war suspicions, he wrote. The means to flush Johnson out lay in stressing conservative economic issues and opposition to "negro suffrage." Above that, the President did appreciate the Democracy's aid. After studying the returns, Blair concluded the local party was on the correct track. Even "our adversaries feel that in the stand made this fall in New York we have laid the foundation of the success when success will be magnificent."[49]

Swallow-tail and Regency editors reflected Barlow's disenchantment because they had pledged so much and received so little. "The Democracy who have lost nothing, can afford, as a party to wait," Cassidy explained as a way of apology. Nevertheless, these men were in no mood to surrender. Echoing Barlow, they continued to support restoration, but slowly withdrew their total identification with the President.[50]

Bennett and Bryant followed their own instincts. No matter how restless Democrats were, they agreed, the party must back Johnson because it lacked alternatives. Where they differed was more important than where they agreed. Bryant again stressed that the President's supporters must adopt "equal rights," while Bennett believed the question centered on state sovereignty. As for party reorganization, Bennett felt it rested on the public's support for Johnson, while Bryant called the process a matter of reviving the old Jacksonian commitment to "impartial human rights."[51]

Tammany and the Woods devoted more attention to the forthcoming municipal election than to postmortems on the previous one. Immediately, political chaos erupted. Four candidates appeared whose support cut across factional lines. The Woods, with Irish support, ran John Hecker, a wealthy reformer, who gained unlikely endorsements from the Citizens' Association, most Fentonians, and many Union Democrats. The Weedites ran another reformer, Marshall Roberts, who had some radical and Union Democratic support. The declining McKeonites renominated Mayor Gunther, who had few other allies. Recorder Hoffman ran for Tammany with support from swallow-tails, a few conservative Republicans, and a sprinkling of Democratic Unionists.

Since Tammany was normally the majority party, Hoffman's fitness for office became the chief issue. Although his opponents acknowledged his "fidelity" and "unblemished character," they questioned whether he had the courage to avoid becoming the "tool of a clique" and claimed Tweed used his respectability to cloak more corruption. Tammanyites and the swallow-tails countered by portraying Hoffman as a reformer "without reproach," dedicated to the principles of local autonomy and home rule, a man whose election, would ensure the city of an administration "of character and of capacity." The *Daily News* supplied the race's most curious aspect. Conveniently dropping its former bitter denunciations of Greeley and Bryant, it denounced Hoffman as an "abolitionist" and warned that he was a nativist because of his prosecution of draft rioters.[52]

The election returns belied Tammany's image as the master of New York City. Out of 81,065 votes, Hoffman won 40.5 percent, to Roberts' 39.1 percent, Hecker's 12.2 percent, and Gunther's 8.2 percent. Without pondering the causes behind Hoffman's narrow triumph, the Hall outlined the thrust of his mayoralty. It announced that his victory meant responsible citizens could create good government based on home rule and decentralization, not state interference or more institutional reforms by "corrupt combination." Furthermore, Tammany trumpeted that Hoffman's success held national significance by showing the President his main base of support in New York lay among Tammanyites. Few misunderstood the Hall's intent. Despite Hoffman's poor showing, it entirely controlled most municipal departments, and it prepared another bid to dominate the entire state party.[53]

Far from clarifying any issues or trends, the state and municipal elections settled few things. If anything, however, the returns proved that Democrats were in serious trouble largely because their cherished goal of party reconstruction was still problematical. To begin with, the party was still disorganized and torn between conflicting power centers in Albany and New York City, and its overlapping interest groups were on a collision course. Moreover, the Democracy lacked a firm self-image since its principles had not yet recovered from the war. Finally in sheer political terms, Democrats lacked a clear perception of public opinion, and it feared Johnson was too vacillating but had no options.

In a major sense, the Democracy was still a casualty of war. The party simply could not revive unless it first resolved a host of crucial national issues. Prior to 1861, the federal government had rarely touched the daily lives of most Americans. But the realities of war and the imperatives of restoring the Southern states, including the question of blacks, shifted the political focus from antebellum localism to postwar federalism. As a tentative solution, Democrats at first hoped Johnson might settle matters. Yet the party faced an outburst of ideas that no reliance on any President could solve. During the past four years, the nation's solutions to the problems posed by the war centered mainly on governmental initiatives. By 1865, Democrats found it difficult to have the American people adjust to party principles based on legislative and constitutional restraint and on a political philosophy which emphasized local autonomy. In short, if the Democracy meant to return to power, it needed a formula for settling the national problems that disrupted the entire organization and a new basis for establishing the legitimacy of its principles.

By the fall of 1865, every Democratic faction advanced its own peculiar approach. Each program, nevertheless, carried with it severe limitations. Tammany reasoned that party reorganization lay in a grassroots program of decentralism and popular responsibility as a model for other states. These ideas were circumscribed because they did not directly address national issues. Barlow and Marble felt reorganization was possible only by rupturing the relationship between Weedites and Johnson and recapturing stray Democrats. That too had inherent flaws. The President seemed intent on good relations with Weedites, and Bryant's insistence on black equality checked the party's need to support Southern whites. Richmond gradually concluded, in contrast, that any factional reshuffling hinged on forming an alliance with Weedites by using Johnson as a catalyst. This plan was also imperfect. The swallow-tails and Blair hated Weedites for past affronts, while Tammany rejected any program the Regency directed. The Democracy might have solved much of this confusion had it considered an alliance with Greeley, thereby splitting the radicals. After all, Greeley did favor sectional reunion coupled with universal amnesty, and he was suddenly popular in the South because he proposed clemency for the imprisoned Jefferson Davis. Negating these were Greeley's capricious nature, his insistence on universal suffrage, and his lifelong opposition to Democrats.[54]

As it turned out, the Union party was equally distracted. Ruptured into radical, moderate, and conservative factions, the entire party — just as did the Democrats — faced three vexatious questions. From the standpoint of the Constitution, did the definition of the people include blacks; from the standpoint of reunion, did the nation favor Presidential restoration or congressional Reconstruction; from the standpoint of power, where did authority rest? Conservatives and moderates placed their faith in Johnson. With his support, they felt the Union party could settle those questions, and, under Seward's prompting, they allied with Union Democrats and flirted with Richmond. Momentarily forced to stay passive until the President sent his first message to Congress, they nonetheless labored hard to break off his relationship with Blair and Democrats. The radicals also awaited Congress. Some of them favored a social revolution. Others were out to preserve the fruits of war through congressional Reconstruction. Still others favored centralist reformism to revive prewar ideals, much as the Fentonians attempted in New York.

Despite their differences in approach, political priorities, and recurring factionalism, Republican Unionists had one thing in common. During the war they had to varying degrees accepted the idea that federal authority was mandatory to ensure Confederate defeat. By setting the precedent for national supervision of, and intervention in state affairs, they had the justification, if they so wished, for aiding the freedman by a program including suffrage, overseeing elections, determining of Reconstruction policies rather than restoration, and launching a Southern social revolution.[55]

3
The Politics of Union: *1866*

AS Congress gathered, all New York politicians waited for two signs to indicate if the President had chosen sides: his annual message and his selection of a new collector. His message, however, crafted by George Bancroft, proved a moderate appeal for restoration that people could interpret in several ways. In it, Johnson sought national unity, summarized the steps he had already taken, and asked for Divine help to transmit "the great inheritance" of state autonomy and "constitutional vigor" to "our posterity."

The President placated the radicals by adding new preconditions to restoration: Southerners must ratify the Thirteenth Amendment, repudiate the Confederate debt and ordinances of secession, and protect freedmen's civil rights. For conservatives, he termed restoration a civil not military process, left suffrage to the states, and implied Congress had a concurrent voice in admitting ex-rebel states. In regard to Democrats, his stand on the military and suffrage, coupled with his defense of state sovereignty, outweighed their annoyance over his refusal to restore *habeas corpus* and his reluctance to prevent Congress's formation of a Joint Committee, under Thaddeus Stevens's sponsorship, to investigate the circumstances surrounding the election of Southern representatives.

Depending on one's viewpoint, the President had revealed either political indecisiveness or political cunning. Unable to resolve the question satisfactorily, each New York faction awaited more specific action and turned toward the collectorship as a second opportunity to flush him out.[1]

What followed was an exercise in confusion. All groups in both parties, excluding the radicals, bombarded the President and his advisors with a series of unsolicited candidates. For the Unionists, Cochrane and Parke Godwin, soon to become the *Evening Post*'s editor in Bryant's absence overseas, proposed a hypothetical person who could reorganize parties around the President's standard. Such a man, Godwin suggested, must not be "identified" with "old factions or cliques." Conservative Republicans, led by Weed and Morgan, submitted a long list of names. Despite the number of candidates, Morgan assumed he could influence the President because Johnson, out of senatorial courtesy, would consult him. Weed was unconvinced and urged Seward to use his prestige. It was vital, Weed wrote, for the "re-organization which must come" for the President to have "reliable" and "efficient" people in the Custom House. Through all this jockeying, however, while Morgan admitted the President "did not intimate *what* he would do," conservatives and moderates assumed he would select a Weedite. Yet by March 1866 the decision was still unresolved, and their political confusion mounted.[2]

Democrats submitted an equally long shopping list of party stalwarts. Moreover, Barlow and Richmond, with Tammany's approval, dispatched emissaries to the President to inform him that while the party gave all the time he wished, it refused to consider a joint Weedite appointee. Blair was also active. He urged Johnson to recognize "the Democracy as his party" by selecting one of the proposed men. Barlow reemphasized that point. In order to realign parties, he implored, the President must name a staunch Democrat who could "control our whole strength and at the same time draw from the ranks of the Republicans." As delay continued, the struggle for the office became so intense that even the optimistic Blair grew discouraged. Yet after one in a series of recurring meetings with Johnson, he informed Tilden that the President was impressed by the need to appoint a Democrat and would undoubtedly comply.[3]

Unknown to New Yorkers, the President had more pressing things on his mind than patronage. Ever since Lincoln's death, politicians had demanded much of the new President. Since he was expected to do contradictory things, Johnson was bound to disappoint them. Yet the sources of Johnson's problem had other roots. In the looming battle over restoration, he tried to avoid alienating any potential backer. But Johnson, by political training, temperament, and political philosophy lacked the ability to carry out such a delicate task. He was a loner, a man who made decisions on his own and stubbornly refused to budge once his mind was set. As the perplexity over the collectorship revealed, Johnson confused people by seeming receptive to their ideas. Very often, however, when he did unexpected things, those people assumed he had lied. To make the situation more difficult, Johnson pictured himself as a noble patriot, a champion of the Constitution, locked in a life and death struggle with personal enemies.

In the process, he misunderstood the dynamics of Unionist factionalism, the determination of conservative and moderate Republicans to protect black civil equality, and the nature of Northern public opinion which backed them. By a process of his own choosing, the President gradually alienated the moderates and conservatives and raised the radicals to a far more important position than they might have enjoyed, and his blunders eventually destroyed the Union coalition. At that point, Johnson had two alternatives: the formation of an independent party centered around the Administration, or total reliance on the Democracy. As it turned out, he equivocated until too late.[4]

The President's crisis came into focus during January and February 1866 when Republican congressional conservatives and moderates formed a package they thought reflected Johnson's wishes. Included were constitutional amendments to create a new formula for representation and to invalidate the rebel debt, a loyalty test was based on ironclad oaths for Southern officials, enlargement and continuance of the Freedmen's Bureau, and a Civil Rights Bill that guaranteed biracial legal equality. None of these bills bore the imprint of radicalism. Their sponsors rejected territorialism, military occupation, and land confiscation and redistribution, and assumed that black suffrage was not part of restoration. These bills indicated two facts. The conservative-moderate coalition controlled Congress, and radicals were on the defensive. Only one major question remained: what would Andrew Johnson do?

Congressional action prompted an outpouring of conflicting political advice from New York. The line of battle settled first on the Freedmen's Bureau Bill. Democratic Unionists and moderates favored it. They also urged Johnson to endorse a policy based on equal protection of the laws coupled with qualified suffrage for loyal blacks who had served in the Union Army. The worst thing the President could do, Cochrane warned, was to veto. The result would split "your friends" and create the impression the Administration favored "Copperhead Democrats" by "being anti-Negro."[5]

Democrats wanted a veto as the initial step in the break between Johnson and the Unionists. The party, Marble wrote, considered the Freedmen's Bureau unconstitutional and "outside the business of government." Better "abolish the Bureau altogether and let the States take care of their blacks," Cassidy added. In that sense, Democrats did not think the local status of blacks was within Congress's purview, and used that issue to isolate Johnson's other backers. The key problem, Warren wrote, was not racial but one based on Democratic principles: "The Southern States have the same right to regulate citizenship that the Northern States exercise, and which they cannot yield without degradation." Bennett had similar advice. Both publicly and privately, he called for a veto on the grounds that the bill was a "preposterous and costly experiment of charity" that was basically discriminatory because Congress aided "fat Southern negroes" while it ignored "destitute and disabled white veterans." As the final ingredient in its strategy to force Johnson to the Democratic side, the party treated the Unionists as if they did not exist, ignored Republican factionalism, and pictured Congress as a radical camp.[6]

Despite their desire to capture the President, many Democrats still had misgivings about his courage and willingness to fight. "We hope much, but we should like to see some immediate action upon which to base our hopes," the *Leader* complained. Other Democrats agreed. Alexander Long lamented, "I have no confidence in him and am sorry to see Southern men committing themselves to his policy." Blair again acted as a peacemaker. To Francis Kernan he wrote that Johnson "is not the least concerned by the war of the Radicals upon him. He rather likes a fight."[7]

The Weedites hoped for moderation. Realizing the bill's popularity among Democratic Unionists, moderates, and conservatives, they reasoned that a veto would brand Johnson antiblack, disillusion many Northerners who felt the government had a moral obligation to help former slaves, and prevent New York conservatives from strengthening the Union party. Seward's opportunity to influence the President came when he asked for advice prior to preparing a veto message. In a draft to Johnson, which the President ignored, Seward suggested that he must stress the Administration's commitment toward protecting blacks, but question the bill's necessity since the present Bureau remained in effect until a proclamation of peace technically ended the war. If such a bill became necessary in the future, Seward concluded, the President should reconsider the matter.[8]

Johnson opened a new political era when he vetoed the bill on the ground that it invalidated state sovereignty and was clearly unconstitutional. Not content with that, the President went beyond the veto's scope by scolding Congress for delaying restoration and by maintaining that the states were fully restored under his direction. Democrats embraced these views and loudly claimed that Johnson had finally chosen sides. They were even more thrilled when he denounced the radicals in bitter, personal terms. The upshot was, Marble concluded, that even "voters of the rudest intelligence" now understood they could not simultaneously support Johnson and Congress "as the Republican party have been pretending to do."[9]

Where the President stood, however, was not as firm as the Democracy assumed. For all their private unhappiness over the President's slighting of Seward's suggestions, the Weedites still clung to the Administration. In a series of public meetings, notably the one at Cooper Union where Seward made the chief address, the Weedites in no uncertain terms backed Johnson and put Democrats on notice they still believed a coalition with him was possible.[10]

The struggle for Johnson's favor once again forced New York politicians to assess the possibility of political reorganization. "What the country needs is a distinct drawing of the line between the supporters of the President and the supporters of the Radical disunionists," the conservative *Journal of Commerce* lectured. That proved easier said than done. The unresolved matter of the collectorship symbolized the transitional state of politics. Before Johnson's veto, both Weedites and Democrats had presented strong cases for their respective candidates. By early March, their attitudes changes. Tilden wrote Blair that the President's "best friends here" wanted delay to allow "cliques and parties" to develop in some concrete form. A similar shift occurred in Blair's thinking. While he still nursed a grudge against Seward as a carryover from their days together in Lincoln's cabinet, Clair now felt he needed Weedite aid for a larger goal, the formation of a new pro-Johnson National Union party. With that in mind, Blair told Barlow that while he regretted "the invasion of the Democratic organization," political necessity forced them to accept the Weedites in the "formation of an administration party." Meantime, Weed was busy. After holding a meeting with Richmond, Weed wrote Seward: "I am in frequent communication with leading Democrats (not copperheads) who are preparing the way for a political reorganization."[11]

Richmond's relationship with Weed abounded with complexity. Richmond encouraged Weed's expectations about fusion in order to disrupt the Union party and win back ex-Democrats. The difficulty Richmond encountered lay in convincing Marble and Barlow to soften their antipathy toward Seward. On the other hand, Weed played games with Richmond. With the Regency's cooperation, he planned to protect Seward from removal, gain moderate Democratic support to beat Fenton, and realign politics around conservative Republican leadership.[12]

So ended round one in what was a continuing battle over party realignments. At this point, attention again shifted to Washington, where Johnson was considering the Civil Rights Bill. Once more, the President's New York backers could not find a common policy. On the Democratic side, Tammany, the Regency, and the swallow-tails felt the bill breached state autonomy, while Ben Wood grumbled that it created artificial racial equality and invited miscegenation. Both the *Herald* and *Evening Post* supported the bill for similar reasons. Each maintained that black civil equality and "impartial justice" were the Thirteenth Amendment's logical consequences. Seward was in a quandary; he disliked the bill's enforcement procedures but approved its objectives. In another proposed draft of a veto message, which Johnson again ignored, Seward tried to preserve the Union party by defending Congress's right to protect black civil rights but implied the bill need modification. Moreover, Seward convinced the hesitant Weed to lobby for a compromise.

Johnson responded with a ringing veto that closely resembled Democratic objections. He termed the bill unconstitutional because it negated state sovereignty and destroyed federalism. Unfortunately for his conservative and moderate supporters, Johnson also gratuitously revealed a hidden insensitivity to the plight of Southern blacks. The bill, he added, was unfair because it gave blacks more advantages than the government "ever provided for the white race."[13]

Political response in New York was immediate and violent. The elated Democrats praised the President without reservation. In defending state authority, the *Argus* claimed in a typical editorial, Johnson labored for national reunion and placed the "question above party." Tammany added that any Democrat who opposed him "digs his own political grave." In a tortuous bit of rationalization, Bennett backed down and praised the President as a prescient statesman who saved the Union from a social revolution. Even better for the party's long-term needs, some Democratic Unionists supported the veto and extolled Johnson for saving "our republican form of government." For the white supremacists, the New York City *Day-Book* called the veto "another terrible blow at the Mongrelists."[14]

The reaction was far different within the Union party. Most conservative and moderate Republicans considered the veto, coming on top of the Freedmen's Bureau situation, an unforgivable mistake. Each bill, they felt, was necessary and justified by the white South's disregard for minimal black rights. As a result, they pleaded with the President for a compromise. "I hope the President will give his friends some elbow room," Weed wrote Senator Morgan. Johnson refused to budge. Under these conditions, many conservatives and moderates were forced into a position more extreme than the one they had started from and indicated the Union party's slow shift to radicalism. Nevertheless, not all of them were prepared to desert the President. Senator Morgan, who voted for the successful override, and Congressman Raymond, who opposed him, along with Weed, now hoped the President might still isolate the radicals by endorsing the proposed Fourteenth Amendment.[15]

Blair followed his own star. Along with congressional conservatives such as Senators James Dixon and James R. Doolittle, he formed a national Johnson club movement as the prelude to a third party dedicated to "sustain the President's policy, leaving the question of names and party organization to the people." Moving cautiously, Blair sounded out Tilden, Barlow, and Richmond who proved receptive. Three hurdles, however, barred the way. Blair reversed his earlier willingness to accept Weedites; he had the President's tacit approval but lacked his active support; and many Tammanyites refused to disband the Democracy. The consequences of these political developments forced a delay in Blair's plan until the issue became clearer.[16]

Meantime, a variety of local issues distracted New Yorkers. In Albany, radical institutional reformers rode high. Central to their program were bills to create a much needed metropolitan health commission, especially because of recurrent cholera attacks, a metropolitan board of control to audit all New York City expenditures, a reorganization of the municipal charter, an excise temperance bill attached to the health commission, and a police commission system for Buffalo. Significantly, the radicals did not advocate or mention changing the state's suffrage requirements.

The colliding forces of reform and partisanship set off a lively debate. Democrats opposed all the bills on the basis of the constitutional right of local autonomy. The health bill, in particular, Cassidy claimed, was a purely partisan measure aimed at "the spoliation of the metropolis." The party further charged that the radicals had a hidden purpose. By establishing centralism, they then intended, Democrats argued, to enfranchise blacks without a public vote. Potential Democratic allies such as the *Herald* and *Evening Post* dissented. They supported the bills and countered that local reforms were necessary. Conservative Republicans had their own concerns. Fearful that the bills' passage would tip the Union party into radical hands, the Weedites deprecated reformism as a political gimmick. This attitude erupted into a bitter quarrel between Greeley and Raymond. The *Tribune* claimed that the conservatives opposed reforms in order to fuse with Democrats, while the *Times* retorted that the radicals planned to manipulate the commission systems "into a party machine."[17]

In February 1866, the Fentonian-controlled legislature passed the Health Bill, and, in April, an amendment to it, the Excise Law. As a reform, the Health Bill was a remarkably progressive measure because it imposed essential sanitary standards on a variety of activities. Politically, however, the new Health Board, consisting of Fenton's appointees, deprived Tammany of all its patronage in naming city health inspectors and weakened the mayor's executive powers by creating another independent commission. The Metropolitan Excise Law, which only applied in the city and bore the imprint of rural hostility, was just as dangerous because it struck at the heart of Tammany's ward networks, the saloons. In addition to creating health codes whose violations could close saloons, the law gave the Board the right to license all liquor establishments and authorized the police to enforce Sunday closings without warrants. The Board generally used its powers in a nonpartisan manner to improve sanitary standards and did substantially increase the city's revenues through license fees. Nevertheless, Democrats were infuriated. On one level, they contended that the legislature intended to divert the Democracy's monopoly of liquor trade profits to the Republican faithful by selective enforcement. Moreover, they assailed the act by insisting Republicans were hypocrites by being purportedly in favor of equal rights but then denying some of those rights because of pious but misplaced sectarianism. Above all, Democrats argued, the act was another example of unwarranted state interference in home rule. Using these ideas to win support, the Democracy successfully stalled the act's operation when Common Pleas Judge Albert Cardozo, Tweed's henchman, declared it unconstitutional and police justices released violators. There matters rested until December 1866, when the Court of Appeals reversed Cardozo.[18]

Taken as a whole, institutional reformism dominated New York politics almost as much as did events in Washington. For Unionists, the entire nature of legislative action enhanced the Fentonian radicals to the point where Weedites lost much prestige. Even more, the Excise Law fit into the Republican party's pietistic strain by appealing to many voters who associated drinking with antiforeignism. To these men, politics and reform were indispensable means to create public virtue. On the other hand, the Excise Law ironically proved just as helpful for most Democrats, Mayor Hoffman in particular. In a series of protest meetings, Hoffman staked his claim to the party's fall gubernatorial nomination by stressing such Democratic principles as home rule and governmental noninterference with private morality. As a result, centralism became a major issue in the fall campaign.[19]

Other problems distracted Democrats. The swallow-tails and the Hall were still uneasy allies. Their mutual enmity reached a new boiling point in April over Barlow's abortive attempt to capture the Tammany Society, the fraternal order whose steering committee, the Council of Sachems, used its ownership of party headquarters, the "Wigwam," to decide the legitimacy of competing party factions.[20]

Fenianism added other complications. In June 1866, some Fenians attempted to invade Canada. Seward, who had a lifelong political and emotional attachment to the Irish, nonetheless condemned the intrusion against a friendly neighbor, and Johnson issued a proclamation warning all citizens to desist from "unlawful proceedings." At first, the majority of Democratic and conservative Republican newspapers, excluding the *Daily News,* condemned the Fenians. Even the *Leader* snickered at them, and mocked their leaders as frauds who raised money among gullible Irishmen for personal use. These views hurt the Democracy. The Irish felt the party had failed them, and their mouthpiece, the *Irish-American,* poured its wrath against the Administration and Tammany. The Hall belatedly attempted to placate the paper by calling on Johnson to protect American citizens arrested in Canada. The effort failed. Instead, the Irish gave their support to the Woods, who had long sympathized with their causes with money and moral support. Thus Fenianism gave both men a new lease on political life.[21]

Johnson's long-delayed appointment of a collector capped the Democracy's woes. While the President kept his own counsel, Richmond had concluded that a political realignment based on a pro-Johnson party was impossible without Weedite aid. On March 16, he and Weed held a secret meeting in which they formed "a plan of political operation for our own state, a plan which, with the support of the Administration, will give a worthy, vigorous and triumphant success," Weed told Seward. Central to the bargain was the appointment of Weedite DeWitt Littlejohn, a former assembly speaker, whom Barlow and Blair had earlier rejected. In April, however, Johnson caught everyone by surprise by nominating Henry Smythe, president of the Central National Bank of New York and Barlow's cousin, whom neither side had considered a viable candidate.[22]

Johnson made a calculated gamble because any man he selected from the lengthy lists the various factions submitted would surely alienate the others. His selection of Smythe, therefore, had certain advantages. Democrats and conservative Republicans alike needed him because of their common patronage desires and hopes to construct a new party. Then, too, Smythe's good business reputation reassured the commercial community that the Custom House was not solely a partisan engine. Yet in another and more critical sense, Johnson's method spoke volumes about his political style. As a lone wolf he lacked the temperamental patience for organization politics and wanted supporters who would vindicate his position, not that of any particular party.[23]

The President's character flaw quickly became apparent. After much grumbling, most Johnsonites in both parties indeed fell into line. Hampered by Smythe's appointment but dependent on his good will, they muted criticism until they saw the drift of his vast patronage policy. Yet Smythe was not a spoils-monger; he disappointed politicians in each camp by making selections on merit alone. Richmond and Weed were equally offended. Since neither man controlled the Custom House, they could not plausibly convince their respective followers to realign politics around a President who promised so much but delivered so little.[24]

Johnson created the most displeasure among Tammanyites. Since the Hall was the key to New York Democratic politics, its support for any realignment was irreplaceable. After looking at the President's record, the *Leader* warned the party against any further reliance upon him. Despite his vetoes, the paper contended, Johnson was "a Republican President," who would not "desert the party that elected him." Seen in that light, "Democrats must let the President alone" and "elect a President of their own, not . . . capture a President elected by the Republicans." Beyond that, the Hall falsely assumed that because Barlow and Smythe were related, Johnson had intervened in local politics by endorsing the Regency and the swallow-tails. Under those conditions, Tammany felt it doubly vital to not abandon the Democracy and elect Hoffman as governor.[25]

Tammany's rejection of Johnson struck a responsive chord among other Democrats. The flush of excitement following his vetoes and his proclamation that formally terminated the war could not obscure the party's unhappiness that he failed to roll back federal centralism, opposed universal amnesty, and seemed bent on prosecuting Jefferson Davis. Equally bad, the President's economic policies fell short of Democratic expectations and inflamed intraparty sectionalism. Eastern banking interests, including Barlow and Belmont, favored Secretary of the Treasury Hugh McCulloch's contractionist program toward greenbacks, while Western Democrats, huddled around Pendleton and Long, were inflationists. Moreover, most Democrats resented Johnson's equivocation on free trade, the National Banking system, and the income tax. Despite their general support for the President's restoration policy, then, many Democrats shared Tammany's nagging doubts. So much in fact that by May 1866 they feared Johnson would never sever his ties with Unionism and even mistrusted Blair.[26]

Suddenly, all the ground rules changed when, in June 1866, the conservative- and moderate-controlled Joint Committee on Reconstruction submitted the Fourteenth Amendment to Congress. Instead of an extreme measure, the amendment reflected Northern reluctance to grapple with black suffrage and set up conditions which the majority of Northerners felt the President, and even sensible white Southerners, would accept. Under the amendment's terms, it nationalized black citizenship, but left specific rights ambiguous and implied that states had certain jurisdiction over such rights; representation hinged on total population, which Congress could reduce if blacks were denied the right to vote; the national debt, but not the Confederate, remained guaranteed; only prior Southern federal and state officeholders who had become rebel officials lost the right to hold office unless Congress granted pardons; and Congress retained enforcement powers. By no means did the amendment bear the radical stamp. In fact, the provision that penalized states for denying citizens the right to vote was a masterly evasion. That is, if Southern states gave its blacks the right to vote their representation in the House of Representatives might increase, while the North, which had proportionally few blacks, could still deny them suffrage without much penalty.[27]

Seward and Raymond, speaking for the Weedites, considered the amendment a judicious compromise and plunged into the delicate task of winning the President's unequivocal backing. Seward publicly minimized the differences between Congress and Johnson, and urged Unionists to reorientate the party around the President and the amendment. Raymond strove for the same end. In Congress, he led efforts to conciliate Johnson. The *Times* also called on the Union party's national executive committee, which Raymond chaired, to rethink issues and form a fresh platform in a national convention "that better understands the political necessities and interests of the hour."[28]

Democrats saw nothing good in the amendment. Consistent with its principles, the party called it unconstitutional because it weakened local power in favor of centralism, unnecessary because the states already had the power to determine citizenship and civil rights, and unfair because Congress set preconditions for the admittance of Southern states that forced them to adopt the amendment. Furthermore, some Democrats opposed the amendment by blatant appeals to racial prejudice, while others used party principles in an unconscious reflection of white supremacy. Even so, the end was the same. They reasoned that the amendment disrupted the social order. Finally, Democrats saw nothing but partisanship behind it. They charged that Republicans, solely to create an artificial Southern party, used blacks as pawns, to the nation's detriment.[29]

The Democracy's opposition rested on a flawed reading of political reality. Falsely assuming that no differences existed among Unionists, Democrats helped soften their internal factionalism by treating them alike. Party newspapers unwisely vilified radicals as "disorganizers" who were no different than prewar secessionists; they belabored Seward and Raymond as "trimmers" and "hypocrites" who could never make up their minds, and foolishly refused to consider the amendment's basically moderate character. In short, by treating the Union party as a monolithic entity, Democrats alienated more and more pro-Johnson Unionists who might have been willing to accept Blair's movement. Equally shortsighted, the Democracy misread Northern public opinion, which gradually accepted the amendment for what it was — a mild compromise that guaranteed local self-determination of suffrage, gave blacks few rights, and allowed ex-rebel states to rejoin the Union with relatively little friction.[30]

The moderate Republican *Evening Post* and pro-Johnson *Herald* understood the realities of Northern politics. Godwin spurned some amendment provisions and agreed with Democrats that they violated state sovereignty. Yet from a practical standpoint, Godwin assumed its acceptance would speed reunion, overturn the Dred Scott decision by giving blacks citizenship "as a simple matter of justice," and thus move on to other pressing issues such as tax reform, free trade, and monetary reforms.[31]

Bennett faced a dilemma of his own making. Originally, he had supported Johnson to enhance the *Herald's* reputation and stimulate sales. By July 1866, however, Bennett discovered the President's loss of popularity. Going through the motions, the paper still backed him, but unknown to the public a crisis gripped its editorial policy. Gradually, James Gordon Bennett, Jr., a man editorial writer W. B. Phillips called "self willed and not very steady or comprehensive in his view," took over the paper's daily operations. Like his father, the younger Bennett prided himself on being a winner. He no longer considered Johnson one. Once committed, Bennett awaited the proper time to dump the President without alienating the public, find the new popular side, and align the *Herald* on that basis.[32]

Concurrently, Blair's national Johnson club movement reached maturity. On June 25, Blair along with a group of congressional Johnson Democrats and conservative Republicans, including Weedites he grudgingly accepted, issued a call for a National Union convention for Philadelphia on August 14. To it, they invited all men who sustained "the Administration in maintaining unbroken the Union of the States under the Constitution." In their call, the sponsors followed the advice of Seward and Raymond by specifically avoiding any criticism of the amendment or other congressional actions.[33]

Although New York Democrats had expected something of this sort for several months, they were divided over what course to pursue. Upstate western Democrats and the Regency embraced National Unionism. As Warren put it, the "real duty of the hour is to divise some method by which the Union men of the whole country can act in harmony." The New York

City Democracy thought otherwise. "There is no reason why Democrats should go to the convention," the *World* retorted. Tammany was blunter. "The Democracy must rely on itself or the future. The call is not issued from any Democratic authority, and will not draw any of the supporters of that great organization," the *Leader* editorialized. To neutralize such criticism, the National Union Club's executive committee pressured the perplexed Democratic chairman, August Belmont, for an endorsement. The real question, Belmont wrote Barlow, was "to decide whether we will follow in their action & thus give up the *National Democratic organization"* or whether to do it alone. For my part, he continued, "*I want only to do what* is best for the Country & what will most effectively kill the Radicals in & out of Congress."[34]

Most of the party's divisions stemmed from uncertainty about Johnson. In late June, the President began to clarify his position. First, he dutifully forwarded the amendment, through Seward, to the states. But Johnson criticized the manner in which Congress had formed it, assailed its terms of ratification, and implied, without being specific, that he disagreed with its provisions. Congressional Democrats responded with a public address endorsing the convention. Johnson was not finished. He soothed Democratic anxieties by assuring prominent party regulars, such as Edmund Burke of New Hampshire, "that he should make the line of demarkation between his friends and enemies evident." After leaving a meeting with him, Burke told former President Franklin Pierce that Johnson's "desire was to disintegrate the Republican party as much as possible. " To that end, he wanted the Democracy's cooperation "in the Philadelphia Convention."[35]

For the moment, the party's uncertainty evaporated. Marble now felt it certain "that this is a movement which all Conservative men may safely encourage," and he noted that it afforded Southerners an opportunity "to receive counsel from [their] friends in the North." Speaking at the Tammany Society's Independence Celebration, Tilden sought the Hall's endorsement. The Democratic party, he said, "is too powerful to be jealous" and would accept "as brethren all who stand with it on the present issues." Blair echoed that reasoning. He wrote Barlow that it was totally unlikely "the limited number of Conservative Republicans" who cooperated "could absorb the Democracy."[36]

Only Tammany Hall held back from the stampede. The entire movement, the *Leader* argued, grew out of Johnson's weakness. The Republicans had expelled him, and he was "too obstinate to rejoin the Democratic party, in which he belongs." As a result, his "silly" plan revolved around organizing a superfluous apparatus, not making a choice within the nation's traditional two-party structure. Thus, he too was inessential. Behind those words, lurked the Hall's real meaning. Tammany rejected National Unionism because of four factors: its success would increase the stature of the swallow-tails and the Regency; it placed the dynamics of party reorganization in hands the Hall did not control; it might force the Democracy to nominate a Johnsonian, perhaps even a Weedite, for governor instead of Hoffman; and its unpopularity among the Irish because of Johnson's suppression of Fenianism gave Tammany a grip to recover their confidence.[37]

Despite the Hall's intransigence, the Democracy's blossoming support for National Unionism had ominous signs for Weedites. Senator Doolittle of Wisconsin and John A. Dix, who now directed the movement's daily operations, wanted the Union party's aid and clung to the hope that Raymond, in his capacity as chairman of its executive committee, would officially endorse the convention. Unknown to them, however, Raymond had second thoughts about the movement, and feared the Democracy might capture the convention. The more Democrats and Union Democrats pressed him, the more Raymond recoiled. His crisis reached a boiling point when Seward asked him to attend and make one of its opening speeches. In his diary, Raymond wrote that he informed Seward he could not because the convention was dominated by "former rebels and their Copperhead associates," who aimed to use the convention "for purposes hostile to the Union party." Seward replied that "the Convention was simply for consultation" and would compromise neither Raymond nor his party.

Still not satisfied, Raymond had an interview with Johnson. Remarkably, the President retracted his pledges to Burke. Johnson said he wanted to maintain the Union party not build a new one, favored congressional control of restoration, and welcomed Democratic support under proper conditions, yet scorned their take-over of the convention. After the meeting, Raymond recorded the "impression" that the President wished to establish a Southern foothold "for the Conservative wing of the Union party" and hoped the convention would "lay the foundation for a National party" capable of absorbing "the Democratic party of the North and West, [and] all of the Union party but the Radicals." Johnson's words revived Raymond's flagging spirits. He decided to attend for the Union party's sake.[38]

Raymond's personal agony was not over. At a Union party congressional caucus, Thaddeus Stevens presented a resolution that demanded the organization censure the convention. Depending on what report people read, Raymond recanted, as Democrats and radicals claimed; or stood his ground, as the *Times* maintained, and defended the convention as a means to expand Union party influence.[39]

Raymond's dilemma symbolized conservative Republican woes. The Weedites, determined to participate, encountered expected radical opposition. But they were unprepared for stiff resistance from many conservative and moderate Republicans. Upstaters from Buffalo to Albany notified Weed and Seward that Johnson's refusal to endorse the amendment indicated that the convention would fall "under the control of men who opposed the War and sympathized with the rebels." Yet Weed paid little heed. "Richmond is here co-operating heartily," he told Seward. The usually shrewd Weed, through perhaps self-deception, blindness, or false reliance on Richmond, simply failed to realize that he was not interested in cooperation but in splitting the Union party and then picking up stray Democrats. Horatio Seymour encouraged the charade. To Blair, he explained: "Good policy demands that conservative Republicans *lead* off. . . . We of Democratic antecedents must readily fall in."[40]

Meantime, the last obstacle to National Unionism fell when Tammany reluctantly bowed to immense pressure and gave the convention its oblique support. The Hall nonetheless had no intention of playing the role of an understudy to either Weed or Richmond, nor did it intend to weaken the Democratic party.[41]

The emergence of National Unionism, however, made the Democracy's knotty political problems infinitely worse. By associating so closely with Johnson, it gained all his assets, but also inherited all his liabilities. As his conflicting promises to

Burke and Raymond so dramatically illustrated, the President was an indecisive man who often told his supporters what they wanted to believe, not what he really thought. Left to himself, the President remained a political isolate whose inflexibility would soon disappoint all the National Unionists. Even worse, while the National Union party did become a vehicle for electing men favorable to his position, Johnson's alienation of moderate Northerners by criticizing the Fourteenth Amendment could not help Democrats. To crown the Democracy's problems, the Peace Democrats did not fade out of the picture as so many men had hoped. Fernando Wood told Johnson, "myself and others have been elected by the people [as] delegates & we do not intend to be excluded." No wonder, then, that the rapidly disillusioned *Herald* predicted that "the combustible element in that convention will, no doubt, ignite and produce a general destruction of all connected to it."[42]

Seward, sitting in his Washington office, anxiously anticipated word from Philadelphia. He did not wait long. "The convention was a far more successful affair than I had hoped to venture," Dix wrote. Raymond was no less optimistic: 'Address and resolutions unanimously adopted and with great enthusiasm." On receipt of these letters, the beaming Seward telegraphed Raymond, "Pride, Passion, Prejudice must perish. Patriotism always lives and must in the end prevail." For all their self-congratulations, however, these men were enmeshed in a tangled web spun by their own delusions. The real fact was that the convention was a Democratic victory and began the Union party's demise.[43]

Even before the convention met, events conspired against the Weedites. Two weeks earlier, a bloody racial riot erupted in New Orleans, instigated by whites who tried to halt a state constitutional convention from enfranchising some blacks and disfranchisng certain former Confederates. Whipping up lingering war hatreds, Greeley charged "the hands of the rebels are again red with loyal blood." The upshot that many Northerners agreed with the radicals that blacks must have more federal protection, beginning with the amendment's adoption, not less as the Johnsonians sought. On top of that, three of the President's cabinet resigned rather than desert the Union party, a move that cast further doubt on national restoration under conservative auspices. From a political standpoint, the swing in public opinion against Weedites now became apparent. Few conservative or moderate Republicans endorsed the convention, other than its organizers, and Democrats dominated its key committees. Just as damaging, the presence as delegates of many former rebels and Peace Democrats made plausible radical charges that the convention was a grand reunion of "traitors" and "disorganizers."[44]

By the time the convention opened, the Democrats were in firm command. On the surface, the meeting proved a huge success for Johnson. Dix's welcoming speech, the platform and Raymond's address poured out a litany of orthodox Presidential programs, including a call for the voluntary adoption of the Fourteenth Amendment. Even more pleasing to Johnson, Wood and Vallandingham withdrew, thus apparently defusing radical charges. Finally, the appearance of many Southern delegates epitomized national reconciliation and indicated the South's apparent practicality.

In contrast, the delegates crushed Raymond no matter his rationalizations. The committee on resolutions watered down his address by specifically erasing his reference to slavery as an evil and his defense of Congress's right to draft amendments. The most serious blow delegates delivered centered on the convention's overall political intent. True, it did not create a new party, nor fresh machinery, but its refusal to endorse the amendment weakened the conservative-moderate alliance in general and the Union party in particular. Marble minced few words. Commenting on the forthcoming state National Union convention, he noted "it assembles under a Democratic call," and invited the Weedites to fuse with the Democracy. In short, the National Union party movement was a cover for the Democratic party, and Democrats used it for their own purposes.[45]

During the next two weeks, the convention's momentum created false optimism. As anticipated, the *Herald* and *Times* supported National Unionism, and even the *Evening Post* attacked radicals. Replying to Greeley's contention that the convention worked counter to the principles of "universal Liberty and Equal Rights," Godwin wrote that "lovers of lawful liberty," who wished to safeguard the Constitution from "its present revolutionary condition" and restore normal relation with loyal Southerners, must support National Unionism.[46]

Godwin's stand fired false Democratic hopes. At this point, Barlow cajoled Collector Smythe that he must use patronage to placate groups "who hate Weed & Seward worse than they do the Radicals," such as Barnburner Republicans, "where two-thirds of our strength is to be found." John Dash Van Buren wrote in a similar vein to Tilden: "What an easy fight we would have to put the party back in power and reform it if only those *Evg Post* barnburners would come back and take the lead." In their elation, the Democrats missed one significant point. The paper backed Nation Unionism, not the Democracy, because it viewed the movement as a prelude to its long-desired hope for a complete political realignment. Yet the Barnburner Republicans soon faced disappointment. National Unionism was not the start of a new third party. As the *Leader* put it, the convention failed to "organize a new party." Under those conditions, the *Evening Post*'s rejection of Johnsonians was merely a matter of time.[47]

Meantime, radicals refurbished the Union party. In conjunction with Southern loyalists they polished plans for their own national convention, and Governor Fenton made inroads among conservatives by successfully asking Senator Morgan to attend. Greeley was equally busy in other directions, exploiting the rift between Johnson and the Fenians. Through Charles G. Halpine, a popular Irish newspaperman, Greeley organized an anti-Tammany slate in the fall elections. Throughout these developments, Raymond and Weed lost prestige as Unionists grew more hostile to National Unionism. The situation became so grave that Raymond was forced to resign his chairmanship of the Union executive committee. Things were so bad, Weed's upstate supporters confessed, that even the most loyal conservative Republicans buckled under radical and anti-Johnsonian Unionist pressure.[48]

At this critical juncture, Democrats, Weedites, and National Unionists suffered a massive setback when Dean Richmond suddenly died. The Democracy lost not only one of its chief sources of finance, but the only man in the party with the finesse to handle such disparate types as Weed and Tweed. Equally discouraging, Richmond's deal with Weed died stillborn, and National Unionism rapidly lost many disgruntled conservatives.

The vicious jockeying for the gubernatorial nomination that followed indicted the immensity of the resultant power vacuum. Prior to his death, Richmond and Weed had agreed to support conservative Democratic senator and anti-Tammanyite Henry Murphy of Brooklyn. Now all bets were off. The purported National Unionists instead pushed forward with a variety of candidates, without reflection on the marked lack of unity within their ranks. Tammany demanded Hoffman; Johnson, the *Herald,* the Weedites, and Godwin preferred Dix; Marble and the swallow-tails boomed Tilden; the leaderless Regency proposed either Seymour or Sanford Church of Rochester. Gradually, Dix emerged as a compromise candidate until the swallow-tails and Tammany formed a marriage of convenience against him; Marble on the basis of Dix's wartime suppression of the *World*, Tammany because of Hoffman.[49]

While the National Unionists bickered, the Union party held its state convention. The radicals took charge. They easily renominated Fenton and formed a clever platform aimed at separating Weed from his followers. To please moderates and conservatives, the platform advocated speedy sectional reunion consistent with "safety" and "constitutional justice," it endorsed the amendment, and, significantly, it was silent about black suffrage. Marble watched with a mounting sense of pleasure. He thought the radicals had played into Democratic hands by renominating Fenton because the Weedites disliked him. At that point, Marble and other Democrats made an error that crippled the Weedite alliance. Convinced that conserative Republicans lacked options, Marble announced no reasons existed "why a regular Democrat should not be taken" for governor against "a narrow, bitter Radical, like Fenton."[50]

Such words fit Tammany's needs. Using a combination of trickery, bribery, and parliamentary maneuvering at their convention, Tweed and Peter B. Sweeny beat off the other contenders and selected Hoffman. As a sop, the delegates named Weedite Robert Pruyn for lieutenant governor. The platform proved a curious document that unwittingly pinpointed National Unionism's fragile nature. The delegates did reaffirm the Philadelphia plank. But at Tammany's insistence, they unnecessarily alienated upstate conservative Republicans and city moderates committed to the Excise Law and institutional reformism by attacking both as invasions of private rights.[51]

The convention ended whatever community of interest the moderates and most conservative Republicans shared with Democrats. The moderates dropped out first. Godwin, after acknowledging Hoffman's "rectitude and courage," blasted Democratic manipulation of National Unionism. In a bitter blow to the party's hopes, Godwin endorsed the entire Union slate and specifically extolled Fenton as "a Barnburner Democrat, of the *Evening Post* school, brought up in the policy of Jackson and Van Buren." The *Times* fell next. Cowed by falling circulation and mounting Unionist contempt, Raymond backtracked by saying the Democrats had seized National Unionism "not to co-operate in carrying it out, but to make it do their own party work." Only Weed stayed firm; he had gone too far to scuttle the movement. In an open letter to Raymond, Weed admitted that the Democracy had ignored Richmond's pledge of a bipartisan fusion. Nonetheless, Weed agonizingly sustained the ticket on the grounds that "the reckless red radicalism which rules the present Congress" endangered national peace. Upon reading the letter, Democrats scurried to reassure the Weedites. Warren, for one, praised Weed in contrast to the "ignoble Raymond" who "spits upon his own platform." Democrats did not require any man "to abandon his party to build up the Democracy," but merely to follow Weed's example to "unite with Democrats" in resisting radicalism and its "revolutionary march."[52]

Democratic actions, however, further weakened Weedites. Tilden, in his capacity as chairman of the National Union state committee, which Democrats controlled, counted on federal patronage to influence voters. While Secretary McCulloch refused to intercede with Smythe, the collector voluntarily purged Unionists. Yet the majority of men he axed were not radicals, who had few jobs in the Custom House, but Weedites. Accordingly, Weed's followers complained to Seward of Democratic perfidy and lambasted their leader for failing to protect them.[53]

Deeper problems emerged. By mid-September, President Johnson's political fiasco in his ill-fated speaking tour convinced the Bennetts the time was ripe to drop him. On September 14, the *Herald* astounded New Yorkers by attacking Johnson as the prime cause of radical ascendancy. The only means to reconcile the sections, it announced, was through the

Fourteenth Amendment. "It is the ultimatum of the victorious North, and the South will lose much and gain nothing by delay in its adoption." The paper further advised Johnson to conciliate Congress by using the prestige of his office on its behalf. Continued opposition helped the radicals. They wished to stymie ratification, pin the blame on the President, and create a vindictive Reconstruction program. The paper then turned to National Unionism and indicated its only positive aspect. By voting against Hoffman, "the people of the State at large" had a unique opportunity to register their opposition "to the band of forty thieves who have governed the city of New York for the past ten years."[54]

Phillips tried to cushion the *Herald*'s about-face by telling Johnson that James Gordon Bennett's "business is in the midst of a mercurial and an excitable people and [he] attracts attention to his paper by doing startling or excitable things." Bennett even wrote the President and expressed his personal regard. These words were beside the point. Despite Marble's attacks on the paper, defending Johnson, John Dash Van Buren put his finger squarely on how well Bennett reflected the public mood. To Francis P. Blair, Senior, Van Buren wrote, "the people believe the President honest" and applaud his integrity, but "there is something wanting to make the masses crystallize around him."[55]

Faced by such odds, the National Unionists built their campaign on a Democratic base. Money was a problem. From all over the state, party workers pleaded to Tilden for cash. Gradually, he managed to find some funds, but not enough, by tapping his own resources, relying on the swallow-tails, and through Tweed and Sweeny. In one way, these financial troubles accentuated the immense consequences of Richmond's death, yet in another they indicated Tilden's emergence. A genius at organization, he formed speakers bureaus, created a statewide network to turn out voters, and gave Tammany free reign to ensure Hoffman the "majority of 50,000" he needed to offset his unpopularity in western New York and "the River counties." Tilden also worked closely with Smythe who, encouraged by Johnson, promised "nothing shall be wanting on *my* part." Even Tammany cooperated, and pledged in congressional races to select "the best men, and to consolidate every interest." By mid-October, a pleased Tilden reported to the President: "Organization throughout the state well advanced. Our people acting everywhere courageously and effectively."[56]

In terms of issues, the National Unionists played on raw emotionalism. To combat the amendment, Democratic newspapers stressed that suffrage, not black civil rights, was the election's chief question. Time and again, these papers charged that the amendment epitomized radical determination to perpetuate "disunion" until "the negro shall be made by the national law the equal of all white men." Hoffman even more vigorously linked racism to the Excise Law. Throughout the canvass, he hammered home the point that the radicals could not consistently support black civil rights and denials of freedom of choice to whites. As Warren put it, the radicals "want to interfere with the rights or private citizens; they want black men to vote and white men to be slaves to their arbitrary laws." Taking their cues from these attacks, German voters deserted the Union party, while the Liquor Dealers Association, along with the Anti-Prohibitionist State Central Committee, endorsed the National Unionist slate. As for the Irish, Democrats sought to stem their defections by blaming Seward for Johnson's anti-Fenianism, while Tilden petitioned the President to release Fenian leaders and restore their arms.[57]

Tactically, however, Democrats handled the situation badly. Voters considered the amendment a reasonable compromise; upstate Republicans favored the Excise Law as a legitimate means of enforcing public virtue; and Weedites resented the attacks on Seward. Before the polls opened, reports to Weed, Seward, and Tilden portended disaster. "Our gains are not as solid and firm as the other side," Cassidy wrote. "The result in Pennsylvania disappoints and distracts me," Weed admitted. We are "in the midst of much discouragement," an upstate Democrat told Tilden. Only illegal methods can save us, others told him; buy votes, "colonize" key districts, use "intimidation," spend freely.[58]

The returns justified this gloom. National Unionism slumped to a stunning defeat. Hoffman did carry the city by more than 50,000 votes but lost to Fenton, and the Union party elected over two-thirds of the state congressional seats. Equally disheartening, the Unionists firmly maintained control over the legislature, which was due to select a new United

States senator. In the city, Tammany suffered a deep blow when Halpine, with radical and Irish support, became city register — a political plum worth more than $40,000 from fees collected.

While National Unionism lay shattered, New York Democrats analyzed the roots of their defeat in hope of laying a solid foundation to rebuild their party. Certain factors were clear; National Unionism had proved a worthless expedient and the Weedite alliance added nothing. But when the Democracy turned for suggestions about a new strategy, conflicting advice filled the air. Warren thought the Democracy should drop Johnson and stop bucking public opinion by now supporting the amendment. Cassidy rejected both suggestions; he asked the President to compromise with Congress. Marble had a totally different approach. He urged white Southerners to defeat the amendment through a policy of passivity and delay. In picturing the scenario, Marble assumed the Democracy could block ratification in the North; when the South held back, a deadlock would ensue and the party could then force Congress to restore the Union on terms less stringent than the Fourteenth Amendment. Tammany and Tweed pursued their own ends. The Hall maintained that Hoffman's huge local plurality made him the state's "most prominent Democrat," one who deserved another shot at governor. Beyond that, Tammany staked its claim to leadership by blasting the Regency and the swallow-tails for leading the Democracy down a false path toward National Unionism. In words that thundered Tweed's challenge, the *Leader* wrote: "Just as there is no place for a State outside the Union, so there is no place for a New York Democrat outside of Tammany Hall."[59]

This lively debate underscored the fact that the Democracy had not yet come to terms with the implications of postwar developments. Repudiated by the voters, infused with unrealistic ideas, living vicariously on past victories, bereft of a vision of the future, unable to breathe life into their principles, Democrats were disarmed by friends and foes alike. But the situation, they realized, was far from hopeless. Their major fault lay in not recognizing that they could not reshape temporizing techniques to conform with new realities. The answer to their policy-making woes lay in using their principles to reestablish party continuity. That, however, raised another problem; finding usable issues that could form the connecting link between the past and the future. In general terms, the Democracy had already uncovered some during the campaign. These included opposition to centralism, the amendment, and black equality. As a result, all Democrats agreed on certain points. The party had not disintegrated; it had upheld traditional principles of strict constructionism and noninterference with state sovereignty; and its objections to black suffrage, while not yet a burning partisan issue because of Unionist avoidance, struck fire among whites in both parties.[60]

The differing ways in which the Democracy's opponents evaluated the returns indicated that their victory might be short-lived despite their gains. The election proved, Godwin wrote, that the public favored moderation through the amendment. Nationally, the Union party ought to avoid extremism, work with Southern loyalists, and establish universal male suffrage by individual state action. Locally, the party must institute "radical reform in the [municipal] system itself" because Tammany was too corrupt. Bennett agreed that the Democracy was "effectively used up," its elements "adrift," but predicted the organization would attempt to resuscitate itself "in a new form" of race-baiting. To counter that, the *Herald* disagreed with moderates and urged Congress to pass "universal suffrage and universal amnesty." Local radicals partially agreed with the paper. Interpreting the election as their mandate, they demanded a comprehensive program aimed at reconstructing Southern society by ending Presidential restoration. Conservatives, moderates, and Democratic Unionists recoiled in dismay, and maintained the nation would not go beyond the Fourteenth Amendment's moderation. This situation gave Weed and Raymond their reprieve. Both strove to restore their Unionist credentials and intended to fight against radical "retribution."[61]

Despite the Union party's victory, then, the logical consequences of these factional disagreements indicated the wartime coalition that had elected Lincoln and Johnson had become obsolete. Moderate and conservative Republicans, along with radicals, for all their differences, still formed the organization's core. But Seward's loyalty to Johnson, coupled with the Weedites' and Democratic Unionists' roles in National Unionism, proved that the party existed in name only. The upshot was that the wartime Union party now faced one of three alternatives — the resurrection of the Republican party, coalition with like-minded Democrats, or reincarnation of 1864 Unionism. But in the fall of 1866, a fusion with Democrats was impossible because of their determination to maintain their organization, and the crisis of 1864 was history. Only reincarnation of the Republican party remained. By December of 1866, therefore, the Union party, as it had existed, ceased, and the Republican party, in spirit if not reality, replaced it.

4
The Politics of Race: *1867–1868*

WHEN Congress opened in December 1866, President Johnson acted as if the past election was meaningless. In his annual message, he castigated the Fourteenth Amendment as unconstitutional, called for the immediate seating of Southern representatives, and considered restoration complete. Nowhere in his address were any words to reassure moderate and conservative Republicans.

In New York, the Regency and swallow-tails commended Johnson, and thought he endorsed Marble's deadlock strategy. In contrast, Bennett and Godwin warned that both the President and the Democracy played into radical hands by not endorsing the amendment. Only Tammany among regular Democrats rejected Johnson's aid. Pursuing its goals of revival under Tweed, the *Leader* wrote: "Mr. Johnson has been dangerous only to his friends . . . .From this city, then, as the citadel of Democracy must come the commencement of the reorganization of the party."[1]

Events during December 1866 and January 1867 looked propitious for Democrats. Johnson vetoed a suffrage bill for the District of Columbia, the Southern states increasingly followed the tactics of deadlock, and the Supreme Court's decision in the Milligan case seemed to end the prospect of the Army's occupation of the South. By late February, the situation changed. Encouraged by Northern anger over what they considered intransigent Southern rejections of lenient treatment, congressional moderates and conservatives, over radical demands for harsher treatment, formed a new Reconstruction program. Passed over Johnson's veto in March, the First Reconstruction Act divided the South into five military districts, established provisional governments run by military governors, and redefined the process of admission by requiring ex-rebel states to allow black suffrage, disfranchise Confederate leaders, and ratify the amendment. Only then could the state be part of the United States and have home rule.

When military Reconstruction first took shape, Democrats were enraged. On reflection, however, some pragmatic New Yorkers were clever enough, as Smythe told Johnson, to realize "it will be regarded nothing short of a *calamity,* if you do not sign it — this being regarded by the people of all parties as the most sound and reasonable bill likely to be passed." Even Democrats as racists as Montgomery Blair pleaded for the same action.[2]

Of these men, Marble and Warren best articulated changing Democratic attitudes. Marble, feeling deadlock was no longer feasible, advised the President to sign the bill. Granting that "negro suffrage" was "the most odious feature of the new scheme," Marble nevertheless felt white Southerners by habit and circumstance could control the black vote. In that sense, suffrage aided Democrats. But if the President balked, and the South fought a fruitless rear guard action, Congress would force suffrage regardless on the states and dominate the grateful blacks to such an extent that they would vote in a Republican bloc. "Denunciation of Congress is idle," Warren added. "There is no alternative, accept the political situation and make the best of it." Furthermore, both men emphasized that continued Southern resistance actually aided Republicans who wished to keep those states out of the Union until after the 1868 national elections. Only by accepting military Reconstruction, they suggested, could the South help itself and elect a Democratic president.[3]

In short, the Democracy seemed on the verge of an incredible new departure on black suffrage. Throughout the war and continuing to early 1867, the party had adamantly rejected suffrage on constitutional, political, and racial grounds. But by March 1867, most pragmatic Democrats saw that black voting in the South, in some form, was a political fact of life, one that the party must accommodate. "Whites are powerless to resist it," Warren observed. "It would be a great mistake . . . to allow the negro to cast a solid vote against white candidates." The worst miscalculation Southern Democrats could make, Marble concurred, lay in allowing Republicans "to band the negroes together, at the outset, as a hostile political organization."[4]

For these reasons, most practical New Yorkers were piqued by Johnson's continued defiance of Congress. Although by no means happy with subsequent Republican efforts to flesh out Reconstruction — a supplemental military bill and registry procedures including ironclad oaths, the Tenure of Office Act, and the Commander of the Army Act — they felt the President's delaying tactics hindered the party and aided Republicans. Marble put the matter trenchantly to Blair by telling him Johnson was a "blunderer" and "politician of common parts," who created his own misfortunes, misfortunes in which the Democracy lacked "the least interest."[5]

Despite these sentiments, not all New York Democrats were prepared to forgo past constitutional or racial misgivings about black suffrage. Nevertheless, Democrats as a whole seemed to have defused an explosive issue. Signs of a party revival abounded. Goodwin and the *Herald* lauded the Democracy's good sense. Weed, who had just taken control of the New York *Commercial Advertiser,* extolled the party's moderation. Even Greeley was impressed. Yet none of these people were blind to the Democracy's reorganization goal and each sought to prevent its success. Northerns were foolish, the *Evening Post* contended, to follow "pigheaded Democrats." Raymond extended that idea by suggesting "nothing but the direct necessity will lead the South into a new alliance with the Northern Democracy." Even so, Democrats were heartened by Republican losses in the Connecticut spring elections when voters defeated a clear radical ticket. Everything now appeared ready to fall into place.[6]

In New York, events looked equally promising. At the start of the legislative secession, the Republicans fell into an ugly family quarrel over electing a new senator. In the thrust-and-cut of personal bitterness, Fenton lost massive prestige when Congressman Roscoe Conkling, the rising star in radical ranks and an open foe, won. That settled, the Fentonians regained lost ground by enacting new institutional reforms such as a tenement law, a free school law, prison reforms, and a state board of charity. At that point, the reformers crowned their efforts by formulating procedures for a state constitutional convention, which the voters had authorized in the fall election. Although they had no way of understanding what the future held, the convention was destined to mark the high-water point of their local dominance.[7]

Democrats, as a reflection of their generally static view of society, tried to prevent the convention with a variety of stalling devices. In a way, the party's hesitancy made sense in political terms. Republicans had rigged in their favor a bill setting a formula for electing delegates in a special April election. Some Republicans tried to cool Democratic anger. "We want no party constitution," Greeley wrote. Democrats doubted his sincerity. "When the time comes, we will force home the responsiblity for all this trickery and wrong doing," Cassidy snapped, "where it belongs, and with powerful effect." On April 23, the voters went to the polls and gave Republicans their ordained majority. The question now became how they intended to use their authority when the convention opened in June.[8]

Meanwhile, Tammany tended to its own needs. In December 1866, Tweed gained another vital office with the election of Richard Connolly as city comptroller. Not only was Connolly important in placating the Irish, but his new office controlled city expenditures, except those of departments the commissioners dominated. Mayor Hoffman was also busy as an administrator and on the hustings. In particular, he gained public admiration for rising above petty ward politics, leaving them in Tweed's hands, and operating as a statesman by continually defending home rule against centralism. In February 1867, Tweed added another important office to his galaxy when Hoffman, with the Board of Aldermen's approval, appointed Peter B. Sweeny, a man Marble praised as businesslike, efficient, and honest, as city chamberlain. Since the law allowed the chamberlain (county treasurer) the right to pocket interest on city deposits in lieu of salary, newspapers noted the post was worth about $100,000 a year, plus nearly $200,000 in interest fees for which the city was currently suing the estate of Sweeny's predecessor, Daniel Delevan. Although Sweeny magnanimously gave up all claims to such monies in favor of a permanent $10,000 salary, the fact that Tweed testified later that Sweeny paid $60,000 to the aldermen for their approval indicated the chamberlain's critical role in fiscal operations. As a result, Sweeny wielded a potent weapon to advance the mayor's gubernatorial candidacy and counter the swallow-tails' wealth, especially with Barlow in poor health and politically disillusioned.[9]

In May, Marble eagerly awaited the implementation of congressional Reconstruction. "The war, as a political issue, is dead," he wrote. "As soon as the southern states have reorganized" and accepted "negro suffrage," the Republicans would lose their "bond of unity" and cease as an organized party. The *Herald* saw the same future. The Republican party "is no longer the party of the people, no longer the vital exponent of the will and thought of the nation" as it had been during the war. Successful Reconstruction proved the party had achieved its ends and lacked any reason for existence.[10]

By June, when congressional Reconstruction machinery was in full gear, things did not go as the New Yorkers anticipated. White southerns despised military supervision of elections and poured their anger against the Republican Union League, which coordinated black voting activities. In response, many of these white Southerners boycotted voter registrations until they realized their tactics strengthened the opposition. By midsummer, Democratic hopes for racial peace and national reunion collapsed. Just as hazardous, many Southern whites now suggested that the section could serve its interests best by remaining outside the Union and accepting indefinite military rule rather than the consequences of Republican Reconstruction.[11]

New York Democrats now faced a crisis of monumental proportions. Rather than blaming white Southerners for the collapse of racial cooperation, Democrats scolded Republicans for organizing blacks into a monolithic voting bloc. The results, Democrats charged, endangered white interests, artifically disrupted the political process, and unconstitutionally distorted the meaning of local sovereignty. Marble now became the party's spokesman for its abrupt shift, which was almost inevitable, away from accepting black suffrage. Congressional Reconstruction, he wrote, instead of "ending our troubles" led irrevocably to "a terrible tragedy, with the extermination of one race or the other for its catastrophe." Democrats cared "little about negro suffrage and would not seriously oppose it if unaccompanied with the disfranchisement of the white man." It was not a question of race, then, in Marble's eyes, but one based on highest motives because the

Democracy opposed Congress's policy of throwing Southern governments "into the hands of the most ignorant and incapable part of their population, and to conduct that section through negro insolence into anarchy." Whatever his high-minded rationale, Marble, like most Democrats, had yielded to political racism.[12]

The *Herald* felt just as betrayed. Convinced like the Democrats that Republicans had manipulated blacks, the paper told the South it should wait for sanity to return in the North rather than accept reunion "on the basis of a controlling Southern negro balance of power." Those factors, the paper suggested, placed Johnson under great pressure to thwart Republicans. The *Herald* reversed its censures of the President and commended his encouragement of southern resistance. Taken as a whole, these appeals to intolerance uncovered a new fact of political life. Racism had emerged as the major issue of the day and the Democracy hoped to become its ultimate beneficiary.[13]

The Democracy's adoption of political racism stemmed from another source, the Republican attempt at the state constitutional convention to end property restrictions for black suffrage. Democrats favored its retention; most Republicans did not. Some Republicans felt potential black voters would counter Tammany. Others viewed local suffrage as the logical continuance of Reconstruction. Still others such as Godwin viewed suffrage as a question of equal rights. When debate began on the question, Horace Greeley, the chairman of the Committee on the Right of Suffrage and the Qualification to Hold Office, presented the majority report. It eliminated all disabilities based on race or color and made a ringing defense of black equality. At the same time, Greeley proposed to halt some of the Democracy's blatant electoral frauds by increasing the period between naturalization and voting from ten to thirty days, and by disfranchising paupers and criminals.

Democrats rejected the report in a variety of ways. Basically, however, they linked black antisuffrage to their other scores against Republicans. For one thing they argued, the Republican had betrayed gross political intolerance by favoring blacks while harassing white immigrants through a series of registry laws and by attacking the naturalization process. Furthermore, since the thrust of congressional Reconstruction lay in treating black suffrage as a national issue "no longer within State jurisdiction," Democrats ironically rejected their defense of state sovereignty and told local Republicans they had no authority to enfranchise New York blacks. Even more, if the Republicans were sincere in establishing the principle of universal suffrage, they must also endorse women's suffrage, which they had not, and cease restricting voting by criminals and paupers, the "victims of circumstance." Finally, Democrats contended that the Committee on Cities sought to make the commission system a constitutional article, in effect disfranchising the entire population of New York City. "If the whole people in this city are incapable of governing themselves like the other municipalities of this State," Marble noted, "the doctrine of human equality is a sham and a few thousand negroes may as well rest under disabilities as a million white inhabitants of the commercial metropolis of this country."[14]

In the convention, Cassidy presented a minority report which urged the retention of property restrictions unless voters approved a change, in an article separate from the rest of the revised constitution. The Republican majority paid no heed; it realized that the only way black suffrage would pass lay in incorporating the issue within the entire document. Although the Republicans did win floor approval of Greeley's report, delays on other questions made it increasingly clear that the complete constitution could not be ready for submission to voters in time for the fall polls. On September 24, the convention adjourned until November 12, one week after the election.[15]

As the summer wore on, Democrats uncovered another explosive issue against Republicans. Under Democratic prodding at the convention, the Committee on Canals and State Finance unfolded disclosures of systematic frauds in canal construction, which the party linked to Fentonians, who vacated low bids for the merest technicalities in favor of a "Canal Ring." Estimates of losses to the state ranged near $1 million. Tilden led the Democratic attacks against the governor. The safest solutions to the problem, Tilden reported to the committee, lay in improving existing facilities through honest contractors and in having a new incorruptible governor appoint efficient managers. The upshot of these disclosures proved disastrous to all Republicans. Despite the fact that some Democrats were implicated in the Canal Ring, the corruption issue tarnished radical reformism, especially in regard to its commission system, which now seemed less idealistic and more partisan. After all, Democrats said, institutional reformers were defrauding the state of money in the same way they defrauded the city of home rule.[16]

The summer of 1867 was a transitional period in state politics. While Republican fortunes ebbed, Democratic prospects waxed because of the party's opposition to black suffrage and canal corruption. Of the two issues, however, racial prejudice proved the key to Democratic resurgence, a fact that became clearer in the light of a growing rupture within the Republican party concerning black suffrage. During the convention, Republican delegates had unanimously supported the Greeley report, but the party's grassroots response was far different. From across the state, Democratic Unionists, along with moderates and conservatives, feared that a white backlash would destroy them if they made suffrage a test vote of Republicanism. Rather, they sought to evade the issue through the Fourteenth Amendment. Despite their stand, however, signs indicated the Republicans could not handle the question, and that voters were increasingly moving toward the Democracy. Sensitive as ever to public opinion, the *Herald* observed: "We cannot doubt this desperate experiment of negro supremacy will be emphatically condemned by the vote of New York in our coming November election."[17]

The paper's judgment fit the Democracy's perception of politics. Convinced they rode a crest of public approval, all party factions agreed on a simple strategy for the fall election — exploit racism to crack and defeat Republicans, use the canal frauds to discredit Fenton, and manipulate the Excise Law to prove Republican intolerance of individual freedom of choice. If any New York Democrat disagreed and wanted to stress the party's long-range idea to reorganize politics around economic issues, not racism, a massive sectional disagreement within the national organization over funding the national debt made the sure issue of white supremacy even more attractive.

For some time, Midwestern Democrats, particularly former Ohio Peace Democrats headed by Long, Pendleton, and Washington McLean, editor of the *Cincinnati Enquirer,* regarded government bonds as an example of unwarranted wartime measures with whose absence they might have arranged a negotiated peace. Moreover, they felt that paying the bonds in gold unfairly rewarded Eastern capitalists and penalized poor farmers. Instead, they favored the "Pendleton Plan," which proposed that that part of the national debt held by national banks, the principal on the 5-20 bonds, he paid in greenbacks. The money the government saved in not paying gold on interest, coupled with other federal revenue economies, would then form a sinking fund, convertible to greenbacks, to pay the remainder of the national debt.[18]

New York Democrats recoiled in distaste. They privately rejected the plan because of its inflationary nature and its tacit denial that the government had a moral obligation to pay the national debt in gold, both of which countered traditional principles. On top of these, New Yorkers resented the Plan's obvious bias against Eastern bankers, notably Belmont, and they scorned its Peace Democratic origins. Moreover, they felt the Plan concealed Pendleton's bid for the presidency, a bid most local leaders considered disastrous because of his wartime record. For the sake of party unity, however, Democrats publicly treated the plan with circumspection. In an editorial which satisfied Pendleton, since it did not reject his proposal, Marble called for more study. Even so, he intimated without reproach that New Yorkers, out of regard for "national honor and a punctilious" respect for public "faith" in the bonds, disagreed with the Ohioans. These words, however, did little to ease the tension over the issue. Given the circumstances, the party could not debate economic issues; its only alternative was racial politics.[19]

Republicans held their state convention first in the critical fall election of 1867. The party, however, was mired with problems. Seeing no distinction between their own personal needs and political victory, the delegates split along factional and personal lines. As a sign of more trouble ahead, the party further ruptured over black suffrage. Instead of backing the issue, as the Fentonians wished, Conkling's supporters forged a plank that called for suffrage in vague terms that failed to specify when and how Republicans planned to implement "impartial suffrage." As for the thorny question of canal frauds, the delegates blundered by dropping several state officials who turned out, Weed noted, to be just the ones who had most "firmly resisted" corruption. Politicans so bent on self-destruction could not avoid other errors. Intent on defusing the criticism of the Excise Law, they antagonized both prohibitionists and antiprohibitionists by another plank that said the police must not deprive citizens of "the right to public or private recreation or pastime on any day of the week," provided they did not "violate public decorum, or the proper respect due to public worship."[20]

The Democracy howled in derision. Party newspapers flayed Republicans for cowardice on suffrage, complicity in the Canal Ring, and confusion over private rights. In a preview of the fall canvass, Marble said that the platform had not condemned Democrats, but Republicans. "Sunday liquor laws! Who passed them? Official corruption! Who perpetrated it? Negro suffrage! Who refused to submit to it?"[21]

The Democratic convention was a study in party harmony except for one minor problem that indicated the continual power struggle between Tammany and the Regency-swallowtail alliance. Tweed wanted Hoffman as permanent chairman to enhance his prestige; the others favored Seymour to rebuke the Hall. Tweed, however, backed down when a count revealed a majority for Seymour, and glumly watched as Hoffman became temporary chairman. The mayor made the most of his opportunity. In a wide-ranging speech that touched on every point that Seymour later made, Hoffman reinforced his image as the party's best vote-getter. That aside, the platform was brief and direct. Among its parts were calls for retrenchment and economy in government, rejection of congressional Reconstruction, condemnation of the Excise Law, a standard defense of adopted citizens and private rights, and a strongly-worded plank that pictured the Republican refusal "to submit the question of negro suffrage to the people as a cowardly evasion of a paramount issue on the pending struggle." In assessing the convention, Marble emphasized how vital racism loomed in the party's eyes. Admitting the importance of the Canal Ring and the Excise Law, he nonetheless termed them "subordinate questions and side issues." Towering above them and "disintegrating the Republican party of the State" was the question of black political status, both in the South and the North.[22]

During September and October 1867, a national trend in state elections developed against Republicans in other states, particularly in those where black suffrage was involved, such as Ohio. To make matters bleaker, local Republicans were on the unpopular side of most issues. Canal corruption was too blatant to rationalize away, and Democrats wasted few chances to underscore the link between dishonest contractors and Republican officials. Moreover, Greeley's maverick streak, which had caused the party much grief in the past, resurfaced. While conservatives and moderates, along with even the Fentonians, tried to avoid suffrage as a test of popular support, Greeley defied them by calling it the election's chief issue. Then, too, Greeley flouted party wishes by making temperance almost as important. He alienated the Irish and Germans by smearing all foes of the Excise Law as "non-Christians" who "desecrated the Sabbath," and, at a mass prohibitionist rally at Cooper Union, he assailed all who rejected the law as people who "tolerated lawlessness."[23]

While Democrats did not value the political dimensions of antitemperance as deeply as those of antisuffrage, Greeley's campaign opened new vistas. At first, the Democracy concentrated on racism and agreed with Greeley that suffrage was the election's "main issue." Thus, voters had a simple choice between "civilization versus barbarism." Yet as Greeley and his prohibitionist supporters raised the Excise Law to a peak of public awareness, Democrats turned to what they called a "subsidiary local question." Initially, the party termed the law "an annoying grievance which ought to be redressed" and cynically suggested upstate Republicans ought to make it statewide so that all could share its blessings. By November, however, the Democracy realized the opportunity Greeley handed them to win votes. The result was a marriage of antitemperance and racism. Marble twisted the two together: "The odious excise law is a twig from the same tree that protrudes its intermeddling branches through everybody's windows, and forces its crude fruit into Southern ballot-boxes as well as Northern beer-cups." Yet the temperance question had a sharp edge; some Democrats, such as Homer Nelson, the candidate for secretary of state, assured prohibitionists that they sympathized with their goals. Under those circumstances, the party retreated back to racism, as the *Irish-American* approvingly noted, because nothing else "so potent" as universal suffrage disgusted "white men of the North." Banners at Tammany's last campaign rally reflected that attitude: "No Suffrage Nor Negro Equality! White Man's Government for White Men! White Men Shall Rule America!" On the eve of the election, a confident Cassidy told Marble, "We shall carry the state ticket & with it a majority of the Assembly."[24]

The extent of Democratic victories exceeded all expectations. The party elected its entire state ticket by an average of 40,000, gained control of the assembly by eighteen seats, and reduced Republican dominance of the senate to two. Democrats were delighted. In an off-year election, they had made startling statewide gains and given Republicans their worst drubbing since 1856. Amidst this jubilation, five political facts were clear: while the canal frauds and Excise Law contributed to the Democratic landslide, racism routed the Republicans; Johnson gained no credit among New Yorkers for influencing events; institutional reformism had run its course; state senator Tweed accelerated his drive to dominate the state party; and the election marked a turning point in local politics.[25]

Since Democratic triumphs throughout the North signaled a massive swing of public opinion against Republicans, the Democracy's main concern lay in consolidating gains through a new program. As Warren insisted to Marble, "We cannot wait for the development of Radical policy, & content ourselves with mere resistance." Marble needed little prompting. Setting a line other state party newspapers adopted, he pointed out that the Democracy won because of Republican mistakes. In the future, Democrats must grasp the initiative by espousing fresh, "live issues." Along that line, Marble suggested a new approach to reunion, the party's "paramount interest." In order to weaken the radicals and speed readmission, he urged white Southerners to accept probationary black suffrage similar to that applied to immigrants, which, after blacks proved their worth, would become universal. In exchange, the North would grant universal amnesty, end white disfranchisements, and adopt three parts of the Confederate Constitution, a six year term for the President, item vetoes, and a two-thirds vote to pass appropriation bills. Furthermore, Marble suggested the Democracy soften its racism by imploring white Southerners to grant blacks full civil equality, thus making the Fourteenth Amendment unnecessary.[26]

The *World's* new departure drew a negative response from outside the state. In Pennsylvania, elder party leader James Buchanan grumbled that the Democracy could not abandon racism because it had "been the principle cause of [our] triumph everywhere." In Kentucky, William B. Haldeman, editor of the moderate *Louisville Courier,* told Marble that even though his proposals made sense, "the hereditary prejudice of our people" prevented compromise. In the South, Democrats acted out their disapproval. They continued to boycott elections, refused to cooperate with Reconstruction governments, and counted on the Northern white backlash to stymie the Republicans. In the Midwest, chiefly Ohio, the party also rejected Marble's advice, concentrated on racism, and used economic issues to boom Pendleton's presidential candidacy.[27]

By late December, the New Yorkers surrendered. Black suffrage, they now wrote, was synonymous with social equality and miscegenation. "The unreasoning, fanatical elevation of the negro is not so disgraceful a sight, as the tyrannical oppression of the white man," Warren claimed. "The Republican party is planting itself squarely upon the negro-suffrage issue, and upon that issue will contest the next Presidential election," Marble announced. "The repugnance to negroes [is] implanted by nature." We "cannot abolish the distinction of race, for it is a distinction established by GOD himself." In sum, outside reaction forced the New York Democracy to retain political racism as a potent issue, one that seemed destined to climax the party's comeback in 1868.[28]

With the lines separating parties now defined in their minds, New York Democrats turned to president-making. Seymour assumed that the local Democracy, although lacking a candidate of its own, would, if united, wield great power because of the state's electoral vote. Even so, Seymour feared Tammany's thirst for domination. "We do not want new leaders," he told Tilden. To ensure their position, the Regency and the swallowtails mapped out a fresh plan of operation. To thwart Tweed's covert attempt to buy the *Albany Argus,* they bought Richmond's shares for Cassidy. Moreover, they pressed Tilden "to give up railroads, & take to politics exclusively." While Tilden rejected their plea, he did use his state chairmanship to prevent a premature commitment to any candidate. Finally city swallow-tails worked through the Bennetts and Charles Halpine to caution Easterners about the dangers in "repudiation" of government bonds. There was another side of policy-making that the swallow-tails and the Regency chose to ignore — finding a suitable presidential candidate. While it was apparent that Pendleton was extremely popular in the Midwest and among former New York Peace Democrats, many other Democrats favored Ulysses S. Grant. Hoping for direction, Samuel S. Cox asked Marble "who is the coming man? Is he on horseback? Or is he a civilian?" This question underscored a fatal flaw in the posture of the Regency and the swallow-tails. Not only had no candidate emerged from the pack in preconvention jockeying, but such a man was not even in sight. The result was that the Regency and swallow-tails drifted with events and played a waiting game in the expectation of jumping on a bandwagon when an apparent winner emerged.[29]

Meantime, Tammany avoided presidential politics and Tweed concentrated on Hoffman's reelection. The Hall's only foe was overconfidence, not the mayor's opponents, Fernando Wood and the radical reformer William Darling. The election was preordained. Hoffman carried every ward and won by 69.4 percent of the votes cast. Few Democrats doubted the importance of Hoffman's victory. The elated *Leader* placed a tombstone over Wood's career, and demanded the party acknowledge a new power equation in the state by an early renomination of Hoffman for governor. Even the Regency and the swallow-tails were subdued. Cassidy praised "the young gallant standard-bearer of our cause," while Marble flattered him as "an able and honest man and an efficient public servant." Left unsaid was their inability to halt Tweed. In contrast, Tweed was ready to challenge other power-brokers for control of the entire state party. Fully the master of the city and county, bankrolled by his close working agreement with the Erie Railroad directors, ready to boss the legislators by force of will and bribery if necessary, he and Sweeny dreamed a sweet dream: the election of Hoffman as governor in 1868 and, after a successful administration, the presidency in 1872.[30]

On the other side, Republicans were in disarray. Conceding their losses were part of a national trend, Republican moderates and conservatives locked with radicals in a bitter intraparty battle, whose stakes were the organization's destiny. The two main questions that divided the factions were black suffrage and the coming presidential election. In general, conservatives and moderates, Raymond wrote, feared the "potent" cry of "negro supremacy" that Democrats raised. Instead, these men sought a new formula for suffrage based upon "intelligence and education." Radicals refused; such evasion they thought "false and cowardly." For the presidency, the conservatives and moderates boomed Grant, while the radicals advanced Chief Justice Salmon P. Chase.[31]

By February 1868, radical hopes for dominating the New York party lay in shambles. The Conklingites undercut Governor Fenton; the Republican state convention endorsed Grant largely because of Weed's spadework; and Democrats in the legislature blocked any fresh institutional reforms. In an even-more shattering blow to radical prestige, the constitutional convention finished work by cutting the new document into three parts—a special judiciary article, the main body, and a black suffrage clause—for separate voter submission. Both parties, however, delayed the submission until 1869 because they feared injecting the question into a presidential year, particularly since neither knew the national platforms and candidates of their respective parties. While this evasion was politically expedient, it did indicate the radicals' shaky position within their party.[32]

As the forthcoming presidential election year of 1868 became the center of politicking, it appeared that Democrats had chosen wisely and well in becoming the party of political racism. On the surface, they had split the Republicans, isolated the radicals, forestalled local black suffrage, stalemated the Fourteenth Amendment's adoption, and checked institutional reformers. Only the choice of a frontrunner for the nomination remained. Whatever his identity, however, he had to satisfy certain needs. Locally, this hypothetical man had to broaden the Democracy's base of support by winning over old Barnburner Republicans and Democratic Unionists. Nationally, he had to be a fiscal moderate, attractive to Southerners, a person with an impeccable war record, and capable of ending the issues of war, restoring the Union, and moving on to new questions. Only future events could uncover that paragon.

Until July 1868, the pattern and rhythm of New York Democratic politics revolved around one simple question — who would the party nominate for president? What made that question complex, however, lay in four unresolved issues fundamentally tied to the nomination: the party's relationship with President Johnson, economic policies, congressional Reconstruction, and the factional struggle between Tammany and the Regency-swallow-tail alliance. Amidst this uncertainty, one fact was manifest — Democrats were no longer concerned with party survival. Political and social racism, linked with the public's rejection of radicalism, party leaders judged, had reconstituted the Democracy into an effective national organization, thus ending war-related issues. On such a basis, Democrats were confident they could win the presidency.

By mid-February, after fluctuating in a love-hate relationship with the President for almost three years, the Democracy generally dismissed him as a possible candidate and avoided any association with his Administration. The situation did not appreciably change with Johnson's impeachment trial. During the proceedings, Democrats denied that Johnson was a surrogate Democrat. Turning the question around, the party maintained that congressional impeachers really sought to "subvert the Constitution, to destroy the institutions of government, and to fill the land with bloodshed and anarchy by enfranchising an ignorant and degraded class, and giving them a voice in the conduct of the nation."[33]

In May, when impeachment failed, Democratic attitudes underwent a subtle change in style, but not substance. Democrats now argued that Johnson's acquittal vindicated the party's strictures against centralism and indicated a continued trend against Republicans. Under these conditions, Cassidy said, only the election of a Democrat would "rescue, at the eleventh hour, the form of government bequeathed by the fathers of the Republic." As for Johnson, Tilden shrewdly noted the Democracy still appreciated his obstructionist tactics in Reconstruction policies. But Tilden added that his exoneration was less a personal triumph than a defense of constitutional guarantees. In sum, the party struck a balance between defending the office of President and the man who was President without being associated with him.[34]

These developments had one unforeseen side-effect, the Democracy's reassessment of Chief Justice Chase. Before the trial, Democrats had dismissed him as a militant radical, a possible Republican presidential nominee, with an unacceptable record on finance and racial matters. Yet as the trial progressed, Chase revealed a hidden streak of constitutional conservatism and judicial fairness that alienated radicals and amazed Democrats. As a result, some New Yorkers, especially John Dash Van Buren, the younger Bennett, and Bryant, began a boomlet for his nomination, either by Democrats or Republicans. By May, the Chase bandwagon gained momentum, but most Democrats were puzzled about his aims. Aware that his candidacy sowed confusion within the Republican party, Warren told Marble the movement had many political dimensions as yet undecipherable. "There can be no harm grown out of the talk, and much practical good may come of it."[35]

Democrats found economic issues just as perplexing as Chase's candidacy. In January, Marble attempted to lay the Pendleton Plan to rest. The Plan, he wrote, harbored explosive class questions that pitted rich against poor, creditor against debtor. Rather than stimulate further divisiveness, the Democracy must remain silent on fiscal questions during the coming campaign. When the state convention met, however, Horatio Seymour muddled the issue. The Democracy's only sensible policy, he maintained, lay in its long-time Jacksonian devotion to a hard money system, achieved through federal fiscal retrenchment and reduction of taxes. Former Democratic Unionists such as John Dix, now looking for a new political home, welcomed this revival of traditional principles. Yet national chairman August Belmont agreed with the *World*. Say little about financial matters, he pleaded to Marble, "but pitch into negro suffrage, reconstruction outrages & disgraceful extravagance." To confuse the problem even more, Western Democrats, while they appreciated the importance of racism, held out for Pendleton's Plan. Speaking for him, Washington McLean chastised Marble for surrendering to "Bankers and Bondholders." Silence on that topic, McLean warned, "would defeat us in every western state. The question must be met with boldness — no dodging, no equivocation."[36]

Had it not been for Republican refinement of Reconstruction procedures, financial differences might have convulsed Democrats. Congressional moderates and conservatives, fearful that a continued boycott by Southern whites unnecessarily delayed readmission of several states, passed a bill which changed the formula for ratification of state constitutions from a majority of the registered voters to a majority of the actual ones. By March, Southern Reconstruction began in earnest. White Democrats, forced to abandon deadlock, now attempted in some states to contest for the black vote, and in others used violence and intimidation. By July, Congress had readmitted all but three states; a combination of blacks, Republicans, and old Southern Whigs controlled the others, and, in the process, the Fourteenth Amendment became part of the Constitution.

In carrying out this program, Republicans triggered a new outburst of Democratic hostility. As if anticipating the presidential campaign, the Democrats growled that ignorant blacks aided by venal transient Northerners (carpetbaggers) and corrupt Southern white turncoats (scalawags), placed the South on the verge of barbarism solely to record instant Republican electoral majorities. The Ku Klux Klan's emergence gave Northern Democrats a further opportunity to realign their organization as the white man's party. The Klan's activities, New Yorkers swore, flowed directly from white reaction against the Union League's manipulation of blacks. In that view, the Klan stood for law and order and represented a legitimate alternative to the military's intrusion in state affairs.[37]

The Democracy's commitment to racism became even clearer because of Tilden. In a message to local committeemen, he wrote: "Our position must be *condemnation and reversal of negro suffrage in the states.*" Any Democratic faltering "shall not only fail to meet the necessities of the present condition of the country" but "prove a great political blunder." The state convention to elect national delegates gave Tilden another forum to stress political white supremacy. In a speech that outlined the thrust of the Democracy's grievances, he flayed Republicans for revolutionizing every aspect of American society through centralism, militarism, and enforced racial commingling. Democratic newspapers endorsed Tilden's racism. Whites, they stressed, hated "Africanization" in the South and were determined to preserve the principle of self-government. In contrast, Republicans used blacks for partisan ends, favored miscegenation, and were too timid to press for suffrage in Northern states. "Go before the country like a man with your flag," Marble taunted. "Proclaim your purpose to bring the negro into the State and into the Family, and let the American people pass upon you in the daylight, not the dark."[38]

Meanwhile, Tweed was busy in other matters. In the legislature, he quickly made his presence felt by hand-picking William Hitchman as assembly speaker over John Flagg, the Regency's choice. Tweed's stature increased even more in the senate where he became a key member of several committees. Yet his real blossoming as a power-broker above all other New York Democrats stemmed from the battle for control of the Erie Railroad between Jay Gould and Cornelius Vanderbilt. The Erie War provoked a public scandal that involved stock manipulation, injunctions and counter-injunctions issued by tainted judges, and naked political clout. Tweed was in the thick of battle. He backed Gould, used pet judges to thwart Vanderbilt, and in the end he and Sweeny became directors of the Erie for services rendered. In addition to making a great deal of money from Gould, Tweed now had more financial backing to challenge Tilden and the swallow-tails.

Tammany did not drift with Tweed away. Under the leadership of Hoffman, Sweeny, and Abraham Oakey Hall, a former Weedite and future mayor, the General Committee stabilized politics by absorbing the now dead Charles G. Halpine's followers and welcomed support from the chastened Fernando Wood, who needed Tammany's aid in his bid for Congress. Only the Irish remained aloof. Still disgruntled over the Hall's belated defense of Fenianism, the *Irish-American* adopted a wait-and-see attitude. Despite that, Tammany stayed patient since it knew the Irish lacked alternatives.[39]

Hoffman pushed ahead on his own. In January and February, he made a series of speeches in Pennsylvania, Connecticut, and particularly New Hampshire where his efforts helped defeat Republican incumbents. As the effervescent Hall explained to Marble, "Hoffman can do the statemanship & I the grand and lofty tumbling." As signs multiplied of more public backing, the mayor's confidence grew. He told a friend of Seymour, sure to relay the message, "that he expected the nomination of Governor to be conceded to him."[40]

Throughout these maneuvers, Tammany strove to stifle all innuendoes of municipal corruption by presenting a stiffly upright public image. Tweed acted as a reformer out to save self-government from Republican centralism; Hoffman postured as a fiscal conservative, statesmanlike and moderate; while Tammany reminded the party that it deserved credit for reorganization. In February, the National Executive Committee crowned their efforts by awarding the convention to New York City in the building the Tammany Society had just erected as its new home.

All these developments placed the Republican party in an uncomfortable political position. Fearful of losing the presidency, each party faction slowly patched up differences for the sake of victory. "The Chicago Convention will be no place for recrimination or denunciation," the Weedite *Commercial Advertiser* announced. The platform that delegates formulated was filled with that spirit. They evaded the question of spreading black suffrage to the North, and adopted a probusiness economic package, including planks that denounced the Pendleton Plan as a form of "repudiation" and called for rapid repayment of the "public indebtedness" according to both the "letter" and "spirit of the laws under which it was contracted." Then, as the party of peace, sobriety, and reunion, the Republicans nominated Grant for president and rejected Fenton as his running mate in favor of Senator Schuyler Colfax of Indiana.[41]

Democrats whooped with happiness. Grant, the *Leader* snorted, was a better judge "upon the relative qualities of whiskey" than national issues, while Marble crowed that the platform was "a jumble of inconsistencies" that would drive "from the party all the reasonable independent men who have belonged to it." Yet Grant proved a stronger candidate than Democrats suspected. As a symbol of Union victory, he was strong in the North among veterans and patriots. Even in the South his popularity grew because his campaign slogan of "Let us have Peace" appealed to many white Democrats. But worst of all from the Democracy's standpoint, his silence on black suffrage robbed the party of its key issue by making political racism a unworkable issue. Even radicals, who did not trust him and disliked the platform, gradually fell into line.[42]

It now became more imperative for Democrats to find an attractive candidate. As the quest expanded, New Yorkers were at a disadvantage since they lacked a favorite son. As a remedy, Tammanyites, along with upstaters such as Warren, Kernan, and Cassidy, boosted Seymour. The former governor rebuffed them. Seymour's backers, however, did not take him at face value because he had made the same basic refusal speech in almost every campaign dating back to his first statewide gubernatorial race in 1850. Calvert Comstock, Cassidy's partner, told him that events indicated the convention will "arrive spontaneously at the conclusion to nominate you. If so it is a duty of patriotism to accept & you must do it." On the other hand, Tilden, Belmont, and Marble were cool. They agreed that Seymour, though a fine man, could not win; rather, they sought a candidate who might yet divide Republicans.[43]

As the dream of president-making unfolded in New York, Tilden, Barlow, Belmont, and Marble seriously weakened the alliance between the Regency and the swallow-tails by rejecting Seymour. Yet because the stakes were so high, these men took the risk. At least they knew whom they did not want — Pendleton or General Frank P. Blair, Montgomery Blair's brother. Yet if the New Yorkers hoped to block the others, they needed a likely replacement. Gradually, Salmon Chase became that man. The Democratic pro-Chase movement began from an unlikely source, Alexander Long, the notorious Peace Democrat and Chase's long-time foe in Ohio politics. In February 1868, Long decided they needed each other; Chase because of his estrangement from the Republicans, Long because the Pendleton crowd had isolated him. The result was Long's suggestion that Chase seek the Democratic nomination. The Chief Justice played coy; feigning indifference, he replied that he might accept a draft if the party came to him with acceptable platform planks. At the same time, Chase made his terms clear: "Suffrage for all; amnesty for all; good money for all; and security for citizens, at home, against military despotism and against governmental invasion." On that basis, Long pushed ahead.[44]

In New York, the effort for Chase developed slowly because of the Democracy's phobia against black suffrage. Behind the scenes, however, Barlow laid the groundwork for the party's adoption of Chase by contacting Southern business acquaintances and seeking to have them moderate opposition to universal suffrage. His efforts failed. Yet John Dash Van Buren, Chase's chief local manager, was not discouraged. At the end of May, he achieved a significant breakthrough when Seymour endorsed Chase and asked Pendleton to withdraw.[45]

Despite that development, Seymour's backers did not relent. In a typical response, Sanford Church told Cassidy the party could never accept Chase as a Democrat because of his stand favoring black suffrage and his identification with Republican wartime fiscal policies. As for Tammany, the *Leader* mounted "Seymour for President" on its masthead, and dismissed Chase as an apostate Democrat without shame or honor. Aware of such opposition, the Chief Justice took matters in hand and utilized Marble to rebuild his political fences. Claiming a lifelong devotion to the Democracy's "political views and sentiments," Chase explained that the extension of slavery issue had forced him into the Republican party. Again playing coy, he continued that he did not seek the nomination, but placed Marble on notice that the Democracy could settle postwar sectional problems because many of its Southern members "are willing to accept universal suffrage & universal amnesty as the basis of reconstruction & restoration." Those declaimers aside, few doubted that the presidential bug had bitten Chase. One Ohio Republican noted that a friend of the Chief Justice told him Chase "*was fully expecting the New York nomination.*"[46]

Chase's candidacy presented Democrats with a strange blend of assets and debits. On the positive side, he would attract some Republicans; moreover, his economic position, hard money and free trade, pleased conservative businessmen, Democratic ideologues, and anti-Pendleton contractionists. Better, the *Herald* observed, the Democracy could neutralize radicalism and begin new political issues by nominating him because in doing so it would "accept the results of the war as facts of history." Another advantage, the paper added, lay in his idea, implicit in the Fourteenth Amendment, that while "freedom and manhood suffrage" were now "unquestioned rights," they were, in line with Democratic principles, under state jurisdiction.[47]

In contrast, a variety of flaws weakened Chase. Westerners regarded him as New York's stalking horse to unseat Pendleton, the Blairs loathed him personally, and many white Southern Democrats refused to cool off the antisuffrage backlash. In Tammany's eyes, rebuffing Chase was less a question of race than part of its unfolding drive to dominate the party. The Hall regarded Seymour, if he lost the presidential nomination, as a likely gubernatorial candidate to block Hoffman. Seen in that light, the Hall had to remove Seymour from the state scene. Taking all these factors into consideration, Chase could only secure the nomination by a skillful juggling act.

Nevertheless, for a time it seemed the Democracy would accept him. After the Republican convention, Chase picked up the type of momentum his backers sought when the *Evening Post* called on Democrats to nominate him. At that point, the party faced an unavoidable choice — which idea, political racism or state determination of suffrage qualifications, provided the best means not only for winning the presidency but for reconstructing the party? Marble tried to ease the Democracy's way. In two key editorials, he developed the theme that Congress had forged de facto suffrage in the South through the Fourteenth Amendment and congressional Reconstruction. Yet, he emphasized, these factors were compatible with the Democratic principle of home rule because local voters, whatever the coercion, determined the qualifications for actual suffrage. Furthermore, he suggested, Democrats need not fear universal black suffrage in the North since Republicans restricted it to the South. Under those conditions, Marble concluded by urging that the party's platform "say nothing on the subject" of black suffrage. Having placed the issue before the party, Marble stopped short of a firm endorsement of Chase and awaited Democratic reaction.[48]

Things worked counter to Marble. Southern Democrats censured the *World,* and the Blairs joined them in scorning the idea of replacing the sure issue of race for the questionable one inherent in Chase's nomination. Upstate Democrats were just as adamant, backed Tammany's efforts for Seymour, and, worst of all, forced Tilden to run a favorite son candidate for president, Sanford Church, whom most politicians recognized as Seymour's stand-in. Suddenly, the *World* caved in, partly because of the avalanche of criticism, partly because of Marble's withdrawal from politics following his wife's death. On June 15, three weeks before the convention, the paper announced that Democrats could not support Chase as long as he regarded black suffrage "as a blessing" rather than an atrocious blunder. The only way that black suffrage could be "uprooted" lay in a Democratic victory. Chase's only hope now rested on a deadlock.[49]

During the first week of July, New York City thronged with many diverse Democrats, as if hope existed that the party's revitalization was complete. As it turned out, that expectation failed. On Reconstruction, the platform backed immediate reunion, universal amnesty, and abolition of all government agencies that fostered "negro supremacy." Additionally, the delegates assailed centralism and military despotism, and implied that the nation must undo all previous Reconstruction measures, which they termed "null and void." The suffrage section reflected the latent politics of race rather than overt white supremacy, largely because delegates realized the Republicans made the issue moot in nominating Grant. Using generalities in a long plank, the delegates defended home rule and concluded the government acted despotically in depriving states "of this right." Nonetheless, most Democrats realized these words covered, in code terms, their objections to universal black suffrage. Finally, the platform approved the Pendleton Plan, but ambiguously proposed that if bonds did not specify payment "in coin" they ought to "be paid in the lawful money of the United States."[50]

Taken as a whole, the platform looked more to the past than the future. Beyond that, the party, bound as it was by its political philosophy and need to assuage its Southern wing, resisted a basically moderate Republican solution, one it could finesse, once the individual states became sovereign, in favor of another that was basically retrograde. For in the most pragmatic sense, congressional Reconstruction and the Republican platform implied home rule and rejected federal guarantees of black suffrage. That solution was Chase's message, a message the party chose to ignore. As a result, Democratic principles still did not work. That is, blinded by resentment against Congress and tied to racism, Democrats simply failed to come to terms with either their principles or political reality.

The delegates then stumbled through twenty-two ballots before the "spontaneous" floor movement Calvert Comstock had predicted developed for Seymour. Given the state of intraparty factionalism, his nomination fit momentary needs. Seymour, a compromise selection, aggrieved Pendleton by his hard money stance; but his war record did console former Peace Democrats and Southerners, and his party regularity soothed others. Frank Blair's nomination as his running mate was another matter. Before the convention, Blair wrote an open letter to James Brodhead of Missouri in which he passionately attacked every aspect of congressional Reconstruction and promised to "allow white people to reorganize their own government." Blair's flagrant racism revolted moderates such as Marble; his stand on Reconstruction stunned conservatives who feared that some Republicans might now propose a constitutional amendment guaranteeing black suffrage; and his hostility to all Republicans rankled Democratic strategists who hoped to widen the party's base.[51]

The bracing effect of the Democracy's mistakes intoxicated Republicans. Seymour's war record, they accused, proved the party was unregenerate. As for his chronic foot-dragging, they insinuated it stemmed from family insanity. Beyond those, they contemptuously showed his inconsistency as a hard money man running on a soft money plank. When it came to Blair, Republican derision knew no bounds. They blasted him as a reactionary whose only goal was to revive "hatred, proscription and defiance of the law." When Greeley reviewed the whole ticket and the platform, he summed up the gist of the Republican campaign. "The Democracy propose to overthrow the loyal governments by force of arms; to repudiate our just debts; to make rebellion honorable; to blot from our history its noblest pages; and to place the country under the men who conspired for its overthrow in the hour of its deepest agony."[52]

The New York Democracy had mixed reactions. Aware of the gravity of Republican charges, Barlow tried to see the situation in the best light. "Our ticket here [New York City] creates almost universal despair," he told Tilden, "but so it was when [James K.] Polk was nominated." Sam Ward tumbled into gloom. The Republicans, he informed Barlow, are "jubilant over our nominations." In contrast, Tammany was exultant. While not enthused about Blair, the *Leader* gushed praise for Seymour. More important, however, was Tammany's challenge to the swallow-tails: "Give us John T. Hoffman for Governor, with Horatio Seymour for President, and the City of New York cannot fail to roll up a majority of one hundred thousand for our State and national tickets."[53]

Horatio Seymour capped the Democracy's confusion. Although caught up in the excitement of his nomination, he became increasingly despondent because he had repeatedly denied his candidacy. Unwilling to expose himself to taunts of insincerity, Seymour turned to his friends for advice and delayed a formal acceptance. This in turn encouraged many of Chase's die-hard backers who hoped for his withdrawal in favor of the Chief Justice. By the end of July, Seymour finally accepted the inevitable, but he scarcely inspired fellow Democrats. To Barlow, he explained: "I think we shall carry the country. This faith does not spring from my desire for I shrink from victory more than I do from defeat."[54]

Fearful that Seymour's lagging spirits could not stimulate party workers, New York Democrats relied on organizational machinery to mobilize voters. Under Tilden's leadership upstate, the state committee assessed contributions from each assembly district, published position papers, formed a speakers bureau, and arranged tours for prominent Democrats to visit Seymour in Utica. In the city, with the fastidious Tilden's gaze averted, Tammany marshalled the voters and swelled the electorate by a massive, possibly illegal, naturalization effort. Two tasks remained, namely, gaining endorsements from Johnson and Chase. Tilden took the initiative. He dispatched Montgomery Blair and Barlow to plead Seymour's case to the President, and ingratiatingly wrote Johnson the party ran on issues "that will make you illustrious in history." By September, the President yielded and used federal patronage on the Democracy's behalf. Chase proved harder to crack. Under great Republican pressure to endorse Grant, the Chief Justice was appalled at the Democratic platform, angry at Blair, and chagrined that the party had rebuffed him. With those factors in mind, Chase stayed silent, a move that encouraged Long and Van Buren well into October to continue their Quixotic attempt to force Seymour's abdication.[55]

As the campaign developed, Democratic efforts collapsed under the weight of their own contradictions. Nothing better illustrated the party's problems than the issue of racial politics. Consistent with their success in 1867, Democrats wanted to make antisuffrage their major issue. They failed because of the Republican platform's equivocation and Grant's tenuous relationship to congressional Reconstruction and the radicals. From the standpoint of practicality moreover, the Democracy had to back off from blatant racism because of the number of Southern black voters. As the *Leader* noted, Seymour needed the South's electoral vote; hence, race-baiting, such as Blair's, increased Republican strength. It made far more sense, Warren also admitted, for white Southerners to compete for blacks than to surrender them to Republicans. Unfortunately, such advice fell on deaf ears in the white South and among Blair's supporters.[56]

Clashing Democratic opinions over inflationary currency proved just as troublesome. Even though Seymour's strategists emphasized his fiscal conservatism and Republican overspending, Midwestern Democrats refused to budge on the Pendleton Plan. Accordingly, when the *Argus* wrote that Seymour's triumph would usher in an "era of retrenchment, sound currency and fiscal responsibility," Greeley replied that his election "will be the triumph of that sneaking, cowardly form of repudiation termed paying the five twenties in greenbacks."[57]

Democrats floundered as badly on Reconstruction. Since the platform reiterated the party's rejection of Republican policies without proposing alternatives beyond self-determination by Southern whites, voters sought clues to Democratic programs. They looked no further than Blair, whose statements indicated he favored long-disgraced Confederates, had no quarrel with white violence, and favored easy reconciliation by treating blacks no differently than prewar slaves. His words disenchanted many Northerners, and Republicans preyed on him. Blair's willingness to disperse legitimate Southern governments, they charged, was all too reminiscent of slavery, in contrast to Grant's disposition to temper justice with wisdom by seeking sectional harmony.[58]

By September, the outline of Democratic disasters became clear. As expected, Republicans won in Vermont, but their majorities exceeded expectations. The Maine elections were equally discouraging for Democrats. With their campaign skidding downward at a sickening rate, the Democracy poured efforts into three bellwether states they had to carry, Pennsylvania, Ohio, and Indiana. In mid-October, havoc struck. Republicans carried all three; they now had the motive force to win most of the North including New York. Senator Morgan had no doubts. Writing to Weed, who was in London, he said: "If the frauds in *this* [New York City] and other cities are not too great, we shall triumph everywhere."[59]

While the virus of declining morale infected the Democracy, Tammany Hall remained immune. At the state convention, Tweed met a momentary setback when the Kings County delegation assailed Tammany's corruption and demanded the selection of Brooklyn's Henry Murphy instead of Hoffman. This outburst failed to halt the Hall's steamroller, and Hoffman won by acclamation. For the sake of consistency, the state platform replicated the national one except for two planks the Hall inserted to appease good government forces — a statewide uniform registry system and a uniform excise law.[60]

What followed was an exercise full of sound, fury, corruption, and vituperation. Both sides used the same tactics of saturating the public mind with questions about the personal qualities of the opposition's gubernatorial candidates. Democrats attacked John Griswold, a former War Democrat who ran with Dix's blessing, as a dishonest businessman who supplied Union troops with inferior goods that led to unnecessary deaths. Republicans spared no efforts to smear Hoffman. In a representative editorial, the *Evening Post* wrote: "To give this State to Hoffman and the [Tammany] Ring would increase our taxes enormously, and expose us to still further evils," Tweed followed another course. In a massive effort that bordered on the spectacular, Tammanyite judges John McCunn and George Barnard helped the Hall purportedly naturalize over 60,000 new citizens during October. Republicans were aware of these frauds, but powerless.[61]

At this point in mid-October, national Democratic problems spilled over on the state party. Since the defeats in other states, rumors swirled through the Democracy concerning an eleventh-hour change in the ticket by replacing Blair, who had become the focal point of Republican attacks. McLean and Long, however, favored a more drastic step. Using a network of friends and collaborators, they contended the Democracy must change the entire national slate and substitute Chase for Seymour. These rumblings gained credence when Chase still did not endorse Seymour and Long continued to stress the Chief Justice's availability. Seymour was furious. Dropping his role of martyr, he lashed out at the "falsehoods" Chase's supporters spread about his supposedly cheating the Chief Justice out of the nomination. It was far better, Seymour scolded, for Chase "to call off his Dogs" and embrace the ticket as an honorable man. Barlow came to the opposite conclusion. Convinced that the Democracy was plummeting to defeat, he called on Tilden and other Regency leaders to drop both Seymour and Blair and replace them with Chase and John Quincy Adams II of Massachusetts. By doing that, Barlow felt, Democrats could "carry a majority of Congress, put an end to Radical rule, lay the foundation for a great party, broad and deep; & do our Country a lasting service."[62]

Manton Marble needed no prompting. Following the convention, his paper treated the campaign with indifference. "The New York *World* is destroying us," Montgomery Blair complained; even Warren chided Marble for creating the impression the New York Democracy "do not stand by the platform." On October 15, acting without Barlow's advice, Marble astounded the party by making public what had been privately whispered. The time had come, he editorialized, for the Democracy to realize the inevitable prospect of defeat. "The Youthful, Indomitable Democracy" must face the future by accepting congressional Reconstruction, dropping racial politics, laying aside all issues connected with the past, and rebuilding the party on the basis of its "vigorous, youthful, aspiring elements." Although he did not make the point specifically, Marble left his readers with the clear impression he favored a quick change in the national ticket.[63]

The party's response devastated Marble. Although Chase's supporters assured him the *World* "almost certainly saves us," every state Democratic newspaper censured him, the national committee treated him as an ingrate, and Barlow professed astonishment at his presumptuousness. Instead, party leaders agreed with Kernan, Seymour's close friend, that all efforts to alter the ticket were "impracticable and would be unsuccessful." Thoroughly vanquished, Marble ended his insurgency.

Even so, the mere fact that some Democrats felt compelled to drop Seymour barely three weeks before the end of the canvass indicated the confusion that still gripped the party.[64]

When the returns were in, Grant won but Seymour ran better than most people thought possible. Although he lost in the Electoral College, 214 to 80, Seymour did well in the popular vote throughout the nation and might have carried the South if not for black suffrage and white disfranchisement. Locally, both Hoffman and Seymour carried the state by paper-thin margins; Seymour by 50.55 percent, Hoffman by 51.6 percent. Despite that, the Republicans won both legislative branches, thus ensuring the election of a new United States senator, and they elected eighteen out of thirty-one congressmen. In the long run, then, Democrats might console themselves with partial victories, such as Hoffman's, or explain away their defeat by pointing to heavy black voting in the South. Nonetheless, the fact remained that while individual pockets of Democratic strength provided building blocks for the future, the present belonged to Republicans.[65]

5

Tammany's Reconstruction: *1868–1870*

T*AMMANY* steered to the future, convinced that it had the party in tow. In order to do so, the Hall had a clear vision of how to end the legacy of Civil War and the uncertainties of reunion. Aware of past ideas implicit in the Fourteenth Amendment and Chase's candidacy, the Hall accepted the idea that once the Southern states were restored the national government lacked the right to interfere with domestic concerns. As a result, Tammany felt the part must allow President-elect Grant the latitude to carry out his promise of sectional peace.

Tammany recognized another fact. Once congressional Reconstruction ran its course, the Republican concept of an activist government was no longer needed and the party faced an identity crisis. In its place, Hoffman prepared a counterphilosophy based on Jacksonianism. Consistent with principles, Hoffman insisted that the Democracy's reliance on home rule, laissez-faire, decentralism, grassroots responsibility, and free trade not only afforded the nation a new program for post-Reconstruction America, but indicated that the party's full restoration was a matter of continuity involving traditional values. One final point stood out. If Reconstruction was over, politics in the future, stripped of the emotions that molded the thinking and behavior of Americans for two generations, became a matter of organizational politics — politics concentrating on the allocation of power, politics where party machinery spelled success. In New York, and perhaps the nation, few politicians understood the process better than Tammany Hall. When the *Leader* suggested that the entire Democracy emulate the methods the Hall used to redeem "New York from the thralldom of Radical tyranny," then, the paper's meaning began a new round in party reconstruction.[1]

This new phase of the New York Democracy's reconstruction began and ended with William M. Tweed. In the city, he controlled the municipal and county governments either directly through patronage or indirectly through his henchmen. Moreover, he dominated Tammany Hall as chairman of the General Committee and the Tammany Society as grand sachem. Expanding his scope even further, Tweed sat on the board of directors of several important business institutions such as banks, railroads, gas, insurance, and a printing company. Even more, Tweed possessed the most important ingredient any politician needed — luck. Whether intentionally or not, he and Tammany had discredited Seymour as the party's titular leader. As for the swallow-tails, they had lost massive prestige because of supporting Chase and Marble's revolt against the ticket. Even the Regency, which had long checked the Hall, was now adrift because the cautious Tilden had not chosen between being a full-time lawyer or a full-time politician. To cap Tweed's position, Tammany's long association with the principle of home rule, which Southern Democrats considered synonymous with state sovereignty and white supremacy, provided the lever to reestablish the party's traditional links with the South.

The increasing professionalization of politics additionally strengthened Tweed. By 1869, Tammany was a mature political machine. It controlled voters by catering to their peculiar needs, bribing others, absorbing dissenters such as the Woods, giving help to ethnic and religious groups, performing vital urban services through an activist government that financed the city by mounting bonded indebtedness, and supplying businessmen with special favors. In that sense, the Hall acted as a cohesive and coordinating agency within a fragmented city to create stability out of pluralism.

On the state level, the machine controlled New York as no other urban group ever had. In Albany, Tweed's instinctive understanding of the nature of power — and, in some cases, bribery and corruption, which the greedy "Black Horse Cavalry" in the legislature had almost sanctioned as a norm — expanded the Hall's power. As for the new governor, Hoffman, although honest and ethical, had revealed a streak of complaisance that led him to accept Tweed's methods and results without question. All signs indicated, then, that Tweed could expand operations with scant opposition. Armed with funds from the Erie Railroad, the city treasury, and businessmen seeking favors, an assured 50,000 vote majority at his beck and call, and an army of patronage jobs to dispense, Tweed *was* the most important politician in New York, and, by extension, a vital power-broker, even a king-maker, in the national Democracy.[2]

Even so, Tweed was vulnerable in several major ways. For one thing, the antiurban bias of upstate Democrats was wide and deep. For another, the swallow-tails rejected his pretensions and some placed devotion to honest government above loyalty to party. For a third, Tilden secretly awaited the opportunity to strike him down. Tweed also created his own problems. His sprawling superstructure in the General Committee was too diffused and tempted ambitious ward politicians to challenge him. Above that, few people, perhaps not even Tweed himself, knew if he was more concerned with the use of power than its privileges. In other words, the question remained unanswered whether the machine's price for order — public works it awarded with silent kickbacks, spiraling municipal debts, the growing sums of money it garnered by often unscrupulous means to pay for running party machinery, the use of private and public corruption for getting things done in the absence of rational government agencies — was a political method or a sign of personal venality.[3]

Shortly after the election, whatever thoughts Tammany entertained about directing the Democracy's state and national revival ran into a distracting byproduct of that campaign, electoral frauds. This episode not only revealed Tweed's latent political liabilities but handed Republicans an opportunity to regain lost ground.

Ever since the first political system emerged in the 1790s, politicians of all factional labels had "corrupted the purity of the ballot-box." The problem, however, was that the Hall was more imaginative, successful, and shameless than its foes. In the month of October 1868, Tammany outdid itself to such an extent that public and private indignation demanded a halt to such illegal, if customary, practices. In the next few weeks, Republicans decided to give the public irrefutable proof of Tammany's chicanery. Their purpose was not only to discredit

Tweed, but to expand the question into a demand for a new national electoral system to set up uniform voting procedures aimed at lessening the Democracy's influence in urban areas, much as they had attempted in past state registry laws. Under the auspices of the stiffly upright and respectable Republican Union Club, John Davenport, a young partisan investigator, turned up evidence that certain wards had more voters than residents, that Tammany sold naturalization certificates, and that Tammany judges had illegally made over 60,000 new citizens.[4]

The Democratic party, especially Tammany, wanted the public to ignore the spreading scandal. Even the swallow-tails preferred to overlook misconduct on the Hall's part, since they had condoned it by silence. The Union Club's disclosures proved it plainly impossible. Faced with a ghastly mess that refused to die, the Democracy at first attempted to cover it up through a grand jury investigation, headed by Judge George Barnard who had gained immense notoriety by running one of the naturalization mills. Predictably, the grand jury found an excuse for doing nothing, since it discovered no indictable offenses. Realizing that they must at all costs avoid giving the appearance of guilt, Democrats took the offensive. To divert attention, they accused the Union Club of partisanship, claimed Republicans committed "the grossest frauds" in Pennsylvania and the reconstructed states, and used the *Irish-American* to bait the investigators as nativists.

In December 1868, the problem reached fever pitch when Congress responded to the Union Club's memorial for an examination of the evidence. The subsequent special committee, headed by William Lawrence of Ohio, contained five Republicans and two Democrats, all from rural areas. As the men set to work, Tammany put on a brave front. It forecast that the committee would absolve Democrats, while Republican frauds "will prove of the most startling and astounding character." There matters rested for two months.[5]

The Democracy was vulnerable in another way. Reconstruction was not over. Despite the seeming finality of congressional Reconstruction, many Southern Democrats fought to deny Republicans what they considered the legitimate consequences of war — Southern white acceptance of black legal, civil, and political equality, the right of those men who had reconstructed the South to rule, and the legitimacy of the Southern Republican party. Even more, Southern white Democratic attacks on Reconstruction state governments proved that racism was undiminished. The upshot was a new congressional flurry of action. Some Republicans felt the Fourteenth Amendment was deficient in protecting both reconstructed governments and black suffrage. Others thought the party had not yet fulfilled its obligation to equal rights. Still others, convinced the nation at large suffered because of the disproportionate attention to black rights, wanted to remove suffrage as an issue and move on to what they considered necessary reforms, such as lowering the tariff and instituting an effective civil service system. Prodded by this blend of high idealism, low partisanship, and incipient reformism, congressional Republicans passed the Fifteenth Amendment.[6]

What emerged was a compromise based on negatives. That is, the amendment denied states the right to limit male suffrange on grounds of color, race, or previous condition of servitude. Specific provisions excluded proved more important than those included. States still retained sovereignty over defining voter qualifications; the amendment lacked clarity over enforcement, and it did not explicitly void discriminatory state suffrage laws. In sum, the amendment did not create universal male suffrage, but only its possibility.[7]

Nevertheless, New York Democrats were overwhelmed with fury. Angrily, the party reverted to the emotion-laden politics of race, on four grounds: the amendment negated state sovereignty; it violated the Republican platform of 1868; it extended federal centralism; and it went counter to the thesis of black cultural inferiority. The *Herald* tried to use its influence for moderation by stressing that the amendment was a meaningless concession to Republicans. The paper admitted that perhaps Congress asked too much from a proud white population who had been acculturated to consider blacks inferiors. But it maintained that whites in their sovereign states could effectively control blacks, even with suffrage, through economic coercion rather than racial violence. In a remarkable reading of the future, the paper noted that, since the Republicans had failed to establish the freedman's economic independence, a black "can be readily gained over at the ballot box by his white employer." Since "the southern negro vote is subject to the controlling southern white element . . . even under universal negro suffrage, we expect that by the year 1870 the whole South will be in the hands of the Democracy." The difficulty with this advice, however, lay with the Democracy, North and South, which could not reconcile itself to federal centralism. Under these conditions, Democratic principles and racism were paradoxically responsible for keeping alive the bitter heritage of war.[8]

Few New Yorkers knew what to expect as Hoffman took office, and many prepared for the worst. Believing he had measured his man correctly, Greeley spoke for the skeptics. Hoffman, he predicted, was Tweed's compliant tool and would surrender the state to Tammany's "vast array of thieves, emigrant-swindlers, sailor-pluckers, blacklegs, pocketbook-choppers, baggage-smashers, and brothel-keepers." Yet, Hoffman brought several unappreciated virtues into the governorship: a keen legal mind, an expertness in public finance, a reputation for personal honesty, long training in professional politics, and a determination to carve out an independent position to prove the doubters wrong.[9]

The governor's legislative message, brief and to the point, proved a masterful document. As a reformer, Hoffman took great care in preparing an outline of his administration based on the Jacksonian ideas of decentralism, efficient but frugal government, local autonomy, fiscal sobriety, and honesty through the ethical awarding of canal contracts and the elimination of special legislation for favored lobbyists. Such a model, he suggested, might permanently revive the state as well as national Democracy. Surprisingly, his address sparked enthusiasm from both sides of the political fence. Only the *Herald* was unimpressed. "Mr. Hoffman has begun his official career very well in this message and we hope he may end with deeds as well as words."[10]

In sharp contrast to Hoffman's auspicious start, Republicans became embroiled in a bitter family feud that enhanced the governor's image and even made Tweed seem more respectable. With a federal senatorship at stake, Republicans fractured over factional and personal lines between incumbent Edwin D. Morgan and Fenton. In the end, Fenton won amid cries of fraud, vote-buying and corruption. On one hand, this power struggle set the stage for another: a battle between Senators Conkling and Fenton for control of federal patronage. On the other, the smoldering resentment between Morgan and Fenton boded ill for state harmony. Democrats wasted little time in turning this situation to their advantage. Since a "clique of office-seekers and corruptionists" dominated Republicanism, Cassidy wrote, "this scandalous party will never reform itself." The result was, Marble agreed, that the Republican party had played itself out, and "there will be a great stampede of honest men from the Republican ranks" into the Democracy.[11]

With everything falling into place for the party, Marble prepared to reassert the swallow-tails' position. As his pretext, Marble announced in early January 1869 that he intended to place "Democratic ideas" in "new lights" by a fresh approach "in harmony with all that is valuable in the progressive spirit of the age." One way lay in emphasizing economic issues such as free trade, laissez-faire, antimonopolism, sound money, and rapid repayment of the national debt. A second new departure lay in ending racial politics. When the Fifteenth Amendment went out to state legislatures, Democrats fought its ratification. By June, the amendment's adoption seemed certain. At that point, Marble felt it foolish to oppose an issue the public approved. For the present, he suggested the party accept black suffrage where it existed, fight against its extension on the basis of anticentralism, and defeat the state constitutional section abolishing black property qualifications. But, in the long run, he wanted to remove the race issue "from the domain of politics." If the party did so, it could move beyond obsolete issues and put its Jacksonian principles to work on other questions.[12]

Encouraged by Joseph Warren's favorable reception to that idea, Marble pressed on to his final goal, dismantling Tammany's influence in party affairs. For a time, it seemed his attack on the "Ring" might win party support. In early January, Tweed sought to capture the city board of education and its $3 million yearly budget by placing an underling as its clerk. Marble sounded the alarm. He charged that William Hitchman, the new clerk, belonged to the "corrupt set of men" who brought "shame upon all of the Democrats of this metropolis." Taken aback, Tweed shifted to the legislature where he transformed the situation by drafting a bill to appoint a new board.

Marble turned to the governor for aid. Hoffman, he wrote, "is an honest Democrat. And no friend of his could wish him a better occasion for a crushing veto."[13]

Marble miscalculated. Shocked at the *World*'s involvement of Hoffman in an affair that could only hurt the party and grateful to Tweed for financial aid, Cassidy set the tone for a subsequent parade of reprimands on Marble. In a sharply worded letter to him, Cassidy wrote he saw no great "Municipal reform" at work in the school issue. Rather, the attacks had degenerated into an effort to diminish "Hoffman whose administration is a turning point in our party history." As his parting shot, Cassidy ended "your old associates must be compelled to disclaim your opinions, when they dissent from them; and to deny your leadership." Democratic legislators picked up the scent. In an official party statement, they censured the *World* for personal "caprices" and urged Democrats through the state to support the more reliable *Argus*. The pack now smelled blood. As a way to appease Tweed and show loyalty to Hoffman, a group of upstate editors joined the *Leader*'s call to blackball the *World* because "its immediate managers were in the employ of parties openly inimical to Democratic interests."[14]

All this proved that Marble had underestimated Tweed. The legislature now passed the bill with Hoffman's approval. Little remained for Marble but to accept defeat as a good sport, seek to reingratiate his paper with the party, and await a shift in fortune to again assail Tammany. In the meantime, he had forfeited any chance to rearrange the Democracy in a new direction other than Tweed's, and the swallow-tails were thoroughly cowed.

At the same time, Governor Hoffman missed no steps in his steady climb to eminence. By 1869, one of the dreariest aspects of New York politics was the legislative practice, employed by corruptionists in both parties, of introducing and passing special class bills, sometimes harmful to the public interest, often for a bribe. During his first months in office, Hoffman vetoed a variety of such bills and amazed even the most skeptical observers. His honeymoon ended in May 1869 with his approval of the Erie Classification Bill at the behest of Tweed and Sweeny. While this bill purported to alter the board each year while maintaining continuity in management, its real purpose lay in keeping Jay Gould and his cronies in power. They could now use any tactic, including cheating other Erie stockholders out of legitimate profits, to enrich themselves.

This alliance between financial sharks and the state government raised a storm of protest. Hoffman paid the price in a huge loss of prestige. For example, the *Evening Post* wrote that the governor "has fallen back in popular esteem, into that general ruck of pretentious politicians, who try to substitute profession for practice and fine words for acts." Democrats protested; they claimed that except for one minor misstep, Hoffman had proven he worked "for the public's good." No matter the defense, Hoffman's image indeed suffered. Soon, other evidence appeared that he was not his own man. Again to please Tweed, the governor vetoed a "purity in election" law that made it a felony for a judge to issue false certificates of naturalization, appointed Cardozo and Barnard to the general terms of the state Supreme Court, and approved an increase in city taxes that benefited Tammany. By June, despite all his achievements, Hoffman seemed no better than a caricature of his former image.[15]

The Lawrence Committee also hurt Tammany. When the committee held local hearings, Davenport supplied it with a mass of circumstantial evidence clearly aimed at establishing Democratic misdeeds. On that basis, the Republican majority filed a report accusing the Hall of "fradulent and fictitious" naturalizations numbering 63,343, while absolving Republicans of comparable trickery. In response, the minority report put the figure at less than 1,600 and suggested that whatever corruption existed rested in both parties. The reports stimulated open acrimony. Republicans launched a full-throated attack at Tammany's corruption and maintained that Hoffman's election was suspect. Democrats cried that partisanship, antiurbanism, and nativism, mixed with envy, influenced the majority report. In the final analysis, however, the disposition of the dispute rested in Congress, not New York, where Republicans sought an excuse to pass a national election law to stymie Democratic urban strongholds.[16]

Luckily for Democrats, the continuing intraparty uproar among Republicans diverted attention. A political novice, President Grant was besieged and perplexed by conflicting patronage demands from New York. While conservative Republicans lusted to avenge Morgan, Raymond's sudden death left them with leaders out of office, like Seward, or too old, like Weed. As they floundered, Conkling's supporters began an inquiry into Fenton's fitness for office based on innuendoes of bribery. At the same time, Conkling gradually froze Fenton out by ingratiating himself with Grant and proposing to use the cohesive power of spoils to revitalize the organization. Making the situation even more muddy, Greeley, inconsistent as ever, craved public office from a President he disliked, called for home rule and universal amnesty in the South, in effect aiding Democrats, and gradually sought a new force in local politics "free from the corruptionists" he claimed ruled the party. Under these conditions, Grant was in an impossible situation no matter what he did. Summing up the party's mood, the *New York Sun,* an original Grant backer, moaned that the President "has failed to meet the expectations of great numbers of those who elevated him." No words could have been sweeter to Democrats. "The feuds between the Republican factions in the state, instead of being adjusted, are more bitter than ever," Marble gloated.[17]

In political warfare, the ideal time for a sweeping victory comes when enemies, those inside and outside the party, are distracted. Tweed felt that moment had arrived. To symbolize his grasp over the Democracy and revive Hoffman's reputation, Tweed meant to destroy the swallow-tails. His excuse lay in Marble's quasi-endorsement of the Fifteenth Amendment. The *Leader,* reversing its earlier stand on ending Reconstruction issues, instructed the party not to abandon principles that had "underlined all its platforms. Suffrage must be left to the States themselves." Thus, the *World,* by defying principles, had forfeited its legitimacy. Once upstate editors read the attack, they joined the howl and praised Tammany for purifying the party of apostates. By September, the *World's* position was perilous; its circulation had fallen and its quarterly earnings plummeted by $75,000.[18]

The overconfident Tweed now blundered. Blaming Belmont and Tilden for the presidential ticket's defeat in 1868 because of their desire to protect corrupt bondholders, Tammany called on the party to remove Belmont from the national executive committee and Tilden as state chairman. With so much at stake, Marble and Belmont studied the Hall's tactics and spotted two flaws — the upstate Democracy's antiurban bias and the party's unwillingness to weaken a successful team effort on the eve of the fall elections. At once, Marble set to work. In a series of editorials, he called on politicans in "country districts" to use their reputation "for probity" and "incorruptibility" to reform the party. He further noted "a vague feeling in the rural districts that certain leaders of the City Democracy are aspiring to an undue ascendancy." In regard to suffrage, he reiterated his earlier stand, but with suitable humility added: "if, unfortunately, we should prove to be mistaken in this opinion we shall quickly accept the result, and forbear further opposition where opposition shall prove manifestly futile." Belmont was equally active. He had Marble and Barlow arrange a public testimonial dinner where political leaders from other states could express their endorsements of his activities in the national committee. "I trust that there is some manhood left among politicians of our State and that they are not at all ready to be hereafter under the heels of Tammany," he told Marble.[19]

Now, it was Tweed's turn to back down. Sweeny, who had been overseas, came home and warned him that he needlessly made the swallow-tails martyrs. Directing a retreat, Sweeny ended the attacks, most of which Mayor Abraham Oakey Hall had written for the *Leader,* and placated Marble in a deal in which Tammany promised to "build up" the *World* and allow it "the treatment to which an acknowledged party organ is entitled." Tilden pressed Marble to accept, since the Hall stifled its attacks on him also. Only managing editor David Croly had reservations. "I do not see how the *World* can afford to come to terms with the ring," he informed Marble. "There is nothing it can offer [that] will compensate for the public discredit of its alliance." Marble, however, much to the disgust of the *Herald, Evening Post,* and *Times,* accepted the bargain since his paper could not afford the struggle. Yet he and Tweed were on an unavoidable collision course.[20]

Few signs of bitterness appeared at the September 1869 Democratic state convention. The delegates renominated the entire state ticket, and formed a platform that bitterly attacked the Administration. While Democrats wanted no fights among themselves, they could not avoid friction on two issues, suffrage and temperance. Behind the scenes, Seymour attempted to forge a plank based on Marble's proposals. Tilden refused. In his opening address, he stigmatized the Fifteenth Amendment as an unconstitutional invasion of states' rights, and the delegates unanimously backed him. On temperance, the Hall sought to rescind the Excise Law. But since many rural Democrats liked its Sabbatarianism, Tammany accepted a substitute which declared that if the legislature wanted such laws, they must be uniform throughout the state.[21]

In marked contrast, the Republican convention proved a fiasco. Meeting in the wake of the infamous "Black Friday" speculation to corner the gold market, which implicated the President, the delegates lacked faith in carrying the ticket. They formed a weak one headed by Greeley for secretary of state when less controversial men turned down the nomination for fear of losing. Even so, Tilden took little for granted. He wanted a smashing victory to redeem his reputation, compromised in the eyes of state committeemen by Tweed's attempted power grab. In a form letter to country chairmen instructing them on maximizing voter turnout, he warned against overconfidence although admitting the Republicans were deeply "demoralized."[22]

As the campaign progressed, Democrats kept close tabs on trends in Ohio, where George H. Pendleton ran for governor on a platform that exploited political white supremacy. His subsequent loss to Rutherford Hayes, a racial moderate, had important local implications. On one level, Hoffman's presidential stock shot up as the leading Democratic frontrunner now that the Ohioan, a potential challenger, had lost his home state. On a second level, many pragmatic Democrats felt Pendleton's defeat reflected the public's desire to end the war's heritage, particularly the political status of blacks. The *Herald* became their mouthpiece. Once again, it lectured the Democracy that racial politics was obsolete, a point that even white Southern Democrats understood. The "true game" now "is to get the negro vote." In New York, Tammany must take the lead in ending the party antisuffrage efforts because voters respected the Hall's commands. By that premise, the ultimate test of Tweed's ability to provide the Democracy with "a general policy or purpose" lay in "no longer fighting against fixed facts." Since the Southern Democracy "have adopted" the black voter, Northern Democrats "will have to recognize him, and the sooner the Tammany sachems take this step . . . the sooner they will be able to lead the Democratic party of the Union on the path of a restoration of power."[23]

For the moment from Tweed's point of view, the paper's suggestions were irrelevant. A brewing rebellion among several ward leaders, brought on primarily because of personal differences, and legitimatized by Tweed's decentralized ward structure, forced him to concentrate on local problems. In a series of miscalculations, Tweed bungled an attempt to gain a reformist image by purging three city senators — Michael Norton, Thomas Creamer, and Henry Genet — who had gained notoriety in the Black Horse Cavalry. Because of the complexity involved in ward politics, Tweed backed down and had the Hall renominate them. But the damage was done. After the election, which all three won, they formed a loose anti-Tweed coalition which included George Purser, a powerful ward leader, John Morrissey, an ambitious former gambler and boxer, now a senator, Ben Wood, never comfortable with Tweed, and Sheriff James O'Brien, who had a personal grudge against Tweed. In themselves, these men had little power, but they did have the ability to embarrass Tweed and underscore his shortcomings. Within a few months they opened, along with some unlikely allies, a new round of intraparty bitterness.[24]

The fall election of 1869 proved a Democratic landslide. Except for the judiciary article, voters rejected the revised constitution, including black suffrage, and Democrats swept the entire state ticket while winning control of both legislative houses. Wasting little time in analysis, Tammany quickly dictated party policy. The legislature, it commanded, must rescind its previous adoption of the Fifteenth Amendment, repeal all "Radical legislation" based on institutional reformism, and form a new city charter geared to home rule.[25]

In a long interview with the *Herald,* Sweeny added further dimensions to the Hall's long-range plans. Making a subtle shift in the party's official racism, he admitted "we ought to get rid of the negro question. It hurts more than the negro vote could injure us. . . . [It] introduces a moral issue — a sentiment of justice — and presents the captivating cry of universal suffrage, which carries away many voters, especially among Germans, and prevents the legitimate political questions of the country from having their just weight before the people." Explaining the question further, he continued that while Tammany still favored having the legislature abrogate the amendment's ratification because of the principle of state sovereignty, Northern Democrats did not fear "the negro vote, and the Southern Democracy have adopted it and turned the negro to a good account." In short, Sweeny argued that political racism no longer made sense. Rather, black suffrage now revolved around the Democracy's ability, as with immigrants, to manipulate voters of different beliefs into an effective coalition. Summarizing his views, Sweeny concluded: "Our boys understand how to get them [blacks]."[26]

Sweeny's official pronouncement indicated Tammany's belief, which Marble and the *Herald* had advanced, and even the *Leader* had earlier stressed, that the Democracy's full political reorganization hinged on ending all Reconstruction issues. The party's Negrophobia had been a step in that direction, but never the full solution because racial politics revived other war-related topics and added credence to Republican charges that Democrats were the unregenerated white South's agents. As a consequence, if the Democracy wanted to gain the presidency in 1872, and Tammany certainly did with Hoffman, it needed a new political departure aimed at four goals. It had to restructure national politics without reference to the past; restore the legitimacy of Jacksonianism; undermine congressional Reconstruction by allowing white Southerners to regain their states while simultaneously subordinating blacks; and prevent any future federal interference in the South by accepting black suffrage even to the extent of Northern Democrats seeking their votes. Moreover, since evidence existed that the crisis of the war and its aftermath had allowed the Republican party's diverse and conflicting interest groups to postpone their latent internecine warfare, Democrats thought that the settlement of all sectional differences would rekindle Republican factionalism and perhaps destroy the party.[27]

While Sweeny's declaration filled Marble with self-righteousness, he nonetheless rejected Tammany's leadership. Determined to break its grasp, Marble again took steps down the long road of political opposition. First, he sought friendship, or at least neutrality, from Hoffman. In that regard, the *World* flattered the governor by predicting that in the final crunch he "will be on the right side." Next, Marble tried to widen the breach between rural Democrats and the Hall by emphasizing the party's latent regional and antiurban jealousies. Finally, Marble wanted unquestioning support from respectable Democrats, notably Tilden, and through him, the state committee. Marble misjudged his man. As early as December 1868, Tilden had confided to Senator Eugene Casserly of California "that the Democratic party would not carry the Tammany Ring and must get rid of it at whatever cost." Despite Tilden's subsequent reputation as a reformer, he was a total political realist. Tilden had spent years solidifying his base within the Democracy, sharpening his skills as a tactician, and developing the ability to organize voters. But more than anything else, Tilden was a disciple of Martin Van Buren — a broker-politician, a compromiser, a patient man, who never anticipated public opinion. Just as his mentor did, Tilden stayed cool and calculating, ready to move when success was assured, but determined to keep his options open if failure or uncertainty loomed. Since those traits controlled his behavior, Tilden did not feel the time was ripe to attack Tweed. Instead, he used Marble as a surrogate and spent his energy preparing an eminent ticket for the April 1870 election for the new Court of Appeals.[28]

Yet Marble was not alone. Among the allies he could count upon were Belmont and Barlow, and from the upstate Democracy, Lieutenant Governor Allen C. Beach and Sanford Church. Two key upstaters remained, however, uncommitted, Warren and Cassidy. Amid this void, Marble cast around for support among legislators and found them in Tweed's recent city opponents, soon called the "Young Democracy." Even so, Marble's position was weak. Belmont was not popular upstate,

Beach and Church busied themselves with the judicial ticket, and the odious reputation of many Young Democrats, whom party workers considered anti-Tweed only on personal grounds, cast doubt on the *World's* self-proclaimed purity and fair-mindedness.[29]

While Marble shored up his position, the Democracy prepared for the legislative session by holding a meeting of party strategists. The principal item on their agenda was the formation of a common program to keep their majorities from fragmenting into feuding factions. With that in mind, they agreed not to push the ideas of any "political clique," and to help the governor form a positive program as a presidential launching pad. Despite Tweed's apparent desire not to foist his wishes on the party, the meeting served as a chilling warning to Marble. As the meeting phrased the options, anyone who deviated from its line was a traitor, not a legitimate dissenter.[30]

With one eye on New York and the other on the nation, Governor Hoffman set the Democracy's tone in a strong message. In local matters, he came on as a Jacksonian reformer. He called for ending special legislation, a stiff new registry law, a commission to revise obsolete state statutes, a statewide excise law run by local groups, and a new, decentralized city charter. Nationally, he contrasted the state's healthy fiscal position with Grant's fumbling economic policies, argued that the public credit demanded hard money, called for antimonopolism through free trade, and took Congress to task for meddling in state affairs. Except for the *Tribune* and *Albany Evening Journal,* newspaper response was again remarkably nonpartisan.[31]

Meantime, Tweed sowed the ground carefully before acting. He handpicked Hitchman as assembly speaker, and carried out the party's commitment against the Fifteenth Amendment. That done, Tweed conciliated the Irish and immigrant supporters by a provision in the 1869-70 tax levy which empowered the city to subsidize nonpublic or charity institutions. Next, he consulted party leaders about his program, and won Cassidy's blessing. Finally, Tweed promised Marble that Sweeny would confer with him and Tilden on the proposed city charter. Watching on the sidelines, the Republicans were thoroughly disarmed. A gloomy Thurlow Weed told Secretary of State Hamilton Fish that their party was so beaten, "dishonored," and "demoralized" that it could not recover in the foreseeable future.[32]

On February 3, 1870, Assemblyman Alexander Frear introduced the long-awaited city charter bill. It proposed a strong mayor, elected for four years, and ended diffusion of responsibility and overlapping jurisdiction by giving him the power to appoint heads of major departments, who in turn had clear duties that freed them from the often corrupt and obstructionist Common Council. The mayor had the right to remove city officials, and the new Board of Aldermen could impeach him. The bill sharply defined expenditures. The aldermen could appropriate money only by a three-quarters vote, but the mayor, comptroller, commissioner of public works, and the president of the park department, who formed a Board of Special Audit, directed payments. The bill next established home rule by abolishing the county Board of Supervisors and the commission system by consolidating the police, fire, health, and excise boards into local departments under the mayor's jurisdiction. As its last provision, the bill authorized new elections once the legislature approved the charter.[33]

The bill proved an ingenious blend of reformism and naked politics. It gave good government forces items they had long coveted — a strong mayor, stricter fiscal controls, accountability, home rule, and an end to diffusion of responsibility. For the party, it decentralized state authority and emphasized the Jacksonian concept of local autonomy. In a larger sense, the bill conceivably set a model for the nation, based on a reformist system of traditional local control, that all Americans might use to deal with their increasingly industrialized, urbanized, technological, and ethnically diverse society. Politically, the bill ensured Tweed's position. He and his henchmen had tight control over all facets of city and county government; by abolishing the Common Council, the Board of Supervisors, and the commissions he ousted Republicans and Young Democrats from office; and his brand of reformism might lead Hoffman to the White House. All that remained was legislative approval.

Public reaction was at first mild since most New Yorkers felt reforms in the city government were long overdue. As expected, Republicans carped that the bill was too drawn-out and complex. But they groped for a consistent policy because the Union Club and even Greeley gave it support. Upstate Democrats, outside of Cassidy, admitted the bill's innovativeness and devotion to principle, yet questioned the Hall's political motives. These reactions perplexed Marble. Initially, he called the bill a starting point for discussion, not a finished product. Sweeny had no quarrel with the *World's* assessment. He explained to the paper's Albany correspondent that haste rather than oversight prevented the promised "consultation," and agreed the bill could be modified.[34]

This episode proved to be the lull before the storm. On February 9 and continuing unabated for the next two months, the *World* declared a "war to the knife" against the "Tammany Ring," and denounced it as an "insuperable barrier to the entrance of old allies or new converts to the ranks of the Democracy." The party itself, Marble wrote, was distinct from the corrupt men who were temporarily in charge. Thus, the responsibility for good government rested with rural Democrats and Governor Hoffman who must lift the "ring's millstone" from the party's neck. Furthermore, Marble sought to win support from workingmen and the business community. "The millions" which the ring had stolen, he charged, "have been sweated out of city deposits, or percentaged out of chairs, plastering, and paving-stones." Finally, in league with the Young Democrats, Marble proposed a series of amendments aimed at keeping the "clique of office-holders from annual re-elections."[35]

Again, Marble found little backing. The *Leader* surprisingly took a detached view, defended home rule, ignored Marble's goading, and called on rural Democrats not to damage the party by consorting with a few unrepresentative malcontents. Warren and Cassidy came out for Tammany, censured Marble for dragging local quarrels into the open where they could only help Republicans, and claimed the bill was so popular that "lobbymen are in a sad plight" because "so little money [is being] used." As a result, even a friend such as Congressman Samuel S. Cox told Marble he was mistaken, while the cynical *Herald* viewed the Democracy's family uproar as a waste of time because it was nothing more than "personal squabbles over the spoils."[36]

The remainder of the battle proved anticlimatic. In March, the Young Democrats introduced a substitute bill, but quickly found themselves outgeneraled. Tweed arrived in Albany with almost unlimited funds, and, according to the *Sun* and Morrissey, spread $200,000 among members of both parties. As a last ditch effort, the Young Democrats, who controlled 187 out of 339 seats in the General Committee, hastily called a special meeting to oust Tweed as chairman. Tweed anticipated them; he had the Tammany Society deny them the use of the Wigwam, the party's sanctuary and the symbol of regularity. Defeated in the city and outspent in Albany, Marble was isolated. With the vote in Albany only a few days off, Tweed ensured even more votes by a deal with Republicans he could not buy to trade their support on the charter for a new registry law which gave them representatives among the board of election inspectors and canvassers in each city precinct. The end came on April 5 when the Frear Bill, slightly amended, passed both houses with huge majorities.[37]

Tweed had two more items to pass, both destined to destroy all his careful plans. In order to flesh out the charter, one created a new Board of Supervisors, consisting of the mayor, recorder, and Board of Aldermen, that approved, with the concurrence of the city comptroller and county auditor, all funds the county might spend in the future. The second created a Board of Audit, formed by the mayor, comptroller, and the president of the defunct Board of Supervisors (Tweed), which certified the payment of county expenditures incurred by the former supervisors.[38]

Tweed's triumph was complete and overwhelming. Even the normally hostile *Times* admitted "the new charter is very generally conceded to be a good one." Other things fell into place. At the end of April, Tweed routed the Young Democracy in the Tammany Society's election of sachems, purged them from the General Committee, and crowned his efforts when the Hall easily swept the field in the special municipal election.[39]

Tweed dealt with Marble in a special way. During an interview published in the *Sun,* Hoffman signaled the *World* to accept the party's will. Terming the struggle over the charter a purely "local quarrel" in which he was not involved, the governor called it a highly "satisfactory" measure and extolled its nonpartisan character, because "prominent men in both parties have been consulted" at every step. Even the *Leader* followed Tweed's well-known conciliatory policy by gently chiding Marble as a political innocent. Mayor Hall, who had a weakness for puns, wrote that the only ring existing in New York was the ring "formed on every sidewalk for the boys to shoot Marbles. We hope none of the New York boys will shoot at the great Marble who places himself in such propinquity to the ring." The *World* conceded. On May 26, Marble asked Sweeny for a conference, which they quickly held with Tweed and Gould. Although no record exists of what occurred, beyond Sweeny's subsequent offer to Marble of a railroad directorship he rejected, the fact remained that the paper yielded to Tweed. Coming on top of everything else, the surrender of the *World* ended all doubts that Tweed had fully reconstructed the Democracy in his image.[40]

Marble's acquiescence, however, was a screen behind which he still hoped to destroy Tammany. Acting as a supplicant, the *World* ingratiatingly urged the party to renominate Hoffman as soon as possible. While others outside his circle interpreted this move as a fawning attempt to curry favor with Tweed, Marble had a more devious purpose in mind. As Croly noted, the *World,* by backing Hoffman in May 1870, "*will kill him in time*" because the paper could later oppose him for president by charging "him with falling short of our high ideals."[41]

These days marked the apex of Hoffman's administration. In dealing with the legislature, he had the considerable advantage of devoted Democratic majorities which beat back Republican attempts to discredit him by a revival of the Erie Classification controversy through the introduction of a new bill. Then, too, the governor gained much prestige in the charter fight by staying neutral, and he won bipartisan applause because of several ringing vetoes of special legislative measures. Furthermore, Hoffman made a compelling gesture to good government forces by appointing an extraordinary commission to review the state's archaic statutes and suggest new laws, headed by David A. Wells, the prominent political economist and free trader. Wells had recently run afoul of the Grant Administration by criticizing its tariff policy. Hoffman had great hopes for him. By selecting Wells, the governor indicated his commitment to reform, and he hoped Wells's popularity among free traders, both Republican and Democrat, would rub off on him.[42]

The temperance question, which had caused so much past Democratic discomfiture, also accrued to the governor's benefit in the form of a revised Excise Law. What emerged from the legislature was a shrewd compromise that satisfied both drys and wets. The new Excise Law, applicable to the entire state, set up boards based on home rule, retained license fees, and removed police involvement. Most critically, the bill so fudged on Sunday sales that prohibitionists, such as the *Evening Journal*, praised "the friends of law and order" in the legislature who "have stood up in behalf of the sanctity of the Sabbath," while antiprohibitionists felt such sales could continue.[43]

Meanwhile, the Democracy ended the politics of race. In March 1870 when the Fifteenth Amendment became official, the party launched a bid for the local black vote by adopting an enforcement bill that ended property qualifications. As the *World* explained, the Democracy could capture the black vote in New York, even though fewer than 2,000 registered in the city and slightly more than 200 in Buffalo, by "some sacrifice of prejudice." The reason for that, Marble continued, lay in the fact that the party had more experience in "managing the vote of ignorant classes," such as immigrants, than did the Republicans. Then too, Warren and the *Herald* felt that ending racial politics destroyed the last barrier that prevented Barnburner and Free Soil Republicans from returning home.[44]

The consequences of the war and reunion, however, still remained. During the spring, congressional Republicans readied two bills ordained to cause havoc in New York politics. In May 1870, Congress passed the Enforcement Act, which protected the constitutional rights of freed blacks as enacted in the three Reconstruction amendments. The beginning sections clarified the Fourteenth by setting up federal machinery to administer the Fifteenth, but two sections — numbers nineteen and twenty — embodied the Lawrence Committee's report. Congressional motivation for these sections stemmed partly from Republican determination to crush the Ku Klux Klan. But a larger reason lay in a partisan attempt to neutralize Northern urban strongholds, such as New York City. In its final form, the Enforcement Act made certain electoral frauds federal offenses if committed in congressional elections. Among these were traditional Tammany tactics such as false registry, repeating, and the use of force to obstruct or menace potential voters. Jurisdiction over such crimes lay in federal courts, and the law authorized federal marshals to supervise elections, appoint deputies, and use federal troops to maintain decorum.

In July, Congress passed the second bill to curb Tammany, the Naturalization Act, which was potentially a far greater threat to urban machines. Under its terms, state courts shared the right to naturalize aliens with federal courts. But it made major changes, as the Lawrence Committee recommended, in provisions with respect to the issuance and false use of naturalization papers, and extended to six months the period between becoming a citizen and voting. Furthermore, in any state or national election in cities of over 20,000, a United States circuit court judge, upon the request of two citizens in each electoral district, could appoint commissioners, one from each party, who, along with federal marshals, supervised registration in the district, challenged voters, assisted in counting votes, and safeguarded the ballot-box. Finally, the bills gave the marshals the right to appoint as many deputies as needed and gave them the authority "to arrest for any offense or breach of the peace committed in their view."[45]

The passage of both bills set off a furious outburst of partisanship. Republicans greeted them as godsends. Greeley predicted that the federal elimination of frauds "in New York City and other strongholds of the Democracy" guaranteed its defeat, and the *Times* hailed the Naturalization Act as the end of Tammany Hall. Democrats were outraged. They denied the need for either law since they claimed that neither the Ku Klux Klan in the South nor electoral frauds in the North existed. To the Republican argument that Congress passed the laws to protect blacks, Democrats answered that since they now courted blacks, the real purpose of both lay in the Republican attempt to frighten off potential Democratic voters. It was far better, Democrats contended, to allow Jacksonian principles, through state registry laws, to handle the problems of illegal naturalization and voting, if indeed they existed.

In the midst of this confrontation, the *Evening Post* strove for moderation by reminding both sides that all "honest men" wanted pure elections. The time for moderation had passed.

Republicans, convinced that recent Democratic victories came from voter frauds and intimidation, had no intention of backing down. Democrats, determined to disprove those charges, intended to maximize their votes in the fall elections to rebuke Congress. Yet each party prepared for the fall canvass with uncertainty as they suddenly plunged ahead into uncharted territory.[46]

New York Republicans needed all the help Congress supplied. In the period between July and September, the entire complexion of party factionalism had changed. Grant threw his support to Conkling by demoting Collector Moses Grinnell, a Fentonian, and replacing him with Thomas Murphy. The selection alienated the party's radical wing. Greeley, for one, was particularly upset. He claimed that Murphy was Tweed's crony and actually a "Tammany Republican," a person who traded Republican secrets for Democratic favors while supporting only token candidates. Fenton was equally furious and awaited the state convention for a showdown. But Conkling was not to be denied. He totally controlled the meeting including nominees and platform, and gained a majority on the state committee under the leadership of Alonzo B. Cornell, the surveyor of the port under Murphy. For the moment, the imperatives of party loyalty forced Greeley and Fenton into line. But the seeds Conkling planted soon bore bitter fruit. Many conservatives and radicals despised his reorganization based on spoils-mongering and were determined to discipline him, at the proper time. Democrats scarcely hid their satisfaction. The Republicans, the *Argus* wrote, were "a menagerie of backbiting politicians, more concerned to circumvent and mortify one another than to organize a campaign against the Democratic party."[47]

Heartened by the Republican's drive toward self-destruction, Democrats carefully planned the fall campaign. In the weeks before their convention, state committeemen held a series of meetings to assess the electoral laws' impact, and decided to campaign on four issues — Hoffman's record, federal invasion of state sovereignty, economic reforms based on free trade and hard money, and the end of racial politics. As they put it, the old "dogma that this is a 'white man's government,' is an obsolete idea as far as it means that no man of color is to participate in it." Beyond that, Tammany ruled every aspect of party behavior because all of its foes had frustrated themselves. Marble lost more standing by supporting the French in the Franco-Prussian war while the party generally backed the Germans. The Young Democracy compounded its exile by seeking an accommodation with Republicans. When rebuffed, the Young Democrats, now called the Apollo Hall Democracy after their meeting place, refused to cooperate with the regular Democrats. As for Tilden, who kept his state committee chairmanship, he maintained his cover, served Tweed's interests as a respectable front, and, just as did the Apolloites, waited a shift in the political spectrum.[48]

The convention confirmed what everybody knew. Tweed rode high, and the delegates accepted his wishes. The party renominated all incumbent state officials, and adopted a platform based on its preconvention strategy. Of most importance, the planks taken together formed a package of economic reforms that was a statement of Hoffman's proposed presidential campaign. Among them were lower tariffs, antimonopolism, a gold standard, retrenchment in federal spending, and fair taxes to aid the working class. In accepting the nomination, the governor emphasized the party's unity and lauded the delegates for not allowing "individual jealousies" to mar the convention's harmony.[49]

As the campaign developed, Tweed directed tactics. Above all, he sought party unity and strove to create the impression that the organization was responsive to the people's wishes. To that end, he coopted the Young Democracy by running several of its members for minor city offices, nominated two of its leaders for Congress, and bought off Ben Wood by backing Fernando Wood's bid for congressional reelection. Even more insidiously, Tweed infiltrated the opposition's local convention by having Tammany Republicans put up ineffectual men. On the state level, Tweed's strategy rested on two ideas: Hoffman must run as a statesman, and the party must attack the electoral laws as partisan Republican devices to thwart representative government. The bemused *Herald* watched the "Tammany Regency's" operation and aptly concluded, "the hostile elements are being absorbed into Tammany as little drops of water become fused with big ones."[50]

Under ordinary conditions, the Republican party's palsied situation, coupled with the Democracy's enormous advantages, should have guaranteed its defeat. These were not ordinary times. The Republicans had one trump card to play, the electoral laws, and they meant to use them with or without any sign of Democratic knavery. As early as August 29, the *Times* wrote: "it is hoped that the Republican managers will lose no time in preparing to carry out the provisions of the recent act of Congress, amending the Naturalization laws."[51]

Republicans needed no prompting. In September, Judge Lewis Woodruff set the gears in motion by appointing the deeply partisan Davenport as the commissioner to supervise the laws. Davenport performed to expectation. By October, he named 772 supervisors for the city's 386 precincts, and United States Marshal George Sharpe arranged for 1,200 deputies to keep order on election day. Since the parties split the supervisors, an immediate disagreement erupted concerning their impartiality. The Republicans termed their men "trustworthy" and Democrats "rough-necks." In response, the Democracy retorted that the Republican list "embraces not only roughs and rowdies, but keepers of houses of prostitution, pick-pockets and thieves."[52]

When registration began, Republicans scored a psychological masterstroke when the supervisors arrested five Democrats for false statements, including John McLaughlin, a member of the General Committee. Immediately, the Republicans prosecuted him as an object lesson, and he received a two year jail term prior to election day. To make the message even louder, Republican newspapers in the week before polling listed the names of more than 15,000 men who they claimed were illegally registered and warned that prison awaited any who voted. Adding to the tension, fears mounted of rioting among the rival groups guarding the polls — municipal police dispatched by Mayor Hall, the deputies, a federal force of over 1,000 troops, and the state militia held in readiness.

The moral value of Republican intimidation proved incalculable to the Democracy. Besides giving Democrats an opportunity to drape themselves with the mantle of defenders of civil rights, the Republicans, who for years blamed naturalization frauds for their losses in the city, had boxed themselves in. That is, Republicans expected to win. Greeley argued that the laws did work by pointing out that the courts made fewer than 2,000 new citizens in October compared to more than 60,000 in 1868. As a result, if Republicans lost they had no one to censure.[53]

"The election yesterday was the fairest held in New York for many years," the *Evening Post* reported. "We have had," the *Herald* agreed, "one of the quietest and peaceful elections we have ever known." All things considered, the canvass was a disaster for Republicans. In the city, Tammany won every congressional seat, Mayor Hall was reelected by 24,645, and Hoffman gained a 52,089 majority. Upstate the results were just as impressive; the Democracy retained the legislature and each state office, and Hoffman cruised to another term. While Republicans turned introspective, Joseph Warren looked beyond the returns for their long-range meaning. Speaking for the party, he predicted now that all "the issues which have divided good citizens in the past are settled, all conservative citizens irrespective of former political differences" must unite with the Democrats "in the government of principles on which it [the United States] was established."[54]

This theme bulked large in Hoffman's thinking. In a widely acclaimed victory speech to the Andrew Jackson Association of Albany, he laid out his bid for the presidency. Starting with the premise that the Democracy had reestablished its principles by concentrating on home rule, he emphasized that it "behooves a great party to bury dead issues and to direct the whole force of its energies with the living facts and questions of the day." Old questions — the war's heritage, reunion, black status — were over. New problems — finance and tax reforms, antimonopolism, free trade, decentralism, the need for constitutional government — these were the topics of the future. Even as the governor set his program, Tweed and Sweeny realized a presidential contender was often in a stronger position when he seemed not to seek the office. With that in mind, they explained that while Hoffman was an undoubted candidate, the New York Democracy wanted an open national convention, free of "intrigue or dictation," and they intended to act with "great fairness and discretion."[55]

If the governor's managers refused to allow him to project himself prematurely into the presidential cockpit, the *Herald* had no doubt that Tweed overlooked few opportunities to restructure the national organization. Behind the titular leaders of both parties, it suggested, were the representatives of special interests, the "great railroad corporations" and giant concentrations of wealth, which favored candidates committed to serving big business. "The central forces of this power are in New York and . . . they are in the hands of Tammany Hall." Continuing its assessment, the paper predicted that as the Democracy gained added strength when Southern states reverted to prewar leaders, and when "the laboring blacks are more and more drawn to their common interests with their white employers," the nation would enter into a new period of Democratic supremacy. So, as Hoffman neared the White House, the *Herald* concluded, little save Grant's diminished popularity as a war hero stood in Hoffman's way, either in 1872 or 1876.[56]

6
Tweed's Reorganization Fails: *1871–1872*

R*EPUBLICAN* woes accentuated Tammany's high hopes. By 1871, the party faced a severe crisis. Nothing symbolized its trend toward dissolution more than the burgeoning Liberal Republican movement led by Senator Carl Schurz of Missouri and including such disparate New Yorkers as Greeley, Bryant, and Fenton. The Liberals, fed by mounting disenchantment with Grant and fired by idealism, called for reviving the party by such reforms as civil service, resumption of specie payments, free trade, and a final reconciliation with the white South through a general amnesty.

In New York, however, the Liberal movement was a mood rather than a full-blown revolt because its discordant elements split between Greeley protectionists who were anti-Grant, Fentonians who opposed Grant but feared Greeley's ambition, and Bryant free traders distrustful of the others. In the city, the Liberals further fragmented into two factions: one led by Greeley who tried to purify the party by capturing the state organization, the other formed around the *Evening Post,* dedicated to good government and public service through moral suasion. Opposing them all were the Conklingites, who denied any need to change the status quo and were determined to renominate Grant.

As a national movement, the Liberals sought to remake the Republican party into a progressive force in American life. In New York, local Liberals stressed that idea by emphasizing the need to purge the party of corruptionists and spoils-mongers and replace them with altruistic men. The difficulty they faced lay in the questionable character and reputation of the men who stepped forward to direct them: Greeley, the tired veteran of innumerable causes, a man many people considered a fool at best; John Cochrane, the former Breckinridge Democrat turned Unionist, then radical, who appeared a rank opportunist; and "Hank" Smith, a city police commissioner and supervisor, the epitome of a Tammany Republican.[1]

In January 1871, Greeley and Cochrane formed a Union Republican General Committee, in opposition to the Murphy-led Regulars, dedicated to political purification and reconciliation with the South. The Conklingites, who dominated the state committee under chairman Alonzo B. Cornell, denied the insurgents' legitimacy and demanded they disband. Greeley refused. In a strong protest, he announced that the full organization, at the fall convention, must decide the question. For the embattled Republicans, then, 1871 seemed a year of increased factionalism, increased defeats, and perhaps party destruction.[2]

Congressional Republicans again tried to help. Rather than take sides, they shifted the focus by reviving Reconstruction issues through two bills designed to restore party idealism and inhibit the Democrats. The first, approved by most Liberals, was an expansion of the Naturalization Act, technically part of the Enforcement Law. Under its terms, the bill gave federal supervisors fresh powers, including the right to check registration, make arrests, and inspect ballots and returns. Furthermore, federal district judges, by appointing a chief supervisor (Davenport in New York City), could authorize the use of federal troops under the supervisor's command, and name deputy marshals, through the United States marshal's office, without regard to political affiliation. Thus, it became a federal crime for state officials to obstruct any duties federal or state laws required. Finally, in its most partisan provision, the act applied only to urban areas of 20,000 or more.[3]

The second law, "The Ku Klux Klan Act," split the reformers. It had two aims, one necessary to suppress organized white Southern terrorism against blacks, the second political. The bill gave the President the right to suspend *habeas corpus,* and enforce the Fifteenth Amendment with federal troops, and authorized federal courts to prosecute individuals if they were aware of a conspiracy against blacks but did nothing. The law's second aim, almost indistinguishable from the first, was less high-minded. Since the Klan was virtually an arm of the Southern Democracy, the bill also attempted to rescue tottering Reconstruction governments. If regular Republicans hoped to revive the party around Reconstruction issues, much as they did by waving the bloody shirt, they were disappointed. While some Liberals admired their party's defense of blacks, others such as Greeley denounced the bill as a hindrance to sectional reunion. Moreover, the moderate reformist *Evening Post,* even though it acknowledged the Klan's terrorism, also rejected the law. "Freedom cannot exist under a centralized government," it asserted and suggested that a far better remedy lay in the passage of a general amnesty act to soothe outraged Southern whites.[4]

As Republican ranks thinned, Democratic strategists followed the advice of Hoffman and Warren and hatched a positive program based on Jacksonianism. To end symbolically the issues of the 1860s, they wished to purge blatant racists such as Frank Blair and Copperheads such as Vallandingham. To rally Southern Democrats, they preached the necessity of accepting the finality of congressional Reconstruction. Above all, they sought an accommodation with Liberal Republicans, particularly the Bryant Barnburners, because they shared so much in common — hard money, "obedience to the constitutional amendments," a general amnesty, free trade, and fiscal "retrenchment and reform." None of these moves, however, meant that New York Democrats rejected white supremacy. Under the guise of Jacksonian decentralism, they advocated full home rule for the South, theoretically accepted black suffrage but in practical terms backed Southern white terrorism, and denied any federal effort to prop up Reconstruction governments.[5]

Paradoxically, other Democrats, notably Blair and Vallandingham, were on the same course. In Missouri, Frank Blair cooperated with disgruntled Republicans in a bipartisan campaign based on sectional harmony. The "Missouri Plan" worked so well that the legislature sent him to the Senate. In his maiden speech, Blair presented substantially what New Yorkers proposed — an accommodation with Liberal Republicans. Vallandingham added his own touch. At a county convention in Dayton, Ohio, he offered a "New Departure" which the state party later adopted. In it, he suggested the Democracy accept "the natural and legitimate results of the war" including the three amendments. As a trade-off, the federal government must then guarantee home rule in the South. In that way, the party could approve black suffrage but give white Southerners autonomy over them, absolve the Peace Democrats from Republican charges of obstructionism, and provide the organization with the means toward fresh programs.[6]

Across New York, Democrats felt the New Departure was magnificent in timing and politically impeccable. They were especially pleased that the old Peace Democrats led the attempt to dissolve the bloody shirt. The *Herald,* equally jubilant, extolled the New Departure as a "remarkable" statement considering the source. "With such a platform," the paper noted, "all that remains for the Democrats to do now is to nominate the right man for their Presidential candidate." Governor Hoffman saw his image in the paper's words. In a carefully written letter to Tammany's Independence Day celebration, which Democrats in other states extravagantly praised, he emphasized the party's complete acceptance of the New Departure, and urged all citizens to accept the political and "civil status of the colored man." Yet while he told Democrats to make a sincere effort to win the black vote, he undermined the Fifteenth Amendment by reminding Congress it could not interfere in Southern affairs. On that basis, he concluded the party could then labor for "the principles upon which the government is founded."[7]

Republican reaction indicated an undercurrent of uncertainty and apprehension. As expected, the Conklingites called the New Departure a sham. Behind that charge lay the fears of many other Republicans that if a public opinion accepted the Democratic program, neither black rights nor Reconstructed governments could endure. This feeling particularly vexed the old Barnburner-Free Soilers and their mouthpiece, the *Evening Post.* In one way, the paper questioned the Democracy's sincerity. Moreover, despite Bryant's constant intention to return to the Democracy, under proper circumstances, which now seemed propitious because the party ostensibly accepted the Jacksonian idea of equal rights and free trade, he was enough of a partisan and moralist to reject it because of Tweed. In another way, Bryant was committed to the same reforms as Hoffman and the others. Thus, the paper's rejection of the New Departure left him with no options save Grant and Conkling, both unpalatable. Thoroughly confused, former

Democratic Liberal Republicans awaited new developments before acting. In contrast, Greeley welcomed the New Departure. Speaking at Cooper Union on his return from touring the Southern states, he said that he was tired of refighting the past. The Republican party must accept fresh issues such as sectional harmony, general amnesty, and reform; "otherwise it would have a short lease of power."[8]

Liberal Republican Samuel Bowles, editor of the Springfield, Massachusetts, *Republican,* disagreed with all these assessments. He felt the New Departure might help Northern Democrats erase past mistakes, but would "demoralize them at the South" because it implied acceptance of carpetbag rule without guaranteeing home rule or a general amnesty. On that basis, he and Schurz believed their most fertile area for recruitment lay among Southern whites. Working carefully, Schurz tested this thesis and found it workable. For the next few months, he laid the groundwork for a third party by organizing "Reunion and Reform Associations" in Western and Southern states to unite "liberal elements of both parties." His efforts angered and perplexed many New York Republicans. The Conklingites called him an apostate. Greeley and Fenton wanted to purify the party, not scuttle it. Bryant remained cautious. Democrats faced a conundrum. While they dreaded Schurz's inroads among Southern Democrats, they enjoyed the way he embarrassed Grant. Even so, Democrats wished Schurz, not to establish an independent party, but to coalesce with them. Under these conditions, the Democracy, like Bryant, adopted a wait-and-see stance.[9]

Concurrently, Governor Hoffman during the first seven months of 1871 carved out a record as eminent as he intended it to be. Yet his links to questionable Tammany practices tarnished his image. Despite the discreet efforts Mayor Hall made to repeal the troublesome Erie Classification Act, it remained a stain on Hoffman's record, and, even though he vetoed other bills, the governor accepted several of Tweed's pet projects that were at variance with his rejection of other special legislation. By July 1871, Hoffman made a spiritual break with Tweed to dispel evidence he lacked backbone. The governor rarely attended Tammany Society meetings, avoided Tammany legislators in Albany, and did not even attend the almost obligatory Independence Day celebration. The march of events, however, soon proved that his sudden burst of freedom came too late.[10]

Behind contrived dilettantism, Mayor Hall, who hoped to succeed Hoffman, had an equally compulsive need to achieve a notable record. As the man in charge of administering the hotly contested charter, he faced the unenviable task of satisfying Tweed and ward leaders, municipal reformers, and the swallow-tails. Hall did so in a variety of ways. He filled key municipal departments with efficient men, held down expenses and paid some city bonds, improved services, and confirmed that the charter was an improvement over the defunct commissions. His efforts bore handsome dividends. Outside of the *Times,* which the *Evening Post* claimed had a "peculiar disease of late, known as 'ring on the brain,' " which sickened its objectivity, the mayor amassed strong bipartisan accolades. Yet Hall, like Hoffman, was not a free agent. For better or worse, both men were captives of Tweed and Sweeny.[11]

Throughout his career, Tweed had exhibited the knack of turning political adversities into personal advantages. For most of 1871, he continued. In the city, Tammany's vast amalgam of traditional patronage, augmented by new sources under the charter, and its seemingly impregnable organization, unnerved dissident Democrats, swallow-tails, and Republicans. Tweed compromised others by spreading a wide net of mutual complicity. Some of the city's leading merchants and businessmen, including Barlow, Peter Cooper, and the Citizens' Association, accepted the charter as a model form of good government and became Tweed's accomplices by doing lucrative business with the city, gaining tax breaks, and padding contracts. Most newspapers, including the *World,* fell into the same trap. Tweed bought them off with municipal printing contracts, high-priced advertisements and gifts to key reporters, or by making various newspaper stockholders, including some of the *Times's,* directors of his New York Printing Company. Finally, Tweed garnered massive admiration among the poor and unemployed by ministering to their immediate needs by providing food, bins of coal, and clothing in the midst of a severe winter and a mild recession.[12]

In the legislature, Tweed's peculiar blend of decentralized reformism, bribery, and the ability to stretch collaboration as broadly as possible blended perfectly with long-accepted means of influence peddling. By July 1871, Tweed dominated the city and state as no man before him. Despite the *Herald*'s admonition that Tweed's grip over the legislature harmed the party because its leaders allowed themselves "to be used by ambitious individuals for personal ends," the Republicans were disabled and the Democracy was his creature. But it was his willing creature. Public opinion backed him, and the efforts the Tweed Testimonial Association made to erect a statue of him, which the *Sun* had originally proposed as a joke, was an impressive display of spontaneous affection.[13]

Although Tweed and his dependents had no inkling of impending doom, that July began a sequence of cruel months that undid reputations, nearly destroyed the Democracy, elevated fresh men to prominence, and raised anew the old question of party reconstruction. The Democracy that gradually emerged from this time of trouble bore scant resemblance to Tammany's model.

The first sign of danger began with a clash between the city's Catholic and Protestant Irish over a municipal parade permit for the Orangemen's celebration of the Battle of the Boyne. The police, Mayor Hall, Governor Hoffman, and the state militia completely mixed signals. Aware of past sectarian friction, Superintendent of Police James Kelso, apparently at the behest of Sweeny and Connolly, both Catholics, issued an order under Hall's authority preventing the parade. At once, city newspapers, mostly Protestant, protested that Hall had sold out to Catholics while depriving Orangemen of their civil rights. At that point, Hoffman countermanded Kelso's order, and the parade took place. Along the route, lined by furious Catholics, someone fired a shot, and the militia opened on the crowd, wounding and killing over one hundred persons.

For Tammany's future peace of mind, the riot was incidental to a larger political problem. The *Leader* tried to avoid involving the organization by calling the shooting a "militia riot." But it could not assess blame further because both Hall and Hoffman were culpable. The *Irish-American* was not so inhibited. It absolved Hall from guilt and charged Hoffman with "direct responsibility for all this horrid destruction of life for which he can never atone." The riot's partisan dimensions grew deeper when the mayor, out of his instinct for survival, broke publicly with Hoffman. That left the Republican *Times* as the governor's only defender. Hoffman "has acted like a man," it announced, "Oakey Hall like a blubbering baby."[14]

The Orange Day Riot proved the first tremor in a Democratic earthquake. It ruptured the working alliance between Hoffman and Hall, discredited both in the process, and weakened Tammany. As for the Catholic Irish, they became so embittered with Hoffman that they never again supported him; while nativists in both parties were furious at Tammany's fumbling leaders. Upstate, the riot sundered the Democracy when rural leaders backed the governor and scorned the mayor. To Republicans, the riot proved their charges that Tammanyism and lawlessness were synonymous.

This situation was merely a prelude in the developing Tammany cataclysm. It began in earnest on July 8 when the *Times* launched its famous exposé of Tweed, with documentary evidence supplied by the disgruntled O'Brien, of transcripts from Comptroller Connolly's ledgers. For the next three weeks, culminating in a special supplement of 200,000 copies, printed in German and English, the paper unfolded sorry allegations of padded bills, kickbacks, overpayments for armory rentals, and extravagant prices paid to contractors on the new county court house.[15]

The *Times*'s disclosures, sharpened to a cutting edge by Thomas Nast's cartoons in *Harper's Weekly,* shook Democratic bastions. Tweed's enemies within the party — overt like Marble and the swallow-tails, or covert like Tilden, Kernan, and Church — realized they at last had the weapons to destroy Tweed. Yet his power and influence, in July and August, were actually undiminished, and public opinion, while aroused, had not yet turned. The result was that these men faced a question that was as simple as it was complex: should the party support or repudiate Tweed? There was no easy answer; to support him might mean corporate guilt and annihilate the party if the accusations were correct; to reject him might split the party by alienating his many backers and make him even more powerful if proven innocent. Yet the *Times*'s indictments were so breathtaking and plausible, its evidence so dazzling, that these men lacked the luxury of prolonged indecision or introspection.[16]

The imprecise nature of public opinion during July and August made the Democracy's options doubly difficult. Since 1870, the *Times* had periodically accused Tweed of corruption, and many people had become skeptical about its motives and proof. Playing on that dubiousness, the *Leader* sought absolution by explaining that the *Times*'s crusade stemmed from Republican partisanship and publisher George Jones's personal pique against Mayor Hall for his refusal to pay an inflated *Times* printing bill. If frauds existed, the *Leader* explained, the fault lay with the Republican commission system, which had prevented responsible home rule. At first, each Democratic newspaper, along with the independent *Herald* and even the Republican *Tribune* and *Evening Post,* repeated the *Leader*'s defense in varying forms. On August 19, Tammany claimed the issue settled. The *Leader* wrote that because the editors of these newspapers, who took the pulse of public opinion, cleared Tammany and understood the *Times*'s twisted motives, "we say, you have made our cause your own, and the good that will come of it is that, whether our strength in the city be so great as to make us vain, or not, your cause is ours."[17]

Tammany's attempt to place a lid over the mounting scandal proved an illusion. On August 30, the *Times* printed more disclosures, under the headline of "The Story of the Accounts," which by innuendo and apparent documentary proof branded Tweed and his cronies swindlers beyond doubt. Now, public opinion turned ugly; where many people previously had considered Tweed a public benefactor, they now viewed him as a crook. A similar change took place within the party. Men such as Tilden and Marble were chilled by the *Leader*'s pronouncement that the Democracy and Tweed were synonymous. They now realized that time was swiftly running out.[18]

On September 4, the political turmoil reached a staggering level when a bipartisan group of city reformers, led by former mayor and businessman William Havemeyer, a Democrat, organized the Committee of Seventy. In explaining the genesis of this group, the *Evening Post* noted that its constituency "lay in the whole people." Once formed, the committee divided into subgroups to gather more evidence and make an in-depth investigation of Connolly's ledgers. Potentially more dangerous to Tammany's credentials was a taxpayer's suit instituted by General Committeeman John Foley to prevent the mayor or any of his subordinates from issuing municipal bonds or paying any expenditures. On September 7, Judge Barnard, heretofore Tweed's pawn, granted the injunction, a move that directly reflected the public's changing attitude. The crisis grew. A fiscal storm threatened the city's bonded indebtedness, workers demanded payments which were not forthcoming, and many people, chiefly in upstate districts, found their antiurban bias in vogue.[19]

Marble, Tilden, Warren, and Kernan now realized that time had run out. They knew that politics was an irrational business whose real currency lay in the public's trust in the moral credentials of its leaders. Fearing that Tweed's problems might engulf the entire organization, they could no longer balance the advantages or disadvantages of joining the crusade against him as if it were an abstration. As John A. Dix prompted Tilden, the Democracy had to reassure honest men that the party wanted a "thorough investigation; for independently of the wrong to taxpayers, it must be evident that popular government cannot be maintained unless the authors and shapers of the plunder, of which we have unquestioned evidence, can be discovered and disgraced."[20]

Other factors were at work. As politicians, Democrats under Tilden's gradual leadership shared one common, overriding concern — how to perpetuate a political organization in the face of widespread corruption which threatened to demoralize party workers and disillusion the public to such an extent that the party itself might be destroyed. For in the final analysis, these men had an overwhelming article of belief — a political party had an organic life of its own, a life they had to maintain at all costs. Such a commitment demanded much from a party leader. He had to be firm but fair, discreet but able to exude the impression of openness, patient but decisive, and honorable but with a degree of tolerance for human foibles. Above all, people had to respect him — as a person, as a symbol of party principles, and as the moral incarnation of the voters' inarticulate but firmly held hopes and dreams and illusions. The art of politics under such conditions involved the political techniques of recruitment, organization, patronage, argument, compromise, adaptation, and maneuver. Here Tweed excelled.

These techniques meant nothing, however, unless these politicians and their leaders convinced the voters that their party was a moral organism, deeply concerned with the general good, and firmly tied to the idea that the party used traditional principles and public opinion as it guides to formulate policy. Here Tweed failed. The problem was that he was too successful; the external pressure that an opposition party exerts in a viable two-party system, and the internal forces which dissidents create, which in turn stimulate inward renewal, were not present. Tweed either crushed the opposition, as in the mayoral race of 1870, coopted dissidents, like Marble and the Young Democracy, or bought off Republican legislators. In short, because of Tweed's ability to beat or buy his foes, he lacked the will, or perhaps the need, to police his own impulses, check his henchmen's greed, and prevent the party's moral destruction.

Taken as a whole, then, Tilden and his colleagues, no matter what the legal system decided about Tweed's guilt or innocence, had to save the party by sacrificing him. They had to drive home the point that while some individuals were corruptionists, the Democracy shared none of their shame and had the ability to "punish the inequity which has been practiced in its name." As Warren aptly wrote: "there has been Democratic stealing in the city of New York, and the Democracy of this state will demand the political heads of the thieves."[21]

Of all the men available in the Democracy, Tilden seemed the least likely to handle the enormous challenge awaiting him. From his early life, he had been a political outsider, a man divorced from the hurly-burly of ordinary politics, content to deal only with organizational matters he could quantify and conceptualize. Yet he possessed three qualifications lacking in others and necessary to reconstruct the Democracy: intellectual integrity, instinctive honesty, and moral principles forged in the crucible of Jacksonian Democracy.

The impact of these factors, however, lay in the future. In September of 1871, Tilden was a reluctant, cautious figure, who kept his own counsel and, consistent with his legal training, avoided emotionalism while building an airtight case against Tweed. Such an effort took time, and Tilden delayed at great risk. In a bitter letter never sent, Marble blasted him for apparently doing nothing and losing the initiative. This feeling seemed reasonable. German Democrats, resentful of Irish influence and fearful that the party's reformers were craven, bolted the organization under the leadership of Oswald Ottendorfer, editor of the *New-Yorker Staats-Zeitung*. They joined Apollo Hall in forming an anti-Tammany delegation to the state convention. Equally damaging to Tilden was the attempt of Tweed, Sweeny, and Hall to escape guilt by making Connolly their sacrificial lamb in demanding his resignation.[22]

It was a mistake. The thoroughly frightened Connolly sought Tilden's help. At once, Tilden suggested he stay in office and appoint Andrew H. Green, a man Tilden trusted, as deputy comptroller. By doing so, Tilden assured Connolly, he would have an honest man to keep the others at bay. Left unsaid in the bargain was Tilden's determination to have Green, not outside party forces, take charge of the vital records. On September 18, Connolly agreed.[23]

Again, Tilden took a calculated risk. In the contest between the mayor and comptroller, Belmont and Marble mixed signals with Tilden. They defended Hall, wanted to replace Connolly with either Belmont or George B. McClellan, and attacked Green's appointment. Another of Tilden's potential allies proved a disappointment when Cassidy, a member of the state committee, defended Tweed. "I think Cassidy means in the main to stand up for the right," Seymour explained, "but it is hard for him to strike men [such as Tweed] who have lifted him into wealth when all about him shrink back."[24]

As these developments unfolded, Governor Hoffman lost whatever prestige he had amassed. Instead of a forceful break with Tweed, he spent most of September on tours of county fairs. Cornered by a *Herald* reporter upstate, Hoffman was "reticent" about affairs in the city, claimed newspapers were his only sources of information, and promised to ask the January legislature to authorize a special investigation. The Committee of Seventy refused to let him off the hook; in mid-October a subgroup interviewed him, ostensibly for new information. Fortunately for Hoffman, the swallow-tails' determination to contain the scandal gave him a reprieve. Marble defended his integrity and announced that the governor needed no prompting to deal with the situation. Hoffman got the message. He appointed Charles O'Conor, Tilden's chief legal adviser, as a special state attorney general in charge of civil suits against Tweed and the others to recover misappropriated money. Yet the tide had turned against Hoffman. In breaking so late with Tweed, the governor reinforced the impression that while personally incorruptible he remained Tweed's stooge, even considering his earlier alienation from Tammany, and that he lacked the moral courage to defy Tweed until the march of events made it imperative. While Hoffman's term lasted another year, and while reformers courted him because they feared his veto powers, most politicians conceded the scandal had destroyed the governor's career.[25]

With so much at stake, Tilden laid careful plans for the state convention. Early in September, he issued his usual circular letter to county chairmen. In addition to standard charges against Republican frauds, particularly the commission system, he wrote that "whenever the gangrene of corruption has reached the Democratic party, we must take a knife and cut it out by the roots." As part of his total strategy, Tilden relied on rural delegates, under Kernan and Church, to censure Tweed by replacing the Tammany delegation with one from Apollo Hall. Things unraveled when the state committee met. Three members whom Cassidy controlled offered a substitute that allowed Tammanyites their seats, followed by their withdrawal provided Apolloites would not replace them. Although he held a majority, Tilden backed down. Fearing a confrontation might endanger his tactics, he depended on the rural delegates to back him in a floor fight.[26]

Tweed acted with boldness. Before the convention, the *Leader* placed Democrats on notice that they must give the Hall exclusive recognition because "all the traditional local successes in the glorious past, are now reposed in the keeping of the Tammany General Committee, and . . . they are now held without especial regard to individuals in or out of it." The paper missed the point. Tilden and his supporters had no wish to destroy Tammany. Rather, they wanted to revive its prestige by abstracting Tweedism from the political equation of state politics.[27]

With the lines of battle within the party now clearly drawn, Tilden set in motion an appeal to the bedrock of Democratic beliefs to accomplish the dual tasks of purging Tweed without harming the organization and reemphasizing the validity of traditional principles. As such, his keystone speech was less a statement of immediate programs than a manifesto testifying to the Democracy's moral health. His role was that of a teacher, his lesson written from the copybook of the party's proud heritage.

Beginning with the premise that the old issues connected to the past were settled, he thundered that American institutions of free government were still vulnerable because of a corrupt, irresponsible centralism "incompatible with civil liberties." Under that Republican doctrine, the moral fiber of public life deteriorated, legislative bodies sold themselves to the highest bidder, and self-government became a mockery. Thus, all the corruption in the city flowed from the commission system, which legitimatized "a partnership of plunder between men of both parties." Yet the means of purification were at hand. With almost religious fervor, Tilden emphasized the immutability of Democratic principles and the men who sustained them, principles based on local responsibility and limited government, wielded by persons of public and private probity. "Principles are the test of political character," he ended. "It is time now to proclaim and to enforce the doctrine that whoever plunders the people, though he steals the livery of Heaven to serve the devil in, is no Democrat."[28]

Tilden's message was a powerful and dramatic statement of ideology, cleverly composed to appeal to Democratic emotions and to convince voters that party leaders meant to punish their own malefactors. The address, furthermore, was totally indifferent to Tweed's notable services, particularly his practical approach in putting the philosophy of home rule and decentralism into operation. As a result, Tilden had forged a propaganda line of the highest order. He blamed Republicans for Democratic excesses, blackballed Tweed without directly invoking his name, and gave the Democracy's political philosophy a new birth of respectability.

Those stirring words left the delegates unmoved. Awed by Tweed's imported toughs, afraid of the unknown, and swayed by fears that Republicans would capitalize on a split party, the delegates tailored the convention to Tweed's specifications. They admitted Tammany, allowed it to withdraw without seating Apolloites, and adopted a platform that faintly echoed Tilden by upbraiding Republicans for all corruption, and endorsing the New Departure. Then, in a stunning blow to Tilden, the delegates renominated all incumbents that Tweed supported including the attorney general, whom Tilden wanted to replace with O'Conor. Tilden stormed from the floor. With reporters present, he angrily told his people he refused to back any Tweedite, did not consider the state ticket representative, and intended to vote only for "honest men."[29]

What Tweed won in convention, he lost in the public forum. Party leaders and most workers were now ready to abandon him because they worried that he had enmeshed the entire Democracy in a destructive web of deceit and thievery. If anything, pressure intensified to purge Tweed in order to reestablish the Democracy's moral standing. Consequently, whatever support Tweed had in the press soon evaporated. Outside of the *Leader* and *Irish-American,* every party newspaper concentrated on local races, ignored the state ticket, and called on county conventions to select anti-Tweed candidates. Even Cassidy capitulated. "This is clear," the *Argus* announced. "The present oligarchy in New York is to go out of office."[30]

The campaign became one of Democratic ambiquities. As politicians, Democrats feared any loss of power. Yet Tweed's close identification with the state ticket and the regular organization was suicidal to their best interests. In order to defeat Tweed, Democrats logically had to vote against the ticket, an act which rubbed against the grain of party loyalty, or somehow convince voters that even if those men were elected, the Democracy could miraculously reform itself under the old leadership elite. The situation became stickier when Tweed ran for reelection and Tammany handpicked his assembly candidates. The only way now to prove the party could police itself lay in electing Apollo Hall candidates, including Tilden, most of whom lacked track records as dependable Democrats. Tilden attempted to cut his way out of this thicket when he advocated "a union of all honest men against a combination of plunders." He solved nothing; the ambiguity remained — how could Democratic voters support their party and purge Tweedites at the same time, when habitual discipline cried out for supporting regularly nominated men, no matter the source?[31]

The *Herald* saw the problem in an even larger context. Tweed's rise to prominence, it noted, provided the national party with its most important lever to unseat Grant. Any attempt to alter or destroy that lever necessarily harmed the entire Democracy. Yet New York Democrats could not stop such damage, since the party had already lost in Ohio and Pennsylvania because of "the odious financing of Tammany." The upshot was that "the Democratic party of the Union, sharing in the honors and schemes of Tammany, must share in her disgrace until some atonement is made for her manifest transgressions."

With Tweed's reconstruction of the party dead and Hoffman discredited, then, the paper predicted no Democrat carrying the heavy burden of Tammany could defeat Grant. Under those conditions, the nation verged on a major readjustment of parties. The Republicans and Democrats would shrink into minority statuses because of their respective scandals, and a new third party, formed around Liberal Republicans, would dominate politics since it was untainted by frauds or "the old issues of the war." In a remarkably able reading of the future, the paper concluded "the best course . . . for the Democratic party is, out-and-out a new party movement and a man on their Presidential ticket fresh from the Republican ranks."[32]

Republicans had their own problems. Conkling was convinced the Tweed scandals had ruptured the Democracy beyond repair. Confident of a major turnabout in state politics, he was in no mood to placate either Greeley or Fenton. At the state convention, the delegates followed Conkling's wishes and rejected the Greeleyite delegation. What remained was a group dominated by the senator and his followers — Collector Murphy, Surveyor Cornell, and attorney Chester Allan Arthur — committed to Grant's reelection and totally contemptuous of Liberal Republicans.[33]

The Conklingite regulars created party unity of a sort that could not last. Putting immense pressure on the Liberals, regular leaders stressed party loyalty and cajoled dissidents to drop "petty quarrels" by campaigning against Democratic corruption. The *Evening Post* buckled. Conveniently overlooking Administration frauds, which it had railed against for almost two years, the paper identified Republicanism with good government. "The contest of this year is not merely for office, but for moral power." That placed Greeley in a bind. If he failed to back the state ticket, the regulars had proof that he was a Tammany Republican; if he did support the ticket he would alienate his followers because the men selected were his enemies. In the end, Greeley made an uneasy peace with the regulars by supporting the state ticket while still attacking Grant and Murphy. In legislative races, however, Greeley bolted. The *Tribune* instructed voters to elect "upright and incorruptible" men, such as Tilden, and defeat corruptionists regardless of party. Even so, Greeley hung onto his Republicanism by a thread. The *Times* belittled his sincerity, Murphy dropped his followers in the Custom House, and regulars treated him as a fool.[34]

In the interim, the patient Tilden closed his case against Tweed. With evidence sifted from Green's hold over the ledgers, Tilden issued a stinging affidavit which accused Tweed of using intermediaries to funnel money into his dummy account at the Broadway National Bank. These charges, coming from a Democratic source, settled the issue for many hesitant party workers, especially when Supreme Court Justice Wilton Learned signed a warrant for Tweed's arrest and set bond at $1 million. In a few hours, the sureties arrived and Tweed continued his reelection bid for vindication. But Democratic reformers had him on the run. His arrest proved, the *World* pronounced, "that this notorious thief has no influence in the Democratic party." Thus, voters must select honest men to the legislature with the clear duty of abolishing the Tweed Charter and the Board of Audit, the chief sources of local corruption.[35]

With both parties distracted by internal problems, the election went quietly and Davenport's deputies met minimal resistance. As the *Herald* reasoned, no group could "afford the odium of instigating violence" or stealing votes. The contest in the city was a ringing defeat for Tammany. Apollo Hall elected all fifteen aldermen, thirteen out of twenty-one assistant aldermen, four out of five senators, and five assemblymen, including Tilden. In other assembly races, Tammany won seven seats, Republicans nine. Tammany recovered slightly when Tweed won, but he barely squeaked to victory over two obscure challengers. The story upstate was much the same. The Republicans elected their entire state ticket and won control over the legislature.[36]

The fall elections of 1871 ended the first phase of a major transformation of the two-party system, a phase best characterized by parallel struggles within each party between reformers committed to good government and party loyalists dedicated to normal organizational processes. Of the two parties, however, the Democracy underwent the deepest modification. Over a five-month period not only had the corruption issue eroded Tammany's seemingly impregnable bastions, but it had also unmade and made political leaders.

Within Tweed's circle, the scandal touched and discredited each man. Mayor Hall, who considered himself the "scapegoat of the Ring," remained in office, but faced the embarrassment of three inconclusive trials for dereliction of duty in failing to audit claims. Sweeny fled first to Canada and then Paris. Few shed any tears for Connolly, who stayed under Tilden's protection until an indictment sent him packing overseas. Tweed did not flee, and stubbornly sought vindication in the courts. Politically, whether he was guilty or not was beside the point to most Democrats. He failed to win reelection to a reform General Committee, and Augustus Schell, a prominent businessman and Tildenite, replaced him as the Tammany Society's grand sachem. Even the *Leader* shared Tweed's fate. Party reformers, convinced the paper was too closely linked to Tweed, withdrew advertisements, and, on December 30, 1871, still breathing defiance, the paper folded.[37]

Governor Hoffman strove to refurbish his reputation. In an interview with the Hearld, he again endorsed the New Departure, promised to punish corruptionists by cooperating with Tilden, and stressed that his principles were undiminished as a presidential candidate. When pressed about his relationship with Tweed, however, the governor "said but little." In his annual message, Hoffman developed the themes once so prominent in his bid for higher office. Yet the hour had struck; like the others, Hoffman's time had passed.[38]

The resultant power vacuum in Democratic leadership opened the way for politicians Tweed had checked. Men of dubious probity such as O'Brien, Genet, and Morrissey grappled for power, encouraged by their successful association with Apollo Hall. Others such as Havemeyer used the Committee of Seventy as a launching pad and urged a host of young and ambitious professionals and businessmen, including William C. Whitney, Abraham Lawrence, and William Peckham, to get involved in public affairs. Swallow-tails had a new lease on life. Belmont earned respect for helping ease the city's bond and fiscal crises, and Marble interpreted Tweed's downfall as the *World*'s exoneration. Within Tammany, fresh pretenders, some old warhorses, some new faces, eyed Tweed's mantle. Since the party wanted to cleanse the Hall, not obliterate it, because of its still formidable ability to turn out voters and its direct linkages to the party's august past, swallow-tail reformers led by Tilden and Abram S. Hewitt ignored these aspirants. Instead, they sought a new leader, "honest, able . . . and experienced," a man who had opposed Tweed in the past, a man immigrants trusted, a man who favored good government reforms. They found him in "Honest" John Kelly, a deeply religious Irish Catholic, former city sheriff, and anti-Tweedite, who had luckily spent several years overseas during the Ring's heyday.[39]

Even more significant for the party's future was swallow-tail Samuel J. Tilden's blossoming into the Democracy's driving force. In making sure that Democrats overthrew and prosecuted Tweed, Tilden earned the statewide, then nationwide, respect of party leaders. Just as critical to the Democracy's long-term interests were his three innate personal values, which were absolutely necessary to restore the public's faith in the party's decency.

Apart from those, Tilden set policies in motion that made the Democracy's long-sought political reconstruction possible. First, he recast the nature of party operations through structural reformism in government. As a prototype Democratic reformer, Tilden called for businesslike efficiency, economy, responsibility, and honesty — all carried out by men of substance, honor, and character. In that sense, structural reformers believed that the proper role of government was to serve business needs. Such an attitude struck political gold among many conservatives during the Gilded Age. A second arrangement Tilden sponsored was the Bourbon Democracy, which overlapped the first and provided the party with one of its key guides for the next twenty years. Among the Jacksonian principles that Tilden transmitted to Bourbonism were free trade, honesty in office, laissez-faire, low taxation, opposition to special privilege, hard money, and a conservative defense of individual initiative through the free enterprise system. Finally, Tilden combined traditional principles with machine politics — a major ingredient in the Democracy's post-Reconstruction operation — through his salvaging of Tammany Hall, despite his barely concealed contempt for bossism. In short, Tilden's efforts unleashed powerful forces that completed the Democracy's final reconstruction and, in the long run, directly contributed to Grover Cleveland's presidency. Yet in the fall of 1871, few politicians had any perception of Tilden's fateful importance. Essentially, he was still an unknown, cautious, provincial commodity. As he admitted to Kernan, "we must receive the good which is attainable, and not sacrifice it to what is beyond our control. It may be that opportunity will arrive, but I do not see it as yet."[40]

The Republican party also underwent great changes. Facing a congressional investigation of frauds in the Custom House, local leaders forced Murphy's resignation. In his place, President Grant named Chester Alan Arthur, who oddly had been thought a Tammany Republican because of his legal work for a Tweed-dominated tax commission. Greeley was unimpressed. He labelled Arthur a second-rate Conklingite flunky, questioned the party's will to reform itself, and edged toward a wrenching break with the organization he had done so much to create. He warned Republicans they faced scandals in Washington similar to the storm that had "just plucked Tammany from its roots." On the other side of party factionalism, Conkling consolidated power by isolating the Fentonians and Greeleyites, forming alliances with businessmen, controlling federal patronage, supporting Grant's renomination, and abandoning radical institutional reformism. Just as the Democrats found their man to reorganize politics in Tilden, so had the Republicans in Conkling. What the future held for both, however, remained in doubt.[41]

7
Stopgap Reconstruction: The Elections of 1872

FOR one of the few times since Martin Van Buren formed the New York Democratic party in the 1820s, the local Democracy entered a presidential year without a leading contender or a possible dark horse candidate. Even worse, party leaders were virtual prisoners of the recent scandals and were preoccupied by the transcendent importance of showing their powers of self-renewal by capturing the reform issue. Such was the hard task the party faced because of Tweed. The basic objective of New York Democrats in 1872, therefore, was not presidential politics but instead the need to revive sagging party fortunes in the state.

New York's electoral votes, however, were of prime importance to the national organization. As soon as the shape of Tweed's debacle became apparent, outsiders, chiefly the Blairs, advocated a prescription to revive the organization in time for the fall election. Their doctoring, called the "Passive Policy," was based on the 1870 Missouri Plan; the idea that Democrats must cease all action until after Liberal Republicans nominated a slate, and then, if the platform and candidates were acceptable, the Democracy would coalesce with them against Grant. Such tactics, the Blairs believed, contained several inbuilt advantages. A Democratic endorsement of Liberal Republicans, coupled to the New Departure, would end the nation's polarization over the war and its consequences, thus allowing the Democracy to make peace with those issues, achieve sectional reunion, and move on to new questions.[1]

After their bitter battle to save the party in the previous fall's election, most influential Democrats under Tilden felt the Blairs' medicine was too bitter a reorganization pill. All party journals agreed with Marble, who became the Democracy's spokesman because of his close association with Tilden, that it made sense for Democrats to set aside narrow sentiments of "party spirit and party prejudice," encourage "honest Republicans," and forbear "any obstinacy of preference for favorite candidates for president." Nonetheless, Marble did not feel the Passive Policy germane to New York needs. Instead, he placed priorities on economic and political reforms that would revive party loyalties, particularly through the idea that the Democracy must expand its clean government campaign to all levels of the polity.[2]

Marble's last idea was crucial because it placed the municipal scandal in the perspective of other frauds purportedly existing within the Grant Administration and among carpetbag regimes. In rationalizing the situation, Democrats suggested that the postwar years were a time of a general deterioration in political morality, that corruption was endemic nationally, and that no party or section had a monopoly on public plunder. Yet the seedbed for remedies lay in the ground party reformers had planted in the fall elections; Tilden's clean government efforts geared to traditional Democratic principles and programs. Paradoxically, Tweed became vital in Tilden's reorganization plans. By having eminent Democrats such as O'Conor act as his chief prosecutor, Tilden proved, as Grant must, that the political system would not sanction fraud no matter the cost. "Grant's power rests on as rotten a foundation as Tweed's did," Marble intoned, "and it is destined to as signal an overthrow, by similar means and agencies. The reform trumpet has, as yet, given forth only its preluding notes; the great reverberating blast is to follow."[3]

As for the Liberal Republicans, Democrats accepted their ends but doubted their courage. Writing to Montgomery Blair, Marble cautioned that he and Tilden lacked any illusions about the Liberals' willingness "to cut loose & burn their bridges." Though Governor B. Gratz Brown and Schurz did so in Missouri, Marble asked, where are the others? The problem did not lie among Democrats who were "waiting to be ravished," but with "the lack of audacity" among the bulk of the so-called Liberals. If those men wanted to beat Grant, they must immediately show signs of tangible independence. "If they wait to be bolters after [his renomination] they will be beaten, if indeed they dare to bolt."[4]

Nor were Liberal Republicans enamored of Democrats. Schurz, their spiritual leader, suspected Democratic treachery and doubted they could accept a Liberal even under the best conditions. Reflecting this skepticism, others such as John Bigelow, a Barnburner Republican and later Tilden's major adviser, confessed to Edwin D. Morgan that he considered Democratic support suspicious. Conversely, the Liberal *Evening Post* shrewdly observed that the Passive Policy entrapped Democrats. No matter what they said, the paper predicted, "a few more months of delay and uncertainty in adopting a policy will render them almost impotent in the national canvass, and they will accept the 'passive policy' not as their choice, but on compulsion."[5]

Here Tilden blundered. He viewed the Liberals as similar to the National Union party and assumed Democrats would absorb them. For that reason, Tilden suggested to Cassidy that the state committee delay a meeting until after the Liberals held their national convention in Cincinnati in early May. The party's best course, Tilden claimed, was to wait until it had the "fullest information on the state of opinion and of parties." When the committee gathered on April 11, Tilden prevailed. The committeemen avoided endorsing the Passive Policy, but substantially accepted it by announcing that the party waited to see how "popular opinion" formed.[6]

Whatever benefits the Passive Policy had for Democrats quickly became self-defeating. During the late spring, the Liberal movement spread rapidly in New York among Barnburner and Free Soil Republicans the Democracy coveted, and the Passive Policy made inroads within Southern and Midwestern Democratic strongholds. Such a groundswell frustrated party chieftains' hopes of controlling events. In short, Democratic leaders labored under an illusion; instead of capturing the Liberals, the Liberals verged on capturing them.[7]

After a tour of Midwestern states in April, national chairman Belmont suddenly discovered the Democracy's predicament. Trying to turn the situation to the party's best interests, he began delicate negotiations with Schurz and suggested cooperation was likely provided the Liberals nominated the right man on a satisfactory platform. Belmont then showed his good faith by setting up a timetable that delayed the Democratic convention until after both the Liberal and the regular Republicans met. As for specifics, Belmont suggested a platform denouncing the Administration's "abuses & corruption," its "military despotism" in the South, and its "centralization of power," and called for "general amnesty & a Revenue tariff." On that basis, he told Schurz, "every Democrat throughout the land [stands] ready to vote for your candidates."[8]

No matter how much excitement the Liberal Republicans generated, or how much it attracted Democrats, few politicians knew if it could survive its own internal inconsistencies. In some cases, the reform issue focused on specific interests. In others, Liberal Republicanism took the form of a rebellion against the old parties and the politicians who led them. Even the definition of principles had a cutting edge. Many Liberals, such as David A. Wells, were adamant free traders who refused to support any man tainted by protectionism, such as Greeley. To confuse matters even more, many Liberals were politicians at loose ends, generally former radicals such as Greeley and Fenton, torn between ideals they felt Grant betrayed and fears that deserting the regular organization would destroy what remained of their careers, and uncertain whether they should back reforms that excluded blacks or reforms based on white sectional needs. As those were not enough, still other Liberals were confused about their relationship with Grant. He was still a popular war hero, largely untainted by personal corruption, the leader of a party that glorified the past and prided itself on ending slavery through the now immortal Lincoln. Breaking with those symbols of greatness, many Liberals believed, was spiritually if not practically impossible. As a result, some Liberals did not want Democratic aid and hoped that regular Republicans would nominate their candidate and thus preserve the party.[9]

Equally vexatious, Liberals split into angry quarrels over candidates. By May, two men — Charles Francis Adams of Massachusetts and Horace Greeley — emerged from the pack. Adams was particularly attractive to Democrats. His reputation as a free trader fulfilled one aspect of Democratic needs. Moreover, Belmont and Marble thought his integrity and notable service to the Union during the Civil War as minister to the Court of St. James could neutralize the party's lingering image of treachery. Best of all, Adams had run for vice president in 1848 when Martin Van Buren headed the Free Soil ticket. As a result, many Democrats considered Adams a Republican in name only and supported his nomination as a clever device to regain the *Evening Post* crowd. Unfortunately, Adams soon disillusioned Democrats by proving himself his own worst enemy. He was an enigmatic politician, made few moves to secure the nomination, and even his closest advisers were unsure whether he would accept if selected.

Greeley was a case unto himself. Despite charges of a political conspiracy that later followed his nomination, Greeley in a practical sense had impressive credentials. As the *Leader* noted as early as 1870, Greeley was popular among prohibitionists, former rebels, blacks, people he met on his frequent national tours, idealists who still thrilled to his antislaveryism, regulars grateful for his spadework in creating the Republican party, trade unionists, and protectionists. No man given his long political involvement, however, could escape serious deficiencies as well. During his career he had alienated free traders, the liquor interests, and Catholics. As an editor, his support for many contradictory positions and unpopular causes appeared the work of a crackpot. Then, too, his repeated lust for political office, coupled with his repeated failures, made him seem a perennial loser. Furthermore, Thurlow Weed, an antagonist of deep-seated hatreds, stirred from retirement at the thought of his "monstrous" candidacy, and many Liberals feared that Greeley's reputation detracted attention from needed reforms. To cap his liabilities, most Northern Democrats felt queasy over possibly endorsing a man who had publicly branded them as Copperheads and traitors.[10]

Despite all these defects, many pragmatic Democrats on reflection saw him in a favorable light. Beginning in 1870, when he opened war on Grant and Conkling, the *Tribune* had moderated attacks on Democrats. Outside of protectionism, he stood right on reformism. In the South, white Democrats appreciated his reconciliation efforts. Best of all, Northern Democrats could erase any lingering issues left by the war and Reconstruction by backing a man who symbolized radicalism. As things stood, then, Democrats preferred Adams, but could just as easily swallow Greeley.[11]

Nonetheless, the question remained whether the Liberals welcomed Democratic fusion, and, if so, under what conditions. Men such as Bryant called on the Democracy to disband it if wished to support the Liberals. Others felt even that was insufficient; by habit and training they had opposed Democrats too long to embrace them now without feeling like apostates. Practical Liberals, however, understood they needed the Democrats. Free trader John Dash Van Buren, now active in seeking Democratic fusion with the Liberals, placed the situation in its largest context. "Our only hope of revenue reform is getting the present men out," he told Wells, "& then talk & argument will have a chance." Given those factors, Bowles wrote Schurz, the Liberals could not remain aloof from Democrats for too long. If the regulars renominated Grant, Bowles argued, the Liberals needed Democratic aid in the common cause leading to "a thorough break up and reconstruction of parties." While few Democrats intended to abandon their party, the fact remained that in terms of common issues little separated them from Liberals. The only imponderable remaining was the Liberals' willingness to accept the Democrats as allies, not converts.[12]

While the pace of national politics accelerated, local Democrats picked up the shattered pieces of their party. In this new era of political morality, they faced five immediate tasks to reestablish public faith in the organization. These included repeal of the Erie Classification Bill, restructuring the municipal government, impeachment of corrupt judges, and prosecutions of leading Ring members. While substantial agreement existed on these four, the last job — rebuilding the city organization — proved nettlesome. The problem facing the party lay in contrasting perceptions of politics. The Committee of Seventy favored bipartisan reforms to oust party hacks and to replace them with new, honest, responsible public servants. Apollo Hall planned a complete party realignment based on its anti-Tammanyism. Opposing it were the remnants of Tweed's supporters under Genet, who acted as if nothing had happened. Tilden and Kelly, who controlled Tammany Hall, had their own plans. In the calculus of city politics, they held the advantage because they dominated the Tammany Society, and with it the sachems' vital right to judge party regularity. Because of that, Tilden and Kelly began the job of Tammany's facelifting through the Society and its new grand sachem, Augustus Schell.[13]

In January of 1872, Schell emphasized that the Tammany Society was morally responsible for maintaining party order and stability. As part of that guardianship, he appointed Kelly to head a committee charged with reforming the organization. In early March, Kelly submitted a plan full of platitudes about good government, which the Council approved, that thoroughly changed the city Democracy's decentralized ward network. In its place, Kelly proposed a consolidated hierarchy, with formalized lines of command, and a fixed system of duties. That done, the Council called for a new General Committee election. Moreover, the report, signed by such eminent and incorruptible men as Belmont, Hewitt, Schell, and Barlow, restated the Hall's new-found self-righteousness. "The frauds in our city affairs were discovered by Democrats; were exposed by Democrats; were prosecuted by Democrats; and to Democrats is now given the sacred trust of guarding against those occurrences in the future."[14]

On April 15, the Tammany Society held its annual election. Kelly stacked his ticket, which easily won over Genet's, with men prominent for both their impeccable party standing and prosecution of the Ring. Even the *Times* was impressed. In purging the "old Tammany gang," it noted, the Tammany Society "has taken to heart the lesson of last fall." The new sachems "will do all that great reputations and unblemished names can do to restore Tammany to power and respectability." With such an accolade backing it, considering the source, the Hall boasted that it had rid itself of all thieves. From the ashes of Tweedism, a refurbished Tammany Hall emerged, pledged to good government on the basis of its housecleaning.[15]

Apollo Hall scoffed at Tammany's sudden conversion. Although bombarded by Tilden's men to disband, the Apolloites formed a separate general committee dedicated to "the success of the Democratic principles and the welfare of the city." The Apolloites, however, underestimated the Council of Sachems' resourcefulness. A political machine runs on patronage, voter identification, and tradition, not insurgency or questionable political intransigence. Here, Tammany held the advantage. In addition, Apollo unintentionally helped Tammany because the diffused interest groups within its coalition failed to draw a clear line between legitimate dissent and personal ambition. The more Apolloites criticized the Hall, the more they seemed party traitors. This situation crystallized in May at the state convention for electing national convention delegates. Given the choice between Apollo, which seemed an accident of circumstance, and the revitalized Tammany, the delegates awarded Kelly's group sole recognition. The decision began Apollo Hall's decline. Sensing the drift of party sentiment, many men prominent in the fall fusion battle, Edward Cooper and Abraham Lawrence among them, made their peace with Kelly.[16]

During these developments, the Tilden wing of the party capitalized on Republican failures to institute meaningful reforms. When the legislature began, it became apparent that Republicans in both houses were more intent on reaping political capital out of the municipal scandals than in attempting to correct them. Equally distracting, Republicans bogged down in an intense intramural power struggle between Conklingites and Liberals. In disgust, the *Evening Post* spoke for many Republicans who felt their party had betrayed them. Bryant, back at his editorial desk, agreed with Democrats that the self-proclaimed reformers, "elected upon a single issue," had "deceived" voters for their "own partisan interests."[17]

By default, the initiative fell into Democratic hands, notably those of Governor Hoffman. In a long review of state affairs in his annual message, he urged the legislature to correct the "great wrongs" in the city administration by amendments to the charter that would establish full public control of elective officials. Beyond that, Hoffman warned that the necessity for local "pure and efficient work" could not be divorced from "the equally pressing and difficult work of state reform."[18]

Senator O'Brien acted quickly to enhance Apollo Hall by introducing a bill to repeal the Erie Classification Act. Although the Tildenites resented O'Brien's poaching, they steered the bill through the legislature against Jay Gould's massive lobbying and lavish spending. In the end, what counted was not money but the Erie's connection with Tweed. When the bill passed in March, O'Brien and Apollo gained much esteem. Yet in a practical sense, their triumph was shortlived. When the new board organized, Tammany retained its leverage because the new directors included some of Tilden's closest friends, chiefly Barlow.[19]

When it came to impeaching judges Barnard, McCunn, and Cardozo, Tilden and his protégé, future governor David Bennett Hill, outflanked other reformers. Tilden in particular prepared position papers, worked with legislative leaders, used newspapers to educate the public, and offered advice to impeachment managers. The result led to the judges' removals. But of more importance, Tilden demonstrated to the party that good government activities translated into good politics, thus establishing the fact that the Democracy's search for respectability was bound to father more reforms.[20]

The same formula applied to indictments brought against Hall and Tweed. Led by Tilden and O'Conor, the Democracy defined its court crusade as part of the steady march of party idealism. Under those conditions, the importance of such efforts did not lie in convicting either Hall or Tweed. Rather, Tilden and O'Conor staged the indictments as part of a morality play to underscore their commitment to a good society through the elimination of corrupt individuals. In that effort, Tildenites excluded other reformers.[21]

The Tildenites scored further points through inaction. Since Apollo, the Committee of Seventy, and other reformers had committed themselves to pass a new charter in the previous campaign, they were responsible for a workable revision. In April, after months of haggling and bargaining, the legislature passed the Committee of Seventy's charter. What emerged was a startling departure totally at variance with Hoffman's suggestions. The charter weakened the mayor's powers and divided responsibility among a strengthened bicameral council and a variety of consolidated boards. Moreover, the charter proposed limits on spending for needed public services and legislated out all incumbents by calling for new spring elections, held separately from state and national elections, as soon as the charter became official. The charter's most controversial feature, designed to ensure minority power at Tammany's expense, lay in the use of cumulative or proportional representation. In voting for the council, the charter divided the city into five districts. Electors had nine votes which they could spread among citywide candidates for the forty-five-man aldermanic board.[22]

Outside of the Conklingite *Times* and the Apolloite *Daily News,* the charter drew universal scorn. Even newspapers which had attacked Tammany, such as the *Herald* and *Evening Post,* implored Hoffman for a veto. With responsibility thrust solely into his hands, the governor agonized for twelve days before applying a long, carefully written veto. The charter's provisions, he noted, showed good intentions but revealed a weak grasp of efficient government. It failed to provide for real home rule and did not affix responsibility for possible frauds. The section on cumulative voting was unconstitutional because it suppressed majority rule; and, taken as a whole, the charter harbored a "retrograde spirit" by bringing back the old commission system in disguise. As for the Committee of Seventy, Hoffman praised its dedication, but chided its members as well-meaning novices, not "conversant with public affairs."[23]

The veto proved to be Hoffman's last gasp of popularity. Liberal Republicans, independent reformers, and Democratic newspapers paid glowing tribute to his "reasonable and cogent" arguments and clear sense of "what the City of New York wants." In desperation, the coalition that had forged the charter failed in an override, and made a futile bid to formulate a new one. When the session ended, the *Times,* which had previously avoided any attacks on the governor's connection with Tweed, lost restraint. In June, the paper published vouchers that ostensibly proved that Hoffman, when mayor, permitted illegal expenditures by absenting himself and allowing Tweedites to sign requisitions. Few believed the paper. Detecting malice, not reformism at work, Liberal Republicans and Tildenites vilified the *Times*'s motives and scorned its "reckless" attack on "a great public servant."[24]

By the end of May, every criterion politicians used to test public opinion indicated that the Tildenites had engineered an impressive comeback. In the city, Apollo steadily lost ground, while Kelly restored Tammany's former luster. Through a combination of luck and sound politicking, the Tildenites had draped themselves with the mantle of reform, diminished the Committee of Seventy's credibility, and watched as the *Times* lost prestige by failing to connect Hoffman with Tweed. Only three tasks remained in the Democracy's apparently amazingly short revitalization — the election of a sympathetic president and the recovery of the city and state governments.

The Passive Policy's basic weakness, its failure to form alternatives if the Liberals nominated an unacceptable candidate or drafted an unacceptable platform, burst over the Democracy in early May. The Cincinnati convention selected Horace Greeley on a platform that emphasized worthwhile national reforms which Democrats could accept, but evaded one key item, free trade, by weakly suggesting the solution rested in individual congressional districts. Although Democrats had considered Greeley a possible choice prior to the convention, his actual nomination ended conjecture and forced the party into making a hard decision. Since it was clear that regular Republicans meeting in June would never replace Grant with Greeley, the Democratic predicament boiled down to one simple question: Who was worse for the United States and the Democracy, Greeley or Grant?[25]

The confused Democrats split into four groups. One, led by Marble, certain "no Democrat can or will endorse Greeley," pressed for a straight party nominee. A second, consisting of pragmatists represented by Belmont, felt a separate nomination would ensure Grant's reelection. A third surfaced among Southern Democrats and former Peace Democrats who admired Greeley's stand on sectional reunion and his bail bond for Jefferson Davis. Then, too, they viewed supporting Greeley as a passport to escape the odium of their war records. The fourth, equivocal and drifting, clustered around Tilden, Warren, and Cassidy. For the present, they cautioned Marble to avoid a box until the party at least held its state convention.[26]

If Democrats were confused, some Liberals were outraged. Free traders including Bryant and Wells vented their spleen against an alleged "conspiracy" involving four reform editors, Bowles, Murat Halstead, Horace White, and Henry Watterson — the "Quadrilateral" — that named Greeley. Bryant was particularly furious. In a series of hard-hitting editorials published through May, the *Evening Post* called the nomination a "catastrophe" that reeked of "comedy" if it were not so serious. Still unwilling to surrender to Grant, these men sought to cut out of the thicket by holding a meeting on May 30 at Steinway Hall in the city to plot alternatives. That led to a second gathering three weeks later at the Fifth Avenue Hotel, where free traders from across the nation planned to replace Greeley and form a new ticket.[27]

Of all these men, Carl Schurz felt the most betrayed. The letter-writing debate he set off with Greeley was short but blunt. Schurz denounced the "huckstering" at the convention and the evasion over protectionism as evidences of the Liberals' loss of morality. In reply, Greeley soothed Schurz's hurt, refused to pick up the quarrel, and emphasized the need for party peace. Still not appeased, Schurz corresponded with other malcontents and appeared ready to join them in dumping the ticket. The watchful Montgomery Blair, however, felt Schurz would eventually come around. To Whitelaw Reid, Greeley's chief tactician and interim *Tribune* editor, Blair predicted that Schurz would wheel into line once he and other Liberals realized a rebel ticket ensured Grant's reelection.[28]

Slowly and painfully, most Liberals made peace with Greeley. What tipped the balance for many of them was the feeling that the revulsion stirring within the Democracy among men such as Marble indicated the party's death rattle. If so, that meant a permanent political realignment was at hand. Under these circumstances, much more was at stake than personal grievances against Greeley. There now was a chance to create a new coherent political system based on idealism and reform. By mid-May, Schurz accepted the inevitable, as Blair anticipated, and pledged to confidants his support for the ticket. The busy Reid spread his own salve over wounded spirits. Writing to Bowles, he promised that "Mr. Greeley is heartily willing to pass accounts and start fresh."[29]

By the time the Fifth Avenue Hotel meeting convened, the majority of dissidents lost momentum and agreed not to bolt. Not all Liberals, however, accepted that judgment. Parke Godwin called Greeley a "charlatan from top to bottom," and the *Evening Post,* while admitting Grant's poor record, endorsed him with the rationalization that "considering the circumstances, he has done no great harm." Other potential Liberals followed suit, particularly Thurlow Weed, who placed his remaining prestige behind the President. As a result, if the Greeley-Liberals planned to elect their man, they needed Democrats as much as the Democracy needed them.[30]

The process of accommodation evident among Liberals had its counterpart within the Democracy. Throughout May and June, the *World* peppered Greeley with criticism and maintained that Democrats must stick to principles by selecting a normal ticket. Marble's stand sparked support among the Irish and among Democrats with long memories. Speaking for them, Sam Ward disdainfully told Marble that Greeley's attempt to gain aid from the elitist Union League Club ended in failure because he looked "as filthy & busy as a scavenger just dismounted from a cart." Within that circle, Greeley was considered a dolt, and rumors circulated that Democratic financiers refused to bankroll his hopeless campaign.[31]

These men, however, did not represent the party. Most New York Democrats, forced to make a difficult decision on short notice, looked for sensible advice, not blind prejudice. The *Herald* supplied this need. Probing deeply into the party's mind, it sensed a movement to Greeley among Democrats who assumed they could control him. Thus, "half a loaf is better than no bread." The paper saw other advantages in a Democratic fusion with Liberals. It would rid the Democracy "of all the old impunities of secession and disunion" by supporting a prominent radical Republican, create a fresh "platform of principle" based on new conditions, and give many old Barnburners and Free Soilers an excuse to reunite with their former comrades. Moreover, since the "stupendous Tammany frauds" reversed recent Democratic successes and left the entire party discredited, practical politics dictated that its only hope for victory lay in concentrating the opposition against Grant.[32]

While the paper's influence on Democratic policy-making was difficult to gauge, party leaders echoed its reasoning as they made a wrenching revaluation of Greeley. Publicly, Democratic editors educated the faithful. Cassidy noted Greeley's many "virtues which no eccentricities can cloud." Warren commented that Democrats "no longer regard [him] with the contempt or indifference manifested" earlier. When the state convention met, resistance evaporated. The party accepted the Liberal platform and indirectly endorsed Greeley. The decision was now irreversible. Upstate editors censured the *World*'s "erratic" course as a pro-Grant plot, and the delegates replaced Belmont, assumed to be the influence behind Marble, as a delegate-at-large with Schell. By early July, the *World* knuckled under. "It is too late for any effective opposition to Mr. Greeley's nomination at Baltimore; and any bolt against it is absurd unless it has a fair prospect of driving him out of the field; and of which there is no reasonable chance."[33]

On July 9, the Democratic convention nominated Greeley and approved the Cincinnati platform. In the hectic days that followed, the desire to win worked wonders for the fusionists and helped create a sense of partisan unity. Upstate, both groups coordinated local committees and prepared for an amalgamated state convention. In the city, they handed Kelly the responsibility of reinstating Tammany to "the luster of its better days" by carrying the metropolis for Greeley. Even Belmont, bitter that Schell had replaced him as national chairman, told Marble that the sweep of events indicated Greeley "will be elected & I am glad the 'World' will support him as the *regular* nominee of the party." On the propaganda front, Democratic editors spun out a new line. Marble wrote that the Democracy must win for Greeley to prove to every Northerner and Southerner that the party "sought to heal the wounds of the Civil War and restore harmony between North and South." Cassidy announced that the contest lay between Grant's corruption and Greeley's "liberalizing, reformist spirit." Warren added that his triumph was "destined to give the country lasting peace and deliverance from the heritage of war." Finally, the fusionists aimed at a variety of special interest groups; blacks, workingmen, Germans, and Irish.[34]

Caught up in the stress of organizing their campaign, few Democrats appreciated the irony of the situation. For years, party strategists had assumed the Democracy would rebuild its fortunes by reviving the old Jacksonian coalition with the help of Republican Barnburners and Free Soilers. But as the *Evening Post's* course indicated, most of those men considered Greeley's selection a matter of expediency, not principles. The paradox of the situation lay in the fact that the Democracy did manage to lay one vital question to rest — the heritage of war — by fusion with the symbol of radical Republicanism, but it left unresolved the problem of resuscitating the old Jacksonian party.

Even with Democratic efforts, Greeley's prospects waned with the summer. A group of die-hard Democrats, led by Duncan Blanton of Kentucky and encouraged by Weed, demanded a "straight-out" ticket and held a separate convention in Louisville. To compound the trouble, the Labor Reform party cooperated with them, and ultimately nominated a third ticket headed by Charles O'Conor. Even though he declined, the dissidents refused to accept his withdrawal, and many prominent Democrats, including Belmont, voted for him in protest. More trouble erupted among many former Union Democrats, like Dix, who deserted the Liberals. Worse, Republican editors picked over all of Greeley's multiple inconsistencies, waved the bloody shirt, and made the campaign one of the most vituperative in American history.[35]

The final blow to Democratic hopes came in the South where the black vote rejected Greeley. One Georgia Democrat told Seymour, "the freedmen know no political names but Grant & Lincoln." By August, all signs indicated that the tide had swung against Greeley. Reeling under Republican attacks, Democrats privately gave up any illusion about the national ticket and instead concentrated on saving the state.[36]

Even that prospect looked bleak. With the loss of the Liberals, Republicans put the premium on party unity and stressed reformism. For those reasons, the *Sun* predicted the party would name an upright man for governor, one furthermore who was "a prominent Democrat, with a view of check-mating the liberal movement." Weed now entered the picture and boomed the elderly John A. Dix. This time, Dix fit Republican specifications. A nominal Democrat with close ties to the business community and a known Greeley-hater, his war record and commitment to clean government starkly contrasted with former Peace Democrats and Tweedites. On August 21, the Republicans responded by nominating him. Vivus Smith, the editor of the *Syracuse Journal,* was elated. "The nomination of Dix continues to be considered the play of a trump card," he told Weed. "You see the prominent democratic candidates retiring from the field."[37]

Democrats were furious because they recognized Dix's strength. In an effort to diminish his prospects, party newspapers belittled him as "a bogus reformer" whom Republicans used to mask their "corruption." Yet as William Havemeyer observed, such charges fell flat. "Outside of the Tammany Ring & Greeley Jumble School," the normally Democratic Havemeyer told Dix, all honest men who backed the "cause of good government and reform" endorsed him. Vivus Smith summed up this mood. "The question will be not whom the Democrats will nominate, but who takes the nomination."[38]

Since the Republicans had reappropriated reformism, the fusionists needed a comparable candidate. Complicating this selection was the uncertainty whether that person would be a Democrat or a Liberal. Until Hoffman relieved party leaders by declining another term, on the basis of Irish hostility because of the Orange Day Riot, no prominent Democrat stepped forward. With his retirement, various men found themselves mentioned. Tilden, Seymour, and Cassidy favored Francis Kernan. Kelly wanted Schell. Warren and the King's County organization, hostile to Tammany, favored Church. Hoffman and Marble proposed Lieutenant Governor Beach. The Liberals solved one problem when they conceded the nomination to the Democrats. Yet that merely increased the Democracy's confusion, since each would-be candidate had major liabilities. Beach was too closely associated with Hoffman. Church lacked statewide appeal. Schell was preoccupied with the national election. Kernan, an Irish Catholic, lost stature because of the manner in which Hoffman withdrew. Just as perplexing, rumor-mongers whispered that Tilden used Kernan as a stalking-horse for Beach. Quietly, Tilden quashed the mutterings, and the others silently called off campaign workers and left the field open to Kernan.[39]

Unlike its absorption of the National Union party, the Democracy reached out for a real working relationship with the Liberals locally. Both sides held serious meetings prior to their conventions and agreed on a formula to split state offices and electors. At their subsequent joint convention in Syracuse, the Democratic-Liberals chose Kernan, with Liberal Chauncey M. Depew, later a power in the Republican party, for lieutenant governor, endorsed the Cincinnati Platform, and formed a true fusion ticket. A further sign of amity occurred when Kelly moved Tilden's unanimous selection as state committeeman-at-large.

At first, Kernan's nomination drew universal admiration. The other Democratic contenders pledged full support, Greeley sent his blessing, and Hoffman promised aid. Even the *Evening Post* and *Evening Journal* acknowledged that Kernan's "experience" as a congressman and state senator and "highly respectable character" made him a formidable foe. Left unspoken was Kernan's chief drawback, his religion. Upstate Protestant Democrats, although pleased with his regional identity, nonetheless were stirred by bigotry, spawned in part by Hoffman's indirect but obvious slur on Roman Catholics. Then too, the *Irish-American*'s adamant defense of Kernan backfired among city Protestants who considered his election dangerous to the state's common school system. The more Democrats, and some Republicans such as Bryant, pleaded for toleration, the more nativism increased. As a result, Popery became an invidious but vital campaign issue that both sides exploited. Democrats, particularly Seymour, called for a bloc Irish-Catholic vote and berated Henry Wilson, the Republican vice presidential nominee, as a former Know-Nothing. Republicans cast aspersions on Kernan's obedience to priests, inflamed German Protestant fears, and used the Orange Day Riot to incite latent religious hostility against Catholic lawlessness. By the end of October, political signs indicated a heavy swing towards Dix, and the fusionists resigned themselves to defeat.[40]

Through a process of elimination, Democrats faced staggering losses everywhere they gazed. Under these critical conditions, they had to salvage a modicum of prestige by carrying the party's bastion, New York City. Kelly, aware of the crisis, sought Democratic unity amid mounting and continual difficulties. His chief target was the mayoralty, and he needed a candidate, Marble prompted, "of the first standing," one whose reformism "will be so self-evident that the animosities of last year will fade away." Kelly tried. But after failing to convince the Committee of Seventy and Apollo Hall to form a fusion ticket with Tammany, he sought to finesse both organizations by selecting Abraham Lawrence, a former Apolloite, with impeccable credentials. A pleased Marble praised Kelly's work and concluded "there is no reason to doubt" the Committee of Seventy and Apollo would endorse Lawrence.[41]

Such was not the case. After Apollo named O'Brien for mayor, the Reform Association, composed of the Committee of Seventy, regular Republicans, and Democrats opposed to both halls, nominated William Havemeyer. As if by common agreement, the three tickets fought over two issues: the personal merits of their respective candidates and their exclusive commitment to clean government. Tammany and the Liberals attacked O'Brien as a Republican "dupe" out to deceive "honest Democrats," contended that the "venerable" Havemeyer at age sixty-seven lacked "full vigor" in contrast to Lawrence "in the prime of life," and claimed the reorganized Hall fully supported good government. Apollo praised O'-Brien's efforts in bringing Tweed to justice, belittled Havemeyer and Lawrence as ineffective tools of special interests, and announced that reform would not begin unless voters destroyed the local two-party system. Regular Republicans answered in the same coin. They encouraged O'Brien although privately admitting his election was "unthinkable," boomed Havemeyer as the only man capable of checking the city's "dangerous classes," and chided Lawrence for lending his reputation to Tammany. To emphasize how deeply Tweedism remained inbedded in the public mind, the *Times* fulminated: "Tammany is as rotten at the core today as it was a year ago."[42]

The machine was vulnerable in another way because of Tweed, chiefly over the question of manipulating illegal voters. The fact was clear that Davenport's vast discretionary powers as the chief supervisor of the national election law, along with a new registry law, framed solely for the city, were both direct reactions against Tweed's massive efforts in 1868. With those two cudgels, Warren noted, the Republicans intended not only to prevent incipient frauds, but to intimidate legitimate Democratic voters.

Davenport acted as if he meant to prove the paper correct. Working as if possessed, he appointed inspectors partial to Grant, eliminated Tammany inspectors as unfit, personally checked on voters he felt had illegally registered, and published warnings in Republican newspapers that those men risked arrest if caught voting. In desperation, Marble fumed that Davenport exhibited "the harshest partisanship" possible and revealed "practical treason to liberty and to the laws." Despite such words, Davenport had a major impact on the election. He hurt the fusionists' morale and significantly lowered their registration. Democrats could only fret in frustration.[43]

The election returns were disastrous for the Democratic-Liberals. Havemeyer won with 39.3 percent of the votes cast, to Lawrence's 34.9 percent, and O'Brien's 25.7 percent. In the gubernatorial race, Dix carried the state by 52,469 votes; and

Grant won by almost the same total. Even more shattering, Republicans swept twenty-three out of thirty-two congressional seats, the entire state ticket, and retained the legislature by seventy votes on joint ballot.

For the next few weeks, Democrats mulled over exactly what had happened. Several facts were apparent. In the city, Tammany remained the pivot of the state party, the critical determinant of success or failure. Despite Havemeyer's embarrassing victory, the combined votes for his opponents illustrated that Lawrence lost because of Democratic disunity, not inherent weakness. Moreover, in the face of Davenport's obstructionism, Kernan's religious problems, and Greeley's checkered past, Tammany did manage to give both men slight majorities. As a result, it was clear that the Hall had partially recovered normally Democratic voters lost because of Tweed, that the Democracy needed a healthy Tammany to carry the state, and that the party's two strongmen, Kelly and Tilden, had turned the machine back on the road to respectability. For those reasons, many Democrats felt the election provided a cathartic lesson in party unity. It was the debilitating effect of Tweedism, in short, that gave Tammany's opponents their edge. What the Democracy thus needed was a new means to redraw traditional party lines.[44]

The more Democrats looked, the more encouraged they became. Already the Reform Association showed signs of splitting over the spoils, and Havemeyer created further ill-will by trying to dictate the format of the inevitable revisions of the city charter. Trouble abounded around Dix. Party stalwarts, led by Conkling, were uncertain whether the new governor was a true Republican or a Democrat in disguise, and reformers distrusted his reliance on Weed, who rejected the merit system. Then, too, unanswered questions erupted over how well the elderly Havemeyer and Dix could function once in office.[45]

On the national level, President Grant's reelection was not as harmful to the Democracy as its leaders once thought. By every variable of what constituted executive command, Grant's Administration was a failure and its continuance promised to turn the public against all things Republican. In Congress, his supporters sponsored no constructive legislation, and the major outlines of the Crédit Mobilier frauds promised to take the spotlight off the Tweed issue. Just as satisfying, the scandal involved many leading Republicans, including Dix who had been president of the Union Pacific Railroad. As for the Liberals, few were ready to surrender to the Conklingites. Even better, the repeated failures of carpetbag governments to halt white restoration, coupled to a decline in black voting because of white terrorism and economic coercion, indicated a massive revival of the Southern Democracy.[46]

Lastly, although Greeley's candidacy proved a disaster for Democrats, their fusion with the Liberals was a purge the organization had to swallow in order symbolically to settle all issues connected with the past. The *Evening Post* aptly observed that the Democracy's unflinching support for Greeley completed sectional reunion, forced the regulars to adopt a general amnesty, and heralded the nation's full acceptance of the three Reconstruction amendments. As for the blacks, the paper explained that Northern idealism had faded. Reviewing the last seven years, Bryant announced that Republicans had made good on their promises to sustain civil and political equality for blacks. But now blacks, according to the tenets of social Darwinism, must fend for themselves. In sum, the editorial ended, "the books . . . are closed" on the past, the old "federal union" has been restored, and "let us turn to new duties before us."[47]

This message, which showed the subtle interplay of American racism and American egalitarianism, was exactly what New York Democrats believed. In a series of similar editorials, Warren and Marble both spoke toward the broad spectrum of traditional Democratic ideas by essentially repeating Bryant's observations. With the "Negro question settled," they wrote, the public "will not be required to pick up the dry bones of dead controversies." That meant the Democracy enjoyed an open field for realignment around issues rooted in long-time Democratic principles such as free trade, "banking currency and revenue reforms, and kindred matters." Finally, after praising the Liberals for their fidelity, Marble stated that the Democracy's main task in the days ahead lay in an alignment with men "who held Democratic doctrines before the Republican party was formed, and reinforce them by the numerous recent converts to the sound order of economic and political ideas."[48]

By party consensus, Samuel J. Tilden was the man the times demanded for such a party reconstruction. "You have personally contributed much to clear up the issues in emancipating the Democracy from the Tweed Ring," Montgomery Blair told him. Yet much remained. "The notorious powers of that Ring in the Empire State have been the bane of our politics & we shall never emerge from obloquy with which it loaded us, till we organize upon some searching test measure, which will array all the money classes on one side, & enlist the sympathies of the labor classes on the other. Until such a division is brought about, there will be no democratic triumph."[49]

What Democratic editors and Blair proposed dovetailed into Tilden's ideological perception of politics, a perception he formed in the heat of Jacksonian politics. In essence, they sought to turn the party's clock back to the principles and policies of Jacksonian Democracy and use them as a bridge between the fruitful past and post-Reconstruction America. In doing so, they recognized that certain Jacksonian values made sense in the 1870s — free trade to deny governmental powers that entrenched monopolies, the supremacy of public opinion and rotation-in-office to neutralize the arrogance of elective officials, home rule as a symbol of public participation in decision-making, decentralism to protect individual freedom, and the doctrine of equal rights, theoretically applicable to all citizens, as the ultimate sign of a totally free society. When Blair hoped for a realignment of parties based on the struggle between the "money classes" and the "laboring classes," or when Marble invoked traditional Democratic economic principles, they envisioned the old Jacksonian idea of a political distinction between the "producers" (creative workers) and the "nonproducers" (exploitive capitalists).[50]

By luck, instinct, and ideology, Samuel J. Tilden embodied the moral stature, political training, and sense of purpose necessary to rally the Democracy to a fresh course of action, based on Jacksonian ideals, for a new political generation. To validate that connection, Tilden personally formed a direct link to the past because of his early association with two key New York Jacksonians, Martin Van Buren and Silas Wright, whose names he constantly invoked as Democratic touchstones. Just as promising, with the old issues dead that had sundered the party in the 1850s, Tilden's former links with Republican

Barnburners and Free Soilers seemed to make him the logical person to accomplish the Democracy's long-sought reunion. At the same time, Tilden's ability to inspire voters through traditional principles had a significant effect on his party. After the guilt-ridden shock of Tweed's fall and the numbing defeat of fusion, Tilden spurred Democrats with a renewed feeling that the organization stood for something moral, something in which they could take pride.[51]

The speed with which Democrats rationalized their massive trouncing and outlined their hopes for the future, however, could not obscure the enormity of the Tweed scandals or their shattering impact on the Democracy. The range of Democratic problems was impressive. By the fall of 1872, the party was prostrated, humbled, and divided; every level of important government offices — city, state, and federal — lay in other hands. The corruption issue had alienated Democrats from large sections of the electorate, and while Tilden had the ability to stir voters' minds, few men, perhaps not even himself, knew if he possessed the heart, drive, and ruthless ambition to assert true leadership. Finally, the party lacked an explosively popular issue, or series of issues, to turn the public against Republicans and make its Jacksonian revival operational. Considering all these difficulties, any Democratic optimism was premature at best.

8
The Final Reconstruction: 1873-1874

THE Democracy's major priority in 1873 lay in turning the corruption-in-government issue against Republicans. Fortunately for the party's needs, the Grant Administration was one of the most corrupt in American history. Equally important, scandals such as the Crédit Mobilier, the Salary Grab Act, the John Sanborn fraud, and the electoral trickery that Louisiana Republicans used to upset the popular vote against their gubernatorial candidate touched not only the President's appointees, but the entire Republican party.

Democrats happily stressed every sleazy activity they could find and emphasized that Republican malfeasance proved the most dangerous threat to American liberties. By contrast, Democrats underscored the point that while "the Tammany thieves are now out of office, shorn of their power and incapable of working additional mischief" because of Tilden, no comparable Republican denounced "official bribery." As a result, Democratic wrongdoers faced jail terms due to Democratic probity, while corrupt Republicans, shielded by a conspiracy of mutual complicity, "are still in power and in a position to injure and degrade the nation." Those facts alone, Democrats maintained, were reasons enough to oust all Republicans from office.[1]

Local Republicans tried to salvage what they could from the debris of Grantism. In particular, the *Times* launched a savage assault on Tilden's reformist image. The paper asserted that he had supported Tweed prior to 1871 and lacked the courage to confront him until the last possible moment when victory was assured. On that basis, Tilden did not deserve any credit for the Ring's demise. In fact, the paper continued, Tilden's legal work for the Erie Railroad raised serious questions about his personal honesty. As a satellite of the corrupt Tweed, then, Tilden had nothing in his record to justify his sudden prominence.[2]

The need to counter these charges was a source of great anxiety to Democratic leaders. While Tilden slowly prepared an elaborate account of events, Marble stepped into the void. Using the *Times*'s own editorials dating from 1870, the *World* demonstrated that it had endorsed the Tweed Charter and backed his efforts against the young Democracy. "The Ring which the *Times* denounced," Marble scolded, "was the Ring it had helped to complete domination." Moreover, he asked, if the paper truly wanted good government, why did it not attack Republican "knaves"? Answering himself, Marble concluded that the *Times*'s self-serving silence "thus lends itself to all the uses of the corruptionist cabal of the Republican party."[3]

Tilden's response, published in pamphlet form for the widest circulation, was a stirring defense that followed Marble's approach of damning the *Times* through its own words. In that way, Tilden appealed directly to the public, not merely his party, for a moral reawakening in politics. As expected, Democrats and Liberals approved. The reaction that counted, however, lay among Tilden's old colleagues, the Barnburners. Fortunately, their attitude proved equally positive. The *Evening Post* lauded his "adroit, earnest, sagacious, resolute and patriotic" efforts against Tweed, efforts so outstanding "that no amount of dirt flung by vulgar malevolence could injure him."[4]

Deeply stimulated by this evidence of support, Democrats shifted the focus of their assault against corruption to the legislature where they charged that certain Republican senators had mounted a conspiracy to prevent full disclosures of their involvement in Tweed's bribery. Once more, the *Evening Post* snapped the Democracy's bait. It criticized Republican delaying tactics of an investigation into Tweed's activities as an indication of their party's evasion of "simple justice" and it cautioned Republicans that they must cleanse their organization of "merchantable senators" who still formed "the remnants of the old Tweed Ring in disguise."[5]

Despite these efforts, the Democracy was still beset by a number of problems party leaders could not solve. In the city, the wound between Tammany and Apollo was unhealed, and Mayor Havemeyer checkmated Kelly's reformism by promising to work "free of political bias." Even worse for the Tildenites, Comptroller Green lost public confidence over his tightfisted municipal budgets, which harmed vital city services, and his slowness in meeting city payrolls.

Upstate, Democratic prospects were no brighter. Governor Dix enjoyed widespread approval for endorsing good government. In the legislature, the Republicans easily reappointed Conkling to a second term in the Senate. Then, the Democracy suffered a deep blow when William Cassidy died. To cap the misery, Republican legislators, goaded by the Committee of Seventy and Mayor Havemeyer, prepared a new charter that threatened to limit Tammany's effectiveness and institutionalize an artificial Republican power base.

Along other political lines, troublesome problems emerged. The corruption-in-government issue, which Democrats had heavily counted upon to discredit Grant and neutralize Tweedism, angered the public but did not essentially diminish the President's popularity, or turn the mass of voters against the Administration. Worse, the Republicans exculpated Grant by adopting the earlier Democratic argument, used to explain away Tweedism, that corruption was an unavoidable manifestation of the period's culture. As long as Grant seemed personally innocent, the victim of political naïveté and untrustworthy friends, and as long as general economic prosperity remained high, many people felt the Democracy's carping was in bad taste.[6]

The Democracy faced its deepest challenge when the Republican-controlled legislature made its promised revision of the city charter. Honest reformers viewed the document as a dramatic breakthrough for restoring municipal morality, while most Tammanyites visualized it as an attempt to destroy their party. Both were wrong. The 1873 charter turned out to be a clever synthesis that kept some traditional methods while thoroughly revamping others.

When the bill was first introduced, it contained several radical provisions that upset the delicate balance between the Committee of Seventy, Governor Dix, and partisan Republicans. Among these were sections that created a modified commission system, vast discretionary powers for the superintendent of police, the elimination of all current department heads including Green, the weakening of the mayor's executive powers, particularly that of appointment, and a unicameral Board of Aldermen elected by a proportional system geared to minority interests. Perhaps the bill's most novel wrinkle lay in the Committee of Seventy's idea to return to the days of a government run by professional and business elites. The bill cut the salaries of aldermen and department heads in the hope of dissuading opportunists and luring public-spirited men who regarded municipal work as a duty.[7]

As it turned out, the bill created havoc among its sponsors. Havemeyer bitterly attacked Republicans for diffusing the mayor's powers. In return, Republicans assailed him as an obstructionist. Caught in the middle, Dix disliked giving the superintendent of police more authority, the lack of clear-cut executive responsibility, and the public's minimal control over municipal spending through the new Board of Estimate and Appropriation. But when the governor sought modifications, the Conklingites refused to yield. Democrats quickly responded. They informed Dix he could rely on "their unflinching aid in a veto of the [new] Ring Charter, then a good charter may be framed by a competent body."[8]

In the end, a compromise charter passed the legislature and gained the governor's approval. The final bill contained several key changes: the superintendent of police's powers were not increased, the mayor gained more appointive powers but remained essentially weak, and, amid hard bargaining, several prominent department heads and commissioners, including Hank Smith and Green, retained office. The major change rested in the Board of Estimate and Appropriation's composition; its membership increased from three to four, all but one directly answerable to the public.[9]

The charter proved to be more than Democrats wanted, but much less than they feared. On the negative side, authority and responsibility was too uncertain for efficient government, the mayor lacked executive powers, and the Board of Aldermen represented citywide pressure groups rather than ward interests as under the Tweed Charter. Balancing those, the bill cast doubt on the Conklingites' commitment to good government, cost Havemeyer his Republican support, and stimulated anger between Dix and regular Republicans, destined to harm both.

In again placing the city government at the mercy of the state legislature, the Republicans scored a partisan victory over efficient home rule. But in their inversion of priorities, they blundered badly. For Tammany quickly grasped that the charter, even with its formula for ensuring minority representation, actually strengthened the machine. Because the mayor and boards shared authority, all municipal power became diluted, while responsibility and accountability were uncertain. Such an inefficient system guaranteed Tammany's vital functions as a political machine. It continued to act as a broker between competing groups in a way aldermen could not; it supplied stability to government by electing men with a shared outlook; it catered to local interests that were not represented in the municipal government; and it gave the city a sense of order by centralizing the lines of authority and power, which the charter had dispersed, in itself. As a result, though Tweed's Charter of 1870 represented the best hope for home rule, the Republican Charter of 1873 unwittingly served the machine's interests just as well.[10]

Things did not work out any better in other ways for the Committee of Seventy, Governor Dix, and the Conklingites. Two legislative bills in particular hurt them. One, a local option law, the second a reorganization of the city school system, stemmed from the traditional Republican belief that politics was a vehicle for imposing public virtue and personal reformation on the public. Dix alienated both prohibitionists and Republicans by vetoing the new temperance bill. As for Havemeyer, he offended immigrants with his appointments and through a new school board which seemed less interested in educational reforms than in social control. Each bill played into the Democracy's hands. The party assailed "native-born reformers" as "bigots," and reemphasized that Democratic counter-programs, based on its time-tested principles, were the only safe guarantees of individual liberties and personal autonomy.[11]

The charter also sowed confusion and hurt its sponsors as soon as it became law. Only a late amendment confirmed that Havemeyer could fill his two-year term. Other problems were not so easily resolved. The mayor made appointments without consulting aldermen, other reformers, immigrant blocs, or his political allies. Three choices in particular pleased few people:

police commissioners Oliver Charlick, an old crony, and Republican Hugh Gardner, a former Greeleyite, and police superintendent George Matsell, who had a bad reputation among New Yorkers as a result of his previous tenure as chief of police under Fernando Wood. The situation became stickier when Governor Dix, who disliked spoils-mongering, relied on Weed for advice, much to the chagrin of Conklingite Custom House politicians who now had little say in either state or city patronage.[12]

As an outgrowth of the furor, the aging Havemeyer created the powerful impression in the public mind that all reformers were meddling, ineffectual administrators, unable, the *World* charged, to understand "what is necessary for the working of the different departments." As expected, Democrats found few things agreeable in the mayor's management, and party newspapers interpreted his appointments, along with his obsession with tax cuts and fiscal retrenchment, as shortsighted barriers to both urban growth and key city services. What was unexpected was the shower of abuse that fell on Havemeyer from the groups that had elected him. The *Times* faulted him for hunting "up all his old cronies, from all sorts of forgotten holes and corners" and foisting them "upon the public treasury," while the *Evening Post* damned him with faint praise for making the best of an admittedly bad situation. By August 1873, Havemeyer had few political allies left. Revealing the depth of his unpopularity, Whitelaw Reid editorialized: "Of all the mistakes ever made since the reform campaign opened, the most mischievous — if not disastrous — was the election of Havemeyer."[13]

The mayor's political bankruptcy, combined with Republican miscalculations, enormously increased Democratic hopes of attracting jaded and distrustful voters. On national issues, newspapers focused on the expanding scandals in Washington, and criticized the Administration's favoritism toward businessmen, notably Jay Cooke. The Democracy's major brief against Grant, however, settled on a fresh question, the President's unstated but obvious wish for a third term. Here, the *Herald* was invaluable. Mounting a strong attack on Grant's motives, it wrote that his "Caesarism" indicated "that republican institutions have failed in America." On state issues, Democrats berated Havemeyer as a Republican tool, charged Republicans with fomenting sectarian temperance issues in a cynical attempt to appease bigots, and widened the breach between Dix and the Conklingites by emphasizing Weed's role as the governor's chief patronage agent. In summing up their case, Democrats accentuated the endemic corruption within the Custom House, and questioned the willingness of Republican reformers to cure their own party.[14]

Yet for all their fine prospects, Democrats by the summer of 1873 still had not recovered from the Tweed scandals. Despite all of the opposition's multiple problems, Havemeyer, Dix, and Grant were, after all, still in power and potentially masters of the situation. Equally dampening, Tilden, physically worn by his hectic schedule and in poor health, astounded party workers by suddenly taking a four-month European vacation and offering to resign as state chairman. In short, Democrats had retreated from one setback to another since 1871 and faced an uncertain future. True, they had made a promising start in rebuilding Tammany, lowering Republican prestige, widening the gap between Dix and the Conklingites, and diminishing Havemeyer's reputation. But politically, the Democracy was on the defensive, intent on consolidating dwindling forces, and frustrated in finding issues to create a permanent party reconstruction.

At this critical juncture, Manton Marble made his presence felt. Basic to his ideas was a fresh program geared to Tilden's concept of the continuity and validity inherent in traditional Democratic ideology. The cause behind recent Democratic losses, Marble wrote, was the organization's willingness to act as "a party of expediency," not "a party of principle." The major formula for the future lay in reviving the principle of free trade. But free trade was more than an economic program; taken as a whole, it defined the Democracy's perception of the gateway to a just society. As Marble defined his meaning, free trade meant "Equal Rights before the laws of taxation; Justice in serving to every man the whole reward of his labor; Prosperity to industries and Favor to none." As to specifics, the party must campaign, he continued, on traditional Democratic ideas of limited government, ending protective tariffs, laissez-faire, decentralism, retrenchment in expenditures but not at the needy's expense, and hard currency. Finally, the party must nominate progressively minded candidates "of the highest qualifications," men who had no "grudges to settle and no old scores to obstruct the harmony of the people."[15]

Two factors, the burgeoning Granger movement and Liberal Republicans, complicated Marble's program. The Grangers, mobilizing farmers' grievances and agitating for antimonopoly and antirailroad legislation, seemed ripe for an alliance with Democrats because they shared a common enemy, Republicans, and a common philosophy keyed to equal opportunity. As Marble put it, "free trade is not only synonymous with the enforcement of farmers' rights, but it is the same panacea for all the farmers' wrongs." Any alliance based on those common beliefs, Warren added, must avoid "any suspicion of corrupt complication or combinations." Thus, while Democrats believed that a coalition with Grangers was a natural joining of mutual interests, Marble concluded, "this important result can be served only by the Democracy proving inflexibly true to the Free-Trade principle and maintaining it with constant boldness, fidelity and courage."[16]

Democrats carried the same spirit into their dealings with Liberal Republicans. Originally, some Liberals had bolted their party in the expectation of breaking up the existing two-party system and creating fresh factional alignments. Although that had not occurred, and Democrats made it clear that the Democracy would not disappear, local Liberals kept their dream. They now planned to remodel politics along the example provided by the Democratic party rebellion in Ohio's Allen County, a movement of dissident Liberals and Democrats, opposed to regular organizations and dedicated to reshuffling the two-party system. Unluckily, that dream turned into a nightmare. The Ohio state Democracy quashed the rebels by retaining its organization and naming a straight party ticket on a platform closely resembling Marble's ideas.[17]

This failure staggered New York Liberals. Some simply gave up any idea of changing the system, but others, led by John Cochrane, sought the best deal possible. At first, they proposed a joint convention with Democrats. For a time, the state committee was amenable and considered increasing the number of delegates to appease the Liberals. Kelly, however, killed the bargain by pointing out that it might lead to antiorganization Democrats elected as Liberals. Instead, the state committee issued a call for the regular Democracy to meet, and welcomed Liberals, as individuals, provided they favored "the restoration of pure and economical government" and condemned "monopoly and centralization." Marble put the matter more brusquely; any cooperation Liberals sought must be on Democratic terms and Democratic principles. Infuriated at this rebuff, Cochrane opted for an independent convention to prove the Liberals held the balance of power between the regular parties.[18]

During this period, Kelly consolidated his mastery over the city Democracy. Despite pressure from upstaters, the state committee, and Ben Wood for a fusion with Apollo Hall, Kelly undercut every party attempt to mandate Tammany's actions. In September, the question of which organization represented the city Democracy fell into the delegates' laps at the state convention. The decision was all but predetermined. The *Irish-American* wisely noted that while Apollo had the state committee's blessing for admittance on equal terms with Tammany and luxuriated in massive prestige because of its crusade against Tweed, it nonetheless lacked Tammany's "spirit of thorough discipline, and is deficient in local organization and drill." To remove further suspense, Kelly threatened to bolt if the party recognized Apollo in any manner. With matters put in that way, the delegates admitted only Tammany. Unwilling to accept the finality of that verdict, Apolloites went home determined somehow to force Kelly to accept their legitimacy.[19]

Two weeks before the Democratic convention, the entire nature of politics abruptly shifted following the spectacular failure of banker Jay Cooke's investment schemes. His subsequent bankruptcy sparked a series of other financial collapses that ushered in a depression. Publicly, New York newspapers urged people to stay "cool," and the *Herald* optimistically wrote: "The currents of trade will flow on smoothly, and our merchants, traders and great producing population may smile at the frenzy of the hour in Wall Street." Privately, the story was far different. In typical fear, former collector Thomas Murphy telegraphed the President: "Relief must come immediately or hundreds if not thousands of our best men will be ruined." Daily, conditions grew worse. Worried depositors withdrew funds and more banks closed, investments halted and manufacturers with high inventories cut production, causing growing unemployment, and, as more and more workers lost jobs, purchasing power decreased. Despite the *Herald*'s blithe report, then, the depression's multiple causes and effects eroded the American economy and presaged a catastrophe that reduced many citizens to despair and some to destitution. By the time the Democrats gathered at their convention, although they had no way of knowing the fact since the panic was barely two weeks old, the plummeting economy's political fallout handed the Democracy its long-sought explosive issue to demolish Republicans.[20]

For the first time, Democrats paid themselves the dividends they earned in supporting Greeley, by justifiably consigning to the past all the issues connected with the war, race, and Reconstruction. In their places, the delegates formed a platform, largely crafted by Marble, that stressed the continuity in Democratic politics beginning with the party's Jeffersonian and Jacksonian heritages. The planks called for economic and administrative changes based on traditional "principles enunciated by Thomas Jefferson" — free trade, specie payments, equal justice to all, official integrity and accountability, lowered taxes, decentralism in government, and "absolute acquiescence in the decisions of the majority." Furthermore, after scorching the Republicans for corruption, the platform appealed to the farm vote and the Liberals. It promised aid to Grangers "in their just resistance to the exactions of the monopolists," and invited the Liberals "as worthy coadjutors" to "unite with us" in the effort to "restore pure government." Finally, sensing the political system neared the cutting edge of a new era as a result of the economy's breakdown, a plank criticized "the President's pill for panics — more inflation, more subsidies, more ballooning."[21]

Throughout the fall campaign, party newspapers emphasized the need for Democratic unity and traditional Democratic principles. Marble stressed those values and used the prestige he earned in masterminding the platform to remind Kelly that city Democrats were "decidedly in favor of uniting their strength" against Republicans. As a hint of trouble down the road, Kelly went through the motion of bargaining with Apollo but never seriously considered following Marble's advice. When negotiations predictably broke down, Tammany went it alone and formed a strong ticket for local and judicial offices. Then, with an eye cocked toward good public relations, Kelly put the onus for disunity on Apollo. He explained to reporters that Apollo "did not want the Democrats to be united," while the reformed Tammany scorned any corrupt "bargaining or selling or trading for nominations." Kelly's brief gained strength when the *Tribune* praised the Hall for its excellent choices, excluding that of the unqualified Richard Crocker (a brawling, notorious follower of Kelly, destined to replace him in 1886 as Tammany's leader), for coroner, a post worth $15,000 a year in fees collected and a prime patronage source. Even the hostile *Evening Post* admitted the Hall's selections were "on the whole of a better character than we usually get from Tammany." In the end, Marble backed down and accepted Kelly as the local Democracy's head. Moreover, the *World* placed the burden for unity on Apollo by urging it to support Tammany on Kelly's terms.[22]

Propelled by the need to maintain its political identity, Apollo rejected Marble's advice and fell into Kelly's trap. The bitter O'Brien endorsed the state Democratic ticket, but combined with Republicans on a fusion city slate. Whatever he had in mind his action spelled disaster. Embarrassed reform Republicans denounced the combination as an affront to political purity, while many Apolloites, hypersensitive to the drift of Democratic opinion, "left it *en masse*." Among them, Ben Wood's defection was most damaging. "Apollo Hall, as a Democratic organization, has ceased to exist," he snarled. "The renegades who, in their eager and unscrupulous ambitions, have sought to disintegrate their party with an alliance with its enemies, will find themselves in a position of leaders without followers." By election day, Apollo's political suicide became clearer when Marble instructed voters to back only Tammany and scorn the "mongrel" ticket that the "rotten combination has formed."[23]

The Committee of Seventy also self-destructed. Begun as a moral force in politics, the committee soon lost its thrust, the *Evening Post* noted, and stumbled into the "baser" aspects of partisanship by seeking patronage and aggrandizement. By October, the would-be reformers split over which party to back, how much support the unpopular Havemeyer and Green deserved, and their relationship to former allies, including "trading politicians" such as O'Brien. Watching this confusion, the *Herald* aptly pronounced the committee dead.[24]

By now, two legs of the 1871 triad of antiorganization reformers — the Committee of Seventy and Apollo Hall — had lost out to Kelly and Tilden. Luckily for Democrats, the third leg, reform Republicans under Dix, shared the same fate.

Governor Dix proved a competent administrator, but an indifferent political chieftain. As a result, most Republicans looked to Conkling for leadership. He did not disappoint them. Although not present at the state convention, his henchmen, acting on his order, denied a renomination to Dix's ally, Attorney General Francis Barlow, ostensibly because he had supported Greeley. In reality, Dix knew that Barlow, despite his honest work in ferreting out frauds in canal contracts, had incurred the wrath of Custom House politicians in exposing their questionable involvement in land speculations. Yet while Dix and Weed favored Barlow's retention, they were powerless. Nevertheless, the governor suffered the rebuff with dignity, and told Weed he was "entirely satisifed with the State Ticket." While Dix placed party unity above pride, Conkling's message to reform Republicans was clear — personal loyalty to him, not reform, was the test of fidelity. Under these conditions, the Republican party's reform wing was as badly damaged as its allies.[25]

The Republican campaign began on a sour note, and the party never recovered. Prohibitionists were angry with Dix; the depression tumbled Grant's esteem among party workers; and Republican statewide registrations fell. As disaster loomed, Dix told Weed that the party labored under severe handicaps, the heaviest of which centered in the city where fusion "with the worst elements of the Apollo Hall organization" makes "our promises of reform a delusion and a mockery." Then, to cap the Republicans' plight, a national trend developed toward defeating their incumbents. Local Republicans tried to stem the tide. Newspapers termed the depression a temporary inconvenience, a minor disruption that would shortly end. But as idleness increased, voters, who lacked a real comprehension of the economic forces at work, understood two things — the depression had occurred under a Republican President and the party in power was at fault.[26]

Meanwhile the Liberals adopted all the paraphernalia of a mature third party rather than a faction. In their platform, they attacked Republicans for "public abuses" and slammed Democrats for refusing to cooperate. In nominating their ticket, they followed the implications of reshuffling the two-party system by endorsing two Republicans and five Democrats. But to the Liberals' chagrin, both parties ignored them. If anything, Republicans treated them as apostates, and Democrats discounted their ability to mobilize enough voters to alter the fabric of state politics. Warren noted, "the chances are numerous that the best men will win, no matter what convention nominates or rejects them." Since the Democrats were certain they had the best men, they needed the Liberals not as equals but as supplicants.[27]

Such smugness did not distort the Democracy's sense of political realism. Two factors — a drop in registration and Republican manipulation of voting inspectors — kept party workers scurrying until the polls closed. Since the election took place in an off-year, Democrats expected the decline. Furthermore, by keeping tabs on registration lists, they were elated at signs that proportionally fewer Republicans enrolled than did their own people. The problem of voting inspectors was a much greater obstacle. Using the incumbent's death in the sixth congressional district as a pretext to interfere in a local election over which he lacked jurisdiction, Davenport took charge of the total registration, bullied voters, and appointed citywide inspectors.

Police commissioner Oliver Charlick's involvement, along with Gardner's complaisance, was even more dangerous. Charlick, though a member of Tammany's General Committee, nonetheless sympathized with the Apollo-Republican combination, and he secretly agreed to remove some Tammany inspectors and poll clerks prior to the polls' opening. Kelly, who became aware of the situation only during the last days of the campaign, was unable to stop the commissioners. On election morning, Charlick and Gardner did carry out their plan, without either formal notice or cause, in direct violation of the electoral statute. In the short run, this move hindered Tammany's ability to counter Davenport. But, as Kelly soon discovered, their actions gave the Hall an opportunity after the election to attack the mayor on new grounds.[28]

When the hubbub ended, Democrats scored an impressive turnabout from their dismal losses of the previous two years. Statewide, the party elected its entire ticket and regained the legislature. In the city, Tammany, "true to its time-honored political record," gave the state candidates a majority of over 31,000 votes, and elected seven out of eight judges, the sheriff, county clerk, three coroners, including Croker, one congressman, four out of five state senators, and fourteen out of twenty assemblymen.[29]

The next few days left Democrats euphoric. Major political changes were erupting, changes the party felt accrued to its benefit. Apollo Hall was smashed, and Kelly was supreme in the city. The Liberals retained life because their aid helped Democrats, but their importance as an independent political force was limited. As for the Republicans, they were confused about their defeat and worried that "the severe commercial pressure" had compromised their stature as a national party. Looking beyond the returns, Marble saw a more important factor afoot. Democrats won, he lectured, because of their principles and unity. Now, "after the dead issues of the war are fairly buried," the party had redeemed itself and was ready to regain its pre-1860 majority status "because the people of this country are Democratic in principle."[30]

In coming to terms with the past and developing policies based on continuity in traditional principles and practices, New York Democrats swung onto a new political cycle. In order to complete its reconstruction, however, the Democracy had to solve three lingering problems: how to broaden its appeal; how to neutralize the Republican party's image as the nation's savior; and how to elect a Democratic governor to reassert the New York Democracy's primacy in the presidential sweepstakes. As it turned out, the answer to all three lay in the party's long heritage.

Following the fall election, several important events enhanced the party's new image of respectability. In the city, Kelly ousted Charlick from the General Committee for breaking the electoral law. Just as satisfying, Tweed's conviction for dereliction of duty in failing to audit bills drawn on the city gave the party another opportunity to contrast how the Democracy prosecuted its corruptionists with Republican protection of their own. Moreover, when Henry Genet, the only successful Apollo assembly candidate, who had recently been convicted of misusing city material, escaped prison with the connivance of lame duck Sheriff Matthew Brennan, a Tweedite whom Kelly had replaced, the party emphasized its commitment to good government by demanding Brennan's arrest.[31]

Democratic eyes continued to search and pry for Republican weaknesses. Luckily, the Administration's failure to ease the depression became the ultimate weapon in the Democracy's arsenal. With no end of the misery in sight, with the "widening prospect of a winter of paralysis and suffering" facing the nation, the party demanded relief based on Jacksonian formulas. Almost as if Democratic newspapers relished the rebirth of the party battles of the 1830s, they demanded free trade to reduce the price of domestic commodities in order to stimulate consumption, hard money to stifle the activities of "Wall Street speculators," the destruction of entrenched monopolies, lower taxes for the poor, retrenchment in government based on decentralism, and the separation of federal and state banking by the elimination of the National Banking system.

By far, the largest outpouring of Democratic editorials centered on defending the plight of the state's downtrodden. For those out of work, the party recommended private philanthropy such as Tammany's. For those on the verge of dismissal, the party asked "business houses and factories" to "employ the full number [of workers] on short time" instead of dismissing some. For those with no prospects, "the involuntary vagrants," the party suggested hiring them for city projects, financed by regular taxes, under minimal municipal control. Finally, newspapers throughout the state published names of "respectable men" who needed jobs, and party workers gave the destitute direct relief — food, clothing, and fuel. In all these activities, the Democracy kept a steady eye on the depression's political meaning. The nation's economic problems, it stressed, lay in Republican mismanagement. Since the Administration and Congress governed "upon mere sentiment and the dead past," prosperity would only return with national Democratic victories.[32]

Some of the unemployed turned toward radicalism. In late December, they organized a "Committee of Safety" and proposed extreme solutions for ending the hard times, including direct municipal relief, limitations on all salaries to $5,000 a year, and taxes on surplus wealth. In a city with more than one-quarter of all workers out of jobs, the committee plowed fertile ground. In January 1874, the committee sponsored a protest rally in Tompkins Square without official permission. Late in the morning, a group of police arrived, led by Commissioner Abram Duryea, a martinet who favored military force. Violence erupted when the crowd refused his order to disperse. At that point, the *Herald* reported, the police made "an onslaught on the crowd, using their clubs indiscriminately."[33]

Generally, Democrats sympathized with the workers' plight but abhorred their methods. With the memory of the Paris Commune fresh in their minds, Democrats claimed "foreign communists" duped peaceful Americans. Yet the party criticized unnecessary police brutality, savaged Havemeyer for his insistence that the municipal government had no obligations to help the deserving poor, and used the riot to underscore the wholesale unfitness of the police commissioners.[34]

Taken in context, however, the riot indicated the Democracy's limitations in coping with the depression. Bound by its commitments to negative government and individualism, its principles were too inflexible for any relief beyond customary formulas. Then, too, the party's ideas reflected the nation's limitations. Caught up by social Darwinism, many Americans believed that the economy operated by itself, governed by immutable laws of competition and natural selection, which guaranteed personal initiative and equal opportunity. Impressed by those values, the majority of voters bought the Democracy's contention that the depression was a political problem, capable of curing itself without radical tampering such as the ominous-sounding Committee of Safety suggested. As Tilden put it, Americans could solve the depression by preventing federal interference and "trusting to the people to work out their own prosperity and happiness."[35]

From an economic standpoint, then, the Democrats were hardly better than Republicans in coping with the depression. But from a political standpoint, the Democracy held the advantage. As a protest party, it forced the Republicans to defend their questionable monetary and fiscal policies; it forged alliances with disenchanted Republicans; and its faith in the ability of the people to unravel problems within the framework of traditional American beliefs resonated to popular images. Above all else, Democrats rode the wave of favorable public opinion because voters shared the belief that something was wrong, the Administration was to blame, and only a political change would set things right.

Meanwhile, Democrats pursued their elusive goal of recapturing the old Barnburners and Free Soilers through Dix and Bryant. With that in mind, Marble praised the governor's annual message as a statesmanlike document that revealed his "long association with the Democratic party." Because of the depression, Warren concurred, backsliders such as Dix often reverted in a crisis to "the principles they originally held." Just as encouraging, Bryant flayed Conklingites for their attempts to make the governor a spoils-monger and their foolish desire to draw "an artificial line between two parties or classes." In return, the Conklingites raised Democratic hopes by carping at Dix's lack of sympathy for the new order of Republican machine politics.[36]

During the spring, clues multiplied that Dix was ready to switch sides, primarily because of his differences with Congress over the so-called Inflation Bill of 1874, which attempted to increase the amount of paper money in circulation, as a depression cure-all. New York Democrats adamantly opposed the bill, as did Republican Barnburners and men such as Weed. Secretly, Dix agreed with the noninflationists. A hard money man, he agonized over what course to adopt. Fearing opposition might alienate the President, who was uncommitted, the governor nevertheless wrote Weed that he felt constrained to resist the bill in order "to save the public honor and avert commercial and financial disaster."[37]

On April 7, Dix made his misgivings public by calling on Grant for a veto. The statement galvanized the public. The financial community extolled the governor's "courage," Democratic legislators passed a resolution backing him, and the *Evening Post* gushed praise. Democrats were estatic. Warren observed that the governor, although nominally a Republican, was still guided by "his Democratic training," and Marble added that Dix "had too much of the leaven of Democracy in him" to accept "a proposition so shameful."[38]

In the end, Grant did veto the bill. Even so, Dix denied his actions had any relevance to state politics and refused to make a choice between Conklingites and Democrats. By May, disgusted Democrats ended their courtship. Party newspapers attacked Dix for opposing the proposed Brooklyn Bridge, for supporting a police reorganization bill that deprived aldermen from sharing appointive power with the mayor in the selection of police commissioners, and for being "in league with Custom House rogues." The *Argus* had the last word. "No honest Democrat or true Liberal [Republican] can longer resist the evidence that Governor Dix has abandoned his old-fashioned Democracy, in the insane pursuit of honor which must be profitless, because the price paid is too high."[39]

A similar cycle developed between Democrats and the *Evening Post.* Initially, it seemed the paper headed into the Democracy's embrace because they shared so many similar enemies and goals. Yet as it turned out, Bryant was upset with both political parties and felt voters were "utterly distrustful" of normal partisanship. What irked Bryant most about Democrats was their reiteration of Jacksonian principles, which he felt was a sham. The real Democratic party, he wrote, "which allowed its original principles of equal rights and universal liberty to be swallowed up by slavery and secession," was dead. "Let the people understand this once and for all, and not let themselves be put in awe any longer by men gibbering about ghosts of what once was."[40]

This was more than Marble could stomach. For a dead party, he sneered, the Democracy was a lively cadaver. Its unity was firm, its principles alive, and its strength grew daily because of Republican "desertions." If the Barnburner and Free Soil Republicans were honest, they should reject Bryant's tortured twists and turns, and seek allies with like-minded men in the "faithful" Democracy, "the only nucleus of a sound and healthy political activity."[41]

Whatever thoughts Democrats had about picking up their quondam allies, then, were abandoned in favor of a new tactic, the effort to prove Havemeyer's incompetency in contrast to the party's ability to carve out progressive rule, end social injustice, and prevent political corruption. As the *Herald* pointed out, the Democracy could not reach full stride until it established those points. The city, it maintained, was "the main pivot of the politics of this State. The Democrats cannot carry this State until they give a reasonable guarantee of good government in this city."[42]

When Havemeyer became mayor, the only real question was *how* Democrats would oppose him, not when. At the beginning, opposition proved difficult. Havemeyer proposed a vigorous administration. Working closely with Comptroller Green, he offered a classic program of structural reforms — lowered taxes, reduction of the municipal debt, cutbacks on city improvements, and less political interference with the police. Perhaps with an expanding economy, Havemeyer and Green might have accomplished their goals. But the depression conspired against them. By 1874, the municipal debt increased because of falling revenues, property owners were appalled at higher assessments, and the supposed dose of businesslike efficiency into city government translated into unconcern for the unemployed.

Havemeyer and Green hurt themselves in other ways. In order to implement economies, they sacrificed services and jobs, notably when the mayor vetoed bills to pave and widen uptown streets and refused to increase funds for public charities. These moves angered three powerful interests — west side speculators, downtown commercial groups intent on dock and wharf improvements, and the unemployed. Furthermore, both men alienated voters by opposing a needed rapid transit system. In a way, they were correct; they felt that a bill, which Cornelius Vanderbilt sponsored, gave his private company too much control over public transportation. But when Tammany, reform Republicans, and the state Democratic committee called on Havemeyer to exert leadership by proposing an alternative, he had none. As it turned out, Dix gained credit as a public watchdog by vetoing the bill, while the mayor reaped public contempt for appearing ineffectual.[43]

All these failures fed a steadily building public image of two callous municipal leaders who followed an abstract sense of private morality while ignoring the needs of the community at large. Against this background, Green bore the full weight of contempt because as comptroller he was responsible for determining the city's fiscal health. Yet Tammany treated him cautiously because he was Tilden's man. Even so, the Hall's drift against Green was unmistakable, and the comptroller's key role in the government marked a growing series of policy differences between Kelly and Tilden.

With Green immune to Democratic attacks, Tammany unleashed its fury against the mayor, chiefly over police appointments and criminal procedures. The 1873 Republican legislature, in addition to weakening the Hall's control over the police board, had directly threatened its organizational network by making the previously elective police justices appointive, subject to aldermanic approval, for terms ranging from six to ten years. Since the justices had direct supervision over minor offenders, they deeply affected the everyday lives of ordinary citizens. In the past, Tammany had used the justice system as a political annex, and nominated candidates strictly for political qualifications. What particularly vexed the Hall now was that Havemeyer, after months of bickering with the aldermen, selected a majority of anti-Tammany justices, who immediately undercut the ability of ward leaders to act as intermediaries between the police and offenders.[44]

For that reason, Tammany had to regain its political clout over the police or face partisan strangulation. Kelly began with a flank movement through the Tammany Society. The sachems demanded the mayor make a full investigation of the Charlick-Gardner affair to see if the two commissioners merited removal. While matters rested, Kelly stumbled over a major opportunity to reassert Tammany's position when Hank Smith, president of the board of police commissioners, died. Dix quickly reacted. Hoping to avoid a "fresh embarrassment" for reformism, he dispatched Weed to Havemeyer to impress upon him the need to name an eminent replacement. Tammany had other ideas; it wanted one of its own. Hence, the aldermen refused to confirm any of the mayor's selections, and an impasse developed. Finally, the legislature settled matters, much to Kelly's distress, when it reduced the number of commissioners and stripped the aldermen of their concurrent voice.[45]

The controversy flared anew when Havemeyer appointed Abram Disbecker, a personal friend and former Tweedite, to fill the expired term of commissioner John Russell. The selection drew universal condemnation. The *Times* belittled Disbecker as an "obscure sinecurist"; Governor Dix felt the choice made no sense on either political or reformist grounds; and Tilden and Marble demanded a full reorganization of the entire police system. Only Kelly was thrilled; the mounting criticism weakened the mayor's ability to protect Tammany's chief targets, Charlick and Gardner.[46]

Matters reached the critical stage for Havemeyer in June when the Court of Oyer and Terminer found both men guilty of a misdemeanor and fined them $250 each for breaking the electoral law. At once, they resigned, but rumors circulated that the mayor intended to reappoint them. If public opinion mattered, Havemeyer should have retreated. The *Herald* cautioned that he would strike down "the very foundation of law and order" by his "folly"; Democratic and Republican newspapers warned him to make "upright selections"; and Governor Dix put him on public notice that he must name well-known reformers.[47]

The stubborn Havemeyer defied them all. He replaced Gardner with Charlick, Charlick with Gardner. Again, the mayor ignited a public explosion that helped the Democracy. Without regard to any sense of partisanship, Republican and Democratic newspapers flayed the mayor's "stupidity." The *Herald's* attitude was most pleasing to the Democracy. After pleading with Dix to remove Havemeyer because "he has already disgraced and damaged the city long enough," it noted that "true reform consists in the reforms of parties, for there can be no reform without party. There is great safety in party arrangements against the individual folly of office-holders."[48]

The paper's defense of normal political procedures through the two-party system fit perfectly into the Democracy's theme of political responsibility. Once more conjuring the spirit of Jacksonianism, Democrats argued that real reforms originated in its political philosophy, not in the personal whims of men such as Havemeyer, nor through self-constituted groups such as the Committee of Seventy, lacking an ideological base. In that sense, the party's principles applied to tangible values and concrete needs. Thus, only through Jacksonianism could voters secure true liberty and equality, and free themselves from corruption, privilege, and abuses of power.[49]

By now, Havemeyer realized the Democrats controlled the reform issue. As a result, while he dismissed Kelly's braying for removal as so much rhetoric, the mayor found himself cornered by an aldermanic petition to Dix asking for impeachment based on Havemeyer's appointments of felons to offices of public trust. Belatedly, the mayor fought back. He forced the two commissioners' resignations, and replaced them with Superintendent Matsell and John Voorhis, a former excise commissioner. Then, in an open letter to the governor, Havemeyer defended his administration against entrenched corruptionists, closely linked to Tweed, who schemed to "render every man who makes an honest endeavor for good government, odious." Chiefly, the mayor identified Kelly as the key person who sought to lower him to the level of Tammany's mendacity. Havemeyer adopted a softer tone in a personal letter to state Republican chairman Edwin D. Morgan. Cautioning that Democrats had weakened Dix, the mayor assured Morgan that his personal fate was secondary to the governor's reelection. If, in sacrificing myself, Havemeyer wrote, Dix could prevent "a restoration of power to Tammany," the loss of the mayoralty was a minor price to pay. There matters rested until September.[50]

During this jockeying, two issues the Democracy thought obsolete — racial politics and Reconstruction, particularly in Mississippi — returned to haunt the party. Since 1871, the party had managed to block Senator Charles Sumner's proposed civil rights bill designed to outlaw racial discrimination in public accommodations, including public schools. By 1874, however, several Northern states passed similar bills, and events seemed propitious for congressional action.

Reaction among New York Democrats was a mixed blend of political opportunism, racism, and constitutional conservatism. In a twisted way, all underscored the continuities in Democratic politics. The party opposed the bill on four interrelated grounds. It refused to enhance centralism; it felt further agitation on race a distraction from pressing economic problems; it believed Republicans raised the question to bolster carpetbag governments; and it thought "there is no such thing as social equality asserted in the Declaration or in any American public document of the least authority."[51]

Using his preeminence as Tilden's mouthpiece, Marble outlined the Democracy's position. Democrats, he wrote, defended black political rights and rejected attempts to limit their suffrage because "the more intelligent negroes in many of the Southern States have become allies of the Democratic party." The Democracy accepted "the great results of the war" in respect to individual constitutional rights, and felt them secure from "the schemes of party politics." On the basis of principles, Democrats believed in justice and equal rights for blacks, but not in laws that gave the Reconstruction amendments powers neither Congress nor the people "ever intended." Current guarantees secured black equality; anything more was unconstitutional, as well as immoral, because it went beyond the principle of equality before the law by giving one race, the blacks, more rights than whites, notably immigrants. Dire results would follow, Marble predicted. Racial strife would increase because blacks would gain an inflated idea of their importance; Southern Democrats would in self-defense form "the white man's party," which New Yorkers felt would harm both races; and the entire nation would suffer. In short, Sumner's bill was as pernicious as it was unnecessary.[52]

Essentially, Marble indicated not only the New York Democracy's position, but that of the entire party, and perhaps of white America as well. No longer considering blacks the victims of slavery, Northerners felt the process of Reconstruction had given them the chance to stand on their own feet, without federal help, if they had the innate ability. Democrats denied any hint of racism. They chose to believe that the ending of slavery altered Southern society, forced whites to rethink many presuppositions, and remade the South into a free country, without unfair privileges, where the Constitution and the organic law defended equal rights. The party felt the principle of equal rights was not limited; by providing blacks with this opportunity, the principle remained valid. If blacks failed, it was their fault, not that of the principle.

Sheer politics dictated another wrinkle in the Democracy's thinking. With the erosion of carpetbag governments, black voters lacked any meaningful alternative to the Southern Democracy. Thus, the party's wisest course was home rule, forcing the blacks to vote Democratic or not at all, and preventing any new congressional legislation to undermine white supremacy. In the North, Democrats could then seek the relatively few potential black voters, while at the same time avoiding any rupture with their Southern allies. As a result, the Democracy reverted to another Jacksonian idea: black welfare, particularly in a time of grinding depression, was secondary to the nation's overall needs.[53]

The Democracy's reaction to white terrorism in Mississippi rested on such attitudes. By 1874, Southern Democrats placed New Yorkers on notice of their determination "to throw off . . . the negro yoke." Local Democrats deplored the intimidation of blacks "as nothing less than the old spirit of slavery." Nonetheless, the party condoned such bloodshed out of the compulsions of principles and politics. As their rationale, Democrats explained that because of home rule the government could not intercede, and white violence was an unavoidable reaction against federal centralism. Viewed within that context, local Democrats, and most of the white North as well, accepted events in Mississippi as the price for national reconciliation. They closed their eyes to the plight of blacks, reasoned that terrorism was a political not a racial problem, and sought a better social order through the ideal of self-help implicit in Jacksonism. Such attitudes guided the reconstructed Democracy well into the next century.[54]

By late summer 1874, the state Democracy's political revival became evident when contrasted to the Republican party's woes. On the unpopular side of the depression and the third term issue, wracked by threatened defections among prohibitionists and Grangers, unable to lure Liberals back, and caught in a cruel vise between Conklingite spoils-mongers and Dix's good government forces, Republicans reflected all the symptoms of a party hovering at the edge of disintegration.

Governor Dix's untenable position because of the aldermen's petition to remove Havemeyer best illustrated the sad state of party politics. Dix was in a no-win position: impeachment would strengthen Tammany, contravening the charges would discredit reform Republicans. The governor's dilemma intensified in September when he decided not to remove Havemeyer, reasoning that "his errors" were better "left to popular reproof" than to "executive correction." Angry Democrats quickly underscored Dix's vulnerability. Marble shot back that the governor's refusal was "the best of reasons for discrediting his fitness for the executive chair of the State." No wonder, then, that the *Evening Post,* after surveying Republican prospects, concluded: "The new questions that have arisen, all contribute to unusual uncertainties as to the future in politics."[55]

In order to maintain their momentum, national Democratic leaders met in New York City under the Manhattan Club's auspices and pledged to coordinate state campaigns on "the principles common to the Democracy" from "the time of Jefferson 'till now." The gathering had another dimension vital for local politicians. Since Tweed's reputation caused many "self-respecting" voters to shun Democrats, the *Herald* observed, the party had to make it "not merely evident, but conspicuous, that men of wealth, standing, influence and wide social connections have not retired in apathy or disgust from the Democratic organization." In the sweep of state politics, then, the meeting epitomized that the party had solved one long-term porblem. The swallow-tails had emerged as the Democracy's driving force, under Tilden and Marble, because their respectability was vital to offset Tweedism. In the course of time, however, the same basic conflict remained as before. Kelly, just as Tweed had done, intended to assert Tammany's leadership statewide. Essentially, the party's marriage of convenience could only lead to an explosive divorce.[56]

With politics going so well, Democrats expected to win all fall elections and automatically supply their winning gubernatorial candidate with "the fairest chance for the Presidential nomination in 1876" because New York was the "linchpin" of the national organization. With that in mind, party leaders demanded unity against "our common enemies," prepared to campaign on economic issues, and strove to eliminate any intraparty dissension. Above all, they felt that overconfidence was their greatest foe. In that mood the *Argus* cautioned: "The coming contest in this State is to be no holiday affair."[57]

But Democrats were Democrats. In an organization consisting of so many diverse interest groups, internal policy differences were unavoidable. Just as in the 1840s, the party's regional acrimony over the canal system burst the bonds of cooperation. During the legislative session, a group of Western Democrats and Republicans introduced a canal funding bill, financed by higher taxes, to widen the Erie and lower tolls in order to attract increased traffic. Two factors weighed against them; the notorious reputation of the bipartisan canal ring and

Tilden's feeling that the bill was an invitation to public plunder.

At once, a bitter intramural battle flared. Speaking for the canal groups, Warren sought passage to protect Buffalo's economy in particular and Western New York's in general. Marble, using Tilden's arguments first expressed in the 1867 constitutional convention, countered that such a policy would increase shippers' costs because the canal's operation was inefficient. A better solution lay in improving existing facilities and instituting sound management. Marble also cautioned that any tax boost, in light of the depression and the Democracy's stand on Republican fiscal irresponsibility, would alienate voters.

Warren was untouched but shifted tactics. Using heavy-handed methods, Western Democrats sought to name Sanford Church, the chief justice of the Court of Appeals, as the gubernatorial candidate instead of Tilden, the preconvention favorite. Aware of the danger, Seymour told Tilden that "every canal officer" feared him as governor and worked for Church. To prevent the nomination, they intended to praise his ability, but nonetheless claim that only Church could defeat Dix.[58]

The *Herald* leapt into the controversy. In a series of biting editorials, it repeated the *Times*'s earlier censure of Tilden. On other grounds, the paper criticized him for using his state chairmanship for personal advancement, in contrast to Dean Richmond's dictum, dating back to 1850, that the party's head must harmonize differences, not exacerbate them by taking sides. The *Herald* then insinuated that Havemeyer's failures proved that "Mr. Tilden is no exception to the rule that any who distinguished himself in the reform movement is less popular now" than in 1872. To cap its attack, the paper belittled Tilden as Kelly's "cats-paw." That is, Tammany intended to use him, just as Tweed used "the decorous Mr. Hoffman," in order "to get possession of the city offices" without "regard to the interests of the party in the State." Thus, the paper concluded, the Democracy was foolish to run Tilden "against so popular a man as Dix."[59]

The *Herald*'s rousing words jolted Warren into feverish activity. To enhance Church's credentials, he approached the Liberals for a fusion ticket and pressed upstate delegates to protect the canal system from New York City interests. In late

August, Warren presented his case to the full party. As secretary of the state committee, he personally issued a public statement warning delegates that the "country districts" were "emphatic and unanimous" in "their opinion that the candidate for Governor should be taken from outside of the city of New York."[60]

Warren's defiance, buttressed by the *Herald*'s character assassinations, placed Tilden at the cross roads of his political career. Any hesitation, any timidity, any introspection, validated the whispers (now turned to shouts) about his lack of courage. For that reason alone, friend and foe alike awaited his response; only he could save himself. Tilden did not falter. Using all the contacts he had so assiduously built up over the years, Tilden tested opinion at every organizational level and found his support wider and deeper than either the *Herald* or Warren suspected.

Once Tilden passed the test, his friends swung their weight. In the city, Marble brooked no nonsense. Almost daily, he accentuated Tilden's commitment to traditional principles, his role in ousting Tweed, and his importance in restoring the Democracy's respectability. Upstate, Kernan and Seymour played a similar theme, and paradoxically used rural fears of Tammany to make Tilden appear more virile. They argued that because he had tamed Tweed, upstaters need not fear the Hall's influence over the new administration. Moreover, they claimed he could attract enough independent voters and Liberals to more than offset any Democratic defections. Such contentions worked. In the weeks before the convention, many upstate county chairmen and delegates bombarded the Tildenites with letters that lauded his "courageous and successful attacks upon a corrupt ring," and assured him that rural voters appreciated his ability to "purify the State as you have the City."[61]

By September, these efforts bore handsome dividends. The *Evening Post,* while it made no pretense of endorsing Democrats, made Tilden an exception and implied that Barnburner Republicans could support him. For the Liberals, former German Democrats demanded his nomination, and the *Tribune* argued against Church. Most vital of all, Kelly placed Tammany behind Tilden. Quite simply, Kelly told reporters, "he will be very strong at the polls." As for Tilden's critics, particularly Warren, Kelly dismissed them as corruptionists whose only goal was "to get hold of the contracts given out on the canals."[62]

Western Democrats fought back. In a desperate gamble, Warren, along with several canal board members from Buffalo and Rochester, confronted Tilden in Albany and urged his withdrawal. They also brought along Reuben E. Fenton, who was prepared to have the Liberals endorse Church once Tilden retired. Their gambit failed. Tilden, confident of his convention strength, refused for two reasons: a peremptory retirement would be unfair to "his political associates [who] wished him to run," and it "would be manifestly unjust for a few interested parties thus to forestall the action of the chosen delegates of the party." With the ground cut from beneath them, upstaters maintained Church's availability even as it became increasingly obvious their cause was doomed.[63]

The convention confirmed that Tilden and the swallow-tails dominated the Democracy. In a platform that was almost entirely Marble's work, the party listed the key ideas it planned to use to vault back into state and national power: hard money, free trade, home rule, economy in government, state supervision of corporations, "equal and exact justice to all men," and opposition to inflation and a third term. The delegates then selected Tilden, and placated the Germans, the Liberals, and Westerners by choosing one of them, William Dorsheimer of Buffalo, as his running mate.[64]

Tilden's nomination continued the party's program of redrawing New York's political lines. If upstate mavericks doubted the wisdom of his selection, the reactions of Liberal and regular Republican newspapers proved instructive. The *Sun* surmised that he "will receive the suffrages of thousands who do not belong to either party"; the *Times* pictured him as a "highly respectable candidate" whom no man "need be ashamed to vote for"; and the *Tribune* said "his personal character" lent "a flavor of respectability to his constituency." Equally important, the reformers instrumental in forging the Committee of Seventy and the Independent German Association, under Ottendorfer, endorsed him. As the culmination, many Barnburner and Free Soil Republicans confided to Tilden that he was the first Democrat they could in good conscience support since 1848. Nevertheless, Tilden's candidacy still caused sparks. The *Evening Post* encouraged readers to back

Dix. John McKeon, a long-time anti-Tammanyite, called on the Irish to reject the ticket because he feared Germans overly influenced the party. The *Herald* termed Tilden's nomination a "blunder" and announced that the slate faced certain defeat. Then, too, many politicians wondered whether the canal boosters would support Tilden or bolt.[65]

Compulsory postconvention unity, however, swept through Democratic ranks. The *Irish-American* scorned McKeon's blustering, while August Belmont, who had not forgiven Tilden's secretiveness prior to his attacking Tweed, grudgingly gave his blessing. As for the canal interests, they lacked options. "I think they feel that the blame for your defeat would fall upon them," Seymour explained, "and would in the end do them great harm." Warren indeed wheeled into line. "The fact that the ticket is one which eminently deserves to succeed, begets the determination that it shall succeed." Wisely, Marble avoided any recriminations. The election of 1874 promised to usher in a new era of Democratic triumphs, and the Tildenites were determined to harness all their opportunities to ensure victory.[66]

In short, Tilden might not have been the Democracy's most personally popular leader, because of his nonflamboyant personality and inbred caution, but his nomination culminated the party's reconstruction. At last, the Democracy had nominated a legitimate Jacksonian, committed to the continuities in party policy-making, with vast bipartisan support, who could reestablish the old political coalition the slavery issue had shattered. Only Governor Dix stood between him and that goal.

Organizationally, Tilden ran his own campaign. He personally selected the itineraries of all available speakers, flooded the state with pamphlets, particularly the ones he had written attacking the Ring and the *Times,* took charge of fund-raising, and used his meticulous listing of 50,000 dependable party workers to assign each the task of ascertaining trends and urging all potential voters in his district to support Democrats. As Tilden made clear to one of them, "I do not see how with a good organization to get the voters out, we can fail. This is a great point."[67]

Equally vital, Tilden supervised the party's effort to broaden its base by absorbing the Liberals, the Barnburner-Free Soil Republicans, and the Grangers. After months of flirting with both parties, the Liberal Republicans failed to achieve any consensus. At their convention, the delegates endorsed neither party, but instructed voters to select "honest men." Here, Dorsheimer went to work among his former colleagues and campaigned hard for Tilden. Meantime, Tilden used John Bigelow to sway Bryant. Prompted by Bigelow's report that "every man" on the *Evening Post*'s staff, save the editor, was "crazy to come out squarely for you at once," Tilden called on Bryant. But while Bryant respected Tilden, his fear of losing advertisers, coupled with his emotional loyalty to the Republican party despite his dissatisfactions with its actions, kept the paper in Dix's corner. With that failure, Tilden turned toward Whitelaw Reid, who was more receptive and used the *Tribune* on his behalf even to the extent of voting against Dix. The Grangers proved more elusive. In appealing to the farm vote, Tilden and Seymour stressed the Democracy's compact regarding railroad regulation and Dix's connection with the Union Pacific. Yet while many Grangers appreciated the party's encouragement, they distrusted Tilden's work as a corporation lawyer for railroads and they avoided any firm pledges.[68]

On the other side, Republican political stock had slipped so badly that most of Dix's friends anticipated defeat. Taken as a whole, the party had not solved any of its demoralizing problems: the ill will between Conklingites and reformers, Grant's third term ambitions, the Liberals' independence, the battle between inflationists and noninflationists, and, above all, the public's belief that the Administration was the main culprit behind the nation's depression. That alone was an emotional reason to drive away voters. As if those were not enough, the prohibitionists made good on their threat of a third ticket by trotting out former governor Myron Clark as a spoiler. Just as bad, Democrats blasted away at Dix's vulnerability: his silence on the third term question, his presidency of the Union Pacific, his embarrassing refusal to investigate frauds in the Custom House, his apparent backing of Havemeyer, and his mottled political career as a turncoat who had switched parties constantly since he had deserted Federalism in 1823.

Finally, Dix was a poor campaigner who gave the impression that age had robbed his ambition to the point where he welcomed honorable retirement. As it became increasingly clear that his wishes would soon be granted, state chairman Morgan tried to breathe new life into Republican efforts. He told Dix that reports from upstate districts indicated "more Democrats will vote for him, than he will lose by the Temperance movement." Charles O'Conor read the signs better. "The affairs of the Republican party seem to be going to the dogs," he noted to Tilden.[69]

As the election neared its predictable climax, Havemeyer disrupted the Democracy's smooth campaign. Still smarting over the police commissioner imbroglio, the mayor charged that Kelly, while sheriff, had defrauded the city out of $84,482 through illegal claims, and that his posturing as a reformer was nonsense because he backed thugs such as Richard Croker. "I think that you were worse than Tweed except he was a bigger operator," the mayor snapped. For corroboration, Nelson Waterbury, a long-time Tammanyite foe of Kelly, confirmed Havemeyer's contentions, and said "that Kelly is the public robber the Mayor has depicted him to be."[70]

Bombarded by the press and besieged by reporters for an answer, Kelly first defended himself in public. Denying any malfeasance, he said the receipts were confused because of misleading bookkeeping practices, over which he had lacked supervision, and that certain bills reflected inflationary war costs, run up by a Republican Administration, not corruption. Then, Kelly sued Havemeyer for libel and sought $50,000 in damages. The important verdict was not in the courts but in the forum of public opinion. There Kelly won. As expected, Democratic newspapers praised his reformism, and Marble wrote in a typical editorial that John Kelly "was an honest man if there are honest men living." The key attitude, however, rested with independents and Republicans. There, the mayor had no support; as the *Evening Post* observed, "the public does not seem to take very much care." As the issue dragged on in court, Kelly and Tammany emerged unscathed. As for Havemeyer, denied a renomination by any party, the case physically weakened him, and in late November he died.[71]

Other problems arose for Kelly in the municipal elections. Although he plucked an eminent reformer for mayor in William Wickham, the former Apollo Hall chairman, Kelly blundered in allowing Morrissey to select a questionable person for register. At once, a group of anti-Kelly Tammanyites, led by Waterbury and O'Brien, along with Liberal Republicans under Cochrane, organized the People's Liberal Democratic party. But everything went wrong for them. They failed to make common cause with other Democrats, Republicans would not fully cooperate, and the rebels simply could not match Tammany's muscle.[72]

It was a Democratic year. In the city, Tammany elected Wickham and all eight congressmen, including Samuel S. Cox and Fernando Wood, and eighteen out of twenty-one assemblymen. It gave Tilden a plurality of 42,752. The only blot on its record was the register's loss. Upstate, Democrats retained the legislature, thus ensuring the election of their first United States senator since 1857, carried the entire state ticket, and supplied Tilden with an overall margin of 50,317. Nationally, the New York victory became part of a massive tide that washed away Republicans. In the South, Democrats "redeemed" Arkansas, Texas, and Alabama. In other areas, the party gained seventy-seven seats in the House of Representatives and won in ten critical states which elected new senators. All in all, then, the Democracy's smashing victories presaged their return to the White House in 1876 for the first time in twenty years. "The real victory is to be with the whole country, and the triumph is one which every good citizen has an equal share in, with yourself," the often disappointed Samuel Barlow congratulated Tilden.[73]

In such flamboyant fashion, the Democracy reasserted its mastery of New York, and automatically made Tilden the national party's leading contender for the presidential nomination in 1876. Most striking of all, however, was that after more than two decades of organizational disintegration, Democrats had come to terms with past issues and laid a solid foundation that lasted well into the next century.

In writing an epitaph to the Democracy's failures, the *Herald* noted, "the election is not merely a victory but a revolution." The American people, "magnanimous" and "forgiving," had welcomed back rebels as "our brothers and our fellow-citizens." Henceforth, "the test of political rewards" will be "merit, honesty, capacity, not what was done or said during the civil war." Therefore, "the election . . . destroys all 'war records' as claims for political distinctions." As for the black question, the focal point of past Democratic problems, the "party will have no temptation to deprive the negroes of the right of suffrage" because national leaders "will think it easier to accept negro suffrage and control it than to resist the northern domination which would be reinstated by futile attempts to subvert it."[74]

Tilden recognized the Democracy's almost unlimited vistas. Yet to him, respect for traditional values produced political success as well as moral satisfaction. As a result, he felt that future victories were by no means assured unless the party made voters appreciate that its political program emanated from a sense of righteousness and moral certainty.

In a victory speech at the Manhattan Club on November 9, 1874, Tilden addressed himself directly to the problems that had haunted the Democracy since the outbreak of the Civil War — for what ends did the party exist; what visions of the future did it hold; what principles could it plausibly emphasize; how could the old partisan traditions operate in an expanding and changing society? Since 1861, he argued, the Democracy had revitalized itself by adhering to the politics of continuity. Plotting future strategy, he predicted that "the people of the United States, returning to the great traditions of American free government, will stand by us as we go forward and lead them back to the ideas of Jefferson and the maxims of Jackson." In that sense, Democrats had legitimatized the consistency of their principles and values, such as free trade, constitutionalism, hard money, limited government, special privileges to none and equality of opportunity to all, the responsiveness of public servants to their constituents, laissez-faire economics, local autonomy to preserve nongovernmental interference in private affairs, and honesty among office holders. But Tilden was uninterested in self-flattery. The nation, he continued, still faced a crisis "more transcendent in its importance, in its issues, and in its consequences than any that has existed since the election of Mr. Jefferson in 1800." That crisis lay in the people's fears that the aims "of the patriotic founders of our free institutions shall not be realized." In sum, Democratic victories would be transitory "unless we shall achieve the complete restoration of the original purposes of Thomas Jefferson to the government of the United States." The future of the Democracy, then, just as in the past, rested on its political ideology and the issues it created.[75]

By 1874, the Democracy's reconstruction was complete and remained basically unchanged until early in the next century. Democrats, as in the 1830s, viewed their party as a means by which ordinary people could control power, secure equal rights and personal liberty, and protect the institutions of free government. Politically, the party controlled the six key variables necessary for winning in a two-party system. It had an attractive candidate for the presidency in Tilden; it had funding because of the swallow-tails' wealth; it had the organization through Kelly's Tammany Hall and Tilden's experience; it controlled the issues; it was an integral part of a national organization with affiliations across sectional and regional lines; and its ideology made sense in practical terms.

As the New York Democracy prepared for the Centennial Year of 1876 and beyond, the reconstructed party stressed four basic themes — machine politics, Bourbon Democracy, the validity of traditional principles, and continuities in customary Democratic issues. As an organization of remarkable durability and consistency, the party had survived the crises of sectional disruption, war, and reunion. Now, it emerged in the mid-1870s stronger than it had been since Martin Van Buren's heyday. As such, however, the Democracy keyed to the ideology and issues of the past, which now became the party's goals for the future. Jacksonian programs and beliefs were all interrelated aspects of where the party had been and where it hoped to go.

The Democracy's treatment of blacks and the party's willingness to fuse with discontented Republicans, however, raise a vital question concerning whether Democratic principles were a convenience to mask expediency or a genuine reflection of ideology. Looking at the history of the Democracy during the period from 1861 to 1874 and beyond, commentators have often described the party's policy-making as depending upon manipulating voters, raising false issues to the exclusion of real ones, and exhibiting a dreary pattern of opportunism. These charges are true in a limited sense. Democrats did play the politics of expediency, but they nevertheless drew a distinction between temporary contrivances and universal principles.

Seen in that light, Democratic politics and behavior was the art of the possible; an art where principles set the bounds of partisan activity; an art where expediency was acceptable provided it did not negate doctrine; an art where politicians compromised differences without destroying ideals. Like any political organism, the Democracy was and would be limited by ambiguity, inconsistency, and selfishness. Even more deceptive at times, Democrats failed to distinguish between principle and expediency, and the two often blended into a force with a life of its own, a life that confused voters and often worked counter to party ideology. But in the long run, one remarkable fact about the Democratic party stands clear. Democrats, despite all their faults, had an ideology which played a key role in legitimatizing the party's activities and laid down basic principles of governmental behavior and individual rights. As a result, the party followed a consistent pattern of beliefs and values that stretched from the time of Thomas Jefferson through Andrew Jackson and well into the Twentieth Century.

Under those conditions, the party's reconstruction during the period from 1861 to 1874 did not mark a dividing line in politics, or a break with the past. While the Democracy faced new and continual problems after 1874, it dealt with them in the context of Tilden's speech at the Manhattan Club. Thus, the New York Democracy's experiences during the Civil War and Reconstruction confirmed the strength and resiliency of its basic commitments and organization, not its weaknesses.

Abbreviations in Notes

AHR	*American Historical Review*
ALQ	*Abraham Lincoln Quarterly*
APSR	*American Political Science Review*
CU	Columbia University
CWH	*Civil War History*
HSP	Historical Society of Pennsylvania
JAH	*Journal of American History*
JAS	*Journal of American Studies*
JNH	*Journal of Negro History*
JSH	*Journal of Southern History*
LC	Library of Congress
MHS	Massachusetts Historical Society
MVHR	*Mississippi Valley Historical Review*
NYH	*New York History*
NYHS	New-York Historical Society
NYHSQ	*New-York Historical Society Quarterly*
NYPL	New York Public Library
NYSL	New York State Library
OAHQ	*Ohio Archeological and Historical Quarterly*
OHS	Ohio State Historical Society
PMH	*Pennsylvania Magazine of History*
PSQ	*Political Science Quarterly*
SAQ	*South Atlantic Quarterly*
SU	Syracuse University
UR	University of Rochester

Notes

1. PARTIES IN TRANSITION

1. Daniel S. Dickinson to Thomas A. Olcott, November 17, 1860, Thomas A. Olcott Papers, CU.

2. New York *Herald,* June 10, 1874; Matthew Breen, *Thirty Years of New York Politics Up-To-Date* (New York: Published by the Author, 1899); Gustavus Myers, *The History of Tammany Hall* (New York: Boni & Liveright, 1917); Eric Foner, *Free Soil, Free Labor, Free Men: The Ideology of the Republican Party before the Civil War* (New York: Oxford University Press, 1970); Judah Ginsberg, "Barnburners, Free Soil, and the Republican party," NYH 52 (October 1976): 475-500.

3. William Trimble, "The Social Philosophy of the Loco-Foco Democracy," *The American Journal of Sociology* 26 (May 1921): 705-21; Max Mintz, "Political Ideas of Martin Van Buren," NYH 30 (October 1949): 422-45; Eric Foner, "Racial Assumptions of the New York Free Soilers," NYH 46 (October 1965): 311-29; Robert Kelley, *The Transatlantic Persuasion: The Liberal-Democratic Mind in the Age of Gladstone* (New York: Knopf, 1969); Edward Spann, *Ideals and Politics: New York Intellectuals and the Liberal Democracy, 1820-1880* (Albany: State University of New York Press, 1972).

4. Horatio Seymour to Samuel Barlow, May 15, June 8, 1860, Fairchild Collection, NYHS; Barlow to Erastus Corning, May 19, Edwin Croswell to Corning, May 19, Augustus Schell to Corning, June 28, August 1, August Belmont to Corning, August 1, Erastus Corning Papers, Albany Institute of History and Art; George Sanders to Stephen A. Douglas, May 20, Francis Cutting to Douglas, June 11, Gideon Tucker to Douglas, June 29, 1860, Stephen A. Douglas Papers, University of Chicago; Dickinson to James Buchanan, June 30, 1860, James Buchanan Papers, HSP; James Brady to Samuel Barlow, September 20, 1860, Samuel L. M. Barlow Papers, The Henry E. Huntington Library; *HeRAld,* November 10, 16, 1860; Milledge Bonham, Jr., "New York and the Election of 1860," NYH 15 (April 1934): 124-43; Edward J. Miles, "New York Politics, 1860-1879," in *Richards' Atlas of New York State,* ed. Robert J. Rayback (Phoenix, N.Y.: Frank E. Richards, 1958), p. 37.

5. James Bayard to Barlow, November 29, Judah Benjamin to Barlow, December 9, 21, 23, 1860, Barlow Papers; New York *Daily News,* December 15, 20, 1860, March 21, April 1, 1861; *Herald,* January 8, 9, 1861; New York *Irish-American,* January 19, February 26, 1861; New York *Leader,*

April 13, 1861; James Heslin, " 'Peaceful Compromise' in New York City, 1860-1861," NYHSQ 44 (October 1961): 349-52.

6. *Proceedings of the Democratic State Convention* (Albany, 1861); Joel Silbey, "Parties and Politics in Mid-Nineteenth Century America," *Capital Studies* 1 (Fall 1972): 9-27; Joel Silbey, *A Respectable Minority: The Democratic Party in the Civil War Era, 1860-1868* (New York: W. W. Norton & Co., 1977), pp. 20-48.

7. Moses Grinnell to Lincoln, April 15, Democratic Republican General Committee to Lincoln, April 26, Fernando Wood to Lincoln, April 29, 1861, Robert Todd Lincoln Papers, LC; Buchanan to Dix, April 19, 1861, John A. Dix Papers, CU; *Leader,* April 27, May 4, August 17, 1861; John Stevens, *The Union Defense Committee of the City of New York* (New York: Published by the Committee, 1885), pp. 1-38.

8. *Leader,* April 13, May 18, June 8, 1861; *Daily News,* April 15, 16, 1861; *Journal of Commerce,* April 18, 1861; *Irish-American,* April 20, 1861; John Hardy to Lincoln, April 30, Edwin Morgan to Lincoln, May 13, 1861, Lincoln Papers; John Hubbell, "The Northern Democracy and Party Survival, 1860-1861," *Illinois Quarterly* 36 (September 1973): 22-33.

9. *Albany Argus,* April 15, 19, 30, May 21, 22, 29, June 24, 1861.

10. Albany *Evening Journal,* November 26, 30, December 14, 17, 1860; Thurlow Weed to Morgan, February 11, March 4, April 29, 1861, Edwin D. Morgan Papers, NYSL; Preston King to Lincoln, April 22, 1861, Lincoln Papers; Glyndon G. Van Dusen, *Thurlow Weed: The Wizard of the Lobby* (Boston: Little Brown and Co., 1947), pp. 189-272.

11. New York *Times,* April 13, 21, 24, July 24, September 3, 7, 1861; *Evening Journal,* April 17, 24, September 2, 1861; New York *Evening Post,* April 15, September 2, 1861; David Dudley Field to Lincoln, April 23, King to Lincoln, May 2, 1861, Lincoln Papers; Charles Brown, *William Cullen Bryant* (New York: Charles Scribner's Sons, 1971), pp. 426-38.

12. New York *Tribune,* August 6, 7, 1861; *Times,* August 7, 1861; *Evening Post,* September 2, 1861; Silbey, *Respectable Minority,* p. 57.

13. *Argus,* May 21, 29, September 13, 30, 1861; *Leader,* June 15, July 20, August 10, 1861; *Herald,* August 9, 1861; Weed to Lincoln, August 18, 1861, Lincoln Papers; Weed to Morgan, September 29, 1861, Morgan Papers.

14. Benjamin Wood to Lincoln, August 1, 1861, Lincoln Papers; *Daily News*, September 3, 11, 1861; Richard Curry, " 'The Union As It Was': A Critique of Recent Interpretations of the Copperheads," CWH 13 (March 1967); 23-39.

15. *Times,* August 10, 12, 13, 20, 1861; *Tribune,* August 17, 1861; Samuel Pleasants, *Fernando Wood of New York* (New York: Columbia University Press, 1948), pp. 11-12, 25-101; Frank Klement, *The Copperheads in the Middle West* (Chicago: University of Chicago Press, 1960), pp. 1-132; Robert Rayback, "New York State in the Civil War," NYH 42 (January 1962): 56-70; Robert Azbug, "The Copperheads: Historical Approaches to Civil War Dissent," *Indiana Magazine of History* 66 (March 1970): 40-55; Silbey, *Respectable Minority,* pp. 89-114.

16. Isaac Sherman to Weed, September 8, 1861, Thurlow Weed Papers, UR; *Herald*, September 11, 12, 1861; *Evening Post*, September 12, 1861; *Argus*, September 18, 1861.

17. *Times*, August 16, 1861; *Herald*, September 5, 6, 8, 20, 21, 1861; *Argus*, September 6, 7, 1861; *Leader*, September 12, 21, 1861; James Brooks to Caleb Cushing, September 15, 1861, Caleb Cushing Papers, LC; Sidney Brummer, *Political History of New York State during the Period of the Civil War* (New York: Columbia University Press, 1911), pp. 154-59; Silbey, *Respectable Minority*, pp. 89-114.

18. *Argus*, August 12, September 4, 14, 17, 21, November 4, 1861; *Evening Journal*, August 30, 1861; *Herald*, September 9, 1861; *Leader*, September 21, 1861.

19. *Herald*, October 31, November 4, 8, 1861; *Leader*, November 2, 9, 1861; Dix to Tilden, December 3, 1861, Samuel J. Tilden Papers, NYPL; Croswell to Dix, December 13, 1861, Dix Papers.

20. William Havemeyer to Dix, November 8, 23, 1861, Dix Papers; *Leader*, November 16, December 4, 14, 23, 1861; Fernando Wood to William Seward, November 27, 1861, Fernando Wood Papers, NYPL; Wood to Cushing, November 29, 1861, Cushing Papers; *Irish-American*, November 30, 1861; John Develin to Weed, December 3, 1861, Weed Papers.

21. Ward to Barlow, March 16, 18, 22, April 27, May 3, June 27, Barlow to Ward, April 29, 1862, Barlow Papers; Lately Thomas, *Sam Ward "King of the Lobby"* (Boston: Houghton Mifflin Co., 1965), pp. 234-305.

22. Belmont to Barlow, February 10, April 22, Barlow to Frank Blair, April 24, 1862, Barlow Papers; Belmont to Weed, July 20, 26, 1862, William H. Seward Papers, UR; Lincoln to Belmont, July 31, 1862, Lincoln Papers; Irving Katz, *August Belmont: A Political Biography* (New York: Columbia University Press, 1968), pp. 108-12.

23. Wood to Lincoln, January 15, August 20, Van Evie, Horton and Company to Lincoln, January 23, 1862, Lincoln Papers; *Leader*, January 18, 1862; New York *Caucasian*, January 23, 1862; *Herald*, January 25, 1862; Barlow to Seymour, March 8, 1862, Fairchild Collection.

24. Henry Raymond to James Wadsworth, February 9, 1862, Wadsworth Family Papers, UR; *Argus*, March 8, 24, 28, May 22, 1862; *Tribune*, April 29, 1862; Raymond to Lincoln, May 16, 1862, Lincoln Papers; Brummer, *Political History*, pp. 179-200.

25. Ward to Barlow, April 29, May 3, 1862, Barlow Papers; John Hamilton to Samuel Cox, May 8, 1862, Samuel S. Cox Papers, OHS: Ketchum to Lincoln, May 16, Alexander Stewart to Lincoln, May 21, 1862, Lincoln Papers; *Irish-American*, May 24, 1862; *Leader*, May 24, 1862.

26. Barlow to William Prime, June 23, Barlow to Henry Wadsworth, June 26, 1862, Barlow Papers; *Journal of Commerce*, June 26, 1862; *Times*, July 2, 1862; *Herald*, July 2, 1862; *Leader*, July 5, 26, 1862; *Tammany Society or Columbian Order, Annual Celebration, July 4, 1862* (New York: 1862).

27. Washington Hunt to Morgan, July 13, 1862, Morgan Papers; Sidney Gay to Lincoln, July 30, Ira Harris to Lincoln, October 2, 1862, Lincoln Papers; Weed to Seward, August 23, 1862, Seward Papers; *Journal of Commerce*, August 8, 1862; *Evening Journal*, September 23, October 10, 1862; Butterworth to Barlow, September 23, 1862, Barlow Papers; *Tribune*,

September 23, 1862; *Evening Post,* September 24, October 1, 1862; *Times,* September 30, 1862.

28. Cassidy to Tilden, October 1860, Tilden Papers; Belmont to Barlow, May 24, October 1, Cassidy to Barlow, March 14, 1862, Barlow to Calvert Comstock, June 23, 1863, Barlow Papers; Comstock to Manton Marble, January 23, 1863, Manton Marble Papers, LC; George McJimsey, *Genteel Partisan: Manton Marble, 1834-1917* (Ames, Ia.: Iowa State University Press, 1971), pp. 3-37.

29. *Journal of Commerce,* September 23, 1862; *Argus,* September 24, October 14, 1862; *World,* September 24, 1862; *Herald,* September 30, 1862.

30. Edwards Pierrepont to Dix, September 5, 1862, Dix Papers; Wadsworth to Greeley, September 14, Raymond to Wadsworth, October 4, 1862, Wadsworth Papers; Belmont to Barlow, September 27, 1862, Barlow Papers; Dix to Weed, September 27, Weed to Seward, September 30, Charles Cooke to Weed, October 3, 1862, Weed Papers; Dickinson to John Spencer, October 6, 1862, *The Speeches, Correspondence, Etc. of the Late Daniel S. Dickinson,* ed. John Dickinson, 2 vols. (New York: G. P. Putnam & Sons, 1867), 2: 588.

31. Stevens to Connolly, January 20, 1863, Seymour Papers, NYSL.

32. Prime to Richard Lathers, August 20, 1862, *Reminiscences of Richard Lathers,* ed. Alvan Sanborn (New York: Grafton Press, 1907), pp. 117-18; Tilden to Dix, August 28, Dix to Tilden, September 9, 1862, Tilden Papers; *Tribune,* September 16, 1862; *Evening Journal,* September 26, October 3, 7, 14, 1862; *Times,* October 7, 14, 1862; *Evening Post,* October 23, November 3, 1862.

33. *Herald,* October 4, 5, 19, 1862; *Argus,* October 7, 18, 1862; *World* October 7, 1862; *Daily News,* October 9, 10, 1862; *Journal of Commerce,* October 16, 24, 1862; *Irish American,* November 1, 1862; *Leader,* November 15, 22, 1862.

34. Belmont to Marble, October 2, 1862, Marble Papers; Belmont to Barlow, October 12, 1862, Barlow Papers; Richmond to Corning, October 20, 1862, Corning Papers; Bryant to Lincoln, October 22, 1862, Lincoln Papers; Greeley to Gerrit Smith, October 21, 1862, Gerrit Smith Papers, SU.

35. Weed to Seward, November 5, 1862, Seward Papers; *Evening Journal,* November 5, 8, 1862; *Evening Post,* November 5, 7, 1862; William Allen to Francis Kernan, November 6, 1862; Kernan Family Papers, Cornell University; Field to Lincoln, November 8, Dickinson to Lincoln, November 9, 1862, Lincoln Papers; Seymour to Marble, November 11, 1862, Marble Papers.

36. Arthur Bestor, "The American Civil War as a Constitutional Crisis," AHR 59 (January 1964): 327-52; Leonard Curry, "Congressional Democrats, 1861-1863," CWH 12 (September 1966): 213-19; David Montgomery, *Beyond Equality: Labor and the Radical Republicans, 1862-1872* (New York: Alfred A. Knopf, 1967), pp. 45-89; Leonard Curry, *Blueprint for Modern America: Nonmilitary Legislation of the First Civil War Congress* (Nashville, Tenn.: Vanderbilt University Press, 1968); James Rawley, *The Politics of Union* (Hinsdale, Ill.: The Dryden Press, 1973) pp. 57-118; William Barney, *Flawed Victory* (New York: Praeger Publishers, 1975), pp. 158-95; Silbey, *Respectable Minority,* pp. 62-88.

37. Weed to Seward, January 1, 1863, Seward Papers; *Argus,* January 3, 7, 8, 1863; James Randall, *Lincoln the President, Mainstream* (New York: Dodd, Mead & Co., 1953, pp. 292-93.

38. Lincoln to Weed, January 29, Weed to Lincoln, February 1, 1863, Lincoln Papers; King to Morgan, February 14, 1863, Morgan Papers.

39. *Leader,* February 21, March 14, 28, 1863; Raymond to Seward, March 24, 1863, Seward Papers; William Hamilton to Montgomery Blair, March 30, May 2, 1863, Blair Family Papers, LC.

40. *Herald,* February 15, 1863; Tilden to John Taylor, February 26, 1863, Tilden Papers; Charles Murphy, "Samuel J. Tilden and the Civil War," *South Atlantic Quarterly* 33 (July 1934): 261-271; Frank Freidel, "The Loyal Publication Society: A Pro-Union Propaganda Agency," MVHR 26 (September 1939): 359-76; Basil Leo Lee, *Discontent in New York City* (Washington: Catholic University Press, 1943), pp. 231-32.

41. *Tribune,* March 11, April 8, 1863; *Evening Post,* March 14, 1863; *Leader,* April 4, 1863; Christopher Dell, *Lincoln and the War Democrats* (Rutherford, N.J.: Fairleigh Dickinson Press, 1975), pp. 20-26.

42. *Argus,* May 10, June 4, 15, 1863; John Trimble to Samuel Medary, May 12, 1863, Trimble Papers, OHS; Vallandingham to Marble, May 12, 15, 21, Cox to Marble, June 1, 1863, Marble Papers; Kenneth Bernard, "Lincoln and Civil Liberties," ALQ 6 (September 1951): 359-99.

43. *Argus,* May 26, 27, 28, 1863; *Herald,* June 1, 4, 1863; *Leader,* June 6, 23, 1863; Barnett to Barlow, June 6, 10, 1863, Barlow Papers.

44. Purdy to Seymour, June 26, Opdyke to Seymour, June 30, 1863, Seymour Papers; *Daily News,* June 25, July 8, 11, 13, 1863; Williston Lofton, "Northern Labor and the Negro During the Civil War," JNH 34 (1949): 251-73; Eugene Murdock, "Horatio Seymour and the 1863 Draft," CWH 11 (June 1965): 117-41; Adrian Cooke, *Armies in the Street* (Lexington, Ky.: The University of Kentucky Press, 1974).

45. *World,* July 14, 16, 1863; *Herald,* July 15, 24, 1863; *Times,* July 15, 16, 1863; *Tribune,* July 16, 18, 1863; *Irish-American,* July 18, 25, 1863; *Leader,* August 1, 1863; Seymour to Tilden, August 6, 1863, Seymour Papers; Seymour to Dix, August 7, 1863, Dix Papers.

46. Cooke to Weed, September 3, King to Weed, September 9, 11, 1863, Weed Papers; *Herald,* September 4, 12, 1863; *Argus,* September 4, 5, 10, 1863.

47. *Leader,* September 5, 12, 19, 1863; *Argus,* September 11, 19, 1863; Seymour to Marble, September 17, 1863, Marble Papers.

48. *Herald,* October 6, 8, 9, 10, 13, 15, 1863.

49. Halpine to Dix, October 20, November, Stanton to Dix, November 9, 1863, Dix Papers; *Herald,* November 4, 5, 1863; *Times,* November 12, 16, December 3, 6, 1863; Barnard to Marble, November 18, 1863, Marble Papers; *Irish-American,* December 2, 1863.

50. *World,* November 5, 21, 1863; Marble to McClellan, November 16, 1863, George B. McClellan Papers, LC; McClellan to Barlow, November 28, Barlow to Blair, December 23, Blair to Barlow, December 25, 29, 1863, Barlow Papers; Marble to Wall, March 30, 1864, Marble Papers.

51. *Herald,* December 16, 1863; *Leader,* January 2, 9, 23, 1864; Jerome Mushkat, *Tammany: The Evolution of a Political Machine* (Syracuse, N.Y.: Syracuse University Press, 1971), pp. 355-56.

52. *Leader,* February 20, 27, March 5, 1864; Cassidy to Marble, February 22, 1864, Marble Papers; *Herald,* February 25, 1864; *Argus,* February 25, 1864.

53. Weed to Morgan, January 19, May 27, 1864, Morgan Papers; Raymond to Lincoln, March 10, Lincoln to Weed, March 25, Weed to Lincoln, March 25, Weed to Davis, March 30, April 11, 1864, Lincoln Papers; Kelly to Weed, March 23, 1864, Weed Papers; Louis Gerteis, "Salmon P. Chase, Radicalism, and the Politics of Emancipation," JAH 60 (June 1973): 42-62.

54. *Evening Post,* June 3, 4, 10, 13, 1864; *Evening Journal,* June 11, 18, 25, 28, 1864; Greeley to Morgan, June 15, 1864, Morgan Papers; Greeley to Lincoln, July 7, August 8, 9, Raymond to Lincoln, August 22, 1864, Lincoln Papers; Raymond to Seward, August 5, 1864, Seward Papers; James Gloneck, "Lincoln, Johnson, and the Baltimore Ticket," ALQ 6 (March 1951): 255-71.

55. Blair to Barlow, April 28, May 1, 4, 11, 27, 1864, Barlow Papers.

56. Barlow to Blair, April 29, May 10, 1864, Blair Papers.

57. Barlow to McClellan, May 18, 1864, McClellan Papers; Parker to Marble, May 22, 1864, Marble Papers; Pruyn to Barlow, May 23, Barnett to Barlow, May 24, 1864, Barlow Papers.

58. Blair to Lincoln, August 10, 1864, Lincoln Papers; *Evening Journal,* August 13, 1864; Davidson to Corning, August 13, 1864, Corning Papers; *Evening Post,* August 13, 14, 1864; Weed to Seward, August 22, 1864, Seward Papers; William Zornow, *Lincoln and the Party Divided* (Norman, Okla.: The University of Oklahoma Press, 1954), pp. 105-18.

59. Long to Boys, May 1, 25, August 9, 1864, Alexander S. Boys Papers, OHS; Philo White to Long, June 10, 1864, Alexander Long Papers, Cincinnati Historical Society; Richmond to Marble, June 16, Cox to Marble, August 9, 1864, Marble Papers; Mayo Fesler, "Secret Political Societies in the North During the Civil War," *Indiana Magazine of History* 14 (1918): 183-286.

60. *Herald,* March 13, August 6, 17, 19, 22, 1864; Wood to Lincoln, April 29, October 9, 1864, Lincoln Papers; Barnett to Barlow, June 17, Ward to Barlow, July, 1864, Barlow Papers; *Times,* July 16, 1864; Delevan to Corning, July 16, 1864, Corning Papers.

61. *Argus,* August 18, 20, 1864; Silbey, *Respectable Minority,* pp. 116-17.

62. *Leader,* March 19, 1864; Barlow to McClellan, June 18, 1864, McClellan Papers; Cassidy to Marble, May 21, June 25, 26, 1864, Marble Papers; *Daily Courier,* May 31, June 17, 27, July 2, 12, 21, 22, 27, August 1, 2, 29, 1864; *World,* July 7, August 1, 1864.

63. Pruyn to Marble, June 15, 1864, Marble Papers; A. Oakey Hall to Barlow, June 16, Wood to Barlow, June 16, Pruyn to Barlow, June 18, 1864, Barlow Papers; Vallandingham to Long, June 17, 1864, Long Papers; Pruyn to McClellan, June 19, 1864, McClellan Papers; *World,* August 29, 1864.

64. Barlow to Marble, August 21, 24, 1864, Marble Papers; Belmont to Blair, August 29, 1864, Barlow Papers; Noah Brooks to Lincoln, August 29, 1864, Lincoln Papers.

65. Delevan to McClellan, September 1, Belmont to McClellan, September 3, Barlow to McClellan, September 3, 1864, McClellan Papers; Cassidy to Barlow, September 5, 1864, Barlow Papers; Charles Wilson, "McClellan's Changing View of the Peace Plank of 1864," AHR 38 (April 1933): 498-505; Silbey, *Respectable Minority,* pp. 118-39.

66. *Tribune,* September 5, 1864; *Daily Courier,* September 7, 1864.

67. *Daily News,* September 9, 12, 15, 1864; *Daily Courier,* September 12, 17, 1864; Barlow to McClellan, September 14, 1864, McClellan Papers; *Herald,* September 15, 1864; Harriet Owsley, "Peace and the Presidential Election of 1864," *Tennessee Historical Quarterly* 18 (March 1959): 3-19.

68. *Herald,* September 14, 1864; *Leader,* September 17, 1864.

69. *Tribune,* August 30, September 5, 8, 9, 11, 12, 16, 1864; Weed to Seward, September 10, 30, 1864, Seward Papers; *Commercial Advertiser,* September 17, 1864.

70. Barlow to Richmond, September 13, 1864, Barlow Papers; *Argus,* September 15, 16, 1864; Parker to McClellan, September 16, 1864, McClellan Papers.

71. *Argus,* September 15, 16, 17, 1864; Cassidy to Barlow, September 23, 1864, Barlow Papers; Barlow to McClellan, October 1864, McClellan Papers; Blatchford to Seward, October 1, 1864, Seward Papers; Oscar Winter, "The Soldier Vote in the Election of 1864," NYH 25 (October 1944): 440-58.

72. *Argus,* September 8, 30, October 28, 29, 1864; New York *Weekly Day-Book,* October 1, 1864; Cagger to Barlow, October 3, Pratt to Barlow, October 6, 1864, Barlow Papers; *World,* October 3, 4, 10, 14, 1864; Hunt to Marble, October 7, 1864, Marble Papers; Sidney Kaplan, "The Miscegenation Issue in the Election of 1864," JNH 34 (July 1949): 274-343.

73. Page to Lincoln, October 10, Forney to Lincoln, October 22, 1864, Lincoln Papers; *Herald,* October 21, 28, 29, 1864; *Daily News,* November 1, 2, 1864.

74. *Herald,* November 6, 7, 8, 10, 12, 1864; *Leader,* November 12, 1864; Silbey, *Respectable Minority,* pp. 154-57.

75. Barlow to McClellan, November 9, 1864, McClellan Papers; Bogart to Marble, November 10, 1864, Marble Papers; Blunt to Lincoln, November 11, 1864, Lincoln Papers; Bayard to Barlow, November 12, 1864, Barlow Papers; *Argus,* November 12, 27, 1864; *Daily Courier,* November 30, 1864; Louis Merrill, "General Benjamin Franklin Butler in the Presidential Campaign of 1864," MVHR 33 (March 1948): 537-70.

76. *World,* November 13, 21, 22, 23, 24, 1864; *Times,* November 17, 25, 1864; *Evening Post,* November 20, 21, 28, 29, 1864.

77. *Daily News,* November 3, 10, 12, 15, December 8, 9, 1864; *Herald,* November 9, 1864; *World,* November 9, 1864; *Tribune,* December 1, 1864; *Leader,* December 3, 10, 17, 24, 1864, January 7, February 18, 1865; Leo Hirsch, Jr., "The Negro and New York, 1783-1865," JNH 16 (October 1931): 383-454; P. J. Staudenhaus, "The Popular Origins of the Thirteenth Amendment," *Mid-America* 50 (April 1968): 108-15.

78. Cox to Marble, December 7, 1864, Marble Papers.

79. *Daily Courier,* December 3, 10, 1864; William Hartman, "Custom House Patronage under Lincoln," NYHSQ 41 (October 1957): 440-57; Elliott Barkan, "The Emergence of a Whig Persuasion: Conservatism, Democraticism, and the New York State Whigs," NYH 52 (October 1971): 367-95; James Mohr, *The Radical Republicans and Reform in New York during Reconstruction* (Ithaca, N.Y.: Cornell University Press,1973), pp. 15-20.

2. POLITICAL RESTORATION: 1864-1865

1. *Daily News,* December 12, 17, 19, 22, 1864, February 7, 14, 27, March 6, 20, 1865; *Tribune,* February 1, 1865; Cox to Marble, February 13, 1865, Marble Papers.

2. *Irish-American,* December 17, 1864, January 7, 14, April 1, 1865; *Daily Courier,* December 23, 1864; *Leader,* December 31, 1864, January 7, June 24, 1865.

3. *Leader,* December 3, 10, 1864, January 21, May 27, June 24, July 8, 1865; *Evening Post,* December 28, 1864; *Herald,* November 12, 1865.

4. *Daily Courier,* November 18, 1864, February 2, 7, 1865; Blair to Barlow, January 21, 1865, Barlow Papers; Richmond to Marble, January 23, Warren to Marble, March 23, 1865, Marble Papers; Bilbo to Lincoln, January 26, 1865, Lincoln Papers; *Argus,* February 22, 1865; LaWanda and John Cox, *Politics, Principle, and Prejudice* (New York: Atheneum Press, 1969), pp. 1-30.

5. *Daily News,* December 24, 1864, January 5, 12, February 10, 20, 28, 1865; Cox to Marble, January 13, 1865, Marble Papers; Munnsell to Long, January 16, 1865. Long Papers; Ling to Boys, February 12, 13, 1865, Boys Papers.

6. *Leader,* January 7, 14, 21, 1865.

7. Blair to Barlow, December 1864 or January 1865, January 7, 12, February 9, 1865, Barlow Papers; *Evening Post,* January 10, 17, 1865; Bancroft to Cox, January 28, 1865, *The Life and Letters of George Bancroft,* ed. Mark Anthony DeWolfe Howe, 2 vols. (New York: Charles Scribner's Sons, 1908), 2: 156-58.

8. Cox to Marble, December 21, 1864, January 18, 21, February 13, 1865, Marble Papers; *World,* December 21, 1864, January 9, 10, 13, 17, 20, 23, 1865; Schell to Seward, January 23, 1865, Seward Papers; Blair to Barlow, February 14, 1865, Barlow Papers; Cox and Cox, *Politics,* pp. 18-26.

9. Pruyn to Corning, January 6, 1865, Corning Papers; *Daily News,* February 2, 1865; *World,* February 2, 3, 15, 21, 1865; *Daily Courier,* February 11, 1865; *Leader,* February 4, 18, March 4, 1865; *Herald,* March 1, 3, 1865.

10. *Herald,* May 3, 1865; *Leader,* May 6, 1865; *Irish-American,* July 29, August 9, 1865.

11. *Evening Post,* January 11, 17, February 1, 13, 18, 23, March 1, April 8, 1865.

12. *Herald,* January 2, 10, 24, February 3, 1865; *Evening Post,* January 6, 24, February 20, 1865; *Tribune,* January 23, 25, February 12, 1865; Weed to Morgan, February 3, Greeley to Morgan, February 26, 1865, Morgan Papers; *Times,* February 8, 13, 20, March 25, 1865; Glyndon G. Van Dusen,

William Henry Seward (New York: Oxford University Press, 1967), pp. 421-31; James Mohr, "New York: The Depoliticization of Reform," *Radical Republicans in the North,* ed. James Mohr (Baltimore: Johns Hopkins Press, 1976), pp. 66-68.

13. *World,* January 7, 26, February 9, 28, March 11, 15, 18, April 5, 6, 1865; *Leader,* January 7, February 25, 1865; Bogart to Marble, January 24, 1865, Marble Papers; *Argus,* March 23, 1865; *Daily Courier,* March 28, 1865.

14. *World,* April 3, 5, 6, 16, 1865; Richard Calhoun, "New York City Fire Department Reorganization," NYHSQ 66 (January/April 1976): 7-34.

15. *Daily Courier,* January 30, April 6, 1865; *World,* February 24, March 17, April 8, 1865; *Leader,* April 8, 1865; *Irish-American,* April 8, 1865; *Herald,* April 12, 1865; *Daily News,* April 14, 1865.

16. *World,* March 6, 9, 1865; *Daily News,* March 6, 7, 1865; *Irish-American,* March 11, 1865; *Leader,* March 11, 18, 1865; Albert Castel, "Andrew Johnson: His Historiographical Rise and Fall," *Mid-America* 45 (July 1963): 175-84.

17. Barlow to Blair, April 15, Ganson to Blair, April 17, Blair to Barlow, April 18, 1865, Blair Papers; Comstock to Weed, April 17, 1865, Weed Papers; *Daily Courier,* April 17, 18, 1865; *World,* April 18, 1865.

18. *Leader,* April 22, 1865.

19. Walbridge to Johnson, April 15, Dickinson to Johnson, April 17, 1865, Andrew Johnson Papers, LC; *Herald,* April 16, 17, 18, 20, 27, 1865; *Evening Post,* April 18, 25, 1865; Brooks to Blair, April 19, 1865, Blair Papers; *Daily Courier,* April 19, 23, 1865; *Argus,* April 24, 1865.

20. Blair to Barlow, April 28, 1865, Barlow Papers; Campbell to Weed, May 1, 1865, Weed Papers; *Leader,* May 6, 1865; John Dash Van Buren to Franklin Pierce, July 17, 1865, Pierce Microfilms; *World,* July 18, 1865; Barlow to Blair, July 24, 1865, Johnson Papers.

21. Ganson to Marble, March 4, 1865, Marble Papers; *World,* May 1, 2, 6, 1865; Blair to Barlow, May 13, Barlow to Blair, June 15, July 19, 24, 1865, Johnson Papers; *Argus,* May 19, 1865.

22. *Herald,* June 4, 1865; Blair to Barlow, June 15, 21, July 24, 1865, Barlow Papers; Blair to Johnson, June 16, Barlow to Blair, July 24, Barlow to Pratt, August 7, 1865, Johnson Papers; *Irish-American,* July 22, 1865; *Leader,* August 26, 1865.

23. *Evening Post,* June 12, 1865.

24. *Herald,* May 3, 6, 1865; *Evening Post,* May 12, 13, 1865.

25. *World,* March 18, May 3, 4, 1865; *Express,* May 3, 1865; Cox to Blair, May 16, 1865, Blair Papers; *Evening Post,* May 25, 1865; *Daily Courier,* May 26, 1865.

26. John Dash Van Buren to Blair, May 13, 1865, Blair Papers. John Van Buren died in 1866.

27. LaWanda and John H. Cox, "Nego Suffrage and Republican Politics: The Problem of Motivation in Reconstruction Historiography," JSH 33 (August 1967): 303-30; Phyllis F. Field, "Republicans and Black Suffrage in New York: The Grass Roots Response," CWH 21 (June 1975): 136-47; Herman Belz, *A New Birth of Freedom: The Republican Party and Freedmen's Rights, 1861-1866* (Westport, Conn.: Greenwood Press, 1976).

28. *Irish-American,* June 24, August 19, 1865; *World,* July 1, 26, August 3, 7, 10, September 5, December 20, 1865; *Daily News,* July 6, 11, 21, August 25, September 5, 1865; *Daily Courier,* July 7, 13, 14, August 10, 1865; *Argus,* October 10, 1865.

29. *World,* May 29, 30, 31, June 5, July 10, 1865; *Argus,* May 31, June 2, 1865; Coltman to Johnson, June 5, 1865, Johnson Papers; Jonathan Dorris, "Pardoning the Leaders of the Confederacy," MVHR 15 (June 1928): 3-21; Herman Belz, *Reconstructing the Union* (Ithaca, N.Y.: Cornell University Press, 1969), pp. 277-311.

30. *Evening Post,* May 30, 1865; *Tribune,* May 30, June 4, 1865; Carl Schurz to Johnson, June 6, 1865, Johnson Papers; Ewing to Greeley, June 9, 1865, Greeley Papers, LC; *Times,* June 6, 19, 21, 26, 1865; *Evening Journal,* June 26, 1865.

31. *Herald,* May 24, 27, 30, June 1, 4, 8, 11, 12, 29, July 3, 13, 19, August 14, 18, 19, 1865; Blair to Barlow, July 14, 1865, Barlow Papers; Bennett to Johnson, August 26, Johnson to Bennett, October 6, 1865, Johnson Papers; Marguerite Albjerg, "The New York *Herald* As a Factor in Reconstruction," SAQ 46 (1947): 204-11.

32. Mason to Black, June 14, Blair to Black, August 5, O'Conor to Black, September 25, 1865, Jeremiah Black Papers, LC; Barlow to Blair, June 15, July 24, Barlow to Pratt, August 21, Blair to Johnson, September 12, 1865, Johnson Papers; Blair to Barlow, July 8, 14, 16, 21, August 11, 15, 22, September 11, Barlow to Pratt, August 11, Pratt to Barlow, August 16, Cox to Barlow, August 18, 1865, Barlow Papers; Barlow to Tilden, August 31, 1865, Tilden Papers; Cox and Cox, *Politics,* pp. 68-67.

33. *Leader,* June 10, 17, July 15, 1865; *Herald,* July 11, 21, 31, August 3, 6, 1865.

34. *Leader,* June 10, July 22, 1865; Vallandingham to Long, June 11, 1865, Long Papers; *Daily News,* June 13, 16, 23, 28, 1865; *World,* July 27, August 19, 1865; Ben Wood to Florence, September 27, 1865, Johnson Papers.

35. *Herald,* July 28, 1865; Barlow to Blair, September 11, 1865, Johnson Papers; Weed to Seward, September 23, 30, 1865, Johnson Papers.

36. Dix to Johnson, July 1, Crosswell to Johnson, August 10, Dickinson to Johnson, August 19, 1865, Johnson Papers; Sickles to Seward, August 26, 1865, Seward Papers; Barlow to Morgan, September 11, 1865, Morgan Papers.

37. *World,* September 1, 6, 7, 10, 14, 1865; *Daily Courier,* September 7, 8, 9, 1865.

38. *Herald,* September 5, 7, 8, 9, 10, 12, 1865; *Daily News,* September 7, 12, 1865; *Tribune,* September 9, 1865.

39. Shipman to Johnson, September 8, Barlow to Blair, September 11, 1865, Johnson Papers; Barlow to Shipman, September 11, Barlow to Pratt, September 11, Blair to Barlow, September 13, 1865, Barlow Papers.

40. *Evening Post,* September 14, 18, 20, 21, 1865; Weed to Morgan, September 18, 1865, Morgan Papers; *Tribune,* September 20, 21, 22, 1865; *Times,* September 20, 22, 1865; Weed to Seward, September 23, 30, 1865, Seward Papers.

41. Blair to Barlow, September 15, Shipman to Barlow, September 24, 1865, Barlow Papers; *World*, September 25, 29, October 2, 4, 5, 1865; *Daily Courier*, September 29, October 4, 1865; *Leader*, September 30, October 7, 1865; *Argus*, October 2, 20, 1865.

42. *Herald*, September 22, 28, 30, October 4, 6, 1865.

43. *Times*, September 30, October 3, 10, 15, 18, November 2, 3, 1865; *Herald*, October 2, 7, 9, 11, 30, 31 1865; *Evening Post*, October 3, 12, 16, 21, 23, 1865; *Tribune*, October 7, 18, 23, November 4, 1865; Eric McKitrick, *Andrew Johnson and Reconstruction* (Chicago: The University of Chicago Press, 1960), pp. 15-213.

44. Richmond to Tilden, October 2, 1865, Tilden Papers; Barlow to Houston, October 3, 28, Blair to Barlow, October 6, Barlow to Blair, October 6, 14, Barlow to Taylor, October 21, Shipman to Barlow, October 23, Barlow to Shipman, October 24, Houston to Barlow, November 1, 1865, Barlow Papers; *Evening Post*, October 4, 1865; *Argus*, October 15, 24, 1865; *Leader*, October 21, 1865.

45. *Herald*, October 2, 9, 10, 15, November 3, 1865; *Daily News*, October 17, 19, 1865; *Leader*, October 21, 28, 1865.

46. *Leader*, September 30, November 4, 1865; *Daily Courier*, October 6, 1865; *Irish-American*, October 7, 14, November 4, 1865; *World*, October 14, 17, 19, 1865; *Daily News*, November 2, 1865; *Herald*, November 6, 1865.

47. Weed to Seward, November 8, 1865, Seward Papers; *World*, November 8, 10, 14, 1865.

48. Kelly to Seward, November 8, Weed to Seward, November 11, 14, 1865, Seward Papers; *Times*, November 8, 10, 13, 14, 20, December 2, 7, 30, 1865; *Tribune*, November 9, 12, 26, 1865; Weed to Morgan, December 17, 1865, Morgan Papers.

49. Barlow to Blair, November 8, 13, December 21, Blair to Barlow, November 12, 18, 1865, Barlow Papers.

50. *Argus*, November 8, 12, 1865; *World*, November 8, 15, 28, 1865; *Daily Courier*, November 10, 13, 15, 1865.

51. *Herald*, November 8, 9, 10, 13, 1865; *Evening Post*, November 8, 11, 16, 1865.

52. *Evening Post*, November 22, 29, December 2, 9, 1865; *Daily News*, November 22, 27, December 2, 1865; *Times*, November 24, December 2, 1865; *Leader*, November 25, December 2, 1865; *Irish-American*, November 25, December 2, 1865; *World*, November 27, 1865; Kelly to Morgan, December 3, 1865, Morgan Papers.

53. *Leader*, December 2, 1865.

54. Cochrane to Blair, November 19, Blair to Johnson, November 21, 1865, Johnson Papers; Barlow to Taylor, November 22, Barnett to Barlow, November 24, 1865, Barlow Papers; *Herald*, December 5, 7, 9, 1865; *World*, December 6, 1865; *Leader*, December 9, 16, 30, 1865; Davidson to Corning, December 12, 1865, Corning Papers; Robert Kirkwood, "Horace Greeley and Reconstruction, 1865," NYH 40 (July 1959): 270-80.

55. Greeley to Blair, November 24, 1865, Blair Papers; Garfield to Comly, December 12, 1865, James M. Comly Papers, OHS; Morgan to Weed, December 13, 1865, Weed Papers; Michael Les Benedict, *A Compromise of Principle* (New York: W. W. Norton & Co., 1974), pp. 59-135.

3. THE POLITICS OF UNION: 1866

1. Raymond to Weed, December 3, 1865, Weed Papers; *World,* December 6, 1865; *Herald,* December 6, 9, 1865; *Tribune,* December 6, 8, 1865; *Times,* December 6, 1865; *Daily News,* December 12, 1865; *Leader,* December 16, 1865; Weed to Morgan, December 20, 27, 1865, Morgan Papers; Weed to Seward, December 27, 1865, Seward Papers; Lawrence Gipson, "The Statesmanship of President Johnson: A Study of Presidential Reconstruction Policy," MVHR 2 (December 1915): 363-83.

2. Morgan to Weed, December 3, 13, 20, 1865, January 25, 1866, Weed Papers; Batchford to Seward, December 5, 1865, Weed to Seward, January 28, 29, February 26, March 6, 12, 1866, Seward Papers; Weed to Morgan, December 5, 1865, Morgan Papers; Cochrane to Blair, December 22, Godwin to Johnson, December 25, 1865, Johnson Papers.

3. Barlow to Hughes, December 7, 9, 26, 1865, Barlow to Blair, January 13, 18, 29, Barlow to Van Buren, January 11, Blair to Barlow, January 18, February 12, 1866, Barlow Papers; Barlow to Hughes, December 21, 1865, Johnson Papers; Blair to Tilden, March 14, 1866, Tilden Papers.

4. Kenneth Stampp, *The Era of Reconstruction 1865-1877* (New York: Alfred A. Knopf, 1966), pp. 50-82.

5. Cochrane to Johnson, January 23, February 4, 12, Bennett to Johnson, February 1, Dix to Johnson, February 21, 1866, Johnson Papers; *Herald*, January 29, February 3, 1866; *Evening Post,* February 1, 7, 21, 1866; Michael Les Benedict, *A Compromise of Principle* (New York: W. W. Norton & Co., 1974), pp. 134-161.

6. *Daily Courier,* January 17, 18, 1866; *Argus,* January 17, 21, 24, 1866; *World,* January 23, 29, February 3, 9, 14, 1866; *Times,* February 3, 1866; *Leader,* February 9, 17, 1866; Albert House, Jr., "Northern Congressional Democrats as Defenders of the South During Reconstruction," JSH 6 (February 1940): 51.

7. *Leader,* January 20, February 3, 1866; Long to Boys, January 21, 1866, Boys Papers; Blair to Kernan, February 15, 1866, Kernan Family Papers.

8. LaWanda and John H. Cox, "Andrew Johnson and his Ghost Writers: An Analysis of the Freedmen's Bureau and Civil Rights Veto Messages," MVHR 43 (December 1961): 460-79; W.R. Brock, *An American Crisis: Congressional Reconstruction, 1865-1867* (New York: Harper & Row, 1966), pp. 118-21; Glyndon G. Van Dusen, *William Henry Seward* (New York: Oxford University Press, 1967), pp. 440-52.

9. *Argus,* February 20, 1866; *World,* February 20, 21, 22, 23, 24, 1866; Cox to Marble, February 20, 1866, Marble Papers; Long to Trimble, February 22, 1866, Trimble Papers.

10. Raymond to Johnson, February 22, Seward to Johnson, February 23, Dix to Johnson, March 2, 1866, Johnson Papers; Beekman to Raymond, February 23, 1866, Henry J. Raymond Papers, NYPL; *Times,* February 24, 1866; Weed to Morgan, February 26, 1866, Morgan Papers.

11. *Journal of Commerce,* March 3, 1866; Marble to Blair, March 10, Tilden to Blair, March 10, 1866, Blair Papers; Weed to Seward, March 21, 1866, Seward Papers; Blair to Tilden, March 14, 1866, Tilden Papers; Blair to Barlow, April 7, 1866, Barlow Papers.

12. Weed to Seward, July 25, 1866, Seward Papers; *Argus,* August 28, September 7, 1866; Warren to Marble, September 6, 1866, Marble Papers.

13. *World,* March 15, 20, 1866; *Evening Post,* March 16, 20, 25, 1866; *Herald,* March 17, 28, 1866; *Day-Book,* March 24, 1866; Weed to Seward, March 25, 1866, Seward Papers; *Daily News,* March 27, 1866.

14. *Argus,* March 28, 1866; *World,* March 28, April 2, 1866; *Herald,* March 29, April 2, 1866; *Daily Courier,* March 28, April 7, 1866; Hunt to Johnson, March 29, Brady to Johnson, April 9, 1866, Johnson Papers; *Leader,* March 31, 1866; *Day-Brook,* March 31, April 7, 1866.

15. Seward to Johnson, March 27, 1866, Johnson Papers; Weed to Morgan, March 29, April 1, 1866, Morgan Papers; Raymond to Seward, April, Bilbo to Seward, May 1, 1866, Seward Papers; *Times,* April 7, 9, 1866; Campbell to Doolittle, April 25, 1866, James R. Doolittle Papers, LC; Jacob Cox to Campbell, April 28, 1866, Lewis D. Campbell Papers, OHS.

16. *Herald,* February 11, 1866; Blair to Tilden, April 15, 1866, Tilden Papers; *Daily Courier,* April 27, 28, 1866; Dorsheimer to Blair, May 11, 1866, Blair Papers; Blair to Doolittle, July 20, 1866, Doolittle Papers.

17. *Evening Post,* January 2, 19, 29, February 16, 1866; *Daily Courier,* January 6, 12, 1866; *Leader,* January 6, February 3, 10, 17, 1866; *World,* January 8, 17, 25, March 16, 1866; Kelly to Weed, January 8, Hall to Weed, January 23, 1866, Weed Papers; *Herald,* February 14, March 23, 1866; *Evening Journal,* February 15, March 17, 1866; *Argus,* February 16, 1866; *Tribune,* February 1, 6, 8, 17, 1866; *Times,* February 2, 5, 9, 1866; Howard Kramer, "Effect of the Civil War on the Public Health Movement," MVHR 35 (March 1948): 449-62; James Mohr, *The Radical Republicans and Reform in New York during Reconstruction* (Ithaca, N.Y.: Cornell University Press, 1973), pp. 87-114.

18. *Leader,* January 6, June 9, 1866; *World,* February 16, April 25, 28, June 4, 1866, January 2, 1867; *Times,* April 28, May 3, October 25, November 14, 1866, January 3, 1867; Wilber Miller, *Cops and Bobbies: Police Authority in New York and London, 1830-1870* (Chicago: University of Chicago Press, 1977), pp. 162-64.

19. *Leader*, June 9, October 25, 1866; *Times,* October 25, 1866.

20. *Leader,* April 14, 21, May 19, June 22, 1866.

21. *Leader,* May 12, June 2, 1866; *World,* June 2, 8, 1866; *Argus,* June 6, 1866; *Daily News,* June 20, 1866; *Irish-American,* June 16, 23, July 7, August 4, September 1, 1866; Brian Jenkins, *Fenians and Anglo-American Relations during Reconstruction* (Ithaca, N.Y.: Cornell University Press, 1969), pp. 70-174.

22. Weed to Seward, March 17, 1866, Seward Papers; Halpine to Johnson, March 21, Wood to Johnson, April 5, 1866, Johnson Papers; Barlow to Blair, March 31, Blair to Barlow, April 15, 1866, Barlow Papers; *Herald,* April 6, 19, 1866; Weed to Morgan, April 6, 1866, Morgan Papers; Blair to Johnson, April 9, 1866, Blair Papers; Van Buren to Marble, April 9, 1866, Marble Papers; LaWanda and John H. Cox, *Politics, Principle, and Prejudice 1865-1866* (New York: Atheneum Press, 1969), pp. 123-124.

23. Barlow to Blair, April 14, 1866, Barlow Papers; Smythe to Johnson, April 19, Halpine to Johnson, June 16, 1866, Johnson Papers; Weed to Morgan, April 19, 22, May 4, 1866, Morgan Papers; Weed to Seward, May 4, 1866, Seward Papers; Raymond to Weed, n.d., [June 1866], Weed Papers.

24. *Herald,* April 17, 1866; *World,* April 17, 1866; *Times,* April 17, 1866; *Evening Post,* April 17, 26, 1866; *Argus,* April 19, 1866.

25. *Leader,* March 17, May 19, 1866.

26. *Daily Courier,* April 10, May 3, 1866; Horatio King to James Buchanan, April 12, 1866, *The Works of James Buchanan,* ed. John B. Moore, 12 vols. (Philadelphia: J. B. Lippincott Co., 1911), 11: 413-15; *Daily News,* April 14, 1866; *Argus,* May 5, 1866; *Evening Post,* May 15, 1866; Roy Nichols, "The United States vs. Jefferson Davis," AHR 31 (January 1926): 266-84; Herbert Schell, "Hugh McCulloch and the Treasury Department, 1865-1869," MVHR 17 (December 1930): 404-21.

27. Raymond to Weed, May 2, 1866, Weed Papers; Wood to Pierce, May 29, 1866, Pierce Papers; LaWanda Cox, "The Promise of Land to the Freedman," MVHR 45 (December 1958): 413-40; John Clark, "Radicals and Moderates on the Joint Committee on Reconstruction," *Mid-America* 45 (1959): 175-68; Benedict, *Compromise,* pp. 163-86.

28. Weed to Morgan, May 22, 1866, Morgan Papers; *Times,* May 23, 27, 1866; Jewett to Seward May 23, Weed to Seward, July 1, Ketchum to Seward, July 5, 1866, Seward Papers; Raymond to Weed, June 12, 1866, Weed Papers; Barlow to Blair, June 15, 1866, Barlow Papers; Blair to Doolittle, July 20, 1866, Doolittle Papers; Eric McKitrick, *Andrew Johnson and Reconstruction* (Chicago: University of Chicago Press, 1960), pp. 364-410; Joseph James, *The Framing of the Fourteenth Amendment* (Urbana, Ill.: University of Illinois Press, 1956), p. 128.

29. Dixon to Pierce, May 1, 1866, Pierce Papers; *World,* May 1, 4, 8, 19, 22, 25, June 8, 11, 26, 1866; *Daily Courier,* May 3, 14, 16, 17, June 15, 18, 1866; *Leader,* May 19, 1866; *Argus,* May 21, 27, June 17, 1866; *Daily News,* May 21, 26, June 2, 15, 1866; Cox and Cox, *Politics,* pp. 220-31.

30. *Daily Courier,* June 5, 15, July 3, 1866; *World,* June 16, 26, 1866; Blair to Barlow, June 19, 1866, Barlow Papers; *Evening Post,* June 22, 28, 1866.

31. *Evening Post,* May 1, 5, 9, 13, June 14, 27, July 3, 1866; *Herald,* May 4, 12, 20, June 14, 19, 23, 29, 1866.

32. Phillips to Johnson, June 3, 25, July 1, 1866, Johnson Papers; *Daily Courier,* February 5, 1867.

33. Blair to Tilden, June 17, 1866, Tilden Papers; McClelland to Johnson, June 24, 1866, Johnson Papers; *Argus,* June 26, 28, 1866; James Sellers, "James R. Doolittle," *Wisconsin Magazine of History* 18 (September 1934): 29-30.

34. *World,* May 24, 28, June 27, 28, 1866; *Daily Courier,* June 5, 28, 30, July 2, 1866; Belmont to Barlow, June 26, 1866, Barlow Papers; *Times,* June 28, 1866; *Leader,* June 30, 1866; *Argus,* July 2, 1866; Joel Silbey, *A Respectable Minority: The Democratic Party in the Civil War Era, 1860-1868* (New York: W. W. Norton & Co., 1977), p. 183.

35. *World,* June 23, July 5, 1866; Burke to Pierce, July 5, 27, 1866, Pierce Papers; Brock, *American Crisis,* p. 148.

36. *World,* July 6, 7, 14, 1866; Blair to Barlow, July 5, 27, 1866, Barlow Papers.

37. *Leader,* July 14, 1866.

38. Doolittle to Seward, July 10, 1866, Seward Papers; Dix to Doolittle, July 10, 1866, "Some Political Letters of Reconstruction Days Succeeding the Civil War," ed. Duane Mowry, *American Historical Magazine* 4 (May 1909): 332, "Extracts from the Journal of Henry J. Raymond," *Scribner's Monthly* 20 (June 1880): 276-77; Van Dusen, *Seward,* pp. 454-60.

39. Raymond to Weed, July 12, 1866, *Autobiography of Thurlow Weed,* ed. Harriet Weed, 2 vols. (Boston and New York: Houghton Mifflin and Co., 1883), 1:452; *World,* July 12, 13, 16, 1866; *Daily Courier,* July 13, 16, 1866; *Times,* July 13, 1866.

40. Campbell to Weed, July 10, Hawley to Weed, July 15, Vivus Smith to Weed, July 19, 1866, Weed Papers; Hastings to Seward, July 11, Ord to Seward, July 17, Weed to Dawson, July 24, Weed to Seward, July 25, 1866, Seward Papers; Seymour to Blair, July 25, 1866, Blair Papers.

41. Belmont to Marble, July 16, 17, 1866, Marble Papers; *Leader,* July 21, August 4, 1866.

42. Freeley to Long, July 19, 1866, Long Papers; *Herald,* July 22, 1866; Burke to Blair, July 30, 1866, Blair Papers; Wood to Johnson, August 1, 1866, Johnson Papers; McKitrick, *Johnson,* pp. 364-410.

43. Raymond to Seward, August 16, Seward to Raymond, August 16, Dix to Seward, August 17, Schell to Seward, August 17, 1866, Seward Papers; Dix to Johnson, August 16, 1866, Johnson Papers.

44. Raymond to Marble, August 1, 1866, Marble Papers; *Evening Journal,* August 1, 4, 1866; *Tribune,* August 2, 3, 4, 6, 1866; *Leader,* August 4, 11, 1866; Doolittle to Johnson, August 8, 1866, Johnson Papers.

45. Barlow to Blair, August 9, 1866, Barlow Papers; *World,* August 14, 17, 18, 21, 1866; Barlow to Marble, August 17, 1866, Marble Papers; Howard Beale, *The Critical Year: A Study of Andrew Johnson and Reconstruction* (New York: Frederick Ungar Publishing Co., 1930), pp. 11-38.

46. *Evening Post,* August 16, 17, 21, 25, 1866; *Tribune,* August 16, 17, 1866; *Herald,* August 16, 18, 1866; *Times,* August 18, 21, 1866; *Leader,* August 18, 1866; Smythe to Johnson, August 18, 1866, Johnson Papers; *Argus,* August 21, 1866.

47. *Evening Post,* August 15, 23, 27, 1866; Barlow to Smythe, August 25, 1866, Johnson Papers; Van Buren to Tilden, August 31, 1866, Tilden Papers.

48. Fenton to Morgan, August 17, 1866, Reuben E. Fenton Papers, NYSL; *Irish-American,* August 18, 1866; Raymond to Seward, August 19, Schell to Seward, August 24, 1866, Seward Papers; Follett to Weed, August 21, Bradley to Weed, September 10, Vivus Smith to Weed, October 12, 1866, Weed Papers; *Tribune,* August 26, 27, 1866; Halpine to Greeley, September 8, 1866, Charles G. Halpine Papers, The Henry E. Huntington Library; *Leader,* December 28, 1866.

49. Marble to Warren, n.d. [August 1866], Warren to Marble, September 6, Sweeny to Marble, September 8, 1866, Marble Papers; *Herald,* August 25, September 7, 11, 1866; *Argus,* August 28, 30, 1866; *Daily Courier,* September 3, 4, 7, 1866.

50. *Evening Post,* September 6, 8, 1866; *Tribune,* September 6, 9, 1866; *World,* September 7, 13, 1866; *Herald,* September 9, 1866.

51. *Argus,* September 13, 1866; *Leader,* September 15, 1866; Homer Stebbins, *A Political History of the State of New York, 1865-1868* (New York: Columbia University Press, 1913), pp. 99-112.

52. *Evening Journal,* September 13, 1866; *Times,* September 13, 17, 20, October 2, 1866; *Evening Post,* September 13, 23, October 25, 1866; Cox to Marble, September 18, 21, 1866, Marble Papers; *Daily Courier,* October 11, 1866; Brock, *American Crisis,* p. 157.

53. Barlow to Tilden, September 15, Tilden to McCulloch, September 17, McCulloch to Tilden, October 22, 1866, Tilden Papers; Schell to Seward, October 1, 1866, Seward Papers; Smith to Weed, October 11, Cole to Weed, October 17, 1866, Weed Papers.

54. *Herald,* September 13, 14, 15, 17, 18, 21, 22, 24, 26, October 4, 11, 17, 19, 20, 29, 1866; McKitrick, *Johnson,* pp. 421-45.

55. Phillips to Johnson, September 16, October 7, Bennett to Johnson, October 15, 1866, Johnson Papers; *Herald,* September 15, 22, 1866; Van Buren to Francis P. Blair, Sr., September 21, 1866, Blair Papers.

56. *Leader,* September 20, October 20, 1866; Church to Tilden, September 17, Marble to Tilden, September 21, Tweed to Tilden, September 21, Hoffman to Tilden, September 24, Smythe to Tilden, October 17, Brooks to Tilden, October 20, Kelly to Tilden, October 22, Flower to Tilden, October 22, Seymour to Tilden, October 25, 1866, Tilden Papers; Warren to Marble, October 5, 1866, Marble Papers; Tilden to Johnson, October 14, 1866, Johnson Papers.

57. *World,* September 8, 13, 25, October 2, 3, 9, 11, 15, 18, 22, November 3, 1866; Weed to Seward, September 15, 1866, Seward Papers; *Irish-American,* September 20, October 6, November 3, 1866; Tilden to Johnson, September 20, 1866, Johnson Papers; *Argus,* September 27, October 5, 22, 30, 1866; *Daily Courier,* October 12, 14, 16, 25, 28, November 2, 1866; *Tribune,* October 13, November 1, 1866; Cassidy to Tilden, November 1, 1866, Tilden Papers; *Leader,* November 3, 1866; *Times,* November 6, 1866; Stebbins, *Political History,* pp. 115-42.

58. Weed to Risley, October 12, 1866, Weed Papers; Winfield to Tilden, October 13, Kernan to Tilden, October 17, Earl to Tilden, October 30, 1866, Tilden Papers; Weed to Seward, October 26, 1866, Seward Papers; Cassidy to Seymour, October 27, 1866, Seymour Papers; Charles Cashdollar, "Andrew Johnson and the Philadelphia Election of 1866," PMH 92 (July 1968): 363-83.

59. Hoffman to Tilden, November 7, Church to Tilden, November 10, 1866, Tilden Papers; *World,* November 8, 9, 14, 16, 21, 1866; *Daily Courier,* November 10, 15, 1866; *Leader,* November 10, 17, 1866; Cassidy to Johnson, November 17, 1866, Johnson Papers; William Hanchett, *IRISH Charles G. Halpine in Civil War America* (Syracuse, N.Y.: Syracuse University Press, 1970), pp. 154-60.

60. *Argus,* November 8, 18, 1866; *World,* November 16, 30, December 8, 1866, January 1, 1867; Dix to Doolittle, January 8, 1867, AHM: 335-6; *Herald,* January 14, 19, 1867.

61. *Evening Post,* November 7, 8, 14, 26, December 1, 3, 5, 1866; *Herald,* November 7, 8, 10, 15, 19, 20, 23, 1866; Dix to Johnson, November 8, 1866, Johnson Papers; *Tribune,* November 8, 15, December 5, 1866; *Times,* November 14, 22, December 27, 29, 1866; Smith to Weed, November 23, 1866, Weed Papers; Weed to Seward, November 24, 1866, Seward Papers; Greeley to Laurence, December 16, 1866, Greeley Papers, NYPL.

4. THE POLITICS OF RACE: 1867-1868

1. Chamberlain to Marble, December 2, 1866, Marble Papers; *World,* December 4, 6, 1866; *Evening Post,* December 4, 1866; *Argus,* December 4, 1866; *Herald,* December 6, 7, 1866; *Leader,* December 10, 1866.

2. *Evening Journal,* January 2, 1867; *World,* January 2, 8, 17, 1867; *Argus,* January 5, 9, February 3, 1867; *Leader,* January 5, 1867; *Daily Courier,* January 25, February 9, 1867; Greeley to Blair, February 16, 1867, Blair Papers; Smythe to Johnson, February 25, Blair to Johnson, February 26, 1867, Johnson Papers; William Dunning, "The Second Birth of the Republican Party," AHR 16 (October 1910): 57-64; Charles Lerche, Jr., "Congressional Interpretations of the Guarantee of a Republican Form of Government during Reconstruction," JSH 15 (May 1949): 197-99: Joseph James, "Southern Reaction to the Proposed Fourteenth Amendment," JSH 22 (November 1956): 477-97; Michael Les Benedict, *A Compromise of Principle* (New York: W. W. Norton & Co., 1974), pp. 210-56.

3. Wood to Johnson, February 21, 1867, Johnson Papers; *World,* February 23, 25, 26, 27, 1867; *Daily Courier,* February 25, 26, 1867; *Argus,* February 27, 1867; Marble to Buchanan, February 25, Comstock to Marble, March 1, 1867, Marble Papers.

4. *Daily Courier,* December 13, 1866, March 6, 8, 15, 19, 26, April 11, 1867.

5. Marble to Blair, March 11, 1867, Blair Papers; *World,* March 12, 18, 19, 1867.

6. *Herald,* February 21, 23, April 9, 1867; *Evening Post,* February 23, March 7, 12, 1867; *Tribune,* February 23, 25, March 18, 1867; Hawley to Greeley, March 12, 1867, Greeley Papers, NYPL; *Commercial Advertiser,* March 25, 26, 30, 1867; Frederick Seward to Weed, March 31, 1867, Weed Papers.

7. Greeley to Sedley, January 5, 1867, Greeley Papers, NYPL; *World,* January 10, 1867; *Evening Post,* January 11, 1867; *Leader,* January 12, 1867; James Mohr, "New York State's Free School of Law of 1867," NYHSQ 53 (July 1969): 230-49; David Jordon, *Roscoe Conkling of New York* (Ithaca, N.Y.: Cornell University Press, 1971), pp. 85-105; James Mohr, *The Radical Republicans and Reform in New York during Reconstruction* (Ithaca, N.Y.: Cornell University Press, 1973), pp. 114-209.

8. *Leader,* March 16, 30, April 13, 30, 1867; Dix to Tilden, March 20, Cassidy to Tilden, April 15, 1867, Tilden Papers; *Argus,* March 16, 18, May 1, 1867; *World,*March 20, April 15, 22, May 2, 1867; *Tribune,* March 30, April 24, 1867.

9. *World,* January 1, 2 , May 2, 1867; *Daily Courier,* January 12, 1867; Sweeney to Marble, February 27, Barlow to Marble, September 30, 1867, Marble Papers; *Commercial Advertiser,* April 18, 20, 1867; Alexander Callow, Jr., *The Tweed Ring* (New York: Oxford University Press, 1965), pp, 42-44.

10. *World,* April 6, May 2, 4, 1867; *Herald,* April 27, 29, May 5, 11, 12, 25, 27, 1867.

11. Barlow to Tilden, July 11, 1867, Tilden Papers; *World,* May 21, August 5, 1867; *Daily Courier,* June 3, 6, July 21, 31, 1867; *Leader,* June 20, 1867; *Argus,* July 6, August 7, 8, 1867; William Russ, Jr., "Registration and Disfranchisement under Radical Reconstruction," MVHR 21 (September 1934): 164-80; Jack Scroggs, "Southern Reconstruction: A Radical View," JSH 24 (November 1958): 407-39; Forrest Wood, "On Revising Reconstruction History: Negro Suffrage, White Disfranchisement, and Common Sense," JSH 41 (April 1966): 98-113; Michael Perman, "The South and Congressional Reconstruction Policy, 1866-67," JAS 4 (February 1971): 181-200.

12. *World,* May 21, June 21, July 11, 20, August 12, September 4, 1867.

13. *Herald,* May 19, July 14, 18, 23, 26, August 9, 10, 11, 14, 31, September 1, 5, 9, 1867; Phillips to Johnson, August 7, Halpine to Johnson, August 27, 1867, Johnson Papers.

14. Tilden to Marble, April 23, 1867, Marble Papers; *Tribune,* May 13, 1867; *Evening Post,* May 14, 23, July 25, 1867; *Daily Courier,* May 14, 17, June 3, 20, July 12, 13, 22, 27, 1867; *Leader,* June 18, 25, July 13, August 3, 1867; *Argus,* July 2, 26, 1867; *World,* July 6, 16, 1867; James Mohr, "New York: The Depoliticization of Reform," *Radical Republicans in the North,* ed. James Mohr (Baltimore: Johns Hopkins Press, 1976), pp. 68-69.

15. *Tribune,* July 11, 18, August 7, September 25, 1867; Greeley to Comly, July 30, 1867, Comly Papers; *Leader,* August 10, September 7, 1867; Cassidy to Tilden, August 14, 1867, Tilden Papers; Homer Stebbins, *A Political History of the State of New York, 1865-1868* (New York: Columbia University Press, 1913), pp. 212-66.

16. Wright to Marble, May 16, 1867, Marble Papers; *World,* June 17, August 10, September 17, 21, October 16, 21, 24, 27, 1867; *Evening Post,* June 2, 1867; *Daily Courier,* June 29, July 2, September 2, 1867; Thomas Archdeacon, "The Erie Canal Ring, Samuel J. Tilden, and the Democratic Party," NYH 59 (October 1978): 410-12.

17. *Evening Post,* July 16, August 4, September 2, 1867; *Times,* July 22, September 25, 27, 1867; *Herald,* August 17, 28, 1867; *Argus,* September 5, 26, 1867; Morgan to Johnson, September 12, 1867, Johnson Papers; Weed to Seward, September 16, 1867, Seward Papers; *Commercial Advertiser,* September 25, 1867.

18. *World,* March 9, 19, June 15, 28, September 24, 1867; *Evening Post,* October 3, 8, 13, 28, 1867; McCulloch to Tilden, October 10, 1867, Tilden Papers; Reginald McGrane, "Ohio and the Greenback Movement," MVHR 11 (March 1925): 526-42; Chester Desler, "The Origins and Character of the Pendleton Plan," MVHR 24 (September 1937): 171-84; Robert Sharkey, *Money, Class, and Party* (Baltimore: Johns Hopkins Press, 1959), pp. 97-101; Irwin Unger, *The Greenback Era* (Princeton, N.J.: Princeton University Press, 1959), pp. 78-84.

19. Pendleton to Seymour, October 21, 1867, Seymour Papers; Cox to Marble, November 11, Pendleton to Marble, November 13, Marble to Pendleton, November 23, 1867, Warren to Marble, Janaury 28, 1868, Marble Papers; McLean to Barlow, January 14, 1868, Barlow Papers.

20. *Evening Post,* September 24, 25, 30, 1867; *Tribune,* September 25, 26, 1867; *Commercial Advertiser,* September 26, 27, 1867; Stebbins, *Political History,* pp. 159-70.

21. *Leader,* September 28, 1867; *World,* September 28, October 2, 11, 1867; *Herald,* September 29, October 5, 1867; *Daily Courier,* October 5, 1867; *Argus,* October 5, 9, 1867; Stebbins, *Political History,* pp. 170-83.

23. *Tribune,* October 5, 7, 8, 17, 23, 1867; *Argus,* October 7, 1867; Folger to Morgan, October 11, 1867, Morgan Papers; *Journal of Commerce,* October 12, 1867; *Commercial Advertiser,* October 28, 1867.

24. *Herald,* October 7, 1867; Allen to Tilden, October 10, Church to Tilden, October 18, Wood to Tilden, October 18, Tweed to Tilden, November 1, 1867, Tilden Papers; *World,* October 14, 19, 25, 26, 30, November 1, 1867; *Irish-Citizen,* October 19, November 1, 1867; *Leader,* October 19, 26, November 2, 1867; Cassidy to Marble, October 19, November 1, 1867, Marble Papers; *Irish-American,* November 2, 1867.

25. Hoffman to Johnson, November 5, 1867, Johnson Papers; *Daily Courier,* November 6, 1867; *Argus,* November 6, 1867; Dunbar to Black, November 6, 1867, Black Papers; *Irish-Citizen,* November 9, 1867; *Leader,* November 9, 1867; Michael Les Benedict, "The Rout of Radicalism: Republicans and the Elections of 1867," CWH 18 (December 1972): 334-44.

26. *World,* November 7, 13, 16, 22, 1867; *Argus,* November 7, 9, 10, 16, 1867; *Daily Courier,* November 7, 9, 11, 12, 15, 18, 1867; Warren to Marble, November 9, Tilden to Marble, November 9, 1867, Marble Papers.

27. Buchanan to Schell, November 8, 1867, *The Works of James Buchanan,* ed. John B. Moore 12 vols. (Philadelphia: J. B. Lippincott Co., 1911), 11: 455; Haldeman to Marble, November 13, 1867, Marble Papers.

28. *Daily Courier,* November 21, December 18, 1867; *World,* November 22, December 5, 7, 26, 1867, January 3, 6, 1868.

29. Cox to Marble, November 11, Belmont to Marble, December 12, 16, 1867, Marble Papers; Glover to Johnson, December 5, Halpine to Johnson, December 24, 1867, Johnson Papers; Cassidy to Tilden, December 7, 12, Seymour to Tilden, December 13, 1867, Tilden Papers; Blair to Barlow, December 26, 1867, Barlow Papers.

30. *Daily Courier,* December 4, 1867; *Argus,* December 4, 1867; *World,* December 4, 1867; *Herald,* December 6, 1867; *Leader,* December 7, 28, 1867; Florence Gibson, *The Attitudes of the New York Irish toward State and National Affairs, 1848-1892* (New York: Columbia University Press, 1951), pp. 215-18; John Allswang, *Bosses, Machines, and Urban Voters* (Port Washington, N.Y.: Kennikat Press, 1977), pp. 46-47.

31. *Times,* November 9, 10, 16, December 25, 29, 1867; Patterson to Weed, November 11, 1867, Weed Papers; Weed to Seward, December 6, 1867, Seward Papers; *Commercial Advertiser,* December 8, 1867; *Herald,* December 20, 27, 1867.

32. *Tribune,* November 10, 12, 13, 16, 24, 26, December 2, 10, 1867, January 5, 8, 9, 21, February 10, 25, 1868; Pendleton to Greeley, November 13, 1867, Greeley Papers, LC; *Herald,* December 2, 4, 1867, February 6, 1868; *Argus,* December 10, 1867, February 8, 1868; Hilton to Weed, January 4, 1868, Weed Papers; Stanley Coben, "Northern Business and Radical Reconstruction: A Re-Examination," MVHR 46 (June 1959): 67-90; Peter Kolchin, "The Business Press and Reconstruction, 1865-1868," JSH 33 (May 1967): 183-96; Glenn Linden, "Radicals and Economic Policies: The House of Representatives, 1861-1873," CWH 13 (1967): 51-65.

33. Ward to Barlow, February 25, 27, Smythe to Barlow, April 21, 1868, Barlow Papers; *Argus,* February 25, May 20, 1868; *World,* February 26, 26, March 6, 1868; *Leader,* February 29, March 7, 21, April 18, May 2, 1868; Michael Les Benedict, "A New Look at the Impeachment of Andrew Johnson," PSQ 88 (September 1973): 349-67.

34. Barlow to Tilden, n.d. [April 1868], Tilden Papers; Van Buren to Johnson, May 19, Tilden to Johnson, May 19, Smythe to Johnson, July 6, Phillips to Johnson, July 8, 1868, Johnson Papers; *World,* May 20, 1868; *Argus,* May 20, 26, 1868.

35. *Herald,* March 6, 20, 28, May 4, 6, 7, 10, 29, 30, 1868; *Daily Courier,* March 23, April 4, May 2, 1868; *World,* March 26, 1868; Van Buren to Marble, April, Warren to Marble May, 1868, Marble Papers; Van Buren to Chase, May 9, 1868, Salmon Chase Papers, LC; M. Kathleen Perdue, "Salmon P. Chase and the Impeachment of Andrew Johnson," *Historian* 29 (November 1964): 75-92; Jerome Mushkat, ed. "The Impeachment of Andrew Johnson: A Contemporary View," NYH 48 (July 1967): 275-86.

36. *World,* January 30, April 25, May 9, 1868; Storey to Marble, February 12, Gillet to Marble, February 22, White to Marble, February 26, McLean to Marble, March 22, Belmont to Marble, June 1868, Marble Papers; *Daily Courier,* March 11, 12, June 12, 1868; Dix to Tilden, May 18, 1868, Tilden Papers.

37. *Daily Courier,* March 28, April 8, 1868; *Herald,* March 28, 1868; *World,* April 7, 1868; *Irish-Citizen,* April 11, 1868; *Tribune,* May 25, July 9, 1868; Allen W. Trelease, *Reconstruction: The Great Experiment* (New York: Harper & Row, 1971), pp. 112-46.

38. *World,* February 17, March 19, 30, April 3, 14, 30, June 3, 1868; *Argus,* February 17, June 6, 1868; Tilden to ?, February 28, 1868, Tilden Papers; *Leader,* March 14, April 4, 1868; *Daily Courier,* March 15, April 3, 10, 18, 27, 1868; Blair to Barlow, April 15, 1868, Barlow Papers.

39. *Leader,* December 28, 1867, January 4, 25, May 9, 1868; *Evening Post,* January 3, April 30, May 1, 1868; *Herald,* January 7, 10, 16, 29, 1868; *Times,* February 2, August 7, 1868; *Irish-American,* February 22, May 9, 1868; *Evening Journal,* April 24, 1868; *Irish-Citizen,* May 30, 1868; Stebbins, *Political History,* pp. 267-302; Callow, *Tweed Ring,* pp. 165-66.

40. *Herald,* January 7, March 28, 1868; *Leader,* January 18, 1868; Pierce to Marble, January 30, Hall to Marble, February 17, 1868, Marble Papers; North to Seymour, June 8, 1868, Seymour Papers; Hiram Calkins and DeWitt Van Buren, *Biographical Sketches of John T. Hoffman and Allen C. Beach* (New York: The New York Printing Co., 1868).

41. *Commercial Advertiser,* January 15, 20, May 3, 17, 24, 1868; *Herald,* February 6, 7, May 22, 1868; Casserly to Marble, April 11, 1868, Marble Papers; *Times,* May 9, 23, 1868; *Evening Post,* May 22, 25, July 9, 1868; Rice to Weed, May 23, 1868, Weed Papers.

42. *World,* May 19, 21, 28, 1868; *Tribune,* May 23, 1868; *Leader,* May 28, 1868; Charles Coleman, *The Election of 1868* (New York: Columbia University Press, 1933), pp. 85-101.

43. Connolly to Seymour, January 21, Cassidy to Seymour, May 23, Comstock to Seymour, June 17, 1868, Seymour Papers; Bigler to Tilden, February 3, Seymour to Tilden, March 4, 24, May 9, Allen to Tilden, May 25, Loomis to Tilden, June 8, 1868, Tilden Papers; Kernan to Tilden, March 7, 1868, Kernan Family Papers; *Leader,* March 28, 1868; *Herald,* May 25, June 3, 1868.

44. Chase to Long, February 4, April 8, 15, 19, Long to Chase, April 6, 11, Schuckers to Long, April 30, May 9, Long to Seymour, May 17, 1868, Long Papers; Edward Perzel, "Alexander Long, Salmon Chase, and the Election of 1868," *Bulletin of the Cincinnati Historical Society* 23 (January 1965): 3-10.

45. *World,* March 26, 1868; Brown to Barlow, April 23, May 19, June 5, Reverdy Johnson to Barlow, May 28, 1868, Barlow Papers; Van Buren to Seymour, May 1, 20, 1868, Fairchild Collection; Cisco to Chase, June 1, 1868, Chase Papers; *Leader,* June 6, 13, 26, 1868.

46. Barney to Chase, May 28, 1868, Chase Papers; Chase to Marble, May 30, Doolittle to Marble, May 30, 1868, Marble Papers; Church to Cassidy, June 8, 1868, William Cassidy Papers, NYSL; Van Buren to Seymour, June 9, 1868, Fairchild Collection; A.B. [?] to Comly, June 10, 1868, Comly Papers.

47. *Herald,* June 2, 6, 16, November 4, 5, 7, 18, 1868; Blair to Barlow, June 4, Hatch to Barlow, June 13, 1868, Barlow Papers; *Daily Courier,* June 12, 1868; Barlow to Tilden, June 21, 1868, *Tilden's Letters,* 1: 232-34; Aiken to Cox, June 22, 1868, Cox Papers.

48. Schuckers to Long, June 3, Long Papers; *World,* June 3, 8, 1868; *Evening Post,* June 9, 10, 1868; Ward to Barlow, June 17, 19, 1868, Barlow Papers; Bryant to Chase, June 23, Ward to Chase, June 26, 1868, Chase Papers.

49. *Daily Courier,* June 5, 12, 24, 1868; Blair to Barlow, June 10, Sprague to Barlow, June 23, 1868, Barlow Papers; *Herald,* June 10, July 8, 1868; Dawson to Black, June 14, 1868, Black Papers; *World,* June 15, 17, 19, 22, 1868; *Argus,* June 15, 22, 27, 1868; Cassidy to Seymour, June 18, 1868, Seymour Papers; Van Buren to Seymour, June 19, 1868, Fairchild Collection; Chase to Long, July 1, 1868, Long Papers; Coleman, *Election of 1868,* pp. 102-40, 159-86; George McJimsey, *Genteel Partisan: Manton Marble, 1834-1917* (Ames, Ia.: Iowa State University Press, Iowa State University Press, 1971), pp. 127-29.

50. Edward McPherson, *The Political History of the United States of America during the Period of Reconstruction* (Washington, D.C.: Philip & Solomons, 1871), pp. 367-68.

51. Pendleton to Tilden, July 10, Ketchum to Tilden, November 12, 1868, Tilden Papers; Shipman to Barlow, July 11, 1868, Barlow Papers; Stewart Mitchell, *Horatio Seymour of New York* (Cambridge, Mass.: Harvard University Press, 1938), pp. 411-12; Martin Mantell, *Johnson, Grant, and the Politics of Reconstruction* (New York: Columbia University Press, 1973), pp. 113-28; Joel Silbey, *A Respectable Minority: The Democratic Party in the Civil War Era, 1860-1868* (New York: W. W. Norton & Co., 1977), pp. 204-8.

52. *Evening Journal,* July 12, 1868; *Commercial Advertiser,* July 13, 1868; Lapham to Greeley, July 13, 1868, Greeley Papers, LC; *Tribune,* July 15, 1868; *Times,* July 19, 1868; *Evening Post,* July 24, 1868.

53. Barlow to Tilden, July 10, Hoover to Tilden, July 15, Blair to Tilden, July 15, 1868, Tilden Papers; *Leader,* July 11, 18, 25, 1868; Ward to Barlow, July 14, 1868, Barlow Papers.

54. Sprague to Chase, July 10, Van Buren to Chase, July 16, 1868, Chase Papers; Long to Seymour, July 14, Van Buren to Long, July 24, Rosecrans to Long, August 4, 1868, Long Papers; Ward to Barlow, July 16, 20, 22, Seymour to Barlow, July 22, 1868 Barlow Papers; Seymour to Tilden, July 20, August 7, Belmont to Sweeny, August 3, 1868, Tilden Papers; Sweeny to Seymour, July 28, 1868, Seymour Papers; Perzel, "Chase, Long," pp. 11-18.

55. Cox to Johnson, July 25, Niven to Johnson, July 30, Tilden to Johnson, August 28, September 4, 1868, Johnson Papers; Ward to Marble, August 4, 1868, Marble Papers; Parker to Seymour, August 6, Spencer to Seymour, August 6, 1868, Seymour Papers; Schuckers to Long, August 17, Chase to Long, September 30, 1868, Chase Papers.

56. Blair to Tilden, August 13, 19, Barlow to Tilden, September 21, 1868, Tilden Papers; *Daily Courier,* August 14, 21, September 7, 11, 1868; *Leader,* August 15, 22, 1868; *Argus,* August 22, 29, 1868.

57. *Tribune,* August 11, September 1, 14, 1868; *Argus,* August 17, 20, 1868; Vallandingham to Tilden, September 2, 1868, Tilden Papers.

58. *World,* August 11, 12, 14, 15, 19, 20, September 1, 2, 3, 1868; *Herald,* August 14, 15, 16, 17, 19, 22, 26, 29, September 11, 1868; *Argus,* August 17, 18, 20, September 11, 1868; *Evening Post,* August 18, 22, September 12, 1868; Seymour to Tilden, August 20, 31, 1868, Tilden Papers; *Times,* September 9, 14, 17, 1868.

59. *Daily Courier,* September 4, 7, 17, 18, 26, 28, October 3, 9, 10, 1868; Vallandingham to Seymour, September 7, Church to Seymour, September 19, 1868, Seymour Papers; *World,* September 9, 23, October 7, 13, 15, 18, 1868; Seymour to Tilden, September 15, 24, Barlow to Tilden, September 21, 1868, Tilden Papers; Blair to Barlow, September 19, 1868, Barlow Papers; Morgan to Weed, October 20, 1868, Weed Papers.

60. *Herald,* September 3, 4, 1868; Stebbins, *Political History,* pp. 360-68.

61. Tweed to Marble, September 24, 1868, Marble Papers; *Herald,* September 24, October 23, 26, 1868; *Evening Post,* September 24, October 17, 23, 1868; *Leader,* September 26, October 17, 24, 1868; *World,* October 6, 27, 1868; *Irish-American,* October 10, 24, 31, 1868; John Davenport, *The Electon and Naturalization Frauds in New York City, 1860-1870* (New York: Printed by the Author, 1894), pp. 200-268; Gibson, *New York Irish,* pp. 222-38.

62. Long to Chase, September 10, October 3, 1868, Long Papers; Barney to Seymour, September 10, Van Buren to Seymour, September 24, Seymour to Van Buren, September 24, 1868, Fairchild Collection; Chase to Dana, October 1, 1868, Barlow Papers; Barlow to Tilden, October 14, Strong to Tilden, October 16, 1868, Tilden Papers; Barlow to Kernan, October 14, 1868, Kernan Family Papers.

63. Warren to Marble, September 7, 1868, Marble Papers; Blair to Black, September 19, 1868, Black Papers; *World,* October 15, 1868; McJimsey, *Marble,* pp, 129-31.

64. Kernan to Barlow, October 15, 1868, Barlow Papers; Barlow to Tilden, October 15, Vallandingham to Tilden, October 17, Augustus Schell to Hoover, October 18, 1868, Tilden Papers; Cox to Marble, October 16, Long to Marble, October 17, Tilden to Marble, October 17, 20, 1868, Marble Papers; *World,* October 16, 17, 19, 20, 26, 1868; *Daily Courier,* October 16, 17, 19, 20, 26, 1868; *Daily News,* October 16, 1868; *Leader,* October 17, 24, 1868; *Argus,* October 17, 18, 20, 1868.

65. *Leader,* November 7, 1868; Coleman, *The Election of 1868,* pp. 362-67.

5. TAMMANY'S RECONSTRUCTION: 1869-1870

1. *Leader,* November 7, 14, 21, 28, December 5, 19, 26, 1868, January 9, 16, February 6, 13, 20, 1869; *Daily Courier,* November 9, 1868; *Irish-American,* November 14, 1868; *Herald,* November 30, December 2, 4, 1868, February 19, 1869; Morton Keller, *Affairs of State: Public Life in Late Nineteenth Century America* (Cambridge, Mass.: Harvard University Press, 1977), pp. 238-62.

2. Seymour Mandelbaum, *Boss Tweed's New York* (New York: John Wiley & Sons, 1965), pp. 1-58; Alexander Callow, Jr., *The Tweed Ring* (New York: Oxford University Press, 1969), pp. 3-151; Leo Hershkowitz, *Tweed's New York: Another Look* (New York: Anchor Press, 1977), pp. 111-36. The "Black Horse Cavalry" refers to the practice of some legislators in both parties who sold their votes for a price.

3. Gustavus Myers, "The Secrets of Tammany's Success," *The Forum* 31 (August 1901): 488-500; Alexander Callow, Jr., " 'What Are Young Going to Do About It?': The Crusade against the Tweed Ring," NYHSQ 49 (April 1965): 117-42.

4. *Times,* September 23, October 17, 26, 29, November 5, 14, December 2, 1868; *Herald,* November 2, 1868; *Evening Post,* November 4, 14, 20, 1868; *Commercial Advertiser,* November 4, 5, 1868; *Daily Courier,* November 4, 9, 17, 1868; *Tribune,* November 23, 1868; John Davenport, *The Election and Naturalization Frauds in New York City, 1860-1870* (New York: Published by the Author, 1894), pp. 127-33; 216-34.

5. *Irish-American,* November 7, 14, 21, December 12, 1868; *Argus,* November 9, 1868; *Leader,* November 14, 26, 1868; *World,* November 21, 1868; *Herald,* December 16, 1868.

6. *Evening Post,* December 4, 1868, January 21, April 21, 1869; *World,* January 20, 1869; *Herald,* January 26, 1869; William Gillett, *The Right to Vote: Politics and the Passage of the Fifteenth Amendment* (Baltimore:

Johns Hopkins Press, 1965); Lawanda and John H. Cox, "Negro Suffrage and Republican Politics: The Problem of Motivation in Reconstruction Historiography," JSH 33 (August 1967): 303-30; Glenn Linden, "A Note on Negro Suffrage and Republican Politics," JSH 36 (August 1970): 411-20; Michael Les Benedict, *A Compromise of Principle* (New York: W. W. Norton & Co., 1974), pp. 446-47.

7. Keller, *Affairs of State,* p. 68.

8. *Herald,* November 12, December 1, 1868, January 26, 1869; *World,* January 3, February 1, 3, 21, March 2, 7, 1869; *Irish-American,* January 30, February 6, 1869; *Daily Courier,* February 3, April 2, 1869; *Leader,* February 20, 1869; *Argus,* February 27, April 20, 21, 1869.

9. *Tribune,* November 2, 1868, January 9, 1869; *Times,* January 2, 1869; *Evening Post,* January 4, 1869.

10. *Times,* January 6, 1869; *Evening Post,* January 5, 16, 1869; *Buffalo Commercial Advertiser,* January 6, 1869; *World,* January 6, 1869; *Herald,* January 6, 1869; *Leader,* January 9, 1869.

11. *Argus,* January 5, 17, 26, 1869; *World,* January 7, 18, 1869; *Tribune,* January 18, 1869; Wilder to Morgan, January 19, 1869, Morgan Papers; James Rawley, *Edwin D. Morgan, 1811-1883: Merchant in Politics* (New York: Columbia University Press, 1956), pp. 231-33.

12. *World,* November 19, December 20, 1868, January 2, 5, 6, 9, April 11, May 4, June 25, July 19, 21, 1869; *Herald,* June 18, 1869; *Tribune,* June 22, 23, 1869; Porter to Marble, July 5, 1869, Marble Papers.

13. *World,* January 3, 5, 9, 12, 14, March 20, 25, 28, 1869; Calkins to Marble, March 17, 1869, Marble Papers; *Daily Courier,* July 9, 12, September 3, 1869; George McJimsey, *Genteel Partisan: Manton Marble, 1834-1917* (Ames, Ia.: Iowa State University Press, 1971), pp. 135-36.

14. Hoffman to Marble, January 9, May 16, Chamberlain to Marble, May, Marble to Cassidy, May 9, Cassidy to Marble, May 13, Hurlburt to Marble, June 20, Croly to Marble, July, Bogart to Marble, July 30, 1869, Marble Papers; *World,* May 7, 18, 1869; *Argus,* May 15, 1869; *Evening Post,* May 15, 31, 1869; *Leader,* May 18, 1869; Beach to Tilden, July 30, 1869, Tilden Papers; Diane Ravitch, *The Great School Wars: New York City, 1805-1973* (New York: Basic Books, 1973), pp. 92-95.

15. *Evening Post,* April 14, 15, 17, 19, May 21, 27, July 13, 1869; *Commercial Advertiser,* May 15, 1869; *Argus,* May 15, 16, 1869; *Herald,* May 21, 26, 1869; *World,* May 22, 31, June 3, 1869; Cassidy to Tilden, June 2, 1869, Tilden Papers; *Evening Journal,* June 7, 1869.

16. *Evening Journal,* January 13, 1869; *Leader,* January 16, February 13, 20, 27, 1869; *Irish-American,* February 20, March 6, 1869; *World,* February 22, 1869; *Evening Post,* February 23, 1869; *Herald,* February 14, April 17, 1869; U.S. Congress, House of Representatives, Select Committee on Alleged New York City Election Frauds, *Alleged New York City Election Frauds,* Report No. 31. 40th Congress, 3d Session, 1869, pp. 7-12, 28-31, 111, 148.

17. *Tribune,* March 1, May 3, July 2, 1869; *Evening Post,* March 3, 5, 6, 8, 10, 12, 27, July 7, 1869; *Herald,* March 4, 6, 9, 13, May 3, June 15, July 10, 1869; *World,* March 29, April 2, June 21, 1869; Terwilliger to Morgan, April 5, 1869, Morgan Papers; *Times,* April 17, May 16, June 18, 20, 21, 1869; Bogart to Marble, June 21, 1869, Marble Papers; *Sun,* June 30, 1869.

18. *Leader,* July 24, 31, August 7, 28, September 4, 1869.

19. *World,* August 17, 31, September 5, 8, 10, 20, 1869; *Herald,* August 22, 26, 27, September 14, 16, 18, 1869; *Leader,* August 28, September 11, 18, 1869; *Irish-American,* September 4, 1869; Belmont to Marble, September 1869, Marble Papers; Belmont to Barlow, September 30, 1869, Barlow Papers; Irving Katz, *August Belmont: A Political Biography* (New York: Columbia University Press, 1968), 188-90.

20. *Times,* September 9, 1869; *Leader,* September 11, 1869; Croly to Marble, September 13, Tilden to Marble, September 14, Chamberlain to Marble, September 16, 1869, Marble Papers; *Herald,* September 13, 1869; *World,* September 14, 1869; *Commercial Advertiser,* September 15, 1869.

22. Tilden to ?, September 25, 1869, Tilden Papers; *Commercial Advertiser,* September 26, 1869; *Evening Post,* September 23, 1869; *World,* September 27, 30, 1869; *Argus,* October 4, 1869.

23. *World,* August 17, October 14, 15, 1869; Pendleton to Marble, August 18, 1869, Marble Papers; *Evening Post,* October 13, 1869; *Herald,* October 13, 15, 19, 29, 1869; *Argus,* October 14, 1869.

24. *Irish-American,* October 6, 1869; *Leader,* October 9, 16, 23, 30, 1869; *Herald,* October 26, 1869; *World,* October 29, 1869; Mark Hirsch, "More Light on Boss Tweed," PSQ 60 (June 1945): 267-78.

25. *Leader,* November 6, 10, 24, December 4, 1869; *Irish-American,* November 13, 1869; *Herald,* November 26, 27, December 15, 1869; *Argus,* December 6, 7, 1869.

26. Stephen Hoyes, *The Political Situation Resulting from the Late State Election, (Herald Interview with Peter B. Sweeny)* (New York: The Jackson Association, 1869), pp. 15, 16.

27. Lawrence Grossman, *The Democratic Party and the Negro: Northern and National Politics, 1869-96* (Urbana, Ill.: University of Illinois Press, 1976), pp. 1-21; Keller, *Affairs of State,* pp. 238-83.

28. *World,* November 4, 5, 8, December 3, 7, 10, 1869; Tilden to Marble, March 1, 1870, Marble Papers; Casserly to Tilden, November 21, 1874, Tilden Papers; Alexander Flick, *Samuel J. Tilden: A Study in Political Sagacity* (New York: Dodd, Mead & Co., 1939), pp. 192-206; Mark Hirsch, "Samuel J. Tilden: The Story of a Lost Opportunity," AHR 56 (July 1951): 788-802; Robert Kelley, *The Transatlantic Persuasion: The Liberal-Democratic Mind in the Age of Gladstone* (New York: Knopf, 1969), pp. 238-92.

29. Barlow to Tilden, March, Church to Tilden, May 3, 1870, Tilden Papers; Belmont to Marble, March 1, Beach to Marble, March 4, Tilden to Marble, April 1870, Marble Papers.

30. *Daily Courier,* December 3, 1869.

31. *Leader,* January 1, 1870; *Argus,* January 5, 1870; Chamberlain to Marble, January 1870, Marble Papers; Frank Goodnow, "Municipal Home Rule," PSQ 21 (March 1906): 77-90.

32. *Evening Post,* January 5, 6, 7, 11, 17, 20, 1870; *Tribune,* January 5, 1870; *Evening Journal,* January 5, 1870; Weed to Fish, January 9, 1870, Weed Papers; *Times,* January 11, 1870; *Herald,* January 22, 1870; *Argus,* January 24, 1870; Calkins to Marble, January 29, 1870, Marble Papers; *Leader,* February 5, 1870.

33. *Evening Post,* February 3, 7, 1870; *Leader,* February 12, 1870; Callow, *Tweed Ring,* pp. 224-26.

34. *Times,* February 3, 7, 1870; *World,* February 3, 5, 1870; *Tribune,* February 4, 1870; *Herald,* February 4, 1870; Calkins to Marble, February 7, 1870, Marble Papers.

35. *World,* February 9, 12, 14, 16, 19, March 1, 2, 4, 7, 1870; Bryant to Marble, February 10, Calkins to Marble, February 16, Beach to Marble, February 19, Anderson to Marble, February 20, Bangs to Marble, February 21, Marble to Tilden, March 3, 1870, Marble Papers.

36. *Herald,* February 12, 14, 16, 17, 23, 28, March 5, 1870; *Daily Courier,* February 12, 19, 26, March 5, 9, 11, 1870; *Leader,* February 12, 19, 1870; *Evening Post,* February 14, 15, 25, March 8, 1870; *Argus,* February 15, 18, March 23, 1870; Cox to Marble, February 27, 1870, Marble Papers; *Times,* March 15, 1870; *Sun,* March 23, 25, 1870.

37. *Herald,* March 10, 12, 17, 24, 29, 31, 1870; *Daily Courier,* March 12, 26, 28, 31, 1870; *World,* March 18, 21, 24, 26, 29, 31, 1870; Morrissey to Marble, March 23, 1870, Marble Papers; *Leader,* March 26, 1870; *Sun,* March 27, 1870; A.C. Bernheim, "New York City and the State," PSQ 9 (September 1894): 389-92; Callow, *Tweed Ring,* pp. 222-35. For another view, see Hershkowitz, *Tweed's New York,* pp. 149-65.

38. *Daily Courier,* April 9, 1870; *Evening Post,* April 13, 28, 1870; Denis Lynch, *"Boss" Tweed: The Story of a Grim Generation* (New York: Boni & Liveright, 1927), pp. 325-26; Hershkowitz, *Tweed's New York,* p. 154.

39. *Daily Courier,* March 31, 1870; *Irish-American,* April 2, 9, May 28, 1870; *World,* April 4, 11, 20, 1870; Tilden to Marble, April 5, 1870, Marble Papers; *Times,* April 6, 8, 12, 13, May 20, 21, 1870; *Tribune,* April 7, May 28, 1870.

40. *Sun,* March 30, 1870; *Daily Courier,* March 31, 1870; *Leader,* April 2, 9, 23, 1870; *World,* May 23, 1870; Marble to Sweeny, May 26, Sweeny to Marble, May 26, 1870, Marble Papers; McJimsey, *Marble,* pp. 139-42.

41. *World,* May 23, 1870; Croly to Marble n.d. [probably May] 1870, Marble Papers.

42. Hoffman to Kernan, March 16, 1870, Kernan Family Papers; Tilden to Wells, February 2, Bryant to Wells, June 6, Garfield to Wells, June 13, Hoffman to Wells, June 13, September 10, 27, 1870, David A. Wells Papers, LC; Tom Terrill, "David A. Wells, the Democracy, and Tariff Reductions, 1877-1894," JAH 46 (December 1969): 540-55.

43. *Times,* January 5, February 13, March 13, April 11, 14, 1870; *World,* January 5, April 2, 1870; *Leader,* February 5, April 9, 1870; *Daily Courier,* February 11, April 8, 1870; *Evening Journal,* April 8, 1870; *Tribune,* April 8, 1970: David Ellis, " 'Upstate Hicks' versus 'City Slickers,' " NYHSQ 43 (April 1959): 216; David Ellis, *New York: State and City* (Ithaca, N.Y.: Cornell University Press, 1979), pp. 180-99.

44. *Daily Courier,* February 2, March 1, 10 April 2, May 17, 1870; *World,* January 27, 31, March 8, April 22, May 3, 1870; *Herald,* March 2, April 21, 1870; *Evening Post,* April 1, 1870.

45. Edward McPherson, *The Political History of the United States of America during the Period of Reconstruction* (Washington, D.C.: Philip & Solomons, 1871), pp. 546-57, 616-17; Everett Swinney, "Enforcing the Fifteenth Amendment, 1870-1877," JSH 28 (May 1972): 202-18.

46. *World,* May 23, June 22, August 19, 1870; *Daily Courier,* May 25, 31, June 1, 7, 18, August 5, 1870; *Argus,* May 25, June 18, August 19, September 2, 1870; *Leader,* May 28, 1870; *Times,* June 1, 7, August 10, 1870; *Herald,* June 1, 1870; *Irish-American,* June 4, 11, July 16, 1870; *Evening Post,* June 27, 1870; *Tribune,* August 12, 1870.

47. *Evening Post,* July 1, 2, 9, 12, August 15, 22, September 7, 20, 1870; *Times,* July 2, 13, 24, August 6, 26, 28, September 14, 1870; *Tribune,* June 2, 12, August 27, September 8, October 20, 1870; *Argus,* August 2, September 8, 1870; Grant to Conkling, August 22, 1870, Roscoe Conkling Papers, LC; *World,* September 8, 1870; George Howe, *Chester A. Arthur: A Quarter Century of Machine Politics* (New York: Dodd, Mead & Co., 1934), pp. 40-42.

48. *World,* July 18, August 2, 22, 24, September 5, 17, October 10, 1870; *Herald,* July 18, August 21, 25, September 14, 1870; *Leader,* July 23, September 3, 17, 1870; *Daily Courier,* August 22, 30, 1870; Beebe to Tilden, August 24, Beach to Tilden, September 17, 1870, Tilden Papers; *Argus,* August 30, 31, September 17, 22, 1870; *Evening Post,* August 30, September 1, 7, 1870; *Irish-American,* September 10, 1870.

49. *World,* September 19, 22, 24, 1870; *Argus,* September 23, 1870; *Leader,* September 24, 1870.

50. *Daily Courier,* October 1, 1870; *Daily News,* October 1, 4, 6, 10, 1870; *Irish-American,* October 15, 20, 1870; *Commercial Advertiser,* October 17, 20, 22, 1870; *Herald,* October 20, 21, 27, 1870; *Leader,* October 22, 1870; *World,* October 29, 1870.

51. *Times,* August 29, 1870.

52. *Tribune,* October 7, 1870; *Leader,* October 8, 1870; *World,* October 8, 10, 11, 1870; *Times,* October 10, 1870; *Daily Courier,* October 21, 1870.

53. *Herald,* October 15, 18, 19, 23, 25, 27, November 6, 8, 1870; *Evening Post,* October 19, 28, November 1, 2, 4, 6, 1870; *Leader,* October 22, 1870; *Times,* October 22, November 4, 6, 1870; *Daily Courier,* October 29, 1870; *Argus,* November 2, 9, 1870; *Tribune,* November 5, 7, 8, 1870; *Express,* November 9, 1870.

54. *Evening Post,* November 9, 11, 1870; *Times,* November 9, 1870; *Herald,* November 9, 11, 1870; *World,* November 9, 10, 1870; *Evening Journal,* November 9, 1870; *Daily Courier,* November 10, 1870; *Argus,* November 10, 11, 1870.

55. *Leader,* November 12, 19, December 17, 24, 1870; *Daily Courier,* November 18, 1870; *Irish-American,* November 19, 1870; *World,* November 22, 1870.

56. *Herald,* November 28, 1870; *World,* December 20, 1870.

6. TWEED'S REORGANIZATION FAILS: 1871-1872

1. *Times,* November 10, 1870; *Tribune,* November 10, December 13, 20, 1870, January 6, 1871; *World,* November 11, 1870; *Herald,* December 12, 19, 1870; *Commercial Advertiser,* December 20, 1870; *Daily Courier,* December 22, 1870; Jacob Cox to Schurz, December 27, 1870, March 27, April 14, 1871, Eggelson to Schurz, February 14, Thorss to Schurz, February 23, 1871, Carl Schurz Papers, LC; *Evening Post,* March 22, May 13,

1871; Earle Ross, *The Liberal Republican Movement* (New York: Henry Holt and Company, 1919), pp. 1-16; Patrick Riddelberger, "The Break in the Radical Ranks: Liberals vs. Stalwarts in the Election of 1872," JNH 46 (April 1959): 136-57.

2. *Times,* January 7, 12, 1871; *Daily Courier,* January 9, March 11, 1871; *Leader,* January 14, 1871; *Evening Post,* January 26, 1871; *Tribune,* March 2, 3, 1871; Greeley to Cornell, March 13, Cornell to Greeley, March 14, 1871, Alonzo B. Cornell Papers, Cornell University; DeAlva S. Alexander, *A Political History of the State of New York* (New York: H. Holt & Co., 1909), 3: 250-260.

3. Edward McPherson, *A Hand-Book of Politics for 1872* (Washington, D.C.: Philp & Solomons, 1872), pp. 3-8.

4. *World,* January 20, March 15, 20, April 6, 1871; *Evening Post,* March 8, 15, 24, 29, April 10, 12, 1871; *Herald,* March 8, 9, 24, May 3, 1871; *Leader,* March 11, 1871; *Argus,* March 13, April 10, 1871; *Tribune,* March 16, June 14, 15, 1871; *Irish-American,* April 21, 1871; *Daily Courier,* April 24, June 26, 1871; Allen W. Trelease, *White Terror: The Klu Klux Klan Conspiracy and Southern Reconstruction* (New York: Harper & Row, 1971).

5. *Evening Journal,* January 5, 1871; *World,* January 5, March 10, April 6, 14, 1871; *Daily Courier,* May 2, 3, June 13, 22, 1871.

6. *Herald,* February 4, 17, May 17, 1871; Marble to Blair, February 21, 1871, Blair Papers; Vallandingham to Campbell, May 4, 1871, Campbell Papers; James Vallandingham, *A Life of Clement L. Vallandingham* (Baltimore: Trumball Brothers, 1872), pp. 438-39; Clifford Moore, "Ohio in National Politics, 1865-1896," OAHQ 37 (April-June 1928): 268-72; William Smith, *The Francis Preston Blair Family in Politics* 2 vols. (New York: Macmillan Company, 1933), 2: 431-6; Michael Les Benedict, "Preserving the Constitution: The Conservative Basis of Radical Reconstruction," JAH 61 (June 1974): 65-90.

7. *Daily Courier,* May 20, 23, 27, July 19, 1871; *Herald,* May 20, 23, 31, June 2, 3, 7, 10, 19, July 5, 1871; *World,* May 23, 25, June 3, July 5, 1871; *Leader,* May 27, June 24, July 1, 1871; *Argus,* May 30, June 21, 30, July 5, 1871.

8. *Evening Post,* May 19, 24, June 5, 13, 24, July 2, August 16, 1871; *Tribune,* June 13, 14, 1871; *Daily Courier,* June 13, 15, 1871.

9. Stephens to Blair, May 8, Foote to Schurz, October 6, Schurz to J. Cox, October 14, 22, Duncan to Schurz, December 27, 1871, Schurz Papers; *Leader,* June 17, November 25, 1871; Bowles to Wells, June 20, 1871, Wells Papers; *World,* July 22, 1871; *Journal of Commerce,* September 30, 1871; *Tribune,* October 10, 12, 13, 1871.

10. *World,* January 3, 11, June 15, 1871; *Daily Courier,* January 4, 6, March 7, 8, June 10, 1871; Thompson to Marble, January 6, Hoffman to Marble, January 8, Chamberlain to Marble, n.d. [February], Moore to Marble, March 11, 1871, Marble Papers; *Herald,* February 18, March 1, April 8, May 31, 1871; *Evening Post,* March 21, May 30, 1871; *Argus,* May 30, 1871; *Leader,* July 8, 1871.

11. *Evening Post,* February 4, 6, March 1, 10, April 5, June 13, 20, 1871; *Argus,* February 8, May 20, 1871; *Times,* March 4, May 5, June 13, 1871; *Herald,* April 30, July 15, 1871; *Irish-American,* May 13, June 13, 1871;

World, May 17, June 13, 1871; Croswell Bowen, *The Elegant Oakey* (New York: Oxford University Press, 1956), pp. 70-86.

12. Tilden to Marble, January 7, Sweeny to Marble, March 10, April 26, May 19, 24, 28, 1871, Marble Papers; *Irish-American,* January 23, April 22, 1871; *Leader,* February 25, 1871; Tweed to Barlow, March 2, Stillson to Barlow, April 5, 1871, Barlow Papers; Denis Lynch, "*Boss" Tweed: The Story of a Grim Generation* (New York: Boni & Liveright, 1927), pp. 335-37.

13. *Leader,* January 28, March 18, 25, April 15, June 10, 1871; *Argus,* February 3, April 10, 14, 15, 1871; *Herald,* April 13, 17, 18, 20, 22, May 1, 1871; *Irish-American,* April 22, 1871; *World,* May 8, 1871; Alexander Callow, Jr., *The Tweed Ring* (New York: Oxford University Press, 1969), pp. 244-47; Leo Hershkowitz, *Tweed's New York: Another Look* (New York: Anchor Press, 1977), pp. 162-63.

14. *Irish-American,* July 1, 6, 15, September 21, 1871; *Evening Post,* July 11, 14, 15, 20, 1871; *World,* July 11, 12, 13, 17, 18, 1871; *Herald,* July 11, 12, 13, 1871; *Tribune,* July 13, 1871; *Argus,* July 13, 15, 16, 1871; *Times,* July 13, 14, 1871; *Leader,* July 15, 22, 1871; Joel Headley, *The Great Riots of New York City, 1712-1873* (New York: E. B. Treat, 1873), pp. 289-306.

15. *Times,* July 8, 19, 20, 22, 26, 29, 1871; Callow, *Tweed Ring,* pp. 257-61.

16. Belmont to Marble, July, Chamberlain to Marble, August 8, Bogart to Marble, August 18, 1871, Marble Papers; *Herald,* July 25, 1871; Tilden to Cassidy, August, 1871, *Letters and Literary Memorials of Samuel J. Tilden,* ed. John Bigelow, 2 vols. (New York: Harper & Bros., 1908), 1: 272-4; Church to Tilden, August 1, 1871, ibid., 1: 274; Tilden to Minturn, August 12, Seymour to Tilden, August 12, 1871, Tilden Papers; Hendricks to Doolittle, August 31, 1871, Doolittle Papers.

17. *Leader,* July 22, 29, August 5, 7, 12, 1871; *Times,* July 26, 29, August 1, 9, 10, 1871; *Daily Courier,* July 26, August 1, 10, 17, 21, 1871; *World,* July 27, 29, August 1, 4, 7, 11, 18, 1871; *Herald,* July 28, August 3, 5, 11, 19, 1871; *Argus,* August 2, 3, 9, 1871; *Irish-American,* August 5, 12, 1871.

18. *Times,* August 30, 1871.

19. *Evening Post,* September 3, 5, 7, 12, 1871; *Times,* September 3, 5, 7, 1871; *World,* September 5, 7, 8, 12, 13, 1871; Meyer Berger, *The Story of the New York Times, 1851-1951* (New York: Simon and Schuster, 1951), pp. 44-53; Seymour Mandelbaum, *Boss Tweed's New York* (New York: John Wiley & Sons, 1965), pp. 82-83; Hershkowitz, *Tweed's New York,* pp. 177-204.

20. Dix to Tilden, September 2, George Smith to Tilden, September 11, 1871, Tilden Papers; Croly to Marble, September 6, 1871, Marble Papers; Kernan to O'Conor, September 7, 1871, Kernan Family Papers; Barnett to Barlow, September 8, 1871, Barlow Papers; *Herald,* September 8, 1871.

21. *Daily Courier,* September 13, 15, 18, 1871; *World,* September 14, 15, 18, 1871; *Herald,* September 14, 15, 1871; Bryan to Kernan, September 26, 1871, Kernan Family Papers.

22. Seymour to Tilden, September 5, 1871, Tilden Papers; Sweeny to Marble, September 27, Marble to Tilden, October 11, Bogart to Marble, October 31, 1871, Marble Papers; Beach to Kernan, October 1, 1871, Kernan Family Papers.

23. Parker to Tilden, September 15, Connolly to Tilden, September 16, 1871, Tilden Papers; *Herald,* September 19, 1871; John Bigelow, *The Life of Samuel J. Tilden,* 2 vols. (New York: Harper & Bros., 1895), 1: 189-94.

24. Belmont to Marble, n.d. [September] 1871, Marble Papers; *World,* September 12, 18, 20, 21, 22, 23, 25, October 7, 16, 17, 18, 1871; Seymour to Tilden, October 8, Cassidy to Tilden, October 9, 1871, Tilden Papers; *Argus,* October 24, 25, 1871.

25. *Herald,* September 22, 1871; McKeon to Kernan, September 25, Hoffman to Kernan, September 26, 1871, Kernan Family Papers; *Argus,* October 5, 1871; *Times,* October 18, 19, 1871; *World,* October 19, 1871; *Daily Courier,* October 19, 1871.

26. Tilden to Corning, September 11, 1871, Corning Papers; Tilden to Marble, September 29, 30, 1871, Marble Papers, Kernan to Tilden, September 29, Seymour to Tilden, October 8, Cassidy to Tilden, October 9, 1871, Tilden Papers; Tilden to Kernan, September 30, 1871, *Tilden's Letters,* 1: 282.

27. *Leader,* September 30, 1871.

28. *The Writings and Speeches of Samuel J. Tilden,* ed. John Bigelow, 2 vols. (New York: Harper & Bros., 1885), 1: 488-9; Alexander Flick, *Samuel J. Tilden: A Study in Political Sagacity* (New York: Dodd, Mead & Co., 1939), pp. 218-21.

29. *Herald,* October 4, 5, 6, 1871; *Tribune,* October 5, 6, 1871.

30. *Evening Post,* October 4, 5, 6, 20, 24, 1871; *Daily Courier,* October 6, 7, 8, 9, 10, 12, 21, 25, 1871; *Express,* October 5, 1871; *Herald,* October 6, 7, 8, 9, 10, 12, 21, 25, 1871; *World,* October 6, 7, 1871; *Argus,* October 6, 7, 8, 28, 1871; *Leader,* October 14, 21, 1871; *Irish-American,* October 21, 1871.

31. Beach to Kernan, October 6, 1871, Kernan Family Papers; Stillson to Barlow, October 9, 1871, Barlow Papers; Bogart to Marble, October 10, 1871, Marble Papers; *World,* October 10, 17, 24, November 3, 1871; *Daily Courier,* October 11, 12, 17, 18, 23, 1871; *Tilden's Writings,* 1: 491.

32. *Herald,* October 4, 12, 14, 1871.

33. Conkling to Cornell, August 4, September 18, 1871, Cornell Papers; Day to Schurz, September 2, 1871, Schurz Papers; *Herald,* September 20, 29, 1871; *Tribune,* September 28, 29, 30, 1871; *World,* September 30, 1871; David Jordon, *Roscoe Conkling of New York* (Ithaca, N.Y.: Cornell University Press, 1971), pp. 158-9.

34. *Evening Post,* September 30, November 4, 6, 1871; *Times,* October 2, 4, 6, 15, 1871; *Tribune,* October 4, 10, 14, 16, 18, November 1, 1871; Somes to Greeley, October 18, 1871, Greeley Papers, LC; Conkling to Cornell, October 22, 1871, Cornell Papers.

35. *World,* October 26, 28, November 2, 1871; *Tilden's Writings,* 1: 501-14; Hershkowitz, *Tweed's New York,* pp. 197-205.

36. Phelps to Tilden, November 4, 1871, Tilden Papers; *Herald,* November 6, 7, 8, 9, 10, 1871; *Argus,* November 6, 9, 1871.

37. *Irish-American,* November 18, December 2, 1871; Hall to Marble, November 22, December 1871, Marble Papers; Shultz to Smith, November 27, 1871, Tilden Papers; *Herald,* December 5, 1871; *Leader,* December 30, 1871; Sickles to Barlow, March 24, 1872, Barlow Papers; Mark Hirsch, *William C. Whitney, Modern Warwick* (New York: Dodd, Mead & Co., 1948), pp, 60-68; Bowen, *Oakey Hall,* pp. 118-70.

38. *Herald,* November 27, December 16, 1871; *Argus,* December 7, 1871; *Daily Courier,* January 3, 4, 1872.

39. *World,* November 10, 1871, October 18, 1875; Marble to Wells, November 15, 1871, Wells Papers; Marble to Croly, November 1871, Marble Papers; *Herald,* December 30, 1871, January 7, 1872; J. Fairfax McLaughlin, *The Life and Times of John Kelly* (New York: American News Company, 1885); E. J. Edwards, "Tammany under John Kelly," *McClure's Magazine* 5 (September 1895): 325-32.

40. *Evening Post,* November 15, 1871; O'Conor to Tilden, November 11, December 22, Beach to Tilden, November 27, Seymour to Tilden, December 26, 1871, Tilden Papers; Tilden to Kernan, December 9, 1871, Kernan Family Papers; Tilden to Daniel Manning, October 22, 1882, Grover Cleveland to Kings County Democratic Club, February 2, 1888, Grover Cleveland Papers, LC; Flick, *Tilden,* pp. 225-41.

41. *Tribune,* November 12, 20, 21, 22, December 4, 1871, January 29, 1872; *Daily Courier,* November 24, 1871; Bayard to Tilden, December 21, 1871, Tilden Papers; Ari Hoogenboom, *Outlawing the Spoils: A History of the Civil Service Reform Movement, 1865-1883* (Urbana, Ill.: University of Illinois Press, 1968), pp. 70-101.

7. STOPGAP RECONSTRUCTION: THE ELECTIONS OF 1872

1. *Evening Post,* November 22, 1871; Gideon Welles to Blair, November 27, Blair to Marble, December 13, 1871, Blair Papers; Davis to Marble, December 17, 1871, Marble Papers; *Daily Courier,* January 6, 1872.

2. *World,* November 18, December 1, 18, 1871, January 15, March 29, 1872; Bogart to Marble, November 21, 1871, Belmont to Marble, January 1, 1872, Marble Papers; *Irish-American,* December 2, 1871, January 20, April 6, 1872; *Leader,* December 30, 1871; *Daily Courier,* January 29, 1872; *Daily News,* January 22, 1872; *Argus,* January 29, 1872.

3. *World,* December 18, 1871; *Herald,* April 2, 1872.

4. *World,* November 24, December 22, 1871, March 4, 1872; Marble to Blair, November 28, December 10, Blair to Marble, December 14, 1871, Blair Papers.

5. Ritterly to Schurz, December 25, 1871, Nordhoff to Schurz, March 13, 1872, Schurz Papers; Bigelow to Morgan, January 2, 1872, Morgan Papers; *Evening Post,* April 4, 1872.

6. *World,* February 20, 1872; Tilden to Cassidy, March 25, 1872, Tilden Papers; *Argus,* April 11, 1872; *Irish-American,* April 20, 1872.

7. *World,* January 31, February 2, March 2, 3, April 5, 1872; *Herald,* March 5, 11, 1872.

8. Belmont to Schurz, April 23, 1872, Schurz Papers; Irving Katz, *August Belmont: A Political Biography* (New York: Columbia University Press, 1968), pp. 197-98.

9. Grant to Conkling, January 19, 1872, Conkling Papers; J. Cox to Schurz, February 14, April 15, 1872, Schurz Papers; *Evening Post,* March 14, 20, 1872; Osborne to Wells, March 16, 1872, Wells Papers; Osborne to Adams, April 16, 1872, Adams Family Papers, MHS; James McPherson,

"Grant or Greeley? The Abolitionist Dilemma in the Election of 1872," AHR 71 (October 1965): 43-61.

10. *Leader,* September 3, 1870; *Tribune,* March 6, 1872; *World,* March 12, 14, April 23, 1872; Pierce to Adams, March 28, Wells to Adams, April 17, 1872, Adams Papers; *Herald,* April 18, 20, 1872; Cake to Greeley, April 11, 1872, Greeley Papers, LC; Marble to Schurz, April 23, Schurz to Greeley, May 6, 1872, Schurz Papers; Edgar Wells to Wells, April 15, 1872, Wells Papers; Weed to Patterson, July 7, 1872, Weed Papers; Earle Ross, "Horace Greeley and the South," SAQ 16 (October 1917): 324-38; Harry W. Baehr, Jr., *The New York Tribune since the Civil War* (New York: Dodd, Mead and Co., 1936), pp. 67-108.

11. Davis to Blair, April 17, 1872, Schurz Papers; Belmont to Bowles, May 7, Trumbull to Wells, May 11, 1872, Wells Papers; *Herald,* May 8, 1872.

12. Bartlett to Schurz, February 2, Bowles to Schurz, March 18, 1872, Schurz Papers; J. Cox to Wells, April 4, Van Buren to Wells, April 20, 24, 1872, Wells Papers.

13. *Tribune,* January 7, 1872; *Evening Post,* January 18, 1872; *Daily Courier,* February 24, 1872.

14. *Irish-American,* January 3, 1872; *Herald,* January 12, February 27, March 10, 1872; *Daily Courier,* January 12, March 13, 30, 1872; Small to Marble, February 22, 1872, Marble Papers.

15. *Herald,* April 16, 1872; *Times,* April 16, 17, 1872; *Irish-American,* April 27, 1872.

16. *Daily News,* January 22, 30, February 1, 19, 26, March 20, 21, 1872; *Herald,* February 5, May 16, 1872; *Daily Courier,* April 10, May 15, 1872; *Times,* May 16, 1872; *Argus,* May 16, 1872.

17. *Daily Courier,* January 6, 20, 1872; *Evening Post,* January 8, 9, 29, 1872; *World,* January 10, 30, 1872; *Express,* February 17, 1872.

18. *Argus,* January 3, 1872; Hoffman to Kernan, January 5, 1872, Kernan Family Papers.

19. *Herald,* January 5, 25, February 15, 21, March 1, 8, 15, 1872; Casserly to Barlow, April, Charles Day to Barlow, April 23, 24, 27, June 8, September 18, 1872, Barlow Papers; Edward Hungerford, *Men of Erie* (New York: Random House, 1946), pp. 166-74.

20. John Smith to Tilden, November 22, 1871, O'Conor to Tilden, February 3, 1872, Tilden Papers; *Daily News,* March 21, 1872; *Argus,* May 2, 1872; *The Writings and Speeches of Samuel J. Tilden,* ed. John Bigelow, 2 vols. (New York: Harper & Bros., 1885), 1: 472-75.

21. *Daily Courier,* January 13, March 25, April 11, 1872; *Irish-American,* January 20, March 16, November 2, 1872; *Argus,* January 24, 1872; *Times,* April 13, 1872; *Herald,* October 25, 1872; Hall to Marble, December 3, 1872, Marble Papers.

22. *Daily Courier,* January 23, April 12, 22, 1872; *Tribune,* February 2, 22, 1872; Mark Hirsch, *William C. Whitney, Modern Warwick* (New York: Dodd, Mead & Co., 1948), pp. 63-64.

23. *World,* February 13, 17, 29, April 8, 16, 22, 1872; *Argus,* February 23, May 2, 1872; *Herald,* April 18, 1872; *Evening Post,* May 1, 1872; *Daily Courier,* May 2, 1872.

24. *Tribune,* May 1, 2, 15, June 8, 1872; *Herald,* May 3, 10, 12, 1872; *Evening Post,* May 3, 1872; *Argus,* May 15, June 5, 1872; *Times,* June 4, 5, 6, 26, 27, 1872.

25. Vivus Smith to Weed, April 14, 1872, Weed Papers; Carmichael to Seymour, April 20, 1872, Seymour Papers; Chamberlain to Marble, May 3, 1872, Marble Papers; *Herald,* May 4, 5, 6, 1872; Casserly to Barlow, May 17, 1872, Barlow Papers; Earle Ross, *The Liberal Republican Movement* (New York: Henry Holt and Company, 1919), pp. 86-149.

26. Marble to Chamberlain, May 3, Tilden to Marble, May 15, Belmont to Marble, June 10, 1872, Marble Papers; *Daily News,* May 6, 1872; Forrest to Long, May 18, 1872, Long Papers; Watterson to Smith, May 19, 1872, William H. Smith Papers, OHS; *Argus,* May 22, 1872; Belmont to Lyons, June 3, 1872, Barlow Papers; Joseph Wall, *Henry Watterson: Reconstructed Rebel* (New York: Oxford University Press, 1956), pp. 87-113.

27. *Evening Post,* May 3, 4, 5, 6, 9, 22, June 1, 6, 17, 1872; Pierce to Adams, May 2, 1872, Adams Papers; Tilden to Sands, May 29, 1872, Tilden Papers; *Herald,* May 13, June 4, 1872; Matthew Downey, "Horace Greeley and the Politicans: The Liberal Republican Convention in 1872," JAH 53 (March 1967): 727-70.

28. Schurz to Greeley, May 6, 9, 11, Greeley to Schurz, May 8, 10, 12, 17, 20, Schurz to Sands, May 9, Schurz to Bowles, May 11, 1872, Schurz Papers; Blair to Reid, May 25, 1872, Whitelaw Reid Papers, LC; Baehr, *New York Tribune,* pp. 109-110.

29. Bowles to Wells, May 13, 21, 28, Reid to Bowles, May 14, 26, White to Wells, May 19, J. Cox to Wells, May 25, Reid to Wells, June 25, 1872, Wells Papers; Schurz to Greeley, May 18, White to Schurz, May 25, 1872, Schurz Papers; Reid to Bowles, May 26, Schurz to Blair, May 29, 1872, Reid Papers; Allan Nevins, *The Evening Post: A Century of Journalism* (New York: Boni & Liveright, 1922), pp. 394-400.

30. Sanford to Weed, May 3, 8, Patterson to Weed, June 14, 1872, Weed Papers; Reid to Schurz, May 27, 29, Godwin to Schurz, May 28, Schurz to Godwin, June 23, 1872, Schurz Papers; *Herald,* June 21, 1872; *Evening Post,* June 27, 1872; Claude Fuess, *Carl Schurz, Reformer* (New York: Dodd, Mead & Co., 1932), pp. 195-97.

31. *World,* May 7, 9, 10, 15, 22, 31, June 7, 13, 18, 1872; Croly to Marble, May 10, Bogart to Marble, May 25, Ward to Marble, June 23, 1872, Marble Papers; *Irish-American,* May 18, 1872; Pierrepont to Morgan, July 1, 1872, Morgan Papers.

32. *Herald,* May 9, 17, 25, 27, June 7, 11, 22, 1872.

33. *Argus,* May 6, 18, June 8, 1872; *Daily Courier,* May 8, 9, 16, 18, 22, June 8, 11, 14, 20, 28, 1872; *Express,* May 12, 1872; S. Cox to Weed, May 22, 1872, Weed Papers; *World,* July 1, 3, 1872; Tilden to Casserly, July 3, 1872, Tilden Papers.

34. *World,* July 9, 10, 11, 13, 29, 1872; *Daily Courier,* July 9, 10, 13, 16, 1872; *Argus,* July 9, 13, 28, 30, 1872; Belmont to Marble, July 11, 1872, Marble Papers; Jones to Kernan, July 13, 1872, Kernan Family Papers; *Irish-American,* July 13, 20, 1872.

35. Weed to Dix, June 24, Weed to Patterson, July 4, Patterson to Weed, July 10, Vivus Smith to Weed, July 28, Blanton to Weed, November 5, 1872, Weed Papers; *Daily Courier,* July 11, 18, 22, August 5, 7, 24, 27, September 1, 1872; Dix to Morgan, August 1, Blaine to Morgan, August 2, 10, 1872, Morgan Papers; *World,* August 8, September 4, 1872; Thurman to Tilden, August 20, 1872, Tilden Papers; Bryan to Kernan, August 26, 1872, Kernan Family Papers; David Montgomery, *Beyond Equality; Labor and the Radical Republicans, 1860-1872* (New York: Alfred A. Knopf, 1967), p. 409.

36. Callaway to Seymour, August 8, 1872, Seymour Papers; *World,* August 27, 1872; Chamberlain to Barlow, September 1, 1872, Barlow Papers; Phillips to Tilden, October 9, 1872, Tilden Papers.

37. Dix to Weed, August 5, Reed to Weed, August 28, Vivus Smith to Weed, August 30, 1872, Weed Papers; *Sun,* August 7, 1872; *Herald,* August 21, 22, 1872; Dix to Morgan, August 24, 1872, Morgan Papers; Thurlow Weed, *Autobiography of Thurlow Weed,* ed. Harriet Weed, 2 vols. (Boston and New York: Houghton Mifflin and Co., 1883), 2: 486-87.

38. Havemeyer to Dix, August 22, 1872, Dix Papers; *Daily Courier,* August 23, 24, 29, 1872; Vivus Smith to Weed, August 30, 1872, Weed Papers.

39. Church to Kernan, June 26, Dorsheimer to Kernan, July 22, Comstock to Kernan, August 14, Bryan to Kernan, August 31, 1872, Kernan Family Papers; *World,* July 24, August 13, 1872; Seymour to Tilden, August 20, 29, 1872, Tilden Papers; *Tribune,* August 21, 1872; *Argus,* August 22, 1872; Beach to Marble, August 27, 1872, Marble Papers.

40. Moore to Schurz, September 3, 1872, Schurz Papers; *Daily News,* September 5, 1872; Pechman to Kernan, September 6, Greeley to Kernan, September 10, Hoffman to Kernan, September 11, 1872, Kernan Family Papers; *Evening Post,* September 6, 7, October 14, 1872; *Evening Journal,* September 6, 7, October 22, 1872; *Argus,* September 7, October 10, 11, 31, 1872; Kernan to Tilden, September 17, Seymour to Tilden, October 3, 20, Phillips to Tilden, October 9, 1872, Tilden Papers; *World,* October 9, 14, 18, 1872; Hodge to Weed, October 10, 1872, Weed Papers; *Tribune,* October 12, 1872; Chauncey M. Depew, *My Memories of Eighty Years* (New York: Charles Scribner's Sons, 1924), pp. 91-98; Florence Gibson, *The Attitudes of the New York Irish toward State and National Affairs, 1848-1892* (New York: Columbia University Press, 1951), pp. 288-91.

41. *World,* September 28, October 4, 6, 9, 10, 14, 19, 1872; *Times,* October 5, 12, 1872; Kelly to Smith, October 6, 1872, Tilden Papers; *Daily Courier,* October 14, 1872.

42. *Herald,* September 26, October 27, November 2, 1872; *Evening Post,* September 24, October 4, 6, 11, 15, 23, 24, 26, 1872; *Times,* October 4, 1872; *World,* October 11, 23, 25, 1872; *Irish-American,* October 26, 1872.

43. *Daily Courier,* September 10, October 16, 30, 1872; *World,* September 17, 20, October 16, 28, 29, November 4, 1872; *Tribune,* October 12, 29, 1872; *Herald,* October 26, November 5, 1872; Beach to Tilden, October 21, 1872, Tilden Papers; *Times,* November 2, 1872.

44. *World,* November 6, 7, 9, 14, 22, 1872; *Herald,* November 6, 7, 1872; *Argus,* November 7, 14, 26, 1872; *Irish-American,* November 16, 1872; Havemeyer to Morgan, December 3, 1872, Morgan Papers.

45. *Herald,* November 10, 16, 18, 23, December 27, 1872; *Evening Post,* November 26, December 24, 1872; *World,* November 29, December 10, 1872; *Daily Courier,* December 23, 1872, January 3, 1873; Hastings to Weed, December 30, 1872, Weed Papers.

46. *Daily Courier,* December 2, 6, 20, 1872; *Argus,* December 5, 8, 1872; *Herald,* December 13, 21, 28, 1872; *World,* December 14, 1872; *Irish-American,* December 28, 1872.

47. *Evening Post,* November 12, 1872. See also George Fredrickson, *The Black Image in the White Mind* (New York: Harper & Row, 1971), pp. 165-97.

48. *Daily Courier,* November 6, 20, December 16, 1872; *World,* November 15, 1872.

49. Beach to Marble, December 13, 1872, Marble Papers; Blair to Tilden, December 26, 1872, Tilden Papers.

50. For a discussion of these Jacksonian values, see Marvin Meyers, *The Jacksonian Persuasion* (Stanford, Calif.: Stanford University Press, 1957).

51. Kelley, *The Transatlantic Persuasion,* pp. 238-92. For Tilden ideas, see his *Writings,* particularly 1: 20-247, 394-606; 2: 9-137, 237-95, 366-70, 499-534.

8. THE FINAL RECONSTRUCTION: 1873-1874

1. *World,* January 10, 24, 30, February 1, 14, 18, 19, 21, March 6, 1873; *Irish-American,* January 25, 1873; *Herald,* February 6, 11, 20, 24, 1873; *Daily Courier,* February 1, 14, 19, 21, 1873; Casserly to Marble, January 29, Wood to Marble, February 19, 1873, Marble Papers.

2. *Times,* January 4, 21, February 4, 11, 22, 1873.

3. *World,* February 4, 6, 20, 21, March 14, April 3, 1873; Tilden to Marble, February 2, 1873, Marble Papers.

4. *Evening Post,* February 27, March 11, 1873; Marble to Tilden, February 1, March 3, Reid to Tilden, March 11, 1873; *The Writings and Speeches of Samuel J. Tilden,* ed. John Bigelow, 2 vols. (New York: Harper & Bros., 1885), 1: 533-606.

5. *Daily Courier,* March 18, 29, 1873; *Evening Post,* March 5, 19, April 1, 1873; *World,* March 28, 1873; *Tribune,* March 30, 1873; *Argus,* March 31, 1873.

6. *Herald,* January 1, 7, 9, March 18, 1873; *Daily Courier,* January 3, 24, February 18, 20, 1873; *World,* January 7, 8, February 12, 18, 1873; Marble to Tilden, January, Tilden to Marble, March 20, 1873, Marble Papers; *Times,* February 15, 1873; Dix to Weed, May 8, 1872, Weed Papers; *Tribune,* July 8, 1873.

7. *Evening Post,* January 3, February 5, 17, 1873; *Herald,* January 7, 9, 26, February 17, 1873; *Irish-American,* January 18, 1873; *Argus,* January 31, February 5, 18, 1873; *Times,* February 15, 1873.

8. *World,* February 7, 18, 21, March 3, 6, 10, 18, April 17, 1873; *Daily Courier,* February 22, 25, 28, March 12, 19, 20, 24, 1873; Dix to Morgan, March 5, 1873, Morgan Papers; Tilden to Dix, March 22, 1873, Dix Papers; *Tribune,* April 2, 17, 1873; *Irish-American,* April 5, 1873.

9. *Herald,* February 12, March 2, 3, 17, 26, 1873; *Argus,* April 17, 23, 1873; *Daily Courier,* May 10, 1873.

10. *World,* April 17, 1873; *Daily Courier,* April 18, 19, 1873; *Evening Post,* May 17, June 30, July 1, 2, 4, 7, 1873; *Herald,* June 1, 1873.

11. *Irish-American,* April 19, 26, May 24, June 14, 1873; *Evening Post,* May 8, 17, June 30, 1873; *World,* May 19, 1873; *Daily Courier,* May 22, 29, 31, July 30, 1873; *Herald,* May 25, June 25, 1873; Diane Ravitch, *The Great School Wars: New York City, 1805-1973* (New York: Basic Books, 1973), pp. 99-105.

12. *Herald,* April 27, May 5, 6, 8, 22, 1873; Dix to Weed, May 2, 21, 1873, Weed Papers; *Evening Post,* May 9, 12, 13, 1873; *World,* May 21, June 5, 1873; *Daily Courier,* May 29, 1873; Havemeyer to Tilden, June 10, 1873, Tilden Papers.

13. *World,* May 19, August 2, 1873; *Evening Post,* June 12, 30, 1873; *Irish-American,* June 21, July 26, 1873; *Times,* July 11, 20, 1873; *Tribune,* August 13, 1873; Howard Furer, *William Frederick Havemeyer: A Political Biography* (New York: American Press, 1965), pp. 144-60.

14. *Daily Courier,* June 12, 27, August 18, October 6, 1873; *Irish-American,* June 14, 1873; *World,* June 20, 27, July 8, August 2, 18, 25, 1873; *Herald,* July 5, 8, 23, August 13, 21, 22, September 6, 1873; *Sun,* August 14, 21, 1873; *Times,* September 10, 1873; Kelly to Tilden, October 28, 1873, Tilden Papers.

15. *World,* April 23, May 9, 14, 22, 29, June 6, 13, 28, July 5, 15, August 6, 13, 15, September 1, 1873.

16. *Argus,* May 1, 1873; *Daily Courier,* May 3, 4, August 6, 13, September 1, 1873; *World,* May 6, July 12, 24, August 2, 15, 1873; *Irish-American,* August 9, 16, 1873; Frederick Merk, "Eastern Antecedents of the Grangers," *Agricultural History* 12 (1949): 1-8.

17. *Daily Courier,* June 23, July 4, 6, 9, 11, 28, August 1, 4, 5, 8, 1873; *World,* July 14, 20, 29, August 1, 3, 8, 1873; *Argus,* July 17, August 7, 11, 1873; Utica *Observer,* July 31, August 9, 1873; Beach to Marble, August 9, 1873, Marble Papers.

18. *World,* June 11, August 26, September 2, 3, 4, 1873; *Herald,* August 22, September 4, October 9, 1873; *Argus,* September 1, 22, 1873.

19. *Daily Courier,* June 16, July 7, September 30, 1873; *Herald,* June 22, September 15, 20, 30, October 3, 1873; *World*, June 24, September 8, 30, October 2, 1873; *Daily News,* August 4, 1873; *Irish-American,* September 27, October 4, 1873; *Sun,* September 29, October 5, 1873; *Commercial Advertiser,* October 5, 1873.

20. Murphy to Grant, September 19, 1873, Grant Papers; *Herald,* September 19, 20, 26, October 1, 1873; *Evening Post,* September 20, 22, 23, 24, 26, 1873; *Argus,* September 20, 22, 26, 1873; *World,* September 20, 28, 1873.

21. *Herald,* October 3, 4, 1873; *Irish-American,* October 4, 11, 1873.

22. *World,* October 6, 7, 8, 9, 10, 11, 14, 15, 16, 1873; *Herald,* October 10,-11, 12, 15, 1873; *Tribune,* October 13, 14, 1873; Cox to Marble, October 13, Comstock to Marble, October 18, 1873, Marble Papers; *Evening Post,* October 16, 1873.

23. *Evening Post,* October 20, 25, 1873; *Herald,* October 21, 25, 26, 1873; *Daily Courier,* October 21, 28, 29, 1873; *Irish-American,* October 25, November 1, 1873; *Daily News,* October 17, 1873; *World,* October 28, 29, November 3, 1873.

24. *Evening Post,* October 9, 1873; *Herald,* October 9, 10, 23, 1873.

25. Dix to Weed, September 13, 29, 1873, Weed Papers; Weed to Dix, September 15, Barlow to Dix, September 17, Conkling to Dix, October 2, 1873, Dix Papers; *Evening Post,* September 25, October 1, 2, 1873.

26. *World,* October 11, 15, 18, 20, November 3, 1873; *Argus,* October 14, 17, 24, 1873; Utica *Observer,* October 14, 26, 1873; *Times,* October 18, 1873; *Evening Post,* October 23, November 3, 1873; Dix to Weed, October 29, Smith to Weed, November 9, 1873, Weed Papers.

27. *Evening Post,* October 9, 1873; *Herald,* October 9, 13, November 3, 1873; *World,* October 15, 1873; *Daily Courier,* November 10, 1873.

28. *World,* October 19, November 4, 1873; *Irish-American,* October 25, November 1, 1873; Kelly to Marble, October 27, 1873, Marble Papers.

29. *Herald,* November 6, 1873; *Irish-American,* November 15, 1873.

30. *World,* November 5, 6, 10, 1873; *Argus,* November 5, 6, 21, 1873; *Evening Post,* November 5, 8, 19, 1873; *Times,* November 5, 10, 14, 1873; Kernan to Tilden, November 7, Beach to Tilden, November 11, 1873, Tilden Papers; Cochrane to Schurz, November 20, December 15, 1873, Schurz Papers; Beach to Marble, November 27, 1873, Marble Papers. Tilden, on his return from Europe, had resumed his state chairmanship.

31. *Herald,* November 7, 11, December 2, 1873; *World,* November 22, 1873; *Irish-American,* November 29, 1873; *Daily Courier,* December 22, 25, 1873.

32. *Herald,* November 6, 24, 1873; *World,* November 8, 9, 11, December 9, 11, 1873, January 21, 23, 25, 26, 30, 1874; *Daily Courier,* November 12, 14, December 15, 19, 1873, January 19, 1874; Bigelow to Morgan, November 27, 1873, Morgan Papers.

33. *Herald,* January 14, 1874; Herbert Gutman, "The Tompkins Square 'Riot' in New York City on January 13, 1874: A Reexamination of Its Causes and Its Aftermath," *Labor History* 6 (Winter 1965): 48-55.

34. *World,* January 14, 1874; *Argus,* January 14, 1874; *Daily Courier,* January 20, 1874; *Irish-American,* January 24, 1874.

35. *World,* February 11, March 8, 30, 1874; *Herald,* May 8, 1874; *Evening Post,* June 5, 1874; *Tilden's Writings,* 2:58; Samuel Rezneck, "Distress, Relief, and Discontent in the United States during the Depression of 1873-78," *The Journal of Political Economy* 48 (December 1950): 494-512.

36. *Evening Post,* January 5, 6, 7, February 24, 1874; *World,* January 7, 1874; *Daily Courier,* January 7, 1874; Dix to Weed, February 24, 1874, Weed Papers.

37. Marble to Schurz, January 27, Birney to Schurz, March 27, 1874, Schurz Papers; *Irish-American,* March 7, 1874; *Tribune,* March 14, 1874; *Evening Post,* March 24, 26, 30, April 7, 8, 1874; *Daily Courier,* March 24, 1874; Dix to Weed, March 30, April 25, 1874, Weed Papers; Walter Nugent, *The Money Question during Reconstruction* (New York: W. W. Norton & Co., 1967), pp. 93-94.

38. *World,* April 8, 23, 1874; *Daily Courier,* April 8, 1874; Weed to Dix, April 10, 1874, Weed Papers; *Irish-American,* April 18, 1874; *Evening Post,* April 18, 30, 1874.

39. *Argus,* April 23, May 12, 1874; *Herald,* April 25, 1874; *Times,* May 3, 1874; *Evening Post,* May 7, 1874; *World,* May 8, 9, 13, 1874.

40. *Evening Post,* February 4, 6, 23, March 9, 30, July 27, 1874.

41. *World,* February 6, 26, March 1, April 16, 19, 1874.

42. *Herald,* June 10, 1874.

43. *Herald,* January 1, 23, February 3, 7, March 9, 16, 20, 23, April 10, May 3, 1874; *Evening Post,* March 14, April 4, 1874; Andrews to Marble, June 2, 1874, Marble Papers; Seymour Mandelbaum, *Boss Tweed's New York* (New York: John Wiley & Sons, 1965), pp. 98-110.

44. *Times,* April 8, 10, 24, May 18, July 14, October 24, 26, 1874; James Richardson, "To Control the Police: The New York Police in Historical Perspective," in *Cities in American History,* eds. Kenneth Jackson and Stanley Schultz, (New York: Alfred A. Knopf, 1972), pp. 272-78.

45. *Daily Courier,* February 6, 8, 1874; *Evening Post,* February 9, 1874; *Herald,* February 18, 18, 1874; Dix to Weed, February 24, 1874, Weed Papers; *World,* March 6, April 30, May 9, 1874.

46. *Times,* May 5, 6, 12, 1874; *Argus,* May 11, 1874; *Herald,* May 13, 16, June 10, 1874; *World,* May 14, 23, 1874; Tilden to Marble, May 16, 1874, Marble Papers; Augustine Costello, *Our Police Protectors* (New York: Published by the author, 1885), pp. 263-64.

47. *Herald,* April 21, May 21, 29, June 23, 24, 26, 30, July 1, 2, 3, 1874; *World,* May 23, July 6, 1874; *Times,* July 1, 1874; *Evening Journal,* May 1, 2, 1874; *Argus,* July 2, 1874; *Evening Post,* July 2, 3, 1874; *Irish-American,* July 4, 1874.

48. *Herald,* July 3, 8, 9, 10, 12, 1874; James Richardson, *The New York Police: Colonial Times to 1901* (New York: Oxford University Press, 1970), pp. 216-17.

49. *World,* May 23, July 6, 1874; *Times,* July 3, 1874; *Daily Courier,* July 4, 1874; *Evening Post,* July 5, 1874; *Irish-American,* July 11, 1874.

50. *Tribune,* July 8, 9, 1874; *Times,* July 10, 1874; Dix to Havemeyer, July 10, Havemeyer to Dix, July 27, 1874, Dix Papers; *Herald,* July 28, August 17, 1874; *Evening Post,* August 6, 1874; *World,* August 7, 1874; Havemeyer to Morgan, August 13, 1874, Morgan Papers; Furer, *Havemeyer,* pp. 171-72.

51. *World,* May 2, July 4, 15, 23, August 19, September 1, 1874; *Daily Courier,* May 23, August 12, 1874; *Herald,* May 23, 1874; *Evening Post,* May 25, 1874; *Irish-American,* May 30, 1874; Bertram Wyatt-Brown, "The Civil Rights Act of 1875," *Western Political Quarterly* 18 (December 1965): 763-75; David Donald, *Charles Sumner and The Rights of Man* (New York: Alfred A. Knopf, 1970), pp. 530-87.

52. *World,* May 1, November 11, 1874.

53. *Evening Post,* February 20, May 25, August 13, September 24, October 17, 19, 1874; William Hesseltine, "Economic Factors in the Abandonment of Reconstruction," MVHR 22 (September 1935): 191-210; C. Vann Woodward, "Seeds of Failure in Radical Race Policy," *Proceedings of the American Philosophical Society* 110 (February 1966): 1-9; George Fred-

rickson, *The Black Image in the White Mind* (New York: Harper & Row, 1971), pp. 165-97.

54. *Herald,* February 4, May 24, August 4, 13, 25, 28, September 9, 28, 1874; Forsythe to Marble, February 27, 1874, Marble Papers; *World,* August 19, 26, September 11, 1874; *Irish-American,* August 29, October 31, 1874; *Evening Post,* September 8, October 19, 1874; C. Vann Woodward, *The Strange Career of Jim Crow* (New York: Oxford University Press, 1963), pp. 3-95; Lawrence Grossman, *The Democratic Party and the Negro: Northern and National Politics, 1869-96* (Urbana, Ill.: University of Illinois Press, 1976), pp. 165-97.

55. Reid to Weed, January 6, Dix to Weed, January 9, Dix to H. Smith, September 3, 1874, Weed Papers; *Daily Courier,* February 20, June 13, 17, July 2, August 10, 20, 1874; *World,* February 21, March 2, September 15, 1874; *Evening Post,* June 15, September 15, 1874.

56. *Argus,* April 10, 1874; *Herald,* April 20, May 13, 1874; *World,* May 8, 1874; *Daily Courier,* May 8, 1874; *Irish-American,* May 16, 1874.

57. *Herald,* May 7, 1874; *Argus,* July 2, 3, 1874; Beach to Tilden, July 20, 1874, Tilden Papers.

58. *Daily Courier,* February 27, March 2, 3, 4, 9, August 11, 1874; *World,* February 28, 1874; Smith Weed to Tilden, July 1, Kernan to Tilden, July 21, August 31, Robinson to Tilden, August 21, Seymour to Tilden, August 27, September 11, Jacob Gould to Tilden, September 5, 1874, Tilden Papers.

59. *Herald,* June 10, July 13, 24, August 6, 8, 25, 28, September 1, 5, 9, 1874.

60. *Tribune,* August 11, 1874; *Argus,* August 24, 25, 1874; *Daily Courier,* August 25, 26, 1874.

61. Marble to Tilden, August 7, 1874, Marble Papers; *World,* August 21, 22, September 6, 7, 1874; Mangone to Tilden, August 21, Tilden to Jenkins, August 29, Barlow to Tilden, August 31, Campbell to Tilden, September 10, 1874, Tilden Papers; Tilden to Kernan, September 9, 1874, Kernan Family Papers.

62. *Tribune,* August 16, 17, September 3, 1874; *Evening Post,* August 21, 27, September 7, 8, 1874; *Herald,* September 7, 10, 1874; *World,* September 9, 10, 1874.

63. *Herald,* August 25, September 7, 10, 16, 1874; *Daily Courier,* September 10, 11, 12, 1874; Kernan to Tilden, September 10, Parker to Tilden, September 16, 1874, Tilden Papers; *Argus,* September 10, 1874; *Times,* September 15, 16, 1874; Alexander Flick, *Samuel J. Tilden: A Study in Political Sagacity* (New York: Dodd, Mead & Co., 1939), p. 244.

64. *World,* September 10, 11, 14, 16, 17, 18, 1874.

65. *Tribune,* September 17, 1874; *Times,* September 17, 1874; *Sun,* September 17, 1874; *Evening Post,* September 17, 19, 1874; Roosevelt to Tilden, September 18, Butler to Tilden, September 18, 1874, Tilden Papers; *Herald,* September 18, 1874; *World,* September 19, 22, 1874; *Daily Courier,* September 28, 1874.

66. *Daily Courier,* September 18, 21, 22, 1874; Belmont to Marble, September 19, 1874, Marble Papers; *World,* September 21, 22, 1874; *Irish-American,* September 26, 1874; Seymour to Tilden, October 16, 1874, Tilden Papers; *Argus,* October 30, 1874.

67. Tilden to Birdsall, September 19, Tilden to Cooke, September 19, Tilden to Abbott, September 27, Seymour to Tilden, September 20, October 20, Comstock to Tilden, September 25, Pursell to Tilden, October 2, Tilden to ?, October 10, Dorsheimer to Tilden, October 20, 1874, Tilden Papers; William Hudson, *Random Recollections of an Old Political Reporter* (New York: Cupples and Company, 1911), pp. 45-46.

68. Bigelow to Tilden, September 18, Seymour to Tilden, September 21, Kernan to Tilden, September 22, Dorsheimer to Tilden, October 1, 1874, Tilden Papers; *World,* September 22, 29, 30, 1874; *Irish-American,* September 26, October 18, 1874; *Herald,* September 30, 1874; *Argus,* September 28, 30, 1874; Marble to Tilden, October 1874, Marble Papers; Bingham Duncan, *Whitelaw Reid: Journalist, Politican, Diplomat* (Athens, Ga.: University of Georgia Press, 1974), pp. 65-66.

69. *World,* August 14, September 18, 23, 25, 30, October 1, 2, 7, 8, 19, 1874; *Herald,* September 20, 22, October 22, 1874; *Evening Post,* September 24, October 17, 1874; Dix to Weed, September 26, October 23, 1874, Weed Papers; Seymour to Tilden, October 3, O'Conor to Tilden, October 20, 1874, Tilden Papers; Morgan to Dix, October 7, 22, 1874, Dix Papers; Conkling to Morgan, October 22, 1874, Morgan Papers.

70. *Herald,* September 18, 19, 20, 1874; Furer, *Havemeyer,* p. 173.

71. *World,* September 14, 23, October 2, 3, 4, 9, 17, 27, 28, 1874; *Herald,* September 20, 26, October 1, 2, 13, December 1, 1874; *Irish-American,* September 26, October 10, 1874; *Evening Post,* October 2, 12, December 1, 2, 1874. The libel suit became moot with Havemeyer's death.

72. *World,* October 2, 7, 11, 12, 27, 28, 1874; *Irish-American,* October 10, 17, 24, 1874; *Commercial Advertiser,* October 12, 31, 1874; *Times,* October 21, 26, 1874; Kelly to Marble, October 25, Wickham to Marble, October 28, 1874, Marble Papers.

73. *Herald,* November 4, 1874; *Argus,* November 4, 6, 1874; Barlow to Tilden, November 4, 1874, Tilden Papers; *Irish-American,* November 14, 1874; Albert House, "The Speakership Contest of 1875; Democratic Response to Power," JAH 42 (September 1965): 252-56.

74. *Herald,* November 4, 5, 7, 1874; Kernan to Tilden, November 13, 1874, Tilden Papers.

75. *World,* November 4, 10, 1874; *Argus,* November 5, 10, 14, 1874; Casserly to Marble, November 5, 1874, Marble Papers; *Daily Courier,* November 10, 12, 1874; *Irish-American,* November 14, 1874; Earle Ross, *"Samuel J. Tilden and the Revival of the Democratic Party,"* SAQ 19 (January 1920): 43-54.

A Note on Sources

Since the major sources upon which this study rests are almost primary in nature, the purpose of this note is threefold: first, to acquaint readers with the sources used in this study; second, to evaluate the utility of these sources; third, to give readers an insight into my methods and conclusions.

The bulk of Democratic manuscript collections are uneven or unbalanced. No single collection contains a storehouse of information. Furthermore, evidence exists that many Democrats destroyed letters that might prove embarrassing, particularly in regard to their relationship with William M. Tweed.

The most extensive collections are those of Samuel L. M. Barlow (Henry E. Huntington Library), Andrew Johnson (LC), Manton Marble (LC), and Samuel J. Tilden (NYPL). Each, however, contains certain limitations. The Barlow Papers, although rich in the period from 1858 to 1868, diminish in value thereafter. Moreover, Barlow's letterbooks are fragile and some are almost impossible to use. The Johnson Papers, heavy with incoming mail, have little on the President's personal views. The Marble Papers, on a sustained level, encompass the most information, but at times gaps appear in the outgoing mail. The Tilden Papers are generally disappointing. Culled by John Bigelow and others, who deleted material concerning controversial aspects of Tilden's career, the collection additionally has few letters that Tilden wrote. Even so, enough material remains to provide researchers with a hint of what Tilden and his correspondents planned and their reactions to events.

Other collections provide workable building blocks. The Jeremiah S. Black Papers (LC) have insights on the background of the National Union Party. The Blair Family Papers (LC) are particularly good on wartime politics, the first stages of Presidential restoration, and the Passive Policy. Peace Democratic material may be found in the Alexander S. Boys Papers (OHS), the Lewis D. Campbell Papers (OHS), the Alexander Long Papers (Cincinnati Historical Society), and the Allen C. Thurman Papers (OHS). The Salmon P. Chase Papers (LC and the Cincinnati Historical Society), together with the Long Papers, are invaluable concerning the election of 1868. The Erastus Corning Papers (Albany Institute of History and Art) have few political items but are meaty on the Regency's railroad involvements. These papers may be supplemented by the John V. L. Pruyn diaries (NYSL). The Samuel S. Cox Papers (which the OHS has microfilmed from originals housed in a variety of repositories, chiefly Brown University) are spotty, as is the Caleb Cushing Papers (LC) and the James R. Doolittle Papers (LC). The Horatio Seymour Papers, fragmentary at best, are found in the NYSL and the Fairchild Collection (NYHS). The Charles G. Halpine Papers (copied by the Huntington Library from material in several depositories, notably the Library of Congress) have some political items, while the Washington Hunt Papers (NYSL) have material on the Constitutional Unionists. The Kernan Family Papers (Cornell University) have a scattering of relevant letters and are excellent for the gubernatorial race of 1872. The bulky George B. McClellan Papers (LC) are useful for politics in 1864. A few important items appear in the Franklin Pierce microfilms. The Fernando Wood Papers (NYPL and NYHS) are disappointing in both quality and quantity.

Many New York power-brokers who were influential in Democratic politics left little or no manuscript material. Among them are James Gordon Bennett, William Cullen Bryant, William Cassidy, John Cochrane, Richard Connolly, Daniel S. Dickinson, A. Oakey Hall, John T. Hoffman, John Kelly, Dean Richmond, Peter B. Sweeny, William M. Tweed, John Van Buren, John Dash Van Buren, Joseph Warren, and Benjamin Wood. Similarly, August Belmont, although represented by small collections in the LC, NYHS, and the NYPL, left a void in what should have been a voluminous correspondence. The best means to trace these men's ideas lies in researching collateral collections.

A few collections provide information on particular Democratic activities. Among them are the Grover Cleveland Papers (LC) for Cleveland's indebtedness to Tilden, the Thomas A. Olcott Papers (CU) for Dickinson's view of the state of parties in 1860, and the Gerrit Smith Papers (SU) for Greeley's observation of politics in 1862.

Another major source for studying Democratic activities lies in several collections of key Republicans. The Adams Family Papers (Massachusetts Historical Society), which have been microfilmed, the Whitelaw Reid Papers (LC), the Carl Schurz Papers (LC), and the David A. Wells Papers (LC) are irreplaceable for the Liberal Republican revolt. The Wells Papers, additionally, have some Hoffman letters. The Reuben E. Fenton Papers (NYSL, NYHS, and the Fenton Historical Society in Jamestown, New York) provide little information. The Roscoe Conkling Papers (LC), the Ulysses S. Grant Papers (LC), the Horace Greeley Papers (LC and NYPL), the Henry J. Raymond Papers (NYPL), the Daniel Sickles Papers (LC), and the Wadsworth Family Papers (UR) have some helpful items. Some supplementary letters are found in the James M. Comly Papers and the William Henry Smith Papers, both housed in the OHS. The best sources for studying Republican reaction to Democrats and the general state of politics can be found in the John Dix Papers (CU), the Robert Todd Lincoln Papers (LC), the Edwin D. Morgan Papers (NYSL), and, above all, the William H. Seward and Thurlow Weed Papers in the UR.

One of the major difficulties in conducting a detailed study of the Democracy's day-to-day functions, which involves a close scrutiny of the organizational network of various interest groups, lies in the lack of a single, all-inclusive source. A researcher must thus use a variety of newspapers. In that sense, newspapers play a critical role in uncovering Democratic efforts such as notices of meetings, party goals, election of committeemen, attitudes on issues, and other organizational matters. Two notes of caution must be mentioned. Even though the day of political newspapers that functioned as party organs and propagandists had passed and modern journalism, less dependent on political handouts and more intent on mass circulation and advertisements as sources of revenue, had replaced them, newspapers in the 1860s and 1870s still operated as partisan instruments. Moreover, a researcher must identify each newspaper according to its factional allegiance and assess its importance in determining or reflecting policy. Under these circumstances, the various newspaper cited represented particular groups and faithfully presented their views.

Democrats had the following newspapers: The *Albany Argus* and *New York World* wrote for the Regency and swallowtails. The *Buffalo Daily Courier* spoke to the interests of western Democrats and is excellent for reactions to downstate politics. The New York *Daily News, Day-Book, Express,* and *Journal of Commerce* were conservative organs that followed Peace Democratic ideas during the war and later became apologists for the South. All are vital for understanding intraparty opposition to Tammany Hall, the Regency, and the swallowtails. No study is complete without the *New York Leader,* the spokesman of Tammany Hall. Furthermore, many of its columns were written by influential Tammanyites such as A. Oakey Hall and Peter B. Sweeny. The New York *Irish-American* and *Irish-Citizen* provided an index of Irish political expectations.

Republican newspapers played two vital roles in this study — they criticized Democrats and reacted to Democratic ideas. Again, each newspaper served particular Republican interest groups. The New York *Commercial Advertiser* expressed conservative ideas, notably under Thurlow Weed. The *New York Sun* generally served the same constituency. William Cullen Bryant's *New York Evening Post* fulfilled several functions. In addition to being the organ of Barnburner and Free Soil Republicans, the paper was vital as a mirror of proemancipationism, moderate Republicanism during Restoration and Reconstruction, and the party's declining interest in black rights in the 1870s, and as the articulator of traditional Jacksonianism. The *New York Times* was important because of Henry J. Raymond, notably his role in the Union party and his rise and decline as a leader through his relationship to President Johnson. The *New York Tribune,* under Horace Greeley, was excellent for the changing nature of radical ideas, the characteristics of prohibitionism, and the Liberal Republican revolt. Upstate, the *Albany Evening Journal* was a valuable critic of the *Argus* and *Daily Courier.*

The *New York Herald* is difficult to categorize because of its independence and James Gordon Bennett's many twists and turns. Yet the paper is a key source in any New York political study. As the newspaper of largest circulation in the state, it contained a mass of information about day-to-day politics that other newspapers, including the *World, Leader, Daily Cour-*

ier, and *Argus*, lacked. Furthermore, Bennett's editorial policy, given his need to pose as a molder of public opinion, has invaluable insights into the shifting nature of attitudes. Finally, the paper's correspondents often had inside information of party developments, both Democratic and Republican, that are otherwise unavailable.

Selected Bibliography

Government Documents

U.S. Congress, House, Select Committee on Alleged New York City Election Frauds, *Alleged New York City Election Frauds,* 40th Cong., 3d sess., 1869.

Unpublished Manuscript Collections.

Albany. The Albany Institute of History and Art. Erastus Corning papers.
Albany. New York State Library. Reuben E. Fenton papers.
Albany. New York State Library. William Cassidy papers.
Albany. New York State Library. Washington Hunt papers.
Albany. New York State Library. Edwin D. Morgan papers.
Albany. New York State Library. Horatio Seymour papers.
Boston. Massachusetts Historical Society. The Adams Family papers.
Chicago. University of Chicago Library. Stephen A. Douglas papers.
Cincinnati. Cincinnati Historical Society. Salmon P. Chase papers.
Cincinnati. Cincinnati Historical Society. Alexander Long papers.
Columbus. Ohio Historical Society. John A. Bingham papers.
Columbus. Ohio Historical Society. Alexander S. Boys papers.
Columbus. Ohio Historical Society. Lewis D. Campbell papers.
Columbus. Ohio Historical Society. James M. Comly papers.
Columbus. Ohio Historical Society. Samuel S. Cox papers.
Columbus. Ohio Historical Society. William H. Smith papers.
Columbus. Ohio Historical Society. Allen C. Thurman papers.
Ithaca. Cornell University Library. Alonzo B. Cornell papers.
Ithaca. Cornell University Library. Kernan Family papers.
New York City, Columbia University. John A. Dix papers.
New York City. Columbia University. Thomas A. Olcott papers.
New York City. New-York Historical Society. Fairchild Collection.
New York City. New-York Historical Society. Horatio Seymour papers.

New York City. New-York Historical Society. Fernando Wood papers.
New York City. New York Public Library. Horace Greeley papers.
New York City. New York Public Library. Henry J. Raymond papers.
New York City. New York Public Library. Samuel J. Tilden papers.
New York City. New York Public Library. Fernando Wood papers.
Philadelphia. Historical Society of Pennsylvania. James Buchanan papers.
Rochester. University of Rochester. William H. Seward papers.
Rochester. University of Rochester. Thurlow Weed papers.
Rochester. University of Rochester. Wadsworth Family papers.
San Marino. Henry E. Huntington Library. Samuel L. M. Barlow papers.
San Marino. Henry E. Huntington Library. Charles G. Halpine papers.
Syracuse. Syracuse University. Gerrit Smith papers.
Washington. Library of Congress. Jeremiah S. Black papers.
Washington. Library of Congress. Blair Family papers.
Washington. Library of Congress. Salmon P. Chase papers.
Washington. Library of Congress. Grover Cleveland papers.
Washington. Library of Congress. Roscoe Conkling papers.
Washington. Library of Congress. Caleb Cushing papers.
Washington. Library of Congress. James R. Doolittle papers.
Washington. Library of Congress. William P. Fessenden papers.
Washington. Library of Congress. Ulysses S. Grant papers.
Washington. Library of Congress. Horace Greeley papers.
Washington. Library of Congress. Andrew Johnson papers.
Washington. Library of Congress. Robert Todd Lincoln papers.
Washington. Library of Congress. Manton Marble papers.
Washington. Library of Congress. George B. McClellan papers.
Washington. Library of Congress. Franklin Pierce Papers.
Washington. Library of Congress. Whitelaw Reid papers.
Washington. Library of Congress. Carl Schurz papers.
Washington. Library of Congress. Daniel Sickles papers.
Washington. Library of Congress. David A. Wells papers.

Newspapers

Albany Argus
Albany *Evening Journal*
Buffalo *Daily Courier*
New York *Commercial Advertiser*

New York Daily News
New York *Day-Book*
New York *Evening Post*
New York *Express*
New York *Herald*
New York *Irish-American*
New York *Irish-Citizen*
New York *Journal of Commerce*
New York Leader
New York *Sun*
New York Times
New York Tribune
New York *World*

Published Collections of Works, Diaries, Letters, Memoirs, and Autobiographies

Bancroft, Frederick, ed. *Speeches, Correspondence and Political Papers of Carl Schurz*. 6 vols. New York: G. P. Putnam's Sons, 1913.

Bigelow, John, ed. *Letters and Memorials of Samuel J. Tilden.* 2 vols. New York: Harper and Brothers, 1908.

Bigelow, John, ed. *The Writings and Speeches of Samuel J. Tilden,* 2 vols. New York: Harper and Brothers, 1885.

Brinkerhoff, Roeliff. *Recollections of a Lifetime.* Cincinnati: Robert Clarke Company, 1900.

Dickinson, John, ed. *The Speeches, Correspondence, Etc. of the Late Daniel S. Dickinson.* 2 vols. New York: G. P. Putnam & Sons, 1867.

Depew, Chauncey M. *My Memories of Eighty Years.* New York: Charles Scribner's Sons, 1924

"Extracts from the Journal of Henry J. Raymond." *Scribner's Monthly* 20 (June 1880): 274-79.

Howe, Mark Anthony DeWolfe, ed. *The Life and Letters of George Bancroft,* 2 vols. New York: Charles Scribner's Sons, 1908.

Hudson, William C. *Random Recollections of an Old Political Reporter.* New York: Cupples and Leon, 1911.

Moore, John B., ed. *The Works of James Buchanan Comprising his Speeches, State Papers, and Private Correspondence.* 12 vols. Philadelphia: J. B. Lippincott, 1911.

Morse, John T., ed. *Diary of Gideon Welles.* 3 vols. Boston and New York: Houghton Mifflin, 1911.

Mowry, Duane, ed. "Selections from the Correspondence of the Late Senator James R. Doolittle: Post-Bellum Days." *Magazine of History* 17 (August 1913): 56-64.

Mowry, Duane, ed. "Some Political Letters of Reconstruction Days Succeeding the Civil War." *American Historical Magazine* 4 (May 1909): 331-36.

Mushkat, Jerome, ed. "The Impeachment of Andrew Johnson: A Contemporary View." *New York History* 48 (July 1967): 275-86.

Sanborn, Alvan, ed. *Reminiscences of Richard Lathers*. New York: Grafton Press, 1907.

Weed, Harriet, ed. *Autobiography of Thurlow Weed*. 2 vols. Boston and New York: Houghton Mifflin, 1883.

Articles, Books, and Pamphlets on Contemporary Politics

Bigelow, John. *The Life of Samuel J. Tilden*. 2 vols. New York: Harper and Brothers, 1895.

Breen, Michael. *Thirty Years of New York Politics Up-To-Date*. New York: Published by the Author, 1899.

Calkins, Hiram and Van Buren, DeWitt. *Biographical Sketches of John T. Hoffman and Allen C. Beach*. New York: The New York Printing Company, 1868.

Costello, Augustine E. *Our Police Protectors*. New York: Published by the Author, 1885.

Davenport, John. *The Election and Naturalization Frauds in New York City, 1860-1870*. New York: Published by the Author, 1894.

Edwards, E.J. "Tammany under John Kelly." *McClure's Magazine* 9 (September 1895): 325-32.

Headley, Joel. *The Great Riots of New York City, 1712-1873*. New York: E.B. Treat, 1873.

Hill, Adam S. "The Chicago Convention," *North American Review* 107 (June 1868): 167-86.

Hoyes, Stephen. *The Political Situation Resulting from the Late State Election: Herald Interview with Peter B. Sweeny*. New York: The Jackson Association, 1869.

Maverick, Augustus. *Henry J. Raymond and the New York Press*. Hartford: A.S. Hale and Company, 1870.

McLaughlin, J. Fairfax. *The Life and Times of John Kelly*. New York: The American News Company, 1884.

McLeod, Donald. *Biography of Hon. Fernando Wood, Mayor of the City of New York*. New York: 1856.

McPherson, Edward. *A Hand-Book of Politics for 1872.* Washington, D.C.: Philp & Solomons, 1872.

McPherson, Edward. *Political History of the United States of America During the Period of Reconstruction.* Washington, D.C.: Philp & Solomons, 1871.

Memorial of William Cassidy. Albany: Argus Printing Company, 1873.

Myers, Gustavus. "The Secrets of Tammany's Success." *The Forum* 31 (August 1901): 488-500.

Official Proceedings of the National Democratic Convention Held at New York, July 4-8, 1868. Boston: 1868.

Proceedings of the Democratic State Convention. Albany: 1861.

Stevens, John A. *The Union Defense Committee of the City of New York.* New York: Published by the Committee, 1885.

Tammany Society or Columbian Order, Annual Celebration, July 4, 1862. New York: 1862.

Vallandingham, James L. *A Life of Clement A. Vallandingham.* Baltimore: Trumball Brothers, 1872.

Woods, George B. "The New York Convention." *North American* Review 107 (October 1868): 445-65.

Published Monographs, Biographies, and Synthetic Works

Alexander, DeAlva A. *A Political History of the State of New York.* 4 vols. New York: Henry Holt & Company, 1906-1924.

Allswang, John M. *Bosses, Machines, and Urban Voters: An American Symbiosis.* Port Washington: Kennikat Press, 1977.

Baehr, Harry W., Jr. *The New York Tribune since the Civil War.* New York: Dodd, Mead & Company, 1936.

Barney, William L. *Flawed Victory: A New Perspective on the Civil War.* New York: Praeger, 1975.

Beale, Howard K. *The Critical Year: A Study of Andrew Johnson and Reconstruction.* New York: Frederick Ungar Publishing Company, 1930.

Belz, Herman. *A New Birth of Freedom: The Republican Party and Freedmen's Rights, 1861-1866.* Westport: Greenwood, 1976.

Belz, Herman. *Reconstructing the Union.* Ithaca: Cornell University Press, 1969.

Benedict, Michael Les. *A Compromise of Principle; Congressional Republicans and Reconstruction, 1863-1869.* New York: W. W. Norton & Company, 1974.

Benedict, Michael Les. *The Impeachment and Trial of Andrew Johnson.* New York: W. W. Norton & Company, 1973.

Berger, Meyer. *The Story of the New York Times.* New York: Simon and Schuster, 1951.

Bowen, Croswell. *The Elegant Oakey.* New York: Oxford University Press, 1956.

Brock, W. R. *An American Crisis: Congress and Reconstruction, 1865-1867.* New York: Harper & Row, 1963.

Brown, Charles H. *William Cullen Bryant.* New York: Charles Scribner's Sons, 1971.

Brummer, Sidney. *Political History of New York State during the Period of the Civil War.* New York: Columbia University Press, 1911.

Callow, Alexander B. Jr. *The Tweed Ring.* New York: Oxford University Press, 1965.

Coleman, Charles. *The Election of 1868.* New York: Columbia University Press, 1933.

Cook, Adrian. *Armies in the Street.* Lexington: The University of Kentucky Press, 1974.

Cox, LaWanda and Cox, John H. *Politics, Principle, and Prejudice 1865-1866: Dilemma of Reconstruction America.* New York: Atheneum, 1969.

Craven, Avery. *Reconstruction: The Ending of the Civil War.* New York: Holt, Rinehart & Winston, 1969.

Curry, Leonard. *Blueprint for Modern America: Nonmilitary Legislation of the First Civil War Congress.* Nashville: Vanderbilt University Press, 1968.

Dell, Christopher. *Lincoln and the War Democrats: The Erosion of Conservative Tradition.* Rutherford: Fairleigh Dickinson Press, 1975.

Donald, David H. *Charles Sumner and the Rights of Man.* New York: Afred A. Knopf, 1970.

Duncan, Bingham. *Whitelaw Reid: Journalist, Politican, Diplomat.* Athens: University of Georgia Press, 1975.

Ellis, David. *New York: State and City.* Ithaca: Cornell University Press, 1979.

Flick, Alexander. *Samuel J. Tilden: A Study in Political Sagacity.* New York: Dodd, Mead & Company, 1939.

Foner, Eric. *Free Soil, Free Labor, Free Men: The Ideology of the Republican Party Before the Civil War.* New York: Oxford University Press, 1970.

Fredrickson, George M. The Black Image in the White Mind: The Debate on Afro-American Character and Destiny, 1817-1914. New York: Harper & Row, 1971.

Fuess, Claude. *Carl Schurz: Reformer.* New York: Dodd, Mead & Company, 1932.

Furer, Howard. *William Frederick Havemeyer: A Political Biography*. New York: American Press, 1965.

Gibson, Florence. *The Attitudes of the New York Irish toward State and National Affairs, 1848-1892*. New York: Columbia Univeristy Press, 1951.

Gillett, William. *The Right to Vote: Politics and the Passage of the Fifteenth Amendment*. Baltimore: Johns Hopkins Press, 1965.

Grossman, Lawrence. *The Democratic Party and the Negro: Northern and National Politics, 1868-92*. Urbana: University of Illinois Press, 1976.

Hanchett, William G. *IRISH Charles G. Halpine in Civil War America*. Syracuse: Syracuse University Press, 1970.

Hershkowitz, Leo. *Tweed's New York: Another Look*. New York: Anchor Press, 1977.

Hirsch, Mark. *William C. Whitney: Modern Warwick*. Dodd, Mead & Company, 1948.

Hoogenboom, Ari. *Outlawing the Spoils: A History of the Civil Service Reform Movement, 1865-1883*. Urbana: University of Illinois Press, 1961.

Howe, George. *Chester A. Arthur: A Quarter Century of Machine Politics*. New York: Dodd, Mead & Company, 1934.

Hungerford, Edward. *Men of Erie*. New York: Random House, 1946.

Jackson, Kenneth, and Schultz, Stanley, eds. *Cities in American History*. New York: Afred A. Knopf, 1972.

James, Joseph. *The Framing of the Fourteenth Amendment*. Urbana: University of Illinois Press, 1956.

Jenkins, Brian, *Fenians and Anglo-American Relations during Reconstruction*. Ithaca: Cornell University Press, 1969.

Jones, Robert H. *Disrupted Decades: The Civil War and Reconstruction Years*. New York: Charles Scribner's Sons, 1973.

Jordon, David. *Roscoe Conkling of New York*. Ithaca: Cornell University Press, 1971.

Katz, Irving. *August Belmont: A Political Biography*. New York: Columbia University Press, 1968.

Keller, Morton. *Affairs of State: Public Life in Late Nineteenth Century America*. Cambridge: Belknap Press, 1977.

Kelley, Robert. *The Transatlantic Persuasion: The Liberal-Democratic Mind in the Age of Gladstone*. New York, Knopf, 1969.

Klement, Frank L. *The Copperheads in the Middle West*. Chicago: University of Chicago Press, 1960.

Lee, Basil Leo. *Discontent in New York City, 1861-1865*. Washington, D.C.: Catholic University of America Press, 1943.

Limpus, Lowell. *History of the New York Fire Department.* New York: E. P. Dutton, 1940.

Lynch, Dennis T. *"Boss" Tweed: The Story of a Grim Generation.* New York: Boni & Liveright, 1927.

Mandelbaum, Seymour. *Boss Tweed's New York.* New York: John Wiley & Sons, 1965.

Mantell, Martin. *Johnson, Grant, and the Politics of Reconstruction.* New York: Columbia University Press, 1973.

McJimsey, George T. *Genteel Partisan: Manton Marble, 1834-1917.* Ames: Iowa State University Press, 1971.

McKitrick, Eric. *Andrew Johnson and Reconstruction.* Chicago: University of Chicago Press, 1960.

Meyers, Marvin. *The Jacksonian Persuasion.* Stanford: Stanford University Press, 1957.

Miller, Wilbur. *Cops and Bobbies: Police Authority in New York and London, 1830-1870.* Chicago: University of Chicago Press, 1977.

Mitchell, Stewart. *Horatio Seymour of New York.* Cambridge: Harvard University Press, 1938.

Mohr, James, ed. *Radical Republicans in the North: State Politics During Reconstruction.* Baltimore: Johns Hopkins Press, 1975.

Mohr, James. *The Radical Republicans and Reform in New York during Reconstruction.* Ithaca: Cornell University Press, 1973.

Montgomery, David. *Beyond Equality: Labor and the Radical Republicans, 1862-1872.* New York: Alfred A. Knopf, 1967.

Murdock, Eugene. *One Million Men: The Civil War Draft in the North.* Madison: State Historical Society of Wisconsin Press, 1971.

Mushkat, Jerome. *Tammany: The Evolution of a Political Machine, 1789-1865.* Syracuse: Syracuse University Press, 1971.

Myers, Gustavus. *Tammany Hall.* New York: Boni & Liveright, 1917.

Nevins, Allan. *The Evening Post: A Century of Journalism.* Boni & Liveright, 1924.

Nevins, Allan. *The War for the Union: War Becomes Revolution, 1861-1863.* New York: Charles Scribner's Sons, 1971.

Nugent, Walter. *The Money Question during Reconstruction.* New York: W. W. Norton & Company, 1967.

Perman, Michael. *Reunion without Compromise: The South and Reconstruction, 1865-1868.* Cambridge: Cambridge University Press, 1973.

Pleasants, Samuel. *Fernando Wood of New York.* New York: Columbia University Press, 1948.

Randall, James. *Lincoln the President, Midstream.* New York: Dodd, Mead & Company, 1953.

Ravitch, Diane. *The Great School Wars: New York City, 1805-1973.* New York: Basic Books, 1974.

Rawley, James. *Edwin D. Morgan, 1811-1883: Merchant in Politics.* New York: Columbia University Press, 1956.

Rawley, James. *The Politics of Union: Northern Politics during the Civil War.* Hinsdale: Dryden Press, 1973.

Rayback, Robert J. ed. *Richards' Atlas of New York State.* Phoenix: Frank E. Richards, 1958.

Richardson, James F. *The New York Police: Colonial Times to 1901.* New York: Oxford University Press, 1970.

Ross, Earle D. *The Liberal Republican Movement.* New York: Henry Holt and Company, 1919.

Sharkey, Robert P. *Money, Class, and Party: An Economic Study in Civil War and Reconstruction.* Baltimore: Johns Hopkins Press, 1959.

Silbey, Joel. *A Respectable Minority: The Democratic Party in the Civil War Era, 1860-1868.* New York: W. W. Norton & Company, 1977.

Smith, William. *The Francis Preston Blair Family in Politics.* 2 vols. New York: Macmillan, 1933.

Spann, Edward. *Ideals and Politics: New York Intellectuals and the Liberal Democracy, 1820-1880.* Albany: State University of New York Press, 1972.

Stampp, Kenneth. *The Era of Reconstruction, 1865-1877.* New York: Alfred A. Knopf, 1966.

Stebbins, Homer. *A Political History of the State of New York, 1865-1869.* New York: Columbia University Press, 1913.

Thomas, Lately. *Sam Ward: "King of the Lobby."* Boston: Houghton Mifflin Company, 1965.

Trelease, Allen W. *White Terror: The Ku Klux Klan Conspiracy and Southern Reconstruction.* New York: Harper & Row, 1971.

Unger, Irwin. *The Greenback Era: A Social and Political History of American Finance, 1865-1879.* Princeton: Princeton University Press, 1964.

Van Dusen, Glyndon G. *Horace Greeley: Nineteenth-Century Crusader.* New York: Hill and Wang, 1964.

Van Dusen, Glyndon G. *Thurlow Weed: The Wizard of the Lobby.* Boston: Little, Brown and Company, 1947.

Van Dusen, Glyndon G. *William Henry Seward.* New York: Oxford University Press, 1967.

Wall, Joseph F. *Henry Watterson: Reconstructed Rebel.* New York: Oxford University Press, 1956.

Woodward, C. Vann. *The Strange Career of Jim Crow.* New York: Oxford University Press, 1957.

Zornow, William. *Lincoln and the Party Divided.* Norman: University of Oklahoma Press, 1954.

Articles

Abbott, Martin. "Free Land, Free Labor, and the Freedmen's Bureau." *Agricultural History* 30 (October 1956): 150-56.

Albjerg, Marguerite. "The New York *Herald* as a Factor in Reconstruction." *Journalism Quarterly* 46 (1947): 204-11.

Anderson, George L. "The Proposed Resumption of Silver Payments in 1873." *Pacific Historical Review* 8 (September 1939): 301-16.

Anderson, George L. "The South and Problems of Post-Civil War Finance." *Journal of Southern History* 9 (August 1943): 181-95.

Archdeacon, Thomas. "The Erie Canal, Samuel J. Tilden, and the Democratic Party." *New York History* 59 (October 1978): 410-22.

Azbug, Robert, "The Copperheads: Historical Approaches to Civil War Dissent." *Indiana Magazine of History* 66 (March 1970): 40-55.

Barkam, Elliott. "The Emergence of a Whig Persuasion: Conservatism, Democraticism, and the New York State Whigs." *New York History* 52 (October 1971): 367-95.

Benedict, Michael Les. "A New Look at the Impeachment of Andrew Johnson." *Political Science Quarterly* 88 (September 1973): 349-67.

Benedict, Michael Les. "Preserving the Constitution: The Conservative Basis of Radical Reconstruction." *Journal of American History* 61 (June 1974): 65-90.

Benedict, Michael Les. "The Rout of Radicalism: Republicans and the Elections of 1867." *Civil War History* 18 (December 1972): 334-44.

Bernard, Kenneth. "Lincoln and Civil Liberties." *Abraham Lincoln Quarterly* 6 (September 1951): 375-99.

Bernheim, A.C. "New York City and State." *Political Science Quarterly* 9 (September 1894): 389-402.

Bestor, Arthur. "The American Civil War as a Constitutional Crisis." *American Historical* Review 49 (January 1964): 327-52.

Bogue, Allen. "Bloc and Party in the United States Senate, 1861-1863." *Civil War History* 13 (September 1967): 221-41.

Bonham, Milledge, Jr. "New York and the Election of 1860." *New York History* 15 (April 1934): 124-43.

Brigance, William N. "Jeremiah Black and Andrew Johnson." *Mississippi Valley Historical* Review 29 (September 1932): 205-18.

Brown, Bertram-Wyatt. "The Civil Rights Act of 1875." *Western Political Quarterly* 18 (December 1954): 763-75.

Calhoun, Richard. "New York City Fire Department Reorganization, 1865-1870." *New-York Historical Society Quarterly* 60 (January/April 1976): 7-34.

Callow, Alexander B., Jr. " 'What are you Going to do About it?': The Crusade Against the Tweed Ring." *New-York Historical Society Quarterly* 49 (April 1965): 117-42.

Carleton, William G. "Civil War Dissidence in the North: The Perspective of a Century." *South Atlantic Quarterly* 65 (Summer 1966): 390-402.

Castell, Albert. "Andrew Johnson: His Historiographical Rise and Fall." *Mid-America* 45 (July 1963): 175-84.

Coben, Stanley. "Northeastern Business and Radical Reconstruction: A Re-Examination." *Mississippi Valley Historical Review* 46 (June 1959): 67-90.

Cox, LaWanda. "The Promise of Land to the Freedman." *Mississippi Valley Historical* Review 45 (December 1958): 413-40.

Cox, Lawanda, and Cox, John H. "Negro Suffrage and Republican Politics: The Problem of Motivation in Reconstruction Historiography." *Journal of Southern History* 33 (August 1967): 303-30.

Cox, LaWanda and Cox, John H. "Andrew Johnson and His Ghost Writers: An Analysis of the Freemen's Bureau and Civil Rights Veto Messages." *Mississippi Valley Historical Review* 48 (December 1961): 460-79.

Curry, Leonard. "Congressional Democrats: 1861-1863." *Civil War History* 12 (September 1966): 213-19.

Curry, Richard O. " 'The Union as it Was': A Critique of Recent Interpretations of the Copperheads." *Civil War History* 13 (March 1967): 23-39.

Degler, Carl. "American Political Parties and the Rise of the City: An Interpretation." *Journal of American History* 51 (June 1964): 41-59.

Dorris, Jonathan T. "Pardoning the Leaders of the Confederacy." *Mississippi Valley Historical Review* 15 (June 1928): 3-21.

Dougherty, J. Hampden. "Constitutions of New York." *Political Science Quarterly* 3 (September 1888): 489-519.

Downey, Matthew T. "Horace Greeley and the Politicans: The Liberal Republican Convention in 1872." *Journal of American History* 43 (March 1967): 727-50.

Dudley, Harold M. "The Election of 1864," *Mississippi Valley Historical Review* 18 (March 1932), 500-518.

Dunning, William H. "The Second Birth of the Republican Party." *American Historical Review* 16 (October 1910): 57-63.

Ellis, David. " 'Upstate Hicks' Versus 'City Slickers.' " *New-York Historical Society Quarterly* 43 (April 1959): 202-19.

Fahrney, Robert. "Horace Greeley and the *New York Tribune* in the Civil War." *New York History* 16 (October 1935): 415-35.

Field, Phyllis F. "Republicans and Black Suffrage in New York: The Grass Roots Response." *Civil War History* 21 (June 1975): 136-47.

Fishel, Leslie H. "Northern Prejudice and Negro Suffrage, 1865-1870." *Journal of Negro History* 24 (June 1954): 8-26.

Foner, Eric. "Racial Assumptions of the New York Free Soilers." *New York History* 46 (October 1965): 311-29.

Freidel, Frank. "The Loyal Publication Society: A Pro-Union Propaganda Agency." *Mississippi Valley Historical Review* 26 (September 1939): 359-76.

Gerber, Richard A. "The Liberal Republicans of 1872 in Historiographical Perspective." *Journal of American History* 62 (June 1975): 40-73.

Gerteis, Louis. "Salmon P. Chase, Radicalism, and the Politics of Emancipation." *Journal of American History* 60 (June 1973): 42-62.

Ginsberg, Judah. "Barnburners, Free Soilers, and the Republican Party." *New York History* 52 (October 1976): 475-500.

Gipson, Lawrence H. "The Statesmanship of President Johnson: A Study of the Presidential Reconstruction Policy." *Mississippi Valley Historical Review* 2 (December 1915): 363-83.

Gloneck, James F. "Lincoln, Johnson, and the Baltimore Ticket." *Abraham Lincoln Quarterly* 6 (March 1951): 255-71.

Goodnow, Frank. "Municipal Home Rule." *Political Science Quarterly* 21 (March 1906): 77-90.

Gutman, Herbert G. "The Tompkins Square 'Riot' in New York City on January 13, 1874: A Reexamination of Its Causes and Its Aftermath." *Labor History* 6 (Winter 1965): 48-55.

Hartman, William. "Custom House Patronage under Lincoln." *New-York Historical Society Quarterly* 41 (October 1957): 440-57.

Hartman, William, "The New York Custom House: Seats of Spoils Politics." *New York Historical Society Quarterly* 34 (April 1953): 149-63.

Heslin, James. " 'Peaceful Compromise' in New York City, 1860-1861." *New-York Historical Society Quarterly* 44 (October 1961): 349-62.

Hesseltine, William B. "Economic Factors in the Abandonment of Reconstruction." *Mississippi Valley Historical Review* 22 (September 1935): 191-210.

Hirsch, Leo H., Jr. "The Negro and New York, 1783-1865." *Journal of Negro History* 16 (October 1931): 382-454.

Hirsch, Mark. "More Light on Boss Tweed." *Political Science Quarterly* 60 (June 1945): 267-78.

Hirsch, Mark. "Samuel J. Tilden: The Story of a Lost Opportunity." *American Historical Review* 56 (July 1954): 788-802.

House, Albert V., Jr. "Northern Congressional Democrats as Defenders of the South during Reconstruction." *Journal of Southern History* 6 (February 1940): 46-71.

Hubbell, John. "The Northern Democrats and Party Survival, 1860-1861." *Illinois Quarterly* 36 (September 1973): 22-33.

James, Joseph. "Southern Reaction to the Proposal of the Fourteenth Amendment." *Journal of Southern History* 22 (November 1956): 477-97.

Johnson, Ludwell. "Lincoln's Solution to the Problem of Peace Terms, 1864-1865." *Journal of Southern History* 34 (November 1968): 576-86.

Kaplan, Sidney. "The Miscegenation Issue in the Election of 1864." *Journal of Negro History* 34 (July 1949): 274-343.

Kelly, Alfred H. "The Congressional Controversy over School Segregation, 1867-1875." *American Historical Review* 64 (April 1959): 537-63.

Kirkwood, Robert. "Horace Greeley and Reconstruction, 1865" *New York History* 40 (July 1959): 270-80.

Klement, Frank L. "Economic Aspects of Middle Western Copperheads." *The Historian* 14 (Autumn 1951): 27-44.

Klement, Frank L. "Middle Western Copperheadism and the Genesis of the Granger Movement," *Mississippi Valley Historical Review* 38 (March 1952): 679-94.

Kolchin, Peter. "The Business Press and Reconstruction, 1865-1868." *Journal of Southern History* 33 (May 1967): 183-96.

Kramer, Howard D. "Effect of the Civil War on the Public Health Movement." *Mississippi Valley Historical Review* 35 (March 1948): 449-62.

Linden, Glenn M. "A Note on Negro Suffrage and Republican Politics." *Journal of Southern History* 36 (August 1970): 411-30.

Lofton, Williston. "Northern Labor and the Negro during the Civil War." *Journal of Negro History* 34 (October 1949): 251-73.

Man, Albon P., Jr. "Labor Competition and the New York Draft Riots of 1863." *Journal of Negro History* 36 (October 1951): 375-405.

McGrane, Reginald C. "Ohio and The Greenback Movement." *Mississippi Valley Historical Review* 11 (March 1925): 525-42.

McPherson, James M. "Grant or Greeley? The Abolitionist Dilemma in the Election of 1872." *American Historical Review* 71 (October 1965): 43-61.

Merrill, Louis T. "General Benjamin F. Butler in the Presidential Campaign of 1864." Mississippi Valley Historical Review 33 (March 1947): 537-70.

Mintz, Max. "Political Ideas of Martin Van Buren." *New York History* 30 (October 1949): 422-45.

Mohr, James. "New York State's Free School Law of 1867." *New-York Historical Society Quarterly* 53 (July 1969): 230-49.

Moore, Clifford. "Ohio in National Politics, 1865-1896." *Ohio Archeological and Historical Quarterly* 37 (April-June 1928): 200-427.

Murdock, Eugene. "Horatio Seymour and the 1863 Draft." *Civil War History* 11 (June 1965): 117-41.

Murphy, Charles, "Samuel J. Tilden and the Civil War." *South Atlantic Quarterly* 33 (July 1934): 261-71.

Mushkat, Jerome. "Ben Wood's *Fort Lafayette:* A Source for Studying the Peace Democrats." *Civil War History* 21 (June 1975): 160-71.

Nichols, Roy. "The United States vs. Jefferson Davis." *American Historical Review* 31 (January 1926): 266-84.

Perdue, M. Kathleen. "Salmon P. Chase and the Impeachment of Andrew Johnson." *The Historian* 29 (November 1964): 75-92.

Perman, Michael. "The South and Congressional Reconstruction Policy." *Journal of American Studies* 4 (February 1971): 181-200.

Perzel, Edward S. "Alexander Long, Salmon Chase and the Election of 1868." *Bulletin of the Cincinnati Historical Society* 23 (January 1965): 3-18.

Pratt, John W. "Boss Tweed's Public Welfare Program." *New-York Historical Society Quarterly* 45 (October 1961): 396-411.

Rawley, James. "The General Amnesty Act of 1872: A Note." *Mississippi Valley Historical Review* 47 (December 1960): 480-84.

Rayback, Robert. "New York in the Civil War." *New York History* 42 (January 1961): 56-70.

Rezneck, Samuel. "Distress, Relief, and Discontent in the United States during the Depression of 1873-78." *Journal of Political Economy* 48 (December 1950): 494-512.

Riddelberger, Patrick W. "The Break in Republican Ranks: Liberals vs. Stalwarts in the Election of 1872." *Journal of Negro History* 44 (April 1959) 136-57.

Riddelberger, Patrick W. "The Radicals' Abandonment of the Negro during Reconstruction." *Journal of Negro History* 45 (April 1960): 88-102.

Rorabaugh, William. "Rising Democratic Spirits: Immigrants, Temperance, and Tammany Hall, 1854-1860." *Civil War History* 22 (June 1976): 138-57.

Ross, Earle D. "Horace Greeley and the South." *South Atlantic Quarterly* 16 (October 1917): 324-38.

Ross, Earle D. "Samuel J. Tilden and the Revival of the Democratic Party." *South Atlantic Quarterly* 19 (January 1920): 43-54.

Russ, William, Jr. "Registration and Disfranchisement under Radical Reconstruction." *Mississippi Valley Historical Review* 21 (September 1934): 163-80.

Russ, William, Jr. "Was There Danger of a Second Civil War during Reconstruction?" *Mississippi Valley Historical Review* 25 (June 1938): 39-58.

Schell, Herbert. "Hugh McCulloch and the Treasury Department, 1865-1869." *Mississippi Valley Historical Review* 17 (December 1930): 404-21.

Scroggs, Jack. "Southern Reconstruction: A Radical View." *Journal of Southern History* 24 (November 1958): 407-29.

Sellers, James L. "James R. Doolittle." *Wisconsin Magazine of History* 17 (December 1933): 168-78; (March 1934): 277-306; (June 1934): 393-401; 18 (September 1934): 20-41; (December 1934): 178-87.

Shipley, Max L. "The Background and Legal Aspects of the Pendleton Plan." *Mississippi Valley Historical Review* 24 (September 1937): 329-40.

Silbey, Joel. "Parties and Politics in Mid-Nineteenth Century America." *Capitol Studies* 1 (Fall 1972): 9-27.

Staudenraus, P. J. "The Popular Origins of the Thirteenth Amendment." *Mid-America* 50 (April 1968): 108-15.

Swinney, Everette. "Enforcing the Fifteenth Amendment." *Journal of Southern History* 28 (May 1962): 202-18.

Terrill, Tom E. "David A. Wells, the Democracy, and Tariff Reduction, 1877-1894." *Journal of American History* 46 (December 1969): 540-55.

Thelen, David, and Fishel, Leslie, eds. "Reconstruction in the North: The *World* Looks at New York's Negroes, March 16, 1867." *New York History* 49 (October 1968): 405-40.

Trimble, William. "Diverging Tendencies in the New York Democracy in the Period of the Loco Focos." *American Historical Review* 24 (April 1919): 396-421.

Trimble, William. "The Social Philosophy of the Loco-Foco Democracy." *American Journal of Sociology* 26 (May 1921): 705-21.

Unger, Irwin. "Businessmen and Specie Resumption." *Political Science Quarterly* 74 (March 1959): 46-70.

Wilson, Charles. "McClellan's Changing View of the Peace Plank of 1864." *American Historical Review* 38 (April 1933): 498-505.

Winther, Oscar O. "The Soldier Vote in the Election of 1864." *New York History* 25 (October 1944): 440-58.

Wood, Forrest. "On Revising Reconstruction History: Negro Suffrage, White Disfranchisement, and Common Sense." *Journal of Negro History* 41 (April 1966): 98-113.

Woodward, C. Vann. "The Seeds of Failure in Radical Race Policy." *Proceedings of the American Philosophical Society* 110 (February 1966): 1-9.

Zornow, William. "Clement Vallandingham and the Democratic Party in 1864." *Historical and Philosophical Society of Ohio* 29 (January 1961): 21-37.

Zornow, William. "McClellan and Seymour in the Chicago Convention of 1864." *Journal of the Illinois State Historical Society* 43 (Winter 1950): 282-95.

Index